ACTIVITIES 1940–1944

The Collected Writings of John Maynard Keynes

Keynes with Harry White

THE COLLECTED WRITINGS OF
JOHN MAYNARD KEYNES

VOLUME XXV

ACTIVITIES 1940-1944
SHAPING THE POST-WAR WORLD:
THE CLEARING UNION

EDITED BY
DONALD MOGGRIDGE

MACMILLAN
CAMBRIDGE UNIVERSITY PRESS
FOR THE
ROYAL ECONOMIC SOCIETY

Published for the Royal Economic Society
throughout the world, excluding the U.S.A. and Canada, by
THE MACMILLAN PRESS LTD
London and Basingstoke
Associated companies in Delhi   Dublin   Hong Kong   Johannesburg
Lagos   Melbourne   New York   Singapore   Tokyo
and throughout the U.S.A. and Canada by
THE SYNDICS OF THE CAMBRIDGE UNIVERSITY PRESS
32 East 57th Street, New York, NY 10022, U.S.A.

Printed in Great Britain
at the University Press, Cambridge

British Library Cataloguing in Publication Data
Keynes, John Maynard, *Baron Keynes*
The collected writings of John Maynard Keynes
Vol. XXV: Activites 1940–1944
1. Economics
I. Moggridge, Donald. II. Royal Economic Society
330.15'6   HB171
ISBN 0-333-15658-7

Library of congress cataloguing in publication data
Keynes, John Maynard, 1883–1946.

The collected writings of John Maynard Keynes.

Vol. XXIII has imprint: New York, Cambridge University Press, for
the Royal Economic Society.

Contents: v. 1.   Indian currency and finance.—
v. 2.   The economic consequences of the peace.—
v. 3.   A revision of the treaty. [etc.]
1. Economics—Collected works.   I.   Royal Economic Society, London.
HB171.K44   330.15'6'08   76-13349
ISBN 0-521-22018-1

14. AUG. 1980

CONTENTS

GENERAL INTRODUCTION

This new standard edition of *The Collected Writings of John Maynard Keynes* forms the memorial to him of the Royal Economic Society. He devoted a very large share of his busy life to the Society. In 1911, at the age of twenty-eight, he became editor of the *Economic Journal* in succession to Edgeworth; two years later he was made secretary as well. He held these offices without intermittence until almost the end of his life. Edgeworth, it is true, returned to help him with the editorship from 1919 to 1925; Macgregor took Edgeworth's place until 1934, when Austin Robinson succeeded him and continued to assist Keynes down to 1945. But through all these years Keynes himself carried the major responsibility and made the principal decisions about the articles that were to appear in the *Economic Journal*, without any break save for one or two issues when he was seriously ill in 1937. It was only a few months before his death at Easter 1946 that he was elected president and handed over his editorship to Roy Harrod and the secretaryship to Austin Robinson.

In his dual capacity of editor and secretary Keynes played a major part in framing the policies of the Royal Economic Society. It was very largely due to him that some of the major publishing activities of the Society—Sraffa's edition of Ricardo, Stark's edition of the economic writings of Bentham, and Guillebaud's edition of Marshall, as well as a number of earlier publications in the 1930s—were initiated.

When Keynes died in 1946 it was natural that the Royal Economic Society should wish to commemorate him. It was perhaps equally natural that the Society chose to commemorate him by producing an edition of his collected works. Keynes himself had always taken a joy in fine printing, and the Society, with the help of Messrs Macmillan as publishers and the Cambridge University Press as printers, has been anxious to give Keynes's writings a permanent form that is wholly worthy of him.

The present edition will publish as much as is possible of his work in the field of economics. It will not include any private and personal correspondence or publish letters in the possession of his family. The edition is concerned, that is to say, with Keynes as an economist.

Keynes's writings fall into five broad categories. First there are the books which he wrote and published as books. Second there are collections of articles and pamphlets which he himself made during his lifetime (*Essays in Persuasion* and *Essays in Biography*). Third, there is a very considerable volume of published but uncollected writings—articles written for newspapers, letters to newspapers, articles in journals that have not been included in his two volumes of collections, and various pamphlets. Fourth, there are a few hitherto unpublished writings. Fifth, there is correspondence with economists and concerned with economics or public affairs. It is the intention of this series to publish almost completely the whole of the first four categories listed above. The only exceptions are a few syndicated articles where Keynes wrote almost the same material for publication in different newspapers or in different countries, with minor and unimportant variations. In these cases, this series will publish one only of the variations, choosing the most interesting.

The publication of Keynes's economic correspondence must inevitably be selective. In the day of the typewriter and the filing cabinet and particularly in the case of so active and busy a man, to publish every scrap of paper that he may have dictated about some unimportant or ephemeral matter is impossible. We are aiming to collect and publish as much as possible, however, of the correspondence in which Keynes developed his own ideas in argument with his fellow economists, as well as the more significant correspondence at times when Keynes was in the middle of public affairs.

Apart from his published books, the main sources available to those preparing this series have been two. First, Keynes in his will made Richard Kahn his executor and responsible for his economic papers. They have been placed in the Marshall Library of the University of Cambridge and have been available for this edition. Until 1914 Keynes did not have a secretary and his earliest papers are in the main limited to drafts of important letters that he made in his own handwriting and retained. At that stage most of the correspondence that we possess is represented by what he received rather than by what he wrote. During the war years of 1914–18 and 1940–6 Keynes was serving in the Treasury. With the opening in 1968 of the records under the thirty-year rule, many of the papers that he wrote then and between the wars have become available. From 1919 onwards, throughout the rest of his life, Keynes had the help of a secretary—for many years Mrs Stephens. Thus for the last twenty-five years of his working life we have in most cases the carbon copies of his own letters as well as the originals of the letters that he received.

There were, of course, occasions during this period on which Keynes wrote himself in his own handwriting. In some of these cases, with the help of his correspondents, we have been able to collect the whole of both sides of some important interchange and we have been anxious, in justice to both correspondents, to see that both sides of the correspondence are published in full.

The second main source of information has been a group of scrapbooks kept over a very long period of years by Keynes's mother, Florence Keynes, wife of Neville Keynes. From 1919 onwards these scrapbooks contain almost the whole of Maynard Keynes's more ephemeral writing, his letters to newspapers and a great deal of material which enables one to see not only what he wrote but the reaction of others to his writing. Without these very carefully kept scrapbooks the task of any editor or biographer of Keynes would have been immensely more difficult.

The plan of the edition, as at present intended, is this. It will total thirty volumes. Of these the first eight are Keynes's published books from *Indian Currency and Finance*, in 1913, to the *General Theory* in 1936, with the addition of his *Treatise on Probability*. There next follow, as vols. IX and X, *Essays in Persuasion* and *Essays in Biography*, representing Keynes's own collections of articles. *Essays in Persuasion* differs from the original printing in two respects: it contains the full texts of the articles or pamphlets included in it and not (as in the original printing) abbreviated versions of these articles, and it also contains one or two later articles which are of exactly the same character as those included by Keynes in his original collection. In *Essays in Biography* there have been added a number of biographical studies that Keynes wrote both before and after 1933.

There will follow two volumes, XI–XII, of economic articles and correspondence and a further two volumes, already published, XIII–XIV, covering the development of his thinking as he moved towards the *General Theory*. There are included in these volumes such part of Keynes's economic correspondence as is closely associated with the articles that are printed in them. A supplement to these volumes, XXIX, prints some further material relating to the same issues, which has since been discovered.

The remaining fourteen volumes deal with Keynes's *Activities* during the years from the beginning of his public life in 1905 until his death. In each of the periods into which we divide this material, the volume concerned publishes his more ephemeral writings, all of it hitherto uncollected, his correspondence relating to these activities, and such other material and correspondence as is necessary to the understanding of Keynes's activities. These volumes are edited by Elizabeth Johnson and Donald Moggridge, and it has been their task to trace and interpret Keynes's activities sufficiently to make the material fully intelligible to a later generation. Elizabeth Johnson has been responsible for vols. XV–XVIII, covering Keynes's earlier years and his activities down to the end of World War I reparations and reconstruction. Donald Moggridge is responsible for all the remaining volumes recording Keynes's other activities from 1924 until his death in 1946.

The present plan of publication, with two of the wartime volumes already published, is to complete the record of Keynes's activities during World War II with the group of volumes of which this forms one. These five volumes cover not only the problems of war finance, internal and external, but also his contributions both in the Treasury and at Bretton Woods and elsewhere to the shaping of the post-war world. It will then remain to fill the gap between 1923 and 1939, to print certain of his published articles and the correspondence relating to them which have not appeared elsewhere in this edition, and to publish a volume of his social, political and literary writings.

Those responsible for this edition have been: Lord Kahn, both as Lord Keynes's executor and as a long and intimate friend of Lord Keynes, able to help in the interpreting of much that would be otherwise misunderstood; Sir Roy Harrod as the author of his biography; Austin Robinson as Keynes's co-editor on the *Economic Journal* and successor as Secretary of the Royal Economic Society. Austin Robinson has acted throughout as Managing Editor; Donald Moggridge is now associated with him as Joint Managing Editor.

In the early stages of the work Elizabeth Johnson was assisted by Jane Thistlethwaite, and by Mrs McDonald, who was originally responsible for the systematic ordering of the files of the Keynes papers. Judith Masterman for many years worked with Mrs Johnson on the papers. More recently Susan Wilsher, Margaret Butler and Leonora Woollam have continued the secretarial work. Barbara Lowe has been responsible for the indexing. Susan Howson undertook much of the important final editorial work on the wartime volumes. Since 1977 Judith Allen has been responsible for seeing the volumes through the press.

EDITORIAL NOTE

This volume, the first of three concerned with Keynes's efforts to shape the post-war world, has as its focus the origins of the Clearing Union and the progress of subsequent discussions in both London and Washington up to April 1944. Two further volumes will be concerned with the negotiations surrounding the founding of the International Monetary Fund and World Bank after that date and with Keynes's activities in such areas as employment policy, commodity policy, relief and reparations.

The sources for this volume are Keynes's surviving papers, materials available in the Public Record Office and the papers of colleagues and friends. Where the material used has come from the Public Record Office, the call numbers for the relevant files appear in the List of Documents Reproduced following page 478.

In this and the other wartime volumes, to aid the reader in keeping track of the various personalities who pass through the pages that follow, we have included brief biographical notes on the first occasion on which they appear. These notes are designed to be cumulative over the whole run of wartime volumes.

In this, as in all the similar volumes, in general all of Keynes's own writings are printed in larger type. Keynes's own footnotes are indicated by asterisks or other symbols to distinguish them from the editorial footnotes. All introductory matter and all writings by others than Keynes are printed in smaller type. The only exception to this general rule is that occasional short quotations from a letter from

Keynes to his parents or to a friend, used in introductory passages to clarify a situation, are treated as introductory matter and are printed in the smaller type.

Most of Keynes's letters included in this and other volumes are reprinted from the carbon copies that remain among his papers. In most cases he has added his initials to the carbon in the familiar fashion in which he signed to all his friends. We have no certain means of knowing whether the top copy, sent to the recipient of the letter, carried a more formal signature.

Chapter 1

THE ORIGINS OF THE CLEARING UNION, 1940–1942

The Second World War was not, of course, the first occasion on which Keynes concerned himself with international monetary reform. One need only think of the proposals in *A Tract on Monetary Reform* (*JMK*, Vol. IV, pp. 141–60), *A Treatise on Money* (*JMK*, Vol. VI, pp. 346–67), 'Notes on the Currency Question' (*JMK*, Vol. XXI) and *The Means to Prosperity* (*JMK*, Vol. IX, pp. 355–66).

Apart from occasional discussions with the 'Old Dogs' and parts of *How to Pay for the War* (*JMK*, Vol. IX), Keynes's first essay on the post-war world came as the result of a request from Harold Nicolson[1] of the Ministry of Information. Nicolson told Keynes that the Ministry was contemplating a campaign to counter Dr Funk's[2] proposals for a German 'New Order'. He hoped that Keynes would launch the campaign with a broadcast and enclosed notes prepared for the purpose. Keynes replied:

From a letter to H. NICOLSON, *20 November 1940*

Dear Harold,

The question you raise in your letter of November 19th wants a good deal of consideration. The following are some preliminary notes on it.

(1) The dossier which you sent along with your letter seems to suggest that we should do well to pose as champions of the pre-war economic *status quo* and outbid Funk by offering good old 1920–21 or 1930–33, i.e. gold standard or international exchange *laissez-faire* aggravated by heavy tariffs, unemployment, etc. etc. Is this particularly attractive or good

---

[1] Hon. Harold Nicolson (1886–1968); entered Foreign Office, 1909; diplomatic service, 1910–29; M.P. for W. Leicester, 1935–45; Parliamentary Secretary to Ministry of Information, 1940–1; Governor of the BBC, 1941–8.

[2] Dr Walther Funk, German Minister of Foreign Affairs, 1938–43; President of the Reichsbank, 1939–45.

propaganda? If you think it is, I am certainly not the man to put it across.

Your Department think that they are making a good joke at Funk's expense by saying 'gold will have no place in this brave new world' and quoting German propaganda to the effect that 'gold will no longer control the destinies of a nation' etc. Well, obviously I am not the man to preach the beauties and merits of the pre-war gold standard.

In my opinion about three-quarters of the passages quoted from the German broadcasts would be quite excellent if the name of Great Britain were substituted for Germany or the Axis, as the case may be. If Funk's plan is taken at its face value, it is excellent and just what we ourselves ought to be thinking of doing. If it is to be attacked, the way to do it would be to cast doubt and suspicion on its *bona fides*. The point is, I should have thought, not that what Funk purports to do is objectionable, but what he will actually do...

(5) To sum up, it is my opinion—

(*a*) that we should not pose as champions of the *status quo*;

(*b*) that we should not produce at this stage any post-war economic scheme of our own, if only on the ground that no one I have yet seen has the foggiest idea of what such a plan ought to be (it would be too hypothetical both in the minds of ourselves and of our audience);

(*c*) that so far as exchange goes the right line to take is that in our Spanish article, namely, that we are doing the same thing as Funk, but much better, much more honestly and with much more regard to other people's interests;

(*d*) that the counter-propaganda should take the form of casting doubt, not on the value of what Funk purports to offer, but on his *bona fides* and good intentions.

I do not feel greatly inspired at this moment of time to the composition of a broadcast even on these lines. But, if you press me, I will take my first moments of leisure to attempt a draft and would prefer to see what it looks like before committing myself further.

One of Keynes's enclosures in his letter to Nicolson was a note he had written earlier that month with Mr Playfair, eventually published by the British Embassy in Madrid as counter-propaganda.

¿QUE QUIERE DECIR EL AREA?

Years ago, money was an international thing: if you had the money of one country you could change it into the money of another at a fixed rate, and you never had to think which currency you held. Exchange control changed all that: before anyone accepted payment in a controlled currency, he had to discover where he could spend it and what he could buy with it. One by one, the currencies of the world, like their national economies were becoming independent of one another.

Sterling was one of the last currencies which you could freely change into any other currency and so spend anywhere. The custom of using sterling as an international currency was generations old, all over the world: London was an unrivalled financial centre and it was the most convenient of all currencies for trade between one country and another.

When England, at the beginning of the war, imposed some measure of exchange control, there were many who said that this was the end of the international use of sterling and of the predominant usefulness of the London financial market. Once England had accepted the territorial view of money, people in other countries could not continue to accept it without thinking: it was no longer a universal means of payment, but a means of spending money within a certain area, buying certain commodities and certain services. What was that area, and what were those commodities and services? Were they useful to Spain? These were the questions which had to be answered before it was clear whether Spain could continue to sell her goods and services for sterling as she had done in the past.

The answer came in the 'area pound sterling' which is now

as familiar a conception as the 'pound sterling' sans phrase which everyone knew and used before the war. The English system of exchange control does not mean that the expenditure of the 'area pound' is confined to England. 'Area pounds' can be used throughout a great part of the world. The area it covers is not a political entity, but a group of territories based on economic and financial organisation. Canada and Newfoundland, which are in the British Empire, are not in the sterling area: Egypt and Iraq are in the sterling area, but outside the Empire.

The essential point is this: that the area pound sterling can be used throughout the wide territory which contains vast resources of manufactured products, animal and vegetable products of every type, grown under every climate, and enormous mineral wealth. The Funk mark is inevitably restricted to a narrow geographical and climatic range: whereas the area of the pound sterling comprises territories in every part of the world.

So the 'area pound' is a good name, and lays emphasis on its most important characteristic. It can be used over a wider territory and for more purposes than any other currency. What is the comparison between this and the compensation schemes of Dr Funk? Can Central Europe produce tin, rubber, jute, sisal, vegetable oils? It is some convenience to Germany's customers to have a bureau which will provide the financial machinery for remittance between different regions of a rationed and war-ravaged Europe, cut off from overseas trade. It is a still more obvious convenience to Germany herself to have a financial dodge by which she can acquire the produce of the countries she occupies without having to pay for them in goods. But the real test between the two currencies is what each of them will buy. The Funk mark is, in its essence, an instrument of tribute and corruption; an up-to-date variant of the exchange devices for obtaining something for nothing which Germany has worked so hard in recent years. The area pound sterling remains, in its essence, an instrument of trade which preserves to the full extent that is possible in time of war the former universality and lasting worth of the old pound sterling. Let any Spaniard ask himself which he would rather hold, either for present use or for future value, the area pound or the Funk mark, comparing his recent experience of the various Schacht marks with his experience how even after the war the rights of all foreign holders of the old pound sterling were fully preserved. Can he hesitate?

Spain has a clearing with the United Kingdom. In the normal clearing, there is an exact bilateral arrangement of trade; if this was of the ordinary type, the proceeds of everything which Spain sold to England would have to be spent in England. The existence of the sterling area makes a different system possible, which is far more advantageous to Spain. Part of the proceeds of her sales to England are reserved for purchases there; these serve to buy such necessary goods as coal, machinery, tin smelted in England from ores which come from the sterling area, textiles, chemicals, motor-cars, machinery and tools; but an equal part may be used anywhere in the sterling area, for goods which are vital to the Spanish economy and some of which could not be obtained anywhere else, or only with the greatest difficulty.

Let us examine a few of Spain's greatest needs: which can be purchased with the area pound. It will buy wheat from Egypt and Australia; rubber and tin from the Straits Settlements; jute from India; cotton of different grades from Egypt and India; oilseeds from the British African colonies. This short list, which could be greatly extended, is enough to show the vast difference between the surplus resources of the sterling area and the restricted resources of Germany and the German-occupied territories. However skilled the Germans are at manufacturing substitutes and synthetic imitations, they can never change a part of Europe into an area which can produce vegetable products which grow in tropical, semi-tropical and temperate climates; nor can they manufacture deposits of minerals where they do not exist. The sterling area is not merely useful; it is essential, and those who are deprived of its resources know this best.

But that is not the end of the uses of the area pound. At first it seemed that it might have to be confined to expenditure within the sterling area; but events have shown that other countries, who themselves have equal need of the products of the sterling area, are willing to sell their goods for area pounds. Many deals of this kind have been arranged, and the system is developing day by day. To take one or two examples: Spain has bought from Portugal valuable stocks of colonial products, such as vegetable oils and sisal, and paid for them with area pounds; Chile has sold nitrates to Spain for area pounds; and Spain makes large importations of Bacalao from Newfoundland, Iceland and the Faroe Islands and pays for them out of the Anglo-Spanish Clearing.

Exports to England, therefore, provide a means of payment with which no other controlled currency can be compared. The sterling area is vast, but Spain must naturally think of her old trading connections with Portugal, South America and other countries; and owing to the universal need of area pounds, she is able to keep those up, paying, as she so often has done in the past, in sterling.

This is the answer to the question which many have asked: "What is behind sterling? Is there anything beside the convenience of the London market? Cannot we do without the use of sterling which has become a habit, and shall we not have to do without it now that England has imposed exchange control?"

A particular kind of money is a mere mechanism, which works well or badly. The important thing is the goods which that money will buy: the territorial division of present-day economy makes this clearer than ever. The sterling area is the largest and richest of all the territories which have a controlled economy: and the area pound is a simple mechanism to make the resources of the area available to traders all over the world. When you use it, you use the long-established and smooth, reliable machinery of the City of London, which has grown up on conducting international trade on the simplest, most honourable and cheapest basis. It avoids the complications of barter and compensation, which hide the lack of resources and – too often – the juggling of prices to the organiser's benefit which lie behind them; and owing to its true usefulness and the backing of material behind it, the area pound is naturally maintaining the international position which sterling has always had. It is not sterling itself which is useful; it is the sterling area, to which it is the key, and that is necessary to all the world.

At this point Nicolson's request was caught up with another request. Lord Halifax asked the Chancellor if Keynes would prepare 'some authoritative statement exposing the fallacious character of the German promises' for a 'New Order'. Keynes agreed to do so and drafted a series of 'Proposals to Counter the German "New Order"', first dated 25 November 1940. He circulated the proposals on 1 December with a covering note.

PROPOSALS TO COUNTER THE GERMAN 'NEW ORDER'

German propaganda purports to offer her neighbours a stable currency system, adapted to the commerce of countries which have no gold, and above all a system of economic order and organisation. Its object is to appeal to the wide circles and powerful interests in each country which are inclined in present circumstances to value social security higher than political independence. I have been asked to draft a possible basis for counter-propaganda.

It is not easy to be convincing on a purely negative basis. If we have nothing positive to say, we had better be silent. Tentatively, therefore, I have introduced in what follows some positive declarations. The first step is to examine the advisability of these and perhaps to approve them.

(1) I have assumed that our policy of acquiring surplus commodities, with the intention of putting them at the disposal of Europe after the war, is already a going concern. For a comprehensive policy on these lines the cooperation of U.S.A. is necessary and is not yet obtained. If we are to wait for definite American participation before we commit ourselves, no immediate propaganda on these lines is possible. I do not consider such delay is necessary, because we are already acquiring, and the Empire, taken as a whole, already possesses, sufficient surplus stocks to make a large contribution to Europe's most urgent post-war requirements.

(2) I have assumed that we shall continue our existing exchange controls after the war, and that we do not propose to return to *laissez-faire* currency arrangements on pre-war lines by which goods were freely bought and sold internationally in terms of gold or its equivalent. Since we ourselves will have very little gold left and will owe great quantities of sterling to overseas creditors, this seems only common sense. (This does *not* mean that gold will cease to play its part as a reserve of purchasing power and as a means of settling international indebtedness.) I have, therefore, taken the line that what we offer is the same as what Dr Funk offers, except that we shall do it better and more honestly. This is important. For a proposal to return to the blessings of 1920–33 will not have much propaganda value.

The virtue of free trade depends on international trade being carried on by means of what is, in effect, *barter*. After the last war *laissez-faire* in foreign exchange led to chaos. Tariffs offer no escape from this. But in Germany Schacht and Funk were led by force of necessity to evolve something better. In practice they have used their new system to the detriment of their neighbours. But the underlying idea is

8

sound and good. In the last six months the Treasury and the Bank of England have been building up for this country an exchange system which has borrowed from the German experience all that was good in it. If we are to meet our obligations and avoid chaos in international trade after the war, we shall have to retain this system. But this same system will serve to protect the impoverished European countries and is an essential safeguard against a repetition of what happened last time.

(3) An optimistic assumption as to the ultimate outcome of our financial arrangements with U.S.A. is implicit throughout. To prevent misunderstanding I must emphasise this. But, obviously, there is not much scope for convincing economic propaganda except on this assumption.

(4) I have assumed that, this time, there will be no post-armistice starvation of Germany herself and that she will share, equally with her neighbours, in the surplus stocks; i.e. that *after the war is over* we shall not continue starvation and unemployment as an instrument for enforcing our political settlement. This is necessary, if our propaganda is to have value within Germany itself. It is also important in the minds of those who are fearful that, in the event of our victory, we shall allow a general collapse of organisation and social security in Europe.

(5) In one passage I have gone further than this and have indicated that Germany under new auspices will be allowed to resume that measure of *economic* leadership in Central Europe which flows naturally from her qualifications and geographical position. I cannot see how the rest of Europe can expect effective economic reconstruction if Germany is excluded from it and remains a festering mass in their midst; and an economically reconstructed Germany will necessarily resume leadership. This conclusion is inescapable, unless it is our intention to hand the job over to Russia. To admit it is good European propaganda in every quarter which at-

taches importance to social security. It is compatible with any desired degree of severity in respect of political and military conditions. I am assuming, in short, that our post-war policy towards Germany will favour her economic reconstruction and will concentrate all our punitive and preventive measures in the political and military settlement. It is vital to make this distinction if we are to make effective propaganda on the basis that we too, and indeed that we only, can offer Europe economic health.

It is argued in some quarters that our propaganda should aim at an appeal to revolutionary sentiment in Europe. I believe that this is a mistake. The following is based on the idea that we should do better to compete with Germany, for which we are well-qualified, in an appeal to the craving for social and personal *security*.

I append the following (rather slight) draft to focus discussion, with the idea that its substance could be revised, adapted and greatly improved in the light of such discussion. I have not attempted at this stage, to make the document suitable to any particular orator or to any particular occasion. A campaign of propaganda ought to be initiated by an impressive and authoritative declaration on broad lines, supplying positive basis for the Ministry of Information to build upon. It should be followed up by a continuous bombardment of up-to-date and illustrative details in five-minute weekly broadcasts to all the relevant countries; giving particulars, for example, of our Surplus Commodities Policy at each stage of its development, of the working of our payments agreements in practice, of Germany's exactions and impositions etc., etc.

J. M. KEYNES

1 December 1940

Keynes's Draft Statement ran as follows.

The authors of the Peace Treaty of Versailles made the mistake of neglecting the economic reconstruction of Europe in their preoccupation with political frontiers and safeguards. Much misfortune to all of us has followed from this neglect.

The British Government are determined not to make the same mistake again. Mr Bevin said recently that social security must be the first object of our domestic policy after the war. And social security for the peoples of all the European countries will be our policy abroad not less than at home. Indeed the one is hardly possible without the other; for we are all members of one family. We must make it our business, above most other purposes, to prevent the starvation of the post-armistice period, the currency disorders throughout Europe and the wild fluctuations of employment, markets and prices which were the cause of so much misery in the twenty years between the two wars; and we shall see to it that this shall be compatible with the proper liberty of each country over its own economic fortunes.

Very little reflection is necessary to convince anyone that we, acting in friendly collaboration with the United States, and we alone, will be in a position to implement such a policy. For, irrespective of the nature of the political settlement, Europe will end this war starved and bankrupt of all the foods and raw materials, for supplies of which she was accustomed to depend on the rest of the world. She will have no means, unaided, of breaking the vicious circle. For she will possess no gold worth mentioning and can export very little until she has, first of all, received the necessary raw materials. She will face the vast problem of general demobilisation with an almost total lack of the necessary means to put men to work. The depletion of livestock, seed, manures, and agricultural implements, and the omission during the war of necessary cultivation will leave agriculture as prone as industry. The whole continent will face a situation comparable with the famine in Russia which followed the Revolution in the early twenties. For today no one pretends, whatever else may happen, that Germany can hope to end this war with control over the raw materials of the other continents.

The German Government are attempting to cover up the emptiness of their hands and the bleakness of the prospect by much vague talk about 'the New Order'. Mostly words, no doubt. But let us try to discover its content and compare it with the British policy for Europe.

The most definite of the German plans, so far, is the currency scheme of Dr Funk. The Funk mark pretends to offer a stable currency for post-war purposes. How can this be so if it has no command of resources outside Europe? It has only one merit, namely that it avoids some of the abuses of the old *laissez-faire* international currency arrangements, whereby a country could be bankrupted, not because it lacked exportable goods, but merely because it lacked gold. But let no one suppose that we for our part intend to return to the chaos of the old world. To do so would bankrupt us no less than others. The arrangements we are now slowly perfecting, by which international exchange returns to what it always should have been, namely a means for trading goods against goods, will outlast the war; though in a form which will retain a proper place for gold as a central reserve and as a means of international settlement, completer and more mutually advantageous than is easily worked out in war conditions.

We pledge ourselves to the establishment of a system of international exchange which will open all our markets to every country, great or small, alike, and will give equal access for each to every source of raw material which we can control or influence, on the basis of exchanging goods for goods. We pledge ourselves to radical remedies for our own unemployment and to assist the same object in all other countries both by the means we employ at home and by taking whatever measures are necessary to pass into consumption goods which otherwise could not be produced.

At the start, nevertheless, this will not be enough to fill the vacuum. The liberated European countries will require an initial pool of resources to carry them through the transitional period. We therefore contemplate a European Reconstruction Fund out of which the central bank of each liberated country will be supplied immediately with the credit to purchase food and raw materials from outside.

We shall have the means to do this, because the British Empire will actually possess overseas enormous stocks of food and materials, which we are already accumulating so as to ease the problems of the overseas producers during the war and of reconstructed Europe after the war. The Prime Minister has already made clear the importance he attaches to this. We are now actively engaged in working out the details. And in all this we hope for the collaboration of the United States.

What has Germany to offer on her side? Absolutely nothing. An official of the Reich Economics Ministry, in a moment of hard realism which is, in truth, more characteristic of the German mind than transparent and worn-out propaganda, published recently a statement that the present German rationing system must continue for at least one year after the restoration of peace, and perhaps for several. The huge latent demand for food, clothing and other articles of prime necessity which cannot be satisfied under war conditions will, he went on to say, again become operative after the signature of peace, but the production of such commodities will not for a long while exceed war-time output. All this is not only true, but obvious. Yet can social security survive such conditions, continuing, beyond the disciplined period of war, as a frightful disappointment after the peace?

It is not easy to find much else which is definite in Germany's New Economic Order, except the plan by which high-grade industry is to be mainly concentrated within Germany herself, the satellite and tributary states being compelled to confine themselves to the kinds of production which suit the convenience of Germany and chiefly to agriculture;

and by which the terms of exchange between Germany's high-grade products and the output of the other states will be fixed so as to maintain a standard of life in Germany much above that of her neighbours. Meanwhile all foreign commerce would become a German monopoly. It would be a surprising triumph for propaganda to make an up-to-date version of imperialist exploitation verging on slavery seem attractive to the victims. Superimposed on this there will doubtless be prohibitions against teaching to tributary nationals engineering or any other modern technique, perhaps (since one thing leads to another) including medicine, with the destruction of all local universities and technical schools. In this way intellectual darkness would aggravate low physical standards, in the hope that thus the much-to-be-feared nationalist resorgimentos [sic] might be indefinitely postponed. Finally, to what could all this be the prelude but a new war which would carry overseas the imperialist exploitation which had already devoured Europe without finding satisfaction? Such is 'the New Order'.

No one can suppose that the economic reorganisation of Europe after the British victory will be an easy task. But we shall not shirk our opportunity and our responsibility. The peaceful brotherhood of nations with the proper liberty to each to develop its own balanced economic life and its characteristic culture, will be the object. But it is the transition to this end and the establishment of an international economic system, capable of translating the technical possibilities of production into actual plenty and maintaining the whole population in a continuous fruitful activity, which is difficult. We cannot expect to solve the economic riddle easily or completely. But we alone possess a command of the material means. And, what is perhaps more important, we alone have the will and the intention to evolve a post-war order which seeks no particularist advantage but only that each member of the European family shall realise its own character and perfect its own gifts in liberty of conscience and person. We cannot perform miracles. But we have learnt the lesson of the interregnum between the two wars; and we know that no escape can be found from the curse which has been lying on Europe except by creating and preserving economic health in every country.

From which it follows that this same principle must apply to the German people themselves. Under new leadership they will not be excluded from the benefits of the European Reconstruction Fund or from the comfortable relaxation of the economic revival. On suitable conditions they will receive their proper share of the accumulated stocks of food and materials. Their opportunities of recovery shall not be less than those of their liberated neighbours. It is not our purpose to reverse the roles proposed by Germany for herself and for her neighbours. It would be senseless to suppose that her neighbours can develop an ordered, a prosperous, or a secure life with a crushed and ruined Germany in their midst. Germany must be expected and allowed to assume the measure of economic leadership which flows naturally from her own qualifications and her geographical position. Germany is the worst master the world has yet known. But, on terms of equality, she can be an efficient colleague. Our political and military conditions will be sufficiently strict to make Germany's economic and social recovery safe and beneficial to her neighbours.

The right outcome after the war requires on our part no exceptional unselfishness but merely common sense. It is obvious that we have no motive of self-interest prompting us to the economic exploitation either of Germany or of the rest of Europe. This is not what we want or what we could perform. The lasting settlement and internal peace of the continent as a whole is the only thing which suits us. It is the ultimate source of our strength in the secular European conflicts in which we have played a part, that at the bottom of his heart every participant knows this. To every neutral, satellite or conquered country it is obvious that our victory is, for the most fundamental and unalterable reasons, to their plain advantage; and their only hope. This situation is always the same; and in the end it plays a significant part in the defeat of the aggressor which ultimately ensues.

J. M. K.

The draft was then subjected to Treasury, Bank of England, Foreign Office and Ministry of Economic Warfare comment. As well, Keynes discussed the draft with Mr Harry Hopkins during his January 1941 visit to London to discuss President Roosevelt's lend lease proposals. After comments and revisions to met them, Keynes's proposals went to the Prime Minister on 30 January 1941.

The re-draft that went to Mr Churchill had markedly cut down Keynes's original proposals on post-war currency, although the Governor of the Bank of England had commented:

> The currency system to which the statement pledges us presumably commits us to maintaining exchange control after the war. This is as it should be, but the Cabinet should do it with its eyes open.

Similarly, the specific proposal for a European Reconstruction Fund disappeared although the references to surplus materials remained. Also the passages on Germany became stronger to make it clear that a peace settlement would prevent a repetition of Germany's past behaviour and that starvation and mass unemployment would not be a weapon for use against Germany after the war. Finally the document pledged that the U.K. would begin discussions on post-war relief.

There matters stood until May 1941, beyond a letter of 25 April in which Keynes elaborated some of the currency notions of his earlier drafts.

To F. T. ASHTON-GWATKIN, *25 April 1941*

Dear Mr Ashton-Gwatkin,

The best short replies I can make to the questions you pass on to me in your letter of April 21st are these:

1. My words meant that international capital movements would be restricted so that they would only be allowed in the

event of the country from which capital was moving having a favourable balance with the country to which they were being remitted. In other words they would only be allowed when they were feasible without upsetting the existing equilibrium. In the pre-war system they were unrestricted and we then had to take what steps we could, often inadequate, to adjust other items in the account so as to restore the balance. Whatever one might wish, something of this sort seems to be inevitable, since we shall no longer have a cushion of gold or of other liquid assets, by means of which the immediate effects of unbalanced capital movements can be handled.

2. My proposals certainly imply a continuation of payments agreements or something of the same kind. But I should hope that with experience large elements of a multilateral system could be introduced. That is to say, the aim would be to interfere as little as possible, provided that a balance is maintained with the outside world as a whole. But unquestionably it would involve a discrimination against the United States if she persisted in maintaining an unbalanced creditor position. Again, whether we like it or not, this will be forced on us. We shall have no means after the war out of which we can pay for purchases in the United States except the equivalent of what they buy from us.

3. No doubt our hands would be free to fix the exchange parities of sterling. We should no doubt be most reluctant to do this except by agreement. But this would not be the object, which would be almost the opposite. For, with a proper system of payments agreements which would prevent an unbalanced situation from developing, there would be no longer much object in depreciating the exchange. The method of depreciation is a bad method which one is driven to adopt failing something better. The currency system I have in view would be that something better. If U.S.A. inflates more than we do, we might even *appreciate* sterling.

4. My hope would be that the currency system would cover

the whole of the existing sterling area and possibly other countries. The Dutch and Belgians have both indicated that they might be inclined to join the sterling area for this purpose. The wider the area the better. But the details of this are not yet properly thought out. For it is possible for an unbalanced position to develop within the sterling area as well as outside it. There would have to be some arrangement by which an unbalanced position up to an agreed figure would have to be cared for by credit arrangements. But, if the maximum were reached, then the unbalanced debtor member of the system would have to restrict its purchases until it was in balance again.

5. The arrangements now slowly perfecting relate to the payments agreements which now cover nearly the whole world outside North America. There have been some tentative movements for multilateral clearing in South America. In peace conditions there is no reason why multilateral clearing should not be rapidly developed.

Finally I return to the point that this means 'trading goods against goods'. For under such a system, if, for example, we buy maize from the Argentine and pay in sterling there will be no use that Argentine can make of that sterling except to purchase from the sterling area. It does not mean that there would be direct barter of goods against goods, but that the one trading transaction must necessarily find its counterpart in another trading transaction sooner or later. The foreign owner of sterling can, of course, just leave the balance in London, but there is nothing else he can do with it except to purchase goods.

Under such a system an importing country such as Great Britain automatically becomes an attractive country to buy from. For the mere fact that we are importers on a great scale will furnish the selling country with sterling which has to be spent either here or elsewhere in the sterling area.

It seems to me that something of this kind is practically

inevitable and, properly worked, may prove a great boon. The difficulty is to know quite how far it is safe to go in the direction of complete freedom of transactions within the sterling area. The above system might mean that countries selling to us would use the proceeds for buying from other members of the sterling area. If it turned out that this was chronically so on a large scale, it would mean that freedom within the sterling area would break down to some extent and the arrangements in question would have less universality in practice. That is to say, if things go badly, it might mean that we should have to insist that the Argentine seller of maize must spend his sterling in the United Kingdom. But one would like to aim, if possible, at a wider system and allow him liberty to spend it anywhere in the sterling area until experience shows that this is too ambitious a scheme.

The necessity of some such plan as the above arises essentially from the unbalanced creditor position of the United States. It is a necessary condition of a return to free exchanges that the United States should find some permanent remedy for this unbalanced position. Sooner or later one can only suppose that she will have to do so. But it would be very optimistic to believe that she will find the solution in the immediate post-war period, even if she tries to mitigate her task by making large presents for the reconstruction of Europe.

Yours sincerely,
[copy initialled] J. M. K.

In May 1941, Mr Eden decided to use Keynes's draft as the basis for a speech he was to give at the Mansion House on 29 May. After consulting with officials in Washington, where he was engaged in lend lease discussions, Keynes suggested minor amendments to his draft. He also discussed it with the President.[3] When Mr Eden's speech was delivered, it followed the lines of Keynes's draft, adjusted for changes in circumstances and, as Brendan Bracken put it to Churchill on 20 May, 'well wrapped in Foreign Office wool'.

[3] See *JMK*, vol. XXIII, p. 109.

On his return from Washington in August 1941, Keynes, following the early Article VII discussions, returned to thinking and talking about post-war international currency arrangements. At the end of a week's holiday at Tilton, he reported to Richard Kahn.

From a letter to RICHARD KAHN, *21 August 1941*

I have not got down to the job of putting on paper my ideas about future currency arrangements. But I do not think the discussion can make much progress until I try to make my ideas concrete and press others who have different ideas to do the same.

I have had a long talk with Shackle[4] since I came back. He seemed to be prepared to make conditions as to American co-operation which are quite certain not to be fulfilled. Indeed I am not seriously worried by the rather unexpected apparent strength of the *laissez-faire* school. For I have not the slightest doubt that we shall start in practice *de facto* with a [exchange] control and what actually will be evolved from that in a direction which is extremely unlikely to be *laissez-faire*.

What really does worry me is the job of adapting our *de facto* system to peace-time conditions. The general nature of what we do will be dictated by inescapable facts, but the details present a technical problem of the utmost difficulty.

However, I should very much like to talk all this over with you at an early stage, though I shan't myself know exactly what I have in view until I put pen to paper. My aim will be not to allow Shackle and others to waste too much of my time, but to aim at putting the practical problem in its true light and then concentrate on technical means of solution without bothering myself about ideals, which, whether right or wrong, are in the actual circumstances pure fantasy. In other words, I am inclined to share your belief that when we get down to brass tacks many of the exaggerated differences of opinion will simply disappear.

[4] Robert Jones Shackle (1895–1950); Assistant Principal, Board of Trade, 1920, Principal, 1929, Assistant Secretary, 1935, Principal Assistant Secretary, 1942–7, Under-Secretary, 1947.

The Treasury discussions continued into September. On 8 September, after a weekend of drafting at Tilton, Keynes had finished his first shot at post-war currency policy in the form of two memoranda.[5]

POST-WAR CURRENCY POLICY

I. *The Secular International Problem*

The problem of maintaining equilibrium in the balance of payments between countries has never been solved, since methods of barter gave way to the use of money and bills of exchange. During most of the period in which the modern world has been evolved and the autarky of the middle ages was gradually giving way to the international division of labour and the exploitation of new sources of supply by overseas enterprise, the failure to solve this problem has been a major cause of impoverishment and social discontent and even of wars and revolutions. In the past five hundred years there have been only two periods of about fifty years each (the ages of Elizabeth and Victoria in English chronology) when the use of money for the conduct of international trade can be said to have 'worked',—first whilst the prodigious augmentation of the supply of silver from the new world was substituting the features of inflation for those of deflation (bringing a different sort of evil with it), and again in the second half of the nineteenth century when (for reasons to be developed below) the system of international investment pivoting on London transferred the *onus* of adjustment from the debtor to the creditor position.

To suppose that there exists some smoothly functioning automatic mechanism of adjustment which preserves equilibrium if only we trust to methods of *laissez-faire* is a doc-

---

[5] On 16 September 1941 R. H. Brand sent Keynes a memorandum by E. F. Schumacher, a German Rhodes scholar then working as an agricultural labourer on Brand's farm, entitled 'Some Aspects of Post-war Economic Planning'. This memorandum advocated an international clearing arrangement. There is no record of Keynes's comments on the proposal and no indication that it influenced the development of Keynes's ideas.

trinaire delusion which disregards the lessons of historical experience without having behind it the support of sound theory. So far from currency *laissez-faire* having promoted the international division of labour, which is the avowed goal of *laissez-faire*, it has been a fruitful source of all those clumsy hindrances to trade which suffering communities have devised in their perplexity as being better than nothing in protecting them from the intolerable burdens flowing from currency disorders. Until quite recently, nearly all departures from international *laissez-faire* have tackled the symptoms instead of the cause.

International currency *laissez-faire* was breaking down rapidly before the war. During the war it has disappeared completely. This complete break with the past offers us an opportunity. Things are possible to-day which would have been impossible if they involved the prior disestablishment of a settled system.

Moreover in the interval between the wars the world explored in rapid succession almost, as it were, in an intensive laboratory experiment all the alternative false approaches to the solution—

(i) the idea that a freely fluctuating exchange would discover for itself a position of equilibrium;

(ii) liberal credit and loan arrangements between the creditor and the debtor countries flowing from the mere fact of an unbalanced creditor–debtor position, on the false analogy of superficially similar nineteenth-century transactions between old-established and newly-developing countries where the loans were self-liquidating because they themselves created new sources of payment;

(iii) the theory that the unlimited free flow of gold would automatically bring about adjustments of price-levels and activity in the recipient country which would reverse the pressure;

(iv) the use of deflation, and still worse of *competitive* deflations, to force an adjustment of wage- and price-levels which would force or attract trade into new channels;

(v) the use of deliberate exchange depreciation, and still worse of *competitive* exchange depreciations, to attain the same object;

(vi) the erection of tariffs, preferences, subsidies *et hoc genus omne* to restore the balance of international commerce by restriction and discrimination.

It was only in the last years, almost in the last months, before the crash, that after the above trials and errors Dr Schacht stumbled in desperation on something new which had in it the germs of a good technical idea. This idea was to cut the knot by discarding the use of a currency having international validity and substitute for it what amounted to barter, not indeed between individuals, but between different economic units. In this way he was able to return to the essential character and original purpose of trade whilst discarding the apparatus which had been supposed to facilitate, but was in fact strangling it. This innovation worked well, indeed brilliantly, for those responsible for introducing it, and allowed impoverished Germany to build up reserves without which she could scarcely have embarked on war. But as Mr Henderson remarks, the fact that this method was used in the service of evil must not blind us to its possible technical advantage in the service of a good cause. 'If Germany', he points out, 'had wished for butter instead of guns or aeroplanes, there is no reason to doubt that Dr Schacht's expedients would have enabled her to obtain the butter instead of the metal from overseas.' Moreover the use of this method with reckless disregard to the legitimate interests of the other party concerned is characteristic of the German handling of it and is not inherent, as we ourselves have shown in the variants of the method which we have devised and with the aid of which we are successfully maintaining our financial front even during the war.

I expound in a separate paper a possible means of still retaining a currency having an unrestricted international validity. But the alternative to this is surely not a return to the currency disorders of the epoch between the wars, mitigated and temporarily postponed by some liberal Red Cross work by the United States, but a refinement and improvement of the Schachtian device.

II. *Our Contemporary British Problem*

Unfortunately the technical task of devising a system, by which a state of international balance can be maintained once it has been reached, is made vastly more difficult by the circumstance that we start out from an existing state of extreme disequilibrium. Drastic changes in the channels along which trade is likely to run after the war if left to itself are a prior condition of the initial attainment of equilibrium, which is not quite the same problem as that of maintaining equilibrium after it has been reached. The United States never succeeded in effecting the re-orientation of her domestic economy required by the changed circumstances in which she found herself after the last war. Her necessary task after this war will be still more severe. The solution involves a serious disturbance to the vested interests both of industry and of agriculture of a kind which it would be contrary to the political traditions and national customs of the country to carry through. Her first contribution in this field is not encouraging; for she proposes the enforcement of an agreement to restrict Europe's freedom to feed herself by compelling even the poorest Eastern European states, however impoverished by war, to eat pure white bread, the admixture of any rye or potato flour being made illegal by international convention, and to buy from overseas, instead of growing it, an amount of wheat costing an additional sum as large as the German indemnity ultimately fixed after the last war which we failed to collect, and, if the present price clauses were to remain, a much larger sum than this,—all this for the purpose of maintaining on a profitable basis an export of wheat from the United States which, in the interests of the restoration of international equilibrium, ought to disappear altogether.

It will be better, however, that I should discuss this phase of the problem in terms of the British prospective situation when the war is over.

Mr Henderson has summed up the position thus:-

We must expect to emerge from the war with our balance of payments very seriously deranged. A substantial portion of our export trade was permanently lost as a consequence of the last war; a further substantial portion is likely to be permanently lost as a consequence of the present one. A further substantial portion of our 'invisible exports' in respect both of interest, dividends, and of shipping receipts, is also likely to be lost. On the other hand, our need for imports, both of food and materials, will be abnormally large for some time after the war, and will always remain large if we succeed in maintaining a high standard of life.

The Lord President's economists are, I believe, engaged in preparing a reasoned estimate of the possible magnitude of the gap. Meanwhile it would be a waste of time for me to attempt a close estimate. But, remembering that the gross increase in our exports will have to exceed the net improvement required in the balance of trade by the amount of imported raw materials incorporated in the exports, I shall be surprised if the needed increase does not exceed the pre-war figure in real terms by somewhere between 50 and 100 per cent. What valid reason have we for supposing that an increment of this order will automatically accrue to us under conditions of *laissez-faire* and without the stimulus of special measures on our part?

Of the special measures which it is open to us to employ by far the most potent is to use the importance of the British market to producers of food and raw materials overseas as an inducement to them to make equivalent purchases of manufactured articles from us. The Argentine, for example, cannot hope to market her wheat and maize and meat, none of which are required by the U.S., unless she can sell substantial quantities to Britain. We may have to tell her that we are not in a financial position to purchase these substantial quantities unless she is prepared to expend the proceeds on taking textiles and engineering products from us.

This is a legitimate arrangement greatly in the interests of both parties. Without it trade on the appropriate scale might be impossible and both countries would be condemned to unemployment and impoverishment. It may be the only feasible means of maximising the volume of international exchange. But the technical means for thus arranging to match imports with exports would involve a far-reaching departure from the pre-war system.

A further obstacle to the restoration of *laissez-faire* methods at any rate during the transitional period (say the first five years) after the war is the accumulation in London of very large overseas balances, representing what we have borrowed abroad for war purposes over and above what we have discharged by the liquidation of our pre-war overseas investments. This by itself will render it essential for the maintenance of the war controls for a considerable time afterwards, unless we can replace them by a far-reaching constructive scheme which will offer us the necessary protection.

It is far from certain as yet that there are no other, and better, alternatives. I can imagine more than one fortunate turn of affairs which would greatly mitigate the difficulties which lie ahead. I attempt in a separate paper to sketch an ideal system which would solve the problem of multilateral lines by international agreement. This is an ambitious scheme. But the post-war world must not be content with patchwork. If it can be accepted, several vital purposes will be served. But we have yet to discover whether those in authority in the world mean seriously their brave words about radical post-war innovation.

Meanwhile it would be madness on our part to deprive ourselves of the possibility of action along the above lines until we have a firm assurance of an equally satisfactory solution of a different kind. Anyone who at this stage would agree to sign away our future liberty of action would be as great a traitor to his country as if he were to sign away the British navy before he had a firm assurance of an alternative means of protection. For this is the key problem of our post-war prosperity. If we can solve it, the rest will follow without insuperable difficulty. If we fail, our best hopes of finally abolishing economic want and of providing continuous good employment at a high standard of life will be lost to us. A vast disappointment, social disorders and finally a repudiation of our ill-judged commitments will be the result.

III. *The Analysis of the Problem*

I believe that the main cause of failure (except in special, transient conditions) of the freely convertible international metallic standard (first silver and then gold) can be traced to a single characteristic. I ask close attention to this, because I should argue that this provides the clue to the nature of any alternative which is to be successful.

It is characteristic of a freely convertible international standard that it throws the main burden of adjustment on the country which is in the *debtor* position on the international balance of payments,—that is on the country which is (in this context) by hypothesis the *weaker* and above all the *smaller* in comparison with the other side of the scales which (for this purpose) is the rest of the world.

Take the classical theory that the unlimited free flow of gold automatically brings about adjustments of price-levels and activity between the debtor country and the recipient creditor, which will eventually reverse the pressure. It is usual to-day to object to this theory that it is too dependent on a crude and now abandoned quantity theory of money and that it ignores the lack of elasticity in the social structure of wages and prices. But even to the extent that it holds good in spite of these grave objections, if a country is in economic importance even a fifth of the world as a whole, a given loss of gold will presumably exercise four times as much pressure at home as abroad, with a still greater disparity if it is only a tenth or a twentieth of the world, so that the contribution in terms of the resulting social strains which the debtor country has to make to the restoration of equilibrium by changing its prices and wages is altogether out of proportion to the contribution asked of its creditors. Nor is this all. To begin with, the social strain of an adjustment downwards is much greater than that of an adjustment upwards. And besides this, the process of adjustment is *compulsory* for the debtor and *voluntary* for the creditor. If the creditor does not choose to make, or allow, his share of the adjustment, he suffers no inconvenience. For whilst a country's reserve cannot fall below zero, there is no ceiling which sets an upper limit. The same is true if international loans are to be the means of adjustment. The debtor *must* borrow; the creditor is under no such compulsion.

There is a further consequence, having very great importance, of the main burden of adjustment being on the debtor country which is *small* compared with the world at large; namely, that most of the means of adjustment open to the debtor country are liable to have an adverse effect on its terms of trade. (The best argument in favour of the expedient of tariffs is that it is free from this objection). The effect on the terms of trade is not usually understood by outside opinion; but it has a long history in economic theory and came into particular prominence in the controversy whether Germany would be able to manage the comparatively moderate indemnity which was eventually fixed. The point is, however, easily explained. Domestic deflation, exchange depreciation and the like aim at stimulating exports by reducing their international *price* in terms of imports. The amount of price reduction which will prove necessary to stimulate a sufficient expansion in the *quantity* of exports relatively to imports depends on the elasticity of demand in the world at large for the characteristic products of the country which seeks to increase its sales. If, on account of the nature of the products or of the reluctance of foreign competitors to relinquish their share of the trade, a large reduction in price is necessary to stimulate a sufficient increase in quantity, the country which is forcing its products on the world suffers a severe loss in the proceeds obtained from its *previous* volume of trade. To take the limiting case, if it is necessary to reduce the price in at least the same proportion as that in which the volume is increased, the debtor country is involved in a Sisyphus task and gets no nearer a position of equilibrium however great its efforts. Brazilian coffee may offer an example which approaches the limiting case. But for many agricultural products, quite a reasonable percentage reduction in the price paid by the ultimate consumer may, after deduction of costs of transport and distribution overseas at a fixed rate, present conditions to the ultimate producer which approximate to the limiting case.

Thus it has been an inherent characteristic of the automatic international metallic currency (apart from special circumstances) to force adjustments in the direction most disruptive of social order, and to throw the burden on the countries least able to support it, making the poor poorer.

It may be some confirmation of the importance to be attached to this characteristic of the traditional system that, in the two periods in which the system 'worked', special influences were present which largely removed the burden of pressure, or reversed its direction, as between the debtor country and the creditor or the world at large. In the period of inflation caused by the flow of silver from the new world, the strong, creditor countries, which first received the silver, had to take the initiative in price adjustment. (The same easing factor may have been at work in the vast development of trade and prosperity throughout the Mediterranean countries and beyond which followed the dispersal of the temple hoards of Persia by Alexander the Great.) Again, in the Victorian age the peculiar organisation in London and to a less extent in Paris, the two main creditor centres, by which a flow of gold immediately translated itself, not in the first instance into a change in prices and wages, but into a change in the volume of foreign investment by the creditors, caused the burden to be carried by the stronger shoulders.

I conclude, therefore, that the architects of a successful international system must be guided by these lessons. The object of the new system must be to require the chief initiative from the creditor countries, whilst maintaining enough discipline in the debtor countries to prevent them from exploiting the new ease allowed them in living profligately beyond their means.

There was a further defect in the pre-war system not to be overlooked. It allowed *laissez-faire* in the remittance and acceptance overseas of capital funds for refugee, speculative or investment purposes. During the nineteenth century and up to 1914 the flow of capital funds had been directed from the creditor to the debtor countries, which broadly corresponded to the older and the newer countries, and served at the same time to keep the balance of international payments in equilibrium and to develop resources in undeveloped lands. In the first phase after the last war, the flow of funds continued to be directed from the creditor to the debtor countries, but a large part of the flow, namely from the United States (and also from Great Britain) into Europe ceased to correspond to the development of new resources. In the second phase preceding the present war, complete degeneration set in and capital funds flowed from countries of which the balance of trade was adverse into countries where it was favourable.

This became, in the end, the major cause of instability. If the favourable trade balance of the United States had been the only problem, the newly produced gold in the rest of the world would have been more than sufficient to discharge it. The flow of refugee and speculative funds superimposed on this brought the whole system to ruin.

We have no security against a repetition of this after the present war though not perhaps on the same scale or necessarily in the same direction. (It is easy to conceive conditions in which the American capitalists would be the refugees; and if that were to happen, it would be on a scale to swamp all previous experience.) Social changes affecting the position of the wealth-owning class are likely to occur or (what is worse in the present condition) to be threatened in many countries. The whereabouts of 'the better 'ole' will shift with the speed of the magic carpet. Loose funds may sweep round the world disorganising all steady business.

Nothing is more certain than that the movement of capital funds must be regulated;—which in itself will involve far-reaching departures from *laissez-faire* arrangements.

IV. *The Alternative Before Us*

1. The United States do not at present favour any radical remedy. The suggestions current fall under three heads:-

(i) liberal relief to Europe during the reconstruction period, possibly even extending to a redistribution of a part of her redundant stocks of gold;

(ii) some reduction of tariffs and some restriction in the output of agricultural produce for export;

(iii) a general stimulus to demand by the maintenance of

a high level of domestic employment as the result of adopting various New Deal expedients.

(i) provides no lasting solution; and for ourselves not even a temporary solution unless we are to be beneficiaries on a scale more generous than seems likely. (We shall have been helped during the war; it is the others who will be helped afterwards.) There is little prospect of (ii) on an adequate scale. (iii) would offer great, and perhaps adequate, relief if and when it happens. I should accept the view that (capital movements apart) the more or less continuous maintenance of a high level of employment in U.S.A. would go a long way towards redressing the international balance of payments. But this is a happy outcome on which we cannot yet rely.

2. We shall end the war with a well developed system of payments and clearings agreements in actual operation. This might be evolved into a permanent peace-time scheme which would try to mitigate so far as possible the objectionable features of bilateralism. Much will be possible which would have been impossible if we had to start in peace-time *de novo* with the old system of *laissez-faire* as a going concern. If, in addition, we were to continue bulk purchasing of foodstuffs and raw materials through official bodies under instructions to direct their contracts to countries which were prepared to reciprocate with purchases of our exports, we might succeed in stabilising and balancing our trade at a high level of volume.

This policy is not free from difficulties. I have given enough consideration to the details to be fully conscious of them. But I believe that a serviceable scheme could be worked out.

3. I should prefer, however, to sketch out, first of all, an ideal scheme which would preserve the advantages of an international means of payment universally acceptable, whilst avoiding those features of the old system which did the damage.

I doubt if this plan would prove as helpful to British interests as the second alternative mentioned above during the transitional period whilst we were expanding our exports to the level we shall require in future. Against this we may set the advantages of a better system in the long run.

It is also open to the objection, as the reader will soon discover, that it is complicated and novel and perhaps Utopian in the sense, not that it is impracticable, but that it assumes a higher degree of understanding, of the spirit of bold innovation, and of international co-operation and trust than it is safe or reasonable to assume.

Nevertheless, it is with this scheme that I should approach the United States. For it is an attempt to satisfy their fundamental requirements; it would allow us to subscribe to the blessed word 'discrimination'; and it is, therefore, a system in which they might be more willing to co-operate with enthusiasm. Moreover it is a good schematism by means of which the essence of the problem can be analysed and the essential elements of any satisfactory solution brought into full view. If not this, we can ask, what then? Now that you are fully seized of the essential elements of the problem, what alternative solution do you offer us?

J. M. KEYNES

8.9.41

PROPOSALS FOR AN INTERNATIONAL CURRENCY UNION

A.1. Within any member-country or currency unit the provision of foreign exchange to be concentrated in the hands of its central bank* which would deal with the public through the usual banks. That is to say, a member of the public here

---

* The 'national' unit for the purpose of this Currency Union would comprise the whole of any area having a common currency and banking system. It would be for those concerned in each case to decide to what central bank to adhere. Perhaps we could not expect the new sterling area to be as large as what we now call the sterling area, but we should try to make it as large as possible. Could we persuade Australia, New Zealand and India, and even South Africa, to remain within it? I should have a good try. There would be great practical advantages to them as well as to us and increased financial stability by remaining within it, against which must be set some loss of prestige and independence. In any case, most of the Crown Colonies, especially Malaya and Hong Kong, would presumably remain in the British sterling area, though Ceylon might go in with India (as also Burma) if India stayed out.

desiring to obtain dollars for a specified purpose would instruct his bank to make application to the Bank of England —much as at present.†

2. Internationally all transactions to be cleared between central banks, operating on their accounts with an International Clearing Bank. Central banks would buy and sell their own currencies amongst themselves only against debits and credits to their accounts at the Clearing Bank, designated *Clearing Accounts*, and would not themselves hold any foreign currency as distinct from the permitted foreign accounts of their nationals, except as agents for their Governments where the latter required foreign trading accounts for current purposes.

3. Each central bank to have unqualified control over the *outward* transactions of its nationals, i.e. over the purchase of foreign exchange by them (including, in particular, a control of remittances on capital account), but it must always be prepared to *sell* its own currency to another central bank against a credit to its Clearing Account.

4. Each national currency to have a fixed value (subject to what follows about provisions for change) determined when the Currency Union is set up in terms of the bank money of the Clearing Bank, which would be itself expressed in terms of a unit of gold.

† The question how far this would interfere with the traditional international exchange and acceptance business of London would largely depend on the nature of the regulations *in other countries*. So far as the U.K. is concerned, there would be no greater interference than is inevitable on the assumption that exchange transactions must be examined individually at some stage, perhaps by the banks themselves if they can be fully trusted, in order to exclude unlicensed capital transactions, and that after the war we shall not have adequate liquid resources to allow us to keep outstanding with London finance a volume between £100 million and £200 million of non-domestic bills of exchange (already much diminished from their former figure). We could retain and develop the existing system of authorised dealers who would be permitted to retain floating balances abroad. In this connection also it would be most important that the newly defined sterling area should be as large as possible. It should be noticed that the restrictive conditions are merely *permissive* to the central bank concerned. The Bank of England could issue an open general licence for any such business as the above, should it feel itself strong enough to do so. [Keynes's footnote]

5. A central bank to be entitled to replenish its Clearing Account by paying in gold to the Clearing Bank, but the balance on its Account only to be employed for the purpose of making a transfer to another Clearing Account; so that it could not withdraw gold.

6. Any gold held by the Clearing Bank at the end of each year in excess of the amount of its Reserve Fund may be distributed to those central banks whose Clearing Accounts are in credit in proportion to the amounts of their credit balances, their Clearing Accounts being debited accordingly; no Clearing Bank to be entitled to acquire gold otherwise except from its own nationals (including those of its own commonwealth or dependencies) or for industrial purposes.

B.1. Each central bank to be allotted an index-quota equal to half the sum of its imports and exports (both reckoned exclusive of re-exports) on the average of the previous five years (starting with the five pre-war years, the most remote pre-war year in the average being replaced each year by the latest available post-war year), and to be allowed to overdraw its Clearing Account up to a maximum amount equal to its index-quota, provided that it shall not increase its overdraft by more than a quarter of its index-quota in any year.

2. A central bank whose Clearing Account has been in debit for more than a year by an amount exceeding a *quarter* of its index-quota shall be designated a Deficiency Bank. A Deficiency Bank shall be allowed to reduce the exchange value of its national currency by an amount not exceeding 5 per cent within any year. A Deficiency Bank may borrow from the Clearing Account of a Surplus Bank (see below) on any terms which may be mutually agreed.

3. A central bank whose Clearing Account has been in debit for more than a year by an amount exceeding a *half* of its index-quota shall be designated a Supervised Bank. A Supervised Bank may be *required* by the Governors of the

Clearing Bank to reduce the exchange value of its national currency by amounts not exceeding 5 per cent in any year; to hand over in reduction of its deficiency any free gold in the possession of itself or its Government; and to prohibit outward capital transactions except with the permission of the Governors, who may also disallow at their discretion any other requirement from it for foreign exchange. A Supervised Bank may be requested by the Governors to withdraw from the system in which event its debit balance shall be transferred to the Reserve Fund (see below) of the Clearing Bank.

4. A central bank whose Clearing Account has been in credit for more than a year by an amount exceeding a *quarter* of its index-quota shall be designated a Surplus Bank. A Surplus Bank may increase the exchange value of its national currency by an amount not exceeding 5 per cent within any year. A Surplus Bank *shall* grant a general licence for the withdrawal of foreign-owned balances and investments within its jurisdiction. A Surplus Bank may make advances to the Clearing Account of a Deficiency Bank.

5. A central bank whose Clearing Account has been in credit for more than a year by an amount exceeding a half of its index-quota shall be *required* by the Governors of the Clearing Bank to increase the exchange value of its national currency by 5 per cent, and the requirement shall be repeated after any subsequent year in which the average credit balance has increased by a further 10 per cent of its index-quota since the previous upward adjustment.

6. If at the end of any year the credit balance on the Clearing Account of any central bank exceeds *the full amount* of its index-quota, the excess shall be transferred to the Reserve Fund of the Clearing Bank.

7. A central bank having a credit balance on its Clearing Account may withdraw from the system on a year's notice, but shall surrender its credit balance to the Reserve Fund of the Clearing Bank.

8. At the request of the central bank of the borrower the International Clearing Bank may act as trustee for any foreign loan, including loans between central banks, in which case it shall debit the service of the loan without further specific instruction to the Clearing Account of the central bank of the lender, so long as the debtor is not a Supervised Bank, in which case further transfers shall be at the discretion of the Governors of the Clearing Bank.

C.1. The International Clearing Bank shall establish a Reserve Fund.

2. The Reserve Fund shall be employed as already provided in B.3, 6 and 7.

3. 5 per cent of the average annual excess of the Clearing Account of a Surplus Bank above a quarter of its index-quota and 10 per cent of the excess above a half of its index-quota shall be transferred to the Reserve Fund of the Clearing Bank.

4. No interest shall be allowed by the Clearing Bank on credit balances. But interest shall be charged on debit balances at rates fixed by the Governors which shall be increased as the size of the central bank's debit is increased in proportion to its index-quota. The excess of the interest earnings of the Clearing Bank over its expenses shall be transferred to the Reserve Fund.

5. The Reserve Fund may be applied at the discretion of the Board of Governors for the relief of any central bank in difficulty for special causes beyond its own control or for any other purpose.

D.1. Foreign-owned balances and investments held within the jurisdiction of a central bank at the date of the establishment of the International Clearing Bank shall be frozen in the sense that they shall not be withdrawn thereafter except by permission of the central bank concerned or under the general licence to be granted under B.4 above. The same shall apply to subsequent remittances on capital account but the title to such balances and investments may be freely transferred as between foreign nationals.

2. A central bank shall be entitled at the initiation of the scheme to discharge foreign-owned assets within its jurisdiction held in the form of cash or bank deposits or the securities of its Government by paying an equivalent sum in gold to the central bank of the foreign nationals concerned; and the latter central bank shall be entitled to require such a discharge if the former central bank and its Government possess a gold reserve in excess of its index-quota.

3. If the U.S. is prepared to approve an initial redistribution of its gold reserves, it is suggested that if any country, after the adjustments provided in D.2, has a gold reserve of an amount in excess of its index-quota, a proportion of this excess should be transferred to the Clearing Bank at the outset for the credit of the post-war Relief and Reconstruction Council (see below). This would facilitate post-war reconstruction without throwing any real burden on the U.S. as compared with other creditor countries; for it would involve no charge on the budget and the real burden would be carried not by the U.S. in particular, but by all those creditor countries who as a result of this arrangement might come to possess hereafter larger credit balances with the Clearing Bank than they would have possessed otherwise.

E.1. Clearing Accounts with the International Clearing Bank to be set up only in favour of the central banks of countries adhering to the Currency Union and of certain international bodies such as those specified below.

2. The Clearing Bank to set up an account in favour of the supra-national policing body charged with the duty of preserving the peace and maintaining international order. If any country shall have infringed its properly authorised orders, the policing body shall be entitled to request the

Governors of the Clearing Bank to hold the Clearing Account of the central bank of the delinquent country to its order and permit no further transactions on the account except by its authority.

3. The Clearing Bank to set up an account in favour of the international body charged with post-war relief and reconstruction. It is suggested that this body should pay the proper price for all supplies and services which it may administer, financing the excess of these costs over any sums recovered from the beneficiaries and also the cost of furnishing to certain countries by way of gift an initial credit balance in their Clearing Accounts (should this course of action commend itself) partly by funds received under D.3 above (should this come about) and partly by being allowed an overdraft on its Clearing Account up to an agreed maximum amount, the overdraft to be discharged in subsequent years at the discretion of the Governors of the Clearing Bank either out of their Reserve Fund or out of a special levy (in addition to the regular contributions under C.3) on the surplus credit balances of Surplus Banks not exceeding 5 per cent of such surplus in any year, any undischarged balance being in the nature of a fiduciary issue of the Currency Union. By this means all risk is avoided of any country being required to assume a burdensome commitment for relief and reconstruction, since the resources will be provided in the first instance by those countries having credit balances on their Clearing Accounts for which they have no immediate use and are voluntarily leaving idle, and in the long run by those countries which have a chronic international surplus for which they have no beneficial employment.

4. The Clearing Bank to set up Clearing Accounts in favour of international bodies charged with the management of a Commodity Control, and to finance stocks of commodities held by such bodies by allowing them overdraft facilities on their accounts up to an agreed maximum. By this means the

financial problem of holding pools would be satisfactorily solved.

F.1. The International Clearing Bank shall be managed by a Board of eight Governors and a Chairman. They shall draw up their own rules of procedure and shall settle all matters by a bare majority except that an alteration of an article of the constitution of the Clearing Bank, which may include a change in the gold value of the Clearing Bank's money of account, shall require a two-thirds majority.

2. Any of the articles of the constitution may be modified in its application to a particular central bank by agreement between that bank and a majority of the Board of the Clearing Bank.

3. An independent Chairman of the Board shall be elected annually by the Governors and his election shall cause a vacancy in his place as a Governor if he was previously one of them. He shall have no vote except a casting vote.

4. The eight Governors shall be chosen as follows:– one by the United Kingdom, one by the British Commonwealth outside the United Kingdom, one by the United States, one by Russia, two by the European central banks, one by the South American central banks, and one by the remaining central banks. In choosing the four last-mentioned representatives the central banks concerned shall have a voting power in proportion to their index-quota.

J. M. KEYNES

8.9.41

At the time of their circulation, Keynes's proposals were but one set of several personal documents circulating within the Treasury on post-war currency policy. In addition to these, there was a draft Treasury paper on post-war trade and financial policy, which reflected the current state of Treasury discussions, along with related comments and exchanges between D. H. Robertson, H. D. Henderson and the Bank of England. Initially

Keynes's proposals appeared to receive little notice in the Treasury discussions, the main comments coming from Richard Kahn, James Meade, R. G. Hawtrey[6] and L. P. Thompson,[7] and from H. A. Siepmann[8] of the Bank of England.

Kahn picked Keynes up on a theoretical point, noting that adjustments by creditor countries also affected the terms of trade and suggesting that Keynes's example depended on taking the Anglo-American case as the norm. He also questioned Keynes's gloomy perspective on tariff reductions, asking whether this vitiated the proposals, for if the United States reduced tariffs the scheme would break down.

James Meade made a series of suggestions. He suggested that Keynes make clear provision for current account convertibility as the norm in A3 by requiring such convertibility except when the clearing account of the nation concerned had been in debit for more than one year by an amount exceeding one quarter of its quota. Restrictions, moreover, would not be mandatory. Keynes accepted this suggestion on its merits, as well as on Meade's ground that it would commend itself to the Americans. Meade also suggested provisions in the proposals for transactions with non-member banks, as clause A1 would require such a degree of regulation of external transactions that the United States might not wish to enter the scheme. Keynes also accepted this idea, but was unsure as to its application to the United States as he thought it would only be useful for 'odds and ends countries'.

R. G. Hawtrey criticised the absence of safeguards in the system against persistent debtors, be they weak, reckless, misguided or corrupt; the absence of methods of guarding against changes in the purchasing power of the unit of account; the possible inadequacy of the five per cent per annum limitation to exchange rate changes and the possible insufficiency of the quotas in the scheme.

Keynes's comments from L. P. Thompson, along with a series of questions from Siepmann and other comments raised in the Treasury's discussion of post-war international monetary policy, led him to decide to spend more time explaining and advocating his proposals. The result was a second draft which took account of James Meade's suggestions and contemporary Treasury and Bank of England preoccupations as to the shape of post-war international economic relations. The draft also took account of the

---

[6] Ralph George Hawtrey (1879–1975), Kt. 1956; Treasury, 1904–45, Director of Financial Enquiries, 1919–45.

[7] Later Thompson-McCausland.

[8] Harry Arthur Siepmann (1889–1963); with JMK in Treasury during World War I; Adviser to Governors, Bank of England, 1926, Executive Director, 1945–54.

Hansen–Gulick[9] proposals for the post-war maintenance of full employment aired during the authors' autumn 1941 visit to London.

PROPOSALS FOR AN INTERNATIONAL CURRENCY UNION

In my previous paper I made no attempt to explain or advocate my proposals and merely set out the bare bones of a scheme. It may be useful that I should now clothe it with a little flesh. This paper should be regarded as superseding my earlier proposals.

I

The practical difficulties in the way of Anglo–American economic co-operation after the war should not dissuade us from attaching the highest importance to it. We must do our utmost to secure it, and much will depend on the method of our approach.

It would be a mistake just to set forth the extent and extremity of our post-war difficulties and follow up this complaint with a plea that there is nothing to be done except to leave us a free hand to use all those expedients which we may find useful and necessary in our self-regarding interests. Any statement on these lines should be introduced only in the shape of a warning that we must not be asked to abandon possible safeguards until something better is definitely in sight, or in the shape of a hint of the unsatisfactory outcome to which the failure of a constructive plan might drive us.

It would also be a mistake to invite, of our own motion, direct financial assistance after the war from the United States to ourselves, whether as a gift or a loan without interest or a gratuitous redistribution of gold reserves. The U.S. will consider that we have had our whack in the shape of lend

---

[9] Luther Halsey Gulick (b. 1892); government research administrator; consultant on post-war defense planning, National Resources Planning Board, 1941–3; Special Assistant, U.S. Treasury, 1941–5.

lease and a generous settlement of 'consideration'. If the British Commonwealth stands astride the world with the vast prestige of victors, some natural jealousy will not be absent. We in particular, in a distressed and ruined continent, will not bear the guise of the most suitable claimant for a dole, however real and heavy our difficulties. The assistance for which we can hope must be *indirect* and a consequence of setting the world as a whole on its feet and of laying the foundations of a sounder political economy between all nations.

Finally, it would be a mistake in approaching the United States to put in the forefront proposals for an increased solidarity and significance for the British Commonwealth or the sterling area in isolation from the rest of the world, which would arouse both prejudice and suspicion. Such proposals must be ancillary to, and part of, a more general international scheme.

On the contrary. If we are to attract the interest and enthusiasm of the Americans, we must come with an ambitious plan of an international complexion, suitable to serve the interests of others besides ourselves, which to a hopeful spirit may carry a chance of making the post-war economy of the world more reasonable and promising than it was before,—something capable of wide and various application. I have confidence that Americans can be brought to a sympathetic understanding of our difficulties. But, however hard-up we may be for the time being, we—on the assumption which underlies all our post-war plans—shall be standing on the top of the world, one of the two or three masters of the future. It is not with *our* problems of ways and means that idealistic and internationally-minded Americans will be particularly concerned.

I am ready to admit that I share in these respects the purposes which I attribute to such Americans. I am not much interested in patching up something which is as like as possible to what we are doing now and may with luck and skill just serve our turn. If we sincerely wish to collaborate with them to larger ends, as I do, they will soon discover it,—and they would soon discover the opposite, if that were to be true. This, therefore, is the first criterion on which our proposals must be judged.

But further, it is not as if we had another plan which was, from our own point of view, just right. Nothing of the kind. The more we look at the alternatives, the less we like them. They are neither one thing nor the other, but a patched up contrivance, mainly based on abnormal war experience, which might do well enough to carry us through a transitional period, but are not very likely to evolve into a satisfactory permanent system or one which will fit in with (or help) what may be happening in the rest of the world. The most attractive version assumes a high degree of economic solidarity within the British Commonwealth. With so broad a bottom we might (perhaps) safely stand on it without support from outside. But we should run the risk of isolating ourselves from the United States and the rest of the world without real security that we had constructed a reliable economic union within the Empire.

II

The idea underlying my proposals for a Currency Union is simple, namely to generalise the essential principle of banking, as it is exhibited within any closed system, through the establishment of an International Clearing Bank. This principle is the necessary equality of credits and debits, of assets and liabilities. If no credits can be removed outside the banking system but only transferred within it, the Bank *itself* can never be in difficulties. It can with safety make what advances it wishes to any of its customers with the assurance that the proceeds can only be transferred to the bank account of another customer. Its problem is solely to see to it that its customers behave themselves and that the advances made to each of them are prudent and advisable from the point of view of its customers as a whole.

In only one important respect must an International Bank differ from the model suitable to a national bank within a closed system, namely that much more must be settled by rules and by general principles agreed beforehand and much less by day-to-day discretion. To give confidence in, and understanding of, what is afoot, it is necessary to prescribe beforehand certain definite principles of policy, particularly in regard to the maximum limits of permitted overdraft and the provisions proposed to keep the scale of individual credits and debits within a reasonable amount, so that the system is in stable equilibrium with proper and sufficient measures taken in good time to reverse excessive movements of individual balances in either direction.

The fundamental provisions proposed are given in an Appendix. These are substantially the same as those which I gave in my previous paper. It is now suggested, however, that the International Clearing Bank should be founded by the U.S. and U.K. in the first instance; and more detailed provisions are, therefore, necessary for transactions between members of the Currency Union and non-member banks.

These fundamental provisions cover a somewhat narrower ground than the previous draft, other relevant matters being dealt with in the subsequent sections of the main part of this paper.

I now proceed on the assumption that the reader has already a general acquaintance with the nature of the plan or has first referred to the Appendix—to expound in more detail the primary objects in view and the secondary objects which it could be used to promote.

III

The plan aims at the substitution of an expansionist, in place of a contractionist, pressure on world trade, especially in the first years.

Many countries, including ourselves, will find a difficulty in paying for their imports, and will need time and resources before they can establish a re-adjustment. The efforts of each of these debtor countries to preserve its own equilibrium, by forcing its exports and by cutting off all imports which are not strictly necessary, will aggravate the problem of all the others. On the other hand, if each feels free from undue pressure, the volume of international exchange will be increased and everyone will find it easier to re-establish equilibrium without injury to the standard of life.

Now this can only be accomplished by the countries who-ever they may turn out to be, which are for the time being in the creditor position, showing themselves ready to remain so without exercising a pressure towards contraction, pending the establishment of a new equilibrium.

There are one or two other ways of effecting this. For example, U.S.A. might redistribute her gold. Or there might be a number of bilateral arrangements having the effect of providing international overdrafts, as for example an agreement by the Federal Reserve Board to accumulate, if necessary, a large sterling balance at the Bank of England.

The objection to particular arrangements of this kind is that they are likely to be influenced by extraneous, political reasons and put specific countries into a position of particular obligation towards others; and also that the distribution of the assistance between different countries may not correspond to need and to the actual requirements as they will ultimately develop.

Moreover, for reasons already given, we are not likely to be specially eligible applicants for bounty of this kind. If, for example, the problem were to be met by a redistribution of America's gold, it is unlikely that we should get any of it, partly because we should have so lately received assistance under lend lease, partly because the British Commonwealth are the largest producers of gold, which output would be regarded, rightly or wrongly, as ours at one remove.

It should be much easier, and surely more satisfactory, to persuade the U.S. to enter into a general and collective responsibility, applying to all countries alike, that a country finding itself in a creditor position *against the rest of the world as a whole* should enter into an obligation to dispose of this credit balance and not to allow it meanwhile to exercise a contractionist pressure against the world economy and, by repercussion, against the economy of the creditor country itself. This would give us, and all others, the great assistance of multilateral clearing, whereby (for example) we could offset favourable balances arising out of our exports to Europe against unfavourable balances due to the U.S. or South America or elsewhere. I cannot see how we can hope to afford to start up trade with Europe (which will be of vast importance to us) during the relief and reconstruction period on any other terms.

These advantages of the proposed International Clearing Bank are surely so great that they overshadow most reasons of objection on lesser grounds.

It has been suggested that we should mainly depend on the restriction or prohibition of imports as a means of preserving equilibrium in the international balance of payments. When the Bank of England felt that our gold and dollar resources were falling dangerously low, instead of raising the Bank rate to attract foreign funds or restricting domestic credit to cause a deflation of incomes, or depreciating the exchange to stimulate a more favourable balance, the Bank would notify the Board of Trade that another £25 million or £50 million or £100 million of imports must be cut off. Perhaps this would be the worst method of control of all, since it would have no obvious or direct tendency to reverse the forces which had led up to the dangerous situation and so permit of removal of the restrictions later on.

Apart from this, the opposite remedy is surely the right one. If, indeed, we lack the productive capacity to maintain our standard of life, then a reduction in this standard is not avoidable. If our price levels are hopelessly wrong, a change in the rate of exchange is inevitable. But if we possess the productive capacity and the difficulty is the lack of markets as a result of restrictive policies throughout the world, then the remedy lies in expanding opportunities for export by removal of restrictive pressure, not in contracting imports. I believe that there is great force in Prof. Hansen's contention that the problem of surpluses and unwanted exports will largely disappear if active employment and ample purchasing power can be sustained in the main centres of world trade.

I see no means of offering an inducement to the general expansion of international trade in the right degree except by a broadly based international organisation.

IV

The arrangement by which the members of the Currency Union start with substantial overdraft facilities in hand will be mainly useful in the initial period. Obviously it does not by itself provide any long-term solution; for in due course the more improvident and the more impecunious will have run through their resources. The purpose of the overdraft facilities is mainly to give *time* for the necessary adjustments to be effected, and to secure prior agreement that they *will* be made. It is essential, therefore, that there should be a machinery for making such adjustments.

The proposal differs from the existing state of affairs by putting at least as much pressure of adjustment on the creditor country, as on the debtor. This is an attempt to return to the state of affairs which existed in the nineteenth century when a favourable balance in favour of London and Paris, which were the main creditor centres, immediately produced an expansionist pressure in those markets, but which has been lost since New York succeeded to the position of main creditor, aggravated by the break-down of international borrowing credit and by the flight of loose funds from one depository to another.

I did not contemplate that the sanction, proposed in the first version of this scheme, by which creditor balances in excess of a stipulated amount were confiscated, would ever come into force in practice. For obviously it would always be to the interest of the country concerned to find some way of dealing with the surplus other than that. The object of this and of further provisions was to make sure that some other way could be found. The main point is that the creditor should not be allowed to remain passive. For if he is, an impossible task is laid on the debtor country, which is for that very reason in the weaker position, so that the evils with which we are familiar are very likely to ensue.

There is, moreover, great advantage in an automatic register of the size and the whereabouts of the aggregate debtor and creditor positions respectively. The danger signal is shown to all concerned, clearly for all to see and definitely for all to interpret.

By making possible rules as to when changes in the rates of exchange of a national currency are allowed or prescribed, it much increases the efficacy of small changes such as 5 or 10 per cent. In the first place, it makes the creditor contribute to the change by *appreciating* his currency, which countries, left to themselves, will very seldom do. In the second place, it protects any permitted change from being neutralised by an unjustified competitive depreciation elsewhere.

The criticism least easily answered is that the means of

disciplining a recalcitrant and misbehaving debtor country are inadequate. To answer this fully would lead us into more detail than is appropriate to this stage of the discussion. But broadly the answer would be—

(i) that we should have better powers of discipline than at present;

(ii) that the force of a collective sanction and the injury of expulsion from the system, even though it means an escape from past obligations, are very great;

(iii) that the expenses of failure in a particular case are no more than the system can easily afford; and

(iv) that a small expenditure of faith and a readiness to allow actual experience to decide are not too much to ask, when so much else is at stake.

V

In general, the automatic register of the size and the whereabouts of the debtor and creditor positions allows definite criteria of which countries are entitled to special protection until they have re-adjusted their positions, and which are not.

The special protective expedients which were developed between the two wars were sometimes due to political, social or industrial reasons. But frequently they were nothing more than forced and undesired dodges to protect an unbalanced position.

Thus the new system should make possible undertakings *not* to use protective expedients except when they are required. There should be a general agreement amongst members of the Union to the following effect against every version of discriminatory action:–

(1) No tariffs or preferences* exceeding 25 per cent *ad valorem*;

* The formula I prefer for preferences is that they are permitted up to a figure of 25 per cent between members of political and geographical groups.

(2) No export subsidies either direct or by supplying exporting manufacturers with raw material etc. at prices below the prices at which they are available (apart from differences in cost of transport) for export;

(3) No import quotas or prohibitions;

(4) No barter agreements;

(5) No restrictions on the disposal of receipts arising out of current trade.

This forswearing of discriminatory policies would apply to all states subject—

(1) to their being allowed three (or five) years in which to bring the new policy into full effect;

(2) to their being allowed, if they wish to do so, to fall back on the forbidden protective devices in the event of their central bank becoming a Deficiency Bank.

It should be noted that no rule is proposed against subsidies in favour of domestic producers for domestic consumption, with a countervailing levy when such subsidised goods are exported. This is a necessary safety-valve which provides for protective expedients called for on political, social and industrial grounds. Such subsidies would become the approved way of giving purely domestic protection to an industry which for special reasons ought to be maintained for domestic purposes only.

This provision should enable us to give complete satisfaction to Mr Cordell Hull, since we should be accepting a non-discriminatory international system as the normal and desirable state of affairs.

VI

It is a great advantage of the proposed Currency Union that it restores unfettered multilateral clearing between its members; so that nothing has to be done except where a country is out of balance with the system as a whole.

Compare this with the difficulties and complications of a large number of bilateral agreements. Compare, above all, the provisions by which a country, taking improper advantage of a payments agreement (for the system is, in fact, a *generalised* payments agreement) as Germany did before the war, is dealt with not by a single country (which may not be strong enough to act effectively in isolation or cannot afford to incur the diplomatic odium of isolated action) but by the system as a whole.

If the argument is used that the Currency Union may have difficulty in disciplining a misbehaving country and in avoiding consequential loss, with what much greater force can we urge this objection against a multiplicity of separate bilateral payments agreements.

Thus we should not only return to the advantages of an international gold currency, but we might enjoy them more widely than was ever possible in practice with the old system under which at any given time only a minority of countries were actually working with free exchanges.

VII

I share the view that central control of capital movements, both inward and outward, should be a permanent feature of the post-war system.

If this is to be effective, it involves the *machinery* of exchange control for *all* transactions, even though a general open licence is given for all remittances in respect of current trade. Thus I accept in its entirety what I understand to be the conclusion of the Bank of England on this aspect of the problem.

But control of this kind will be much harder to work, especially in the absence of a postal censorship, by unilateral action than as part of a uniform multilateral agreement by which movements of capital can be controlled *at both ends*. We should, therefore, urge the United States and all other members of the Currency Union to adopt machinery similar to that which we have now gone a long way towards perfecting in this country.

This does not mean that the era of international investment should now be brought to an end. On the contrary, the system proposed should greatly facilitate the restoration of international credit for loan purposes in ways to be discussed below.

The object, and it is a vital object, is to have a means of distinguishing—

(*a*) between movements of floating funds and genuine new investment for developing the world's resources; and

(*b*) between movements, which will help to maintain equilibrium, from surplus countries, to deficiency countries and speculative movements or flights out of deficiency countries or from one surplus country to another.

There is no country which can, in future, safely allow the flight of funds for political reasons or to evade domestic taxation or in anticipation of the owner turning refugee. Equally, there is no country that can safely receive fugitive funds which cannot safely be used for fixed investment and might turn it into a deficiency country against its will and contrary to the real facts. The following general principles are, therefore, essential:–

(i) *All* remittances must be canalised through central banks and the resulting balances cleared by them through the International Clearing Bank.

(ii) No remittances in respect of the outstanding capital of existing or future assets owned by non-residents shall be made except under licence of both the central banks concerned.

(iii) The ownership of such assets may be freely shifted between non-residents, and non-residents may exchange one investment for another within a country.

(iv) The net current income of such assets may be freely

remitted together with an annual amortisation of capital not exceeding (say) 5 per cent.

(v) The offer of investments or assets to non-residents to be newly acquired by them shall require the approval of both the central banks concerned.

(vi) Floating and liquid funds, apart from those required to finance current trade through bills and acceptances and in connection with current banking business approved by the central bank concerned (much as in this country under present conditions) shall only be lent and borrowed between central banks.

These rules would not preclude the issue of general licences of indefinite duration by agreement between the central banks concerned.

VIII

We shall not be the only country which may find difficulties with its balance of payments after the war. Our post-war currency and exchange system should, therefore, be one which is capable of wide, indeed of universal, extension as further countries become ready for it.

I conceive of the new Bank as being brought into existence in the first instance by the United States and the United Kingdom as joint founders of the Club, covering the United States and its possessions and the members of the British Commonwealth. Other members would then be brought in —some from the outset, some as soon as they had established an internal organisation capable of sustaining the obligations of membership. This approach has the great advantage that the United States and the United Kingdom (the latter in consultation with the other members of the British Commonwealth) could settle the charter and the main details of the new body without being subjected to the delays and confused counsels of an international conference. It would also mean that considerable progress could be made irrespective of the nature of the European political settlement and before the conditions of adherence of the European members could be finally determined. Moreover, membership would be thus established as a privilege only open to those who conformed to certain general principles and standards of international economic conduct. I conceive of the management and the effective voting power as being permanently Anglo-American.

An important matter for decision is whether and how far there should be currency unions *within* the international system, or whether individual countries should be accepted for membership. Either system is possible, but there is much to be said in favour of currency unions within the general framework.

One view of the post-war world which I find sympathetic and attractive and fruitful of good consequences is that we should encourage *small* political and cultural units, combined into larger, and more or less closely knit, economic units. It would be a fine thing to have thirty or forty capital cities in Europe, each the centre of a self-governing country entirely free from national minorities (who would be dealt with by migrations where necessary) and the seat of a government and a parliament and a cultural and university centre, each with their own pride and glory and their own characteristics and excellent gifts. But it would be ruinous to have thirty or forty entirely independent economic and currency units. Therefore I would encourage customs unions and customs preferences covering groups of political and geographical units, and also currency unions, railway unions and the like.

Thus it would be preferable, if it were possible, that the members should, in some cases at least, be groups of countries rather than separate units. But this provision is not essential to the scheme. We might start with mixed modes, and it might sometimes be better to begin with separate units with the intention of encouraging subsequent combination rather than to force premature inter-arrangements for which those concerned were not ready. For we have to face the fact that the pooling of balances within a limited area as against the rest of the world represents a high degree of mutual trust and dependence and might be difficult without a single central bank and uniform currency and banking within the whole group.

(Subject to these reserves and hesitations, the ideal arrangement might be one of grouped membership comprising the following:–

1. North America comprising the United States, Canada, Newfoundland and the West Indies.

2. South and Central America comprising South America, Central America and Mexico.

3. The sterling area comprising the United Kingdom, the Crown Colonies (outside N. America), India, Australia, New Zealand, and South Africa.

4. The U.S.S.R.

5. The Germanic countries, including Switzerland, Holland and Austria and the constituents of the former Reich (better than a *purely* German Union excluding Switzerland and Holland).

6. The Scandinavian countries (Norway, Sweden, Denmark, Finland, the Baltic States—if there be such).

7. The Latin Union (France, Belgium, Italy, Spain, Portugal).

8. Central Europe (Poland, Silesia, Bohemia, Slovakia, Hungary).

9. The Balkan Union.

10. The Middle East (Turkey, Egypt, North Africa, the Soudan, Ethiopia, Palestine, Syria, Iraq, Iran).

11. The Far East (China, Japan and Siam).

I beg the reader to consider this passage as a highly substantive proposal. The Currency Union could be developed either along separate nationalistic or along economic federationist lines, according to the way the world works out. My point is that it is not incompatible with a new pattern for the post-war world and can be adjusted either to older or to newer notions.)

Meanwhile there should be no obstacles in the way of the voluntary formation of such groups. In particular, we ourselves should be free to develop special arrangements within the sterling area, provided they were compatible with the general obligations and the provisions against discrimination which we had undertaken towards the membership as a whole. The United States would be equally free to develop special Pan–American economic links. And so would the other members in groups amongst themselves, voluntarily selected or prescribed under the Treaty of Peace.

IX

It has been suggested that so ambitious a proposal is open to criticism on the ground that it requires from the members of the Currency Union a greater surrender of their sovereign rights than they will readily concede.

But, in the first place, no greater surrender is required in point of form than is required in any commercial treaty— certainly not much greater than in the binding undertakings against discrimination which the U.S. is inviting us to make. The obligations will be entered into voluntarily and can be terminated on certain conditions by giving notice.

In the second place a greater surrender of sovereign rights must be in order in the post-war world than has been accepted hitherto. The arrangements proposed could be described as a measure of financial disarmament. They are very mild in comparison with the measures of military disarmament which, it is to be hoped, the world will be asked to accept.

Surely it is an advantage, rather than a disadvantage, of the scheme that it invites the member states and groups to abandon that licence to promote indiscipline, disorder and bad-neighbourliness which, to the general disadvantage, they have been free to exercise hitherto.

There is nothing here which we need be reluctant to accept ourselves or to ask of others. Or if there be anything such, let it be amended.

X

An International Bank might become the instrument and the support of international policies apart from those which it is its primary purpose to promote.

I recapitulate below certain suggestions from my previous paper and make some additions to them. Obviously these suggestions are in no way a necessary part of the plan. But they are illustrations of the additional purposes of high importance and value which the Bank, once established, might be able to serve.

(1) The Bank might set up an account in favour of the international body charged with post-war relief and reconstruction. If necessary, it might supplement contributions received from other sources by granting overdraft facilities in favour of this body, financing relief and reconstruction, so to speak, out of the fiduciary issue of the new currency system, this overdraft being discharged over a period of years out of a levy on the credit balances of Surplus Banks. By this means it is possible to avoid asking any country to assume a burdensome commitment for relief and reconstruction, since the resources would be provided in the first instance by those countries having credit balances on their Clearing Accounts for which they have no immediate use and are voluntarily leaving idle, and in the long run by those countries which have a chronic international surplus for which they have no beneficial employment.

(2) If the United States were to wish to effect a redistribution of gold reserves, the Bank would provide a suitable

channel for the purpose, the gold so re-distributed being credited (e.g.) to the account of the Relief and Reconstruction Authority.

(3) The Bank might set up an account in favour of the supranational policing body charged with the duty of preserving the peace and maintaining international order. If any country were to infringe its properly authorised orders, the policing body might be entitled to request the Governors of the Clearing Bank to hold the Clearing Account of the central bank of the delinquent country to its order and permit no further transactions on the account except by its authority. This would provide an excellent machinery for enforcing a financial blockade.

(4) The Bank might set up an account in favour of international bodies charged with the management of a Commodity Control, and might finance stocks of commodities held by such bodies, allowing them overdraft facilities on their accounts up to an agreed maximum. By this means the financial problem of holding pools and 'ever-normal' granaries would be satisfactorily solved.

(5) The Bank might be closely linked up with a Board for International Investment of the kind proposed by Professors Hansen and Gulick. It might act as the bankers of this Board and collect for them the annual service of their loans by automatically debiting the Clearing Account of the country concerned. The statistics of the Clearing Accounts of the member banks would give a clear indication as to which countries were in a position to finance the Investment Board, with the advantage of shifting the whole system of clearing credits and debits nearer to equilibrium. It might be provided that Surplus Banks of countries which were indebted to the Board should automatically use their surplus to discharge such indebtedness, and that Surplus Banks accumulating credits beyond a stipulated percentage of their quota should

advance such surplus to the Board for further investment by them. (This would be preferable to the previous proposal for the cancellation of such super-surplus balances.)

(6) The Bank might also be closely associated with the Anti-Depression Board, acting in collaboration with this Board and with the International Investment Board and the Commodity Pools to exercise contractionist or expansionist influence on the system as a whole or on particular sections according to the circumstances. It would be easier to give reality and some measure of authority to the advice of the Anti-Depression Board through the International Bank than in any other way.

(7) There are also other methods by which the Clearing Bank could use its influence and its powers to maintain stability of prices and to control the trade cycle.

XI

I conceive of the Bank as essentially under Anglo-American management, especially in its early days. It would be easy to give it a constitution which would ensure this.

Two head offices in New York and in London would be appropriate. The Head Office in London under an English Chairman would deal with the business of banks situated in the British Commonwealth (apart from Canada), Europe and the Middle East. The Head Office in New York under an American Chairman would deal with the business of banks situated in North and South America and the Far East.

The Board of Managers would meet alternately at each of the Head Offices. With modern means of transport and communication by air and with (one would hope) no need for joint meetings more frequently than once a quarter this double-headedness should lead to no practical inconvenience.

Members of the Board would be appointed by the member

banks each of which would have a vote in proportion to its quota. But there might be some provision, at any rate for some years, by which the British and American members when acting in agreement could outvote the rest of the Board.

J. M. KEYNES

18 November 1941

APPENDIX

A

A.1. An International Clearing Bank to be founded by the U.S. and the U.K. This Bank will be entrusted with the management of an International Currency Union to provide bank money, to be designated grammor, for the settlement of international balances, which will be universally accepted as the equivalent of gold and will be ultimately based on it (see A.5 below).

A.2. Other states will be admitted on suitable conditions as full members of the Union, entitled to the facilities from the Clearing Bank to be set forth in B below. Meanwhile all central banks will be entitled to keep an account with the Clearing Bank, and will, indeed, be expected to do so if they wish to do exchange business with members of the Union.

A.3. Within any state (or group of states), which is a member of the Union, the provision of foreign exchange for remittance either to member or non-member states will be concentrated in the hands of its central bank which would deal with the public through the usual banks. That is to say, a member of the public here desiring to obtain dollars for a specified purpose would instruct his bank to make application to the Bank of England—much as at present.

A.4. The balances due to or from any foreign state will be cleared between the central banks concerned, operating on their accounts with the Clearing Bank.

A.5. The national currency of each member state to have a fixed value (subject to what follows about provisions for change) in terms of the bank money (or grammor) of the Clearing Bank, which would be itself expressed in terms of a unit of gold. The central bank of a non-member state may fix the value of its national currency for the purpose of transactions with member states at any figure it wishes in terms of grammor, provided that this figure is the same at any given time in respect of all transactions with member states.

A.6. Any central bank (member or non-member) to be entitled to replenish its Clearing Account by paying in gold to the Clearing Bank, but the balance on its Account only to be employed for the purpose of making a transfer to another Clearing Account; so that it cannot withdraw gold.

A.7. Any gold held by the Clearing Bank at the end of each year in excess of the amount of its Reserve Fund may be distributed to those central banks whose Clearing Accounts are in credit in proportion to the amounts of their credit balances, their Clearing Accounts being debited accordingly; no Clearing Bank of a member state to be entitled to acquire gold otherwise except from its own nationals (including those of its own Commonwealth or dependencies) or for industrial purposes.

B

The following provisions relate only to the central banks of states which are full members of the Union, and are a recapitulation of my previous proposals.

B.1. Each central bank to be allotted an index-quota equal to half the sum of its imports and exports (both reckoned exclusive of re-exports) on the average of the previous five years (starting with the five pre-war years, the most remote pre-war year in the average being replaced each year by the latest available post-war year), and to be allowed to overdraw its Clearing Account up to a maximum amount equal to its index-quota, provided that it shall not increase its overdraft by more than a quarter of its index-quota in any year.

B.2. A central bank whose Clearing Account has been in debit for more than a year by an amount exceeding a *quarter* of its index-quota shall be designated a Deficiency Bank. A Deficiency Bank shall be allowed to reduce the value of its national currency in terms of grammor by an amount not exceeding 5 per cent within any year. A Deficiency Bank may borrow from the Clearing Account of a Surplus Bank (see below) on any terms which may be mutually agreed.

B.3. A central bank whose Clearing Account has been in debit for more than a year by an amount exceeding a *half* of its index-quota shall be designated a Supervised Bank. A Supervised Bank may be *required* by the Governors of the Clearing Bank to reduce the grammor value of its national currency by amounts not exceeding 5 per cent in any year; to hand over in reduction of its deficiency any free gold in the possession of itself or its Government; and to prohibit outward capital transactions except with the permission of the Governors, who may also disallow at their discretion any other requirement from it for foreign exchange. A Supervised Bank may be requested by the Governors to withdraw from the system in which event its debit balance shall be transferred to the Reserve Fund (see below) of the Clearing Bank.

B.4. A Central Bank whose Clearing Account has been in credit for more than a year by an amount exceeding a *quarter* of its index-quota shall be designated a Surplus Bank. A Surplus Bank may increase the exchange value of its national currency by an amount not exceeding 5 per cent within any year. A Surplus Bank *shall* grant a general licence for the withdrawal of foreign-owned balances and investments within its jurisdiction. A Surplus Bank may make advances to the Clearing Account of a Deficiency Bank.

B.5. A central bank whose Clearing Account has been in

credit for more than a year by an amount exceeding a half of its index-quota shall be *required* by the Governors of the Clearing Bank to increase the exchange value of its national currency by 5 per cent, and the requirement shall be repeated after any subsequent year in which the average credit balance has increased by a further 10 per cent of its index-quota since the previous upward adjustment.

B.6. If at the end of any year the credit balance on the Clearing Account of any central bank exceeds *the full amount* of its index-quota, the excess shall be transferred to the Reserve Fund of the Clearing Bank, unless steps have been taken to dispose of it by placing it at the disposal of the International Investment Board or otherwise.

B.7. A central bank having a credit balance on its Clearing Account may withdraw from the system on a year's notice, but shall surrender its credit balance to the reserve fund of the Clearing Bank.

B.8. At the request of the central bank of the borrower the International Clearing Bank may act as trustee for any foreign loan, including loans between central banks, in which case it shall debit the service of the loan without further specific instruction to the Clearing Account of the central bank of the lender, so long as the debtor is not a Supervised Bank, in which case further transfers shall be at the discretion of the Governors of the Clearing Bank.

B.9. The International Clearing Bank shall establish a Reserve Fund.

(i) The reserve fund shall be employed as already provided in B.3, 6 and 7 above.

(ii) 5 per cent of the average annual excess of the Clearing Account of a Surplus Bank above a quarter of its index-quota and 10 per cent of the excess above a half of its index-quota shall be transferred to the Reserve Fund of the Clearing Bank.

(iii) No interest shall be allowed by the Clearing Bank on credit balances. But interest shall be charged on debit balances at rates fixed by the Governors which shall be increased as the size of the central bank's debit is increased in proportion to its index-quota. The excess of the interest earnings of the Clearing Bank over its expenses shall be transferred to the Reserve Fund.

(iv) The Reserve Fund may be applied at the discretion of the Board of Governors for the relief of any central bank in difficulties for special causes beyond its own control or for any other purpose.

C

C.1. There shall be free and unlimited facilities of foreign remittance between member states in respect of all transactions arising out of current trade and current income, widely interpreted so as to cover all items, 'visible' and 'invisible', usually reckoned to be on current income account, subject only to the indulgences proposed in V above in favour of Deficiency Banks, if they should desire to exercise them (or, in case of Supervised Banks, if they are required to exercise them).

C.2. But each member bank shall have unqualified control over the capital transactions of its residents both outward and inward (subject to the obligations of a Surplus Bank), and it shall be entitled to call on the collaboration of other member banks to prevent unlicensed movements. A member bank will be free to give open general licences, provided they do not conflict with the policy of another central bank, in favour of capital transactions of a particular character or to particular destinations. The control of capital transactions will require the machinery of exchange control over *all* transactions if it is to be effective, but the arrangements made will be at the discretion of the member bank concerned.

C.3. Non-resident balances and investments held within the jurisdiction of a member bank at the date of the establishment of the Clearing Bank shall be frozen in the sense that they shall not be withdrawn thereafter except by permission of the member bank concerned or under the general licence to be granted by a Surplus Bank. The same shall apply to subsequent withdrawals on capital account. But the title to such balances and investments may be freely transferred between holders, resident or non-resident.

C.4. A member bank shall be entitled at the initiation of the scheme to discharge foreign-owned assets within its jurisdiction held in the form of cash or bank deposits or the securities of its Government by paying an equivalent sum in gold to the member bank of the foreign nationals concerned; and the latter bank shall be entitled to require such a discharge if the former bank and its Government possess a gold reserve in excess of its index quota.

J. M. K.

It was this second draft of Keynes's proposals that moved them to the centre of subsequent discussions. Up to that time, although Keynes's plan had figured in the discussions of Treasury policy and although it had become more important as the Treasury–Bank meetings proceeded, it had not held the field. However, from the moment of its circulation, Keynes's scheme now became the most prominent.

On 24 November, C. F. Cobbold of the Bank sent Keynes a few reflections on the second draft prior to a meeting the next day. Cobbold argued that the difference between the Bank's position and Keynes's plan lay in means of achieving the same end, with the Bank preferring to start from existing bilateral payments agreements and move towards multilateralism. However, the meeting on 25 November suggested a more fundamental source of disagreement, for the Bank put its faith in a planned system of international trade, while Keynes's scheme abjured in advance the use of many of the devices proposed by the Bank.

Keynes's plan brought out support from others in Whitehall. Professor Robbins found it 'a real release of fresh air in this surcharged and stale atmosphere' and hoped that whatever happened to it a copy might come to the notice of the Prime Minister. D. H. Robertson wrote in a more fulsome vein.

From D. H. ROBERTSON, *27 November 1941*

J. M. K.

I sat up late last night reading your revised 'proposals' with great excitement,—and a growing hope that the spirit of Burke and Adam Smith is on earth again to prevent the affairs of a Great Empire from being settled by the little minds of a gang of bank-clerks who have tasted blood (yes, I know this is unfair!).

And then also a growing hope that we shall choose the right things and not the wrong ones to have such rows with the Americans about as we must have.

I don't know if you saw my *cri-de-cœur* (my only copy attached)[10] on the last version of the Treasury paper,—I now feel it is on a fair way to be answered.

I began to think of an embellishment by which the gold-less countries could pay their entrance fees in staple commodities, but I think you are right to avoid it. The U.S. will *have* to pay most of the entrance fees!

A gold reserve which can never be paid out to *anyone* (except probably the International Bank of Mars) is an odd thought, but probably the right *reductio ad absurdum.*—No doubt a provision could be tacked on to your scheme for revaluing all currencies simultaneously in terms of the grammor if necessary.

I'm not sure that deficit countries ought to be allowed to commit *all* the wickednesses,—only *some* of them, I think!

D. H. R.

James Meade also wrote to provide encouragement.

Suggestions for changes came from S. D. Waley, Lord Catto, Henry Clay, the Board of Trade and R. F. Harrod.[11] Waley asked Keynes whether the scheme went 'too far in reducing the gentle art of central banking to a science conducted by rule of thumb'. He suggested more discretion in the system to allow for cases where lending was not the appropriate solution, greater exchange rate flexibility, a greater range of possible measures for the restoration of equilibrium from the side of surplus countries, more frankness as to the role of gold in the system, and government rather than

[10] Not printed.
[11] Roy Forbes Harrod (1900–78), Kt. 1959; Student of Christ Church, 1924–67; University Lecturer in Economics, Oxford University, 1929–37 and 1946–52; Fellow of Nuffield College, 1938–47, and 1954–8; served under Lord Cherwell on Mr Churchill's private statistical staff in Admiralty, 1940, and in Prime Minister's Office, 1940–6; Nuffield Reader in Economics, 1952–67; Hon. Student of Christ Church, 1967–78.

central bank appointment of the governors of the proposed system. Lord Catto, for his part, suggested greater discretion for the member banks in the system, the deletion of Keynes's proposals concerning supervised banks, the removal of the idea of deficiency banks and alterations in the passage dealing with discrimination. Clay asked for more consideration of measures complementary to exchange rate changes, while the Board of Trade suggested a softening of Keynes's line of discrimination and subsidies and a deletion of the passages dealing with specific customs unions in favour of a general enabling clause.

However, on this draft, as on those which were to follow, R. F. Harrod provided the most copious criticisms and suggestions. He emphasised the desirability of a simple scheme, with as few concessions from surplus countries as were necessary to achieve its main purposes. His suggestions removed the international money, removed the compulsion to deal through central banks, allowed gold acquisition through any channel, and removed the requirements for controlling capital transactions and freezing foreign assets.

In the discussions at this stage, apart from the Bank of England, the official who disagreed most strongly with Keynes's proposals was H. D. Henderson. He had a 'profound aversion' for the proposal that Britain's goals were similar to America's but that she could not state exactly when she could move towards the American ideal owing to her prospective balance of payments position. He was more inclined to abjure barter arrangements and discriminatory import restrictions for a limited, but undefined period, some time after the war, when they would prove unnecessary, and seek a purely Anglo–American arrangement along the lines of the Tripartite Agreement of 1936. He favoured only vague noises as to anything grander.

It was after this range of comment that Keynes again re-drafted his proposals, circulating them after 15 December 1941.

PROPOSALS FOR AN INTERNATIONAL CURRENCY UNION

This paper has been substantially re-written throughout. The principal alterations are to be found in the following passages: p. 3, 2nd para.; p. 4, 1st para.; p. 5 to p. 7, end of 1st para.; p. 10, last para. to p. 13; p. 14, last para. to p. 19, end of 1st para.; p. 21, 2nd and 3rd paras.; p. 24, 2nd para. to end.

I have dispensed with the Appendix on the ground that

particular provisions are either important enough to be discussed in the main text or too much a matter of detail to be
worth taking up at all at this stage.

J. M. K.

15.12.1941

PROPOSALS FOR AN INTERNATIONAL CURRENCY UNION

I

The practical difficulties in the way of Anglo-American economic co-operation after the war should not dissuade us from
attaching the highest importance to it. We must do our utmost
to find common ground, and much will depend on the
method of our approach.

It would be a mistake just to set forth the extent and
extremity of our post-war difficulties and follow up this complaint with a plea that there is nothing to be done except to
leave us a free hand to use all those expedients which we may
find useful and necessary in our self-regarding interests. Any
statement on these lines should be introduced only in the
shape of a warning that we must not be asked to abandon
possible safeguards until something better is definitely in
sight, or in the shape of a hint of the unsatisfactory outcome
to which the failure of a constructive plan might drive us.

It would also be a mistake to invite, of our own motion,
direct financial assistance after the war from the United States
to ourselves, whether as a gift or a loan without interest or
a gratuitous redistribution of gold reserves. The U.S. will
consider that we have had our whack in the shape of lend
lease and a generous settlement of 'consideration'. If the
British Commonwealth stands astride the world with the vast
prestige of victors, though shared with Russia and the United
States herself, some natural jealousy will not be absent.
We in particular, in a distressed and ruined continent, will

not bear the guise of the most suitable claimant for a dole, however real and heavy our difficulties. The assistance for which we can hope must be *indirect* and a consequence of setting the world as a whole on its feet and of laying the foundations of a sounder political economy between all nations.

Finally, it would be a mistake in approaching the United States to put in the forefront proposals for an increased solidarity and significance for the British Commonwealth or the sterling area in isolation from the rest of the world, which would arouse both prejudice and suspicion. Such proposals must be ancillary to, and part of, a more general international scheme.

On the contrary. If we are to attract the interest and enthusiasm of the Americans, we must come with an ambitious plan of an international complexion, suitable to serve the interests of other besides ourselves, which to a hopeful spirit may carry a chance of making the post-war economy of the world more reasonable and promising than it was before,—something capable of wide and various application. I have confidence that Americans can be brought to a sympathetic understanding of our difficulties. But, however hard-up we may be for the time being, we—on the assumption which underlies all our post-war plans—shall be standing on the top of the world, one of the two or three masters of the future. It is not with *our* problems of ways and means that idealistic and internationally-minded Americans will be particularly concerned.

I am ready to admit that I share in these respects the purposes which I attribute to such Americans. I am not much interested in patching up something which is as like as possible to what we are doing now and may with luck and skill just serve our turn. If we sincerely wish to collaborate with them to larger ends, as I do, they will soon discover it,—and they would soon discover the opposite, if that were to be true. This, therefore, is the first criterion on which our proposals must be judged.

But further, it is not as if we had another plan which was, from our point of view, just right. Nothing of the kind. The more we look at the alternatives, the less we like them. They are neither one thing nor the other, but a patched up contrivance, mainly based on abnormal war experience, which might do well enough to carry us through a transitional period, but are not very likely to evolve into a satisfactory permanent system or one which will fit in with (or help) what may be happening in the rest of the world. The most attractive version assumes a high degree of economic solidarity within the British Commonwealth. With so broad a bottom we might (perhaps) safely stand on it without support from outside. But we should run the risk of isolating ourselves from the United States, and the rest of the world without real security that we had constructed a reliable economic union within the Empire.

It is, therefore, an ambitious and far-reaching scheme that I propose in what follows. Certain elements in it are fundamental. Others are not, and are capable of being treated this way or that without impairing the main purpose. If any project of this kind is to see the day, it can only be after it has been worked out by modification and compromise in the light of the preferences and difficulties of those who will have to take responsibility for it. It would obscure the character and possibilities of the scheme if we start off with too much modification and compromise before we have heard the American point of view; and would very likely result in spoiling it in advance with unnecessary and unwanted concessions. But that must not lead to the assumption that the details proposed below are put forward dogmatically. The detailed plan is to afford a basis for discussion, as one variant of a central idea which is capable of being worked out in various ways. It is put forward, not as a cut-and-dried scheme to be formally adopted by the British Government, but for discussion and amendment between all those represented at the conversations as a constructive suggestion which might be found capable of contributing to the solution of the main economic problem which will face not only us but all the world.

II

The fundamental provision of the scheme is the establishment of a Currency Union based on international bankmoney, called (let us say), bancor, fixed (but not unalterable) in terms of gold and accepted as the equivalent of gold by the British Commonwealth and the United States and all members of the Union for the purpose of settling international balances. The central banks of all member states (and also of non-members) would keep accounts with an International Clearing Bank through which they would be entitled to settle their exchange balances with one another at their par value as defined in terms of bancor. Countries having a favourable balance of payments with the rest of the world as a whole would find themselves in possession of a credit balance with the Clearing Bank, and those having an unfavourable balance would have a debit balance. Measures would be necessary (see below) to prevent the piling up of credit and debit balances without limit, and the system would have failed in the long run if it did not possess sufficient capacity for self-equilibrium to prevent this.

The idea underlying such a Currency Union is simple, namely to generalise the essential principle of banking, as it is exhibited within any closed system. This principle is the necessary equality of credits and debits, of assets and liabilities. If no credits can be removed outside the banking system but only transferred within it, the Bank *itself* can never be in difficulties. It can with safety make what advances it wishes to any of its members with the assurance that the proceeds can only be transferred to the bank account of another member. Its problem is solely to see to it that its members behave themselves and that the advances made to each of them are prudent and advisable from the point of view of the Union as a whole.

In only one important respect must an international bank differ from the model suitable to a national bank within a closed system, namely that more must be settled by rules and by general principles agreed beforehand and less by day-to-day discretion. Perhaps the most difficult question to determine is how much to decide by rule and how much by discretion. If rule prevails, the liabilities attaching to membership of the system become clear and definite, whilst the responsibilities of central management are reduced to a minimum. On the other hand, liabilities which would require the surrender by legislation of discretion normally inherent in a government, with the result that in certain circumstances sovereign rights would be infringed, will not be readily undertaken by ourselves or by the United States. If discretion prevails, we have to decide how far the ultimate decision can be left to the individual members and how far to the central management. If the individual members are too free, indiscipline may result and unwarrantable liberties be taken. If it is to the central management that the discretions are given, too heavy a weight of responsibility may rest on it and it may be assuming the exercise of powers which it has not the strength to implement. If rule prevails, the scheme can be made more water-tight theoretically. If discretion prevails, it may work better in practice. All this is the typical problem of any super-national authority. In my first draft I was criticised for leaning too much to the side of rule. In this draft the bias is in the other direction (see Section IV below). For it may be better not to attempt to settle too much in advance of experience and to provide that the plan shall be reconsidered after an initial experimental period of (say) five years. Only by collective wisdom and discussion can the right compromise be secured between law and licence.

It is proposed that the Currency Union should be founded

by the United States and the United Kingdom, which would be designated founder-members and given a special position. Their representatives, and those of other members, on the Governing Board of the Clearing Bank would be appointed by the governments of the several member states; the daily business and technical arrangements being carried out, as at present, by their central banks.

III

The plan aims at the substitution of an expansionist, in place of a contractionist, pressure on world trade.

It effects this by allowing to each member state overdraft facilities of a definite amount, proportionate to the importance of its foreign trade and subject to certain regulative provisions. That is to say, each country is allowed a certain margin of resources and a certain interval of time within which to effect a balance in its economic relations with the rest of the world. These facilities are made possible by the nature of the system itself and do not involve particular indebtedness between one member state and another. A country is in credit or debit with the Currency Union as a whole. This means that the overdraft facilities, whilst a relief to some, are not a real burden to others. For credit balances, just like the importation of actual gold, represent those resources which a country voluntarily chooses to leave idle. They represent a potentiality of purchasing power, which it is entitled to use at any time. Meanwhile, the fact that the creditor country is not choosing to employ this purchasing power would not mean, as it does at present, that it is withdrawn from circulation and exerts a deflationary and contractionist pressure on the whole world including the creditor country itself. No country need be in possession of a credit balance unless it deliberately prefers to sell more than it buys (or lends); no country becomes unliquid or is prevented from employing its credit balance whenever it chooses to do so; and no country suffers injury (but on the contrary) by the fact that the balance, which it does not choose to employ for the time being, is not withdrawn from circulation. In short, the analogy with a national banking system is complete. No depositor in a local bank suffers because the balances, which he leaves idle, are employed to finance the business of someone else. Just as the development of national banking systems served to offset a deflationary pressure which would have prevented otherwise the development of modern industry, so by carrying this analogy into the international field we may hope to offset the contractionist pressure which might otherwise overwhelm in social disorder and disappointment the good hopes of our modern world.

These facilities will be of particular importance in the immediate future. Many countries, including ourselves, will find a difficulty in paying for their imports, and will need time and resources before they can establish a re-adjustment. The efforts of each of these debtor countries to preserve its own equilibrium, by forcing its exports and by cutting off all imports which are not strictly necessary, will aggravate the problem of all the others. On the other hand, if each feels free from undue pressure, the volume of international exchange will be increased and everyone will find it easier to re-establish equilibrium without injury to the standard of life anywhere.

However, this can only be accomplished by the countries whoever they may turn out to be, which are for the time being in the creditor position, showing themselves ready to remain so without exercising a pressure towards contraction, pending the establishment of a new equilibrium.

There are one or two other ways of effecting this. For example, U.S.A. might redistribute her gold. Or there might be a number of bilateral arrangements having the effect of providing international overdrafts, as for example an agreement by the Federal Reserve Board to accumulate, if necessary, to a large sterling balance at the Bank of England.

The objection to particular arrangements of this kind is

that they are likely to be influenced by extraneous, political reasons and put specific countries into a position of particular obligation towards others; and also that the distribution of the assistance between different countries may not correspond to need and to the actual requirements as they will ultimately develop.

Moreover, for reasons already given, we are not likely to be specially eligible applicants for bounty of this kind. If, for example, the problem were to be met by a redistribution of America's gold, it is unlikely that we should get any of it, partly because we should have so lately received assistance under lend lease, partly because the British Commonwealth are the largest producers of gold, which output would be regarded, rightly or wrongly, as ours at one remove.

It should be much easier, and surely more satisfactory, to persuade the U.S. to enter into a general and collective responsibility, applying to all countries alike, that a country finding itself in a creditor position *against the rest of the world as a whole* should enter into an arrangement not to allow this credit balance so long as it chooses to hold it, to exercise a contractionist pressure against the world economy and, by repercussion, against the economy of the creditor country itself. This would give us, and all others, the great assistance of multilateral clearing, whereby (for example) we could offset favourable balances arising out of our exports to Europe against unfavourable balances due to the U.S. or South America or elsewhere. I cannot see how we can hope to afford to start up trade with Europe (which will be of vast importance to us) during the relief and reconstruction period on any other terms.

These advantages of the proposed International Clearing Bank are surely so great that they overshadow most reasons of objection on lesser grounds.

It might be suggested that we should mainly depend on the restriction or prohibition of imports as a means of preserving equilibrium in the international balance of payments. Then if the Bank of England felt that our gold and dollar resources were falling dangerously low, instead of raising the Bank rate to attract foreign funds or restricting domestic credit to cause a deflation of incomes, or depreciating the exchange to stimulate a more favourable balance, the Bank would notify the Board of Trade that another £25 million or £50 million or £100 million of imports must be cut off. Perhaps this would be the worst method of control of all, since it would have no obvious or direct tendency to reverse the forces which had led up to the dangerous situation and so permit of removal of the restrictions later on.

Apart from this, the opposite remedy is surely the right one. If, indeed, we lack the productive capacity to maintain our standard of life, then a reduction in this standard is not avoidable. If our price levels are hopelessly wrong, a change in the rate of exchange is inevitable. But if we possess the productive capacity and the difficulty is the lack of markets as a result of restrictive policies throughout the world, then the remedy lies in expanding opportunities for export by removal of restrictive pressure, not in contracting imports. I believe that there is great force in Prof. Hansen's contention that the problem of surpluses and unwanted exports will largely disappear if active employment and ample purchasing power can be sustained in the main centres of world trade.

I see no means of offering an inducement to the general expansion of international trade in the right degree except by a broadly based international organisation.

IV

The arrangement by which the members of the Currency Union start with substantial overdraft facilities in hand will be mainly useful in the initial period. Obviously it does not by itself provide any long-term solution: for in due course the more improvident and the more impecunious, left to themselves, would have run through their resources. The purpose of the overdraft facilities is mainly to give *time* for the necessary adjustments to be effected, and to secure prior arrangements to secure, so far as possible, that they *will* be made. It is essential therefore, that there should be a machinery for making such adjustments.

The actual proposal put forward below differs in one important respect from the existing state of affairs by putting some part of the responsibility for adjustment on the creditor country, as well as on the debtor. This is an attempt to recover the advantages which were enjoyed in the nineteenth century when a favourable balance in favour of London and Paris, which were the main creditor centres, immediately produced an expansionist pressure in those markets, but which have been lost since New York succeeded to the position of main creditor, this change being aggravated by the break down of international borrowing credit and by the flight of loose funds from one depository to another. The point is that the creditor should not be allowed to remain entirely passive. For if he is, an impossible task may be laid on the debtor country, which is for that very reason in the weaker position, so that the evils with which we are familiar are likely to ensue.

The provisions, tentatively proposed, are the following:–

(1) The amount of the maximum debit balance allowed to any member state shall be determined by reference to the amount of its foreign trade, and designated its *quota*. There is no limit to the amount of the credit balance which may be held.

(2) A member state whose debit balance has exceeded a *quarter* of its quota on the average of at least a year shall be designated a Deficiency Country; and a member state whose credit balance has exceeded a *half* of its quota on the average of at least a year shall be designated a Surplus Country.

78

The regulations which aim at keeping the system of debit and credit balances as near to equilibrium as possible are the following:

(3) A charge of 1 per cent per annum will be payable to the Reserve Fund of the Clearing Bank on the average balance of a member state, whether credit or debit, up to a half of its quota; and of 2 per cent on the average balance, whether credit or debit, in excess of half its quota. Thus only a country which keeps as nearly as possible in a state of international balance on the average of the year, will escape this contribution.

(4) Any member state in debit may borrow from the balances of any member state in credit on such terms as may be mutually agreed. In this way each would avoid the contribution under (3) above.

(5) A member state may not increase its overdraft by more than a quarter of its quota within a year and may not raise its total debit in excess of half its quota, except by permission of the Governing Board of the Clearing Bank, which may attach conditions to such permission.

(6) A member state may not depreciate the rate of exchange of its local currency in terms of bancor, unless it is a Deficiency Country; and the amount of the depreciation within a year shall not exceed 5 per cent without the permission of the Governing Board. The Governing Board may require a stated measure of depreciation as a condition of allowing an overdraft in excess of half of a member's quota, if it deems that to be the suitable remedy. By making possible rules as to when changes in the rates of exchange of a national currency are allowed or prescribed, it much increases the efficiency of small changes such as 5 or 10 per cent; and it protects any permitted change from being neutralised by an unjustified competitive depreciation elsewhere.

(7) A Surplus Country shall discuss with the Governing Board (but shall retain the ultimate decision in its own hands)

what measures would be appropriate to restore the equilibrium of its international balances, including

(*a*) measures for the expansion of domestic credit and domestic demand:

(*b*) the appreciation of its local currency in terms of bancor, or, if preferred, an increase in money-wages;

(*c*) the reduction of excessive tariffs and other discouragements against imports;

(*d*) international loans for the development of backward countries.

(8) The special protective expedients which were developed between the two wars were sometimes due to political, social or industrial reasons. But frequently they were nothing more than forced and undesired dodges to protect an unbalanced position. The new system, by providing an automatic register of the size and whereabouts of the aggregate debtor and creditor positions respectively, will give a clear indication whether a particular country should be allowed to adopt special expedients as a temporary measure to assist in regaining equilibrium in its balance of payments, in spite of a general rule *not* to adopt them. This question is considered in more detail in a separate paper, to which reference should be made.

Apart from such temporary indulgences to a Deficiency Country, and also to founder and member states on their first joining the system to cover the period during which they are bringing the new policy into full effect, the scheme for a Currency Union should look to the ultimate removal of the more dislocating forms of protection and discrimination, and assume the prohibition of some of the worst of them from the outset. There would in this way be definitely prohibited to the members of the Currency Union as amongst themselves, except to a Deficiency Country and temporarily to a new member:–

(i) restrictions on the disposal of receipts arising out of current trade and of 'invisible' income.

It would also be desirable to obtain recognition of the un-desirability in principle of:–

(ii) import restrictions, whether quantitative or in the form of 'duty-quotas' (excluding however prohibitions genuinely designed to safeguard e.g. public health or morals or revenue collection);

(iii) barter arrangements;

(iv) export quotas and discriminatory export taxes;

(v) export subsidies either furnished directly by the state or indirectly under schemes supported or encouraged by the state; and

(vi) excessive tariffs.

In regard to (iii) no barter agreements should be made unless one party to the agreement is a Deficiency Country, and it should be open to any other member state to enter into a barter agreement with the Deficiency Country on equally favourable terms. But these provisions should not be inter-preted to interfere with state trading which has no reciprocal conditions attaching to it.

Subsidies in favour of domestic producers for domestic consumption, with a countervailing levy when such subsi-dised goods are exported, would not be excluded. This is a necessary safety-valve which provides for protective expedi-ents called for on political, social, and industrial grounds. Such subsidies and tariffs would be a permitted way of giving purely domestic protection to an industry which for special reasons ought to be maintained for domestic purposes only. The question of preferences and of other relaxations to most-favoured-nation treatment does not fall within the scope of this paper.

The above provisions should enable us to give substantial satisfaction to Mr Cordell Hull over a wide field, since we should be accepting without reserve a non-discriminatory international system as the normal and desirable state of affairs.

V

It is a great advantage of the proposed Currency Union that it restores unfettered multilateral clearing between its members; so that nothing has to be done except where a country is out of balance with the system as a whole.

Compare this with the difficulties and complications of a large number of bilateral agreements. Compare, above all, the provisions by which a country, taking improper advantage of a payments agreement (for the system is, in fact, a *generalised* payments agreement) as Germany did before the war, is dealt with not by a single country (which may not be strong enough to act effectively in isolation or cannot afford to incur the diplomatic odium of isolated action) but by the system as a whole.

If the argument is used that the Currency Union may have difficulty in disciplining a misbehaving country and in avoiding consequential loss, with what much greater force can we urge this objection against a multiplicity of separate bilateral payments agreements.

Thus we should not only return to the advantages of an international gold currency, but we might enjoy them more widely than was ever possible, in practice with the old system under which at any given time only a minority of countries were actually working with free exchanges.

The advantages of multilateral clearing are of particular importance to London. I would go so far as to say that this is an essential condition of the continued maintenance of London as the banking centre of the sterling area. Under a system of bilateral agreements it would seem inevitable that the sterling area, in the form in which it has been historically developed and as it has been understood and accepted by the Dominions and India, must fall to pieces.

In conditions of multilateral clearing everything would go on exactly as before without our having to ask anyone to accept special or onerous conditions. We should, in this re-spect, be back again in the best days of the gold standard. The traditional advantages of banking in London would be retained, precisely because London has been built up on the basis of an international currency having universal validity.

But if we try to make of the sterling area a compact currency union as against the rest of the world, we shall be putting a greater strain on arrangements, which have been essentially (even in time of war) *informal*, than they can be expected to bear.

It is possible to combine countries, some of which will be in a debtor and some in a creditor position, into a Currency Union which, substantially, covers the world. But surely it is impossible, unless they have a common banking and econ-omic system *also*, to combine them into a currency union not with, but against, the world as a whole. If other members of the sterling area have a favourable balance against the world as a whole, they will lose nothing by keeping them in bancor, which is universally acceptable, until they have occasion to use them. But if the sterling area is turned into a currency union, the members in credit would have to make a forced and *non-liquid* loan of their favourable balances to the members in debit. Incidentally they might find themselves involved in making between them an involuntary loan to London at the rate, perhaps, of £100 million a year cumu-lative. They would have to impose import regulations and restraints on capital movements according as the area as a whole was in debit or credit, irrespective of their own posi-tions. They would have to bound by numerous bilateral agreements negotiated primarily (at least so they would be-lieve) in the interests of London. The sterling resources of creditor Dominions might come to be represented by nothing but blocked balances in a number of doubtfully solvent coun-tries with whom it suited *us* to trade. It is difficult to see how the system could work without a pooling of gold reserves.

It is improbable that South Africa or India would accept such arrangements. We should soon find ourselves, therefore, linked up only with those constituents which were running at a debit, apart from the Crown Colonies, whom, I suppose, we could coerce.

Is it not a delusion to suppose that the *de facto*, but somewhat flimsy and unsatisfactory, arrangements, which are carrying us through the war, on the basis that we do our best to find the other members of the area a limited amount of dollars provided that they lend us a very much larger sum in sterling, can be carried over into the peace and formalised into a working system based on a series of bilateral agreements with the rest of the world combined with a strict control of capital movements outside the area?

The sterling area, if we mean by this the system under which the members of the British Commonwealth do their international banking through London, grew up under conditions of freedom. It lives and breathes by being a voluntary system. It is only in that same atmosphere of the City of London as Liberty Hall administering a universal currency that we can expect to preserve it. The notion that a multilateral plan, based on an international standard, jeopardises the position of the sterling area, must be based on a rigid and (I should have thought) politically impracticable version of the sterling area concept and not on its historical and actual significance. A multilateral plan would be of the greatest possible assistance in maintaining the position of London in relation both to the British Commonwealth and to many other countries which like our way of doing business and would give up most reluctantly the facilities we have given them.

VI

The position of gold would be left substantially unchanged. What, in the long run, the world may decide to do with gold is another matter. The establishment of an International Clearing Bank does not require any significant or immediate change. Indeed by providing an automatic means by which some part of the favourable balances of the creditor countries can be settled, the current gold production of the world and the remnant of gold reserves held outside U.S.A. may yet have a useful part to play. Moreover gold still possesses great psychological value which will not have been diminished by recent events; for the desire to possess a gold reserve against unforeseen contingencies is likely to remain. Gold also has the merit of providing, in point of form whatever the underlying realities may be, an uncontroversial standard of value for international purposes, for which it would not yet be easy to find a serviceable substitute.

I conceive, therefore, that the international bank money which we have designated *bancor*, would be defined in terms of a weight of gold. Since the national currencies of the member states would be given a fixed exchange value in terms of bancor, it follows that they would have a defined gold content which would also be their official buying price for gold above which they must not pay. Any central bank would be entitled to obtain a credit in terms of bancor by paying actual gold into the Clearing Bank.

Central banks would be entitled to retain their separate gold reserves and ship gold to one another against a clearance between them in the books of the Clearing Bank; they could coin gold and put it into circulation and, generally speaking, do what they liked with it.

One restriction only would be necessary. No central bank would be entitled to demand gold from the Clearing Bank against its balance of bancor; for bancor would be available only for transfer to the Clearing Account of another central bank. This need not mean that the Clearing Bank would only receive gold and never pay it out. If the Clearing Bank found itelf in possession of a stock of gold in excess of the amount of its own Reserve, the Governors of the Bank should have the discretion to distribute the surplus between all central banks possessing a credit balance with it, proportionately to such balances, in reduction of their amount.

The value of bancor in terms of gold should be fixed but not unalterably. The two founder states, the United States and the United Kingdom acting in agreement, should have the power to change it. Clearly they should exercise this power if the stocks of gold tendered to the bank were to be super-abundant for their legitimate purposes. No object would be served by attempting further to peer into the future or to attempt to prophesy the ultimate policy of the founder states in this regard.

Changes in the value of the national currencies of member states stand in a different category. For the real significance of such changes is to be found not in relation to gold itself but in relation to the values of other national currencies. The general principles by which such changes should be governed have been discussed in a previous section. It would be undesirable, if it can be avoided, to lay down precise rules in advance, since it is difficult to distinguish by means of a rigid formula the cases in which a change in the rate of exchange will assist the restoration of equilibrium and is the right remedy from those cases where some other type of measure is more appropriate.

VII

I share the view that control of capital movements, both inward and outward, must be a permanent feature of the post-war system,—at least so far as we are concerned.

If this control is to be effective, it probably involves the *machinery* of exchange control for *all* transactions, even though a general open licence is given to all remittances in respect of current trade.

Moreover control of this kind will be more difficult to work, especially in the absence of a postal censorship, by unilateral action than if movements of capital can be controlled *at both ends*. We should therefore, urge the United States and all other members of the Currency Union to adopt machinery similar to that which we have now gone a long way towards perfecting in this country; though this cannot be regarded as *essential* to the proposed Union.

This does not mean that the era of international investment should be brought to an end. On the contrary, the system contemplated should greatly facilitate the restoration of international credit for loan purposes in ways to be discussed below.

The object, and it is a vital object, is to have a means of distinguishing

(*a*) between movements of floating funds and genuine new investment for developing the world's resources; and

(*b*) between movements, which will help to maintain equilibrium, from surplus countries to deficiency countries and speculative movements or flights out of deficiency countries or from one surplus country to another.

There is no country which can, in future, safely allow the flight of funds for political reasons or to evade domestic taxation or in anticipation of the owner turning refugee. Equally, there is no country that can safely receive fugitive funds which cannot safely be used for fixed investment and might turn it into a surplus country against its will and contrary to the real facts.

The general principles of the control of capital movements are dealt with in a separate paper. It is evident that a Currency Union and Clearing Bank would make such control easier.

VIII

We shall not be the only country which may find difficulties with its balance of payments after the war. Our post-war currency and exchange system should, therefore, be one which is capable of wide, indeed of universal, extension as further countries become ready for it.

I conceive of the new bank as being brought into existence by the United States and the United Kingdom as joint founders of the Club, covering the United States and its possessions and the members of the British Commonwealth. Other members would then be brought in—some from the outset, some as soon as they had established an internal organisation capable of sustaining the obligations of membership. This approach has the great advantage that the United States and the United Kingdom (the latter in consultation with the other members of the British Commonwealth) could settle the charter and the main details of the new body without being subjected to the delays and confused counsels of an international conference. It would also mean that considerable progress could be made irrespective of the nature of the European political settlement and before the conditions of adherence of the European members could be finally determined. Moreover, membership would be thus established as a privilege only open to those who conformed to certain general principles and standards of international economic conduct. I conceive of the management and the effective voting power as being permanently Anglo–American.

The effectiveness of the scheme and the economic well-being of the territories concerned would be considerably enhanced if the membership consisted of relatively large units such as might be formed through numbers of small states associating themselves in appropriately constituted currency and customs unions. Subordinate unions should be permitted and indeed encouraged by procedures which preserve the most-favoured-nation principle as a general rule.

In the case of the British Commonwealth, it would be natural (unless they wish otherwise) that the self-governing Dominions and India should be members in their own names but that the United Kingdom and the Crown Colonies should enter the Union as a single banking and currency unit which, for all practical purposes, they are already. This would have the advantage of enabling India and the Dominions to maintain all their existing arrangements with London without having to assume any new burdens or enter into special obligations.

IX

It has been suggested that so ambitious a proposal is open to criticism on the ground that it requires from the members of the Currency Union a greater surrender of their sovereign rights than they will readily concede.

But, in the present version of the plan, no greater surrender is required than in any commercial treaty—certainly not greater than in the binding undertakings against discrimination which the U.S. is inviting us to make. The obligations will be entered into voluntarily and can be terminated on certain conditions by giving notice.

In the second place a greater readiness to accept supernational arrangements must be required in the post-war world than has been shown hitherto. The arrangements proposed could be described as a measure of financial disarmament. They are very mild in comparison with the measures of military disarmament which, it is to be hoped, the world will be asked to accept.

Surely it is an advantage, rather than a disadvantage, of the scheme that it invites the member states and groups to abandon that licence to promote indiscipline, disorder and bad-neighbourliness which, to the general disadvantage, they have been free to exercise hitherto.

There is nothing here which we need be reluctant to accept ourselves or to ask of others. Or if there be anything such, let it be amended.

X

An International Bank might become the instrument and the support of international policies apart from those which it is its primary purpose to promote.

I recapitulate below certain suggestions from my previous paper and make some additions to them. Obviously these suggestions are in no way a necessary part of the plan. But they are illustrations of the additional purposes of high importance and value which the Bank, once established, might be able to serve.

(1) The Bank might set up an account in favour of the international body charged with the post-war relief and reconstruction. If necessary, it might supplement contributions received from other sources by granting overdraft facilities in favour of this body financing relief and reconstruction, this overdraft being discharged over a period of years out of the Reserve Fund of the Bank, or if necessary, out of a levy on the credit balances of Surplus Banks. By this means it is possible to avoid asking any country to assume a burdensome commitment for relief and reconstruction, since the resources would be provided in the first instance by those countries having credit balances on their Clearing Accounts for which they have no immediate use and are voluntarily leaving idle, and in the long run by those countries which have a chronic international surplus for which they have no beneficial employment.

(2) If the United States were to wish to effect a redistribution of gold reserves, the Bank would provide a suitable channel for the purpose, the gold so re-distributed being credited (e.g.) to the account of the Relief and Reconstruction Authority.

(3) The Bank might set up an account in favour of the supra-national policing body charged with the duty of preserving the peace and maintaining international order. If any

country were to infringe its properly authorised orders, the policing body might be entitled to request the Governors of the Clearing Bank to hold the Clearing Account of the central bank of the delinquent country to its order and permit no further transactions on the account except by its authority. This would provide an excellent machinery for enforcing a financial blockade.

(4) The Bank might set up an account in favour of international bodies charged with the management of a Commodity Control, and might finance stocks of commodities held by such bodies, allowing them overdraft facilities on their accounts up to an agreed maximum. But this means the financial problem of holding pools and 'ever-normal granaries' would be satisfactorily solved.

(5) The Bank might be closely linked up with a Board for International Investment. It might act as the bankers of this Board and collect for them the annual service of their loans by automatically debiting the Clearing Account of the country concerned. The statistics of the Clearing Accounts of the member banks would give a reliable indication as to which countries were in a position to finance the Investment Board, with the advantage of shifting the whole system of clearing credits and debits nearer to equilibrium. This important question is the subject of a separate paper.

(6) There are various methods by which the Clearing Bank could use its influence and its powers to maintain stability of prices and to control the trade cycle. If an International Economic Board is established on the lines proposed by Professors Hansen and Gulick, this Board and the Clearing Bank might be expected to work in close collaboration to their mutual great advantage. If an International Investment or Development Corporation is also set up together with a scheme of Commodity Boards for the control of stocks of the staple raw materials, we might come to possess in these four institutions a powerful means of combating the evils of the

trade cycle, by exercising contractionist or expansionist influence on the system as a whole or on particular sections. This, again, is a large and important question which cannot be discussed adequately in this paper; and need not be discussed at length here because it does not raise any important issues affecting the fundamental constitution of the proposed Union. I mention it to complete the picture of the large purposes which the foundation of the Currency Union might be made to serve.

XI

I conceive of the Bank as substantially under Anglo-American management, especially in its early days. It would be easy to give it a constitution which would ensure this. In view of our experience and of our geographical and political position in relation to Europe, the United States and the British Commonwealth, we could justifiably ask that the head office should be situated in London with the Board of Managers meeting alternately here and in Washington.

Members of the Board would be appointed by the Governments of the member states, each of which would have a vote in proportion to its quota. But there should be a provision, at any rate for some years, by which the British and American members when acting in agreement could outvote the rest of the Board.

There is no reason why the central banks of non-member states should not keep Credit Clearing Accounts with the Clearing Bank; and indeed it would be advisable for them to do so for the conduct of their trade with member states. But they would have no say in the management.

Members should be entitled to withdraw from the Union on a year's notice, subject to their making satisfactory arrangements to discharge any debit balance. They would not, of course, be able to employ any credit balance except by making transfers from it, either before or after their withdrawal, to the Clearing Accounts of other central banks.

Similarly it should be within the power of the Governing Board to require the withdrawal of a member subject to the same notice.

XII

In most of its objectives and in many of its methods this paper is in fundamental accord with alternative proposals which have been put forward. The special merits claimed for this particular version include the following:–

For ourselves

(1) Our British problem of gaining enough receipts overseas to balance our import requirements is so acute that we can scarcely hope to solve it except through a scheme which

(a) by a strong expansionist stimulus throughout the world provides willing markets for a largely expanded volume of our exports;

(b) offers facilities for the multilateral clearing of international payments, since we cannot afford to have any of the credit balances, which we may acquire overseas, to be blocked and unavailable as a set off against our debit balances elsewhere;

(c) provides us with a margin during the period before we can re-establish equilibrium by an international scheme which does not require us to ask particular favours or accommodations from the U.S. but merely gives to us, and requires of us, the same facilities for the expansion of international trade and the maintenance of international equilibrium which all the countries will be asked to receive and to allow;

(d) affords us the possibility of subsequent rectifications of the rate of exchange against the rest of the world without the risk of competitive depreciations or of complaints by other countries in the event of the initial value of sterling proving to be higher than the level at which we can balance our overseas trade.

(2) A multilateral system preserves, to the full extent com-

patible with the control of capital movements, the traditional freedom of London as a financial centre. Above all it allows the historical continuity of the sterling area in the same form and with the same absence of restraint as heretofore. For it is evident that any system of numerous bilateral agreements would put in great jeopardy not only the sterling area but the whole position of London as an international centre.

For the U.S. and the world at large

(1) It provides a general framework by the aid of which *all* countries can hope to rehabilitate their currencies.

(2) It offers a criterion by the help of which we can satisfy American aspirations, which we ourselves share not less than Mr Hull and Mr Sumner Welles, for the greater freedom of international trade supported by firm undertakings.

(3) It is a plan which can be used to further such general world purposes as (*a*) post-war relief and reconstruction; (*b*) international T.V.A.; (*c*) the finance of commodity agreements; (*d*) the preservation of peace; (*e*) the control of the trade cycle and the stabilisation of prices, and, generally (*f*) the maintenance of active employment everywhere.

(4) It is capable of arousing enthusiasm because it makes a beginning at the construction of the future government of the world between nations and 'the winning of the peace', in a sphere not the least important because the conditions and the atmosphere are thereby created in which much else is made easier.

J. M. KEYNES

15 December 1941

Before running off the stencils of his third draft, Keynes, at Sir Richard Hopkins' suggestion, showed a carbon of the scheme to R. F. Harrod. To Harrod's suggestions, which are summarised in footnotes where necessary, Keynes replied.

To R. F. HARROD, *16 December 1941*

Dear Roy,

Thank you very much for your further notes. My reactions to them are the following:–

1. It is of course fundamental that bancor should not be convertible into gold. I take it your point is that there should be some provision to prevent gold from in fact having a value in terms of bancor in excess of par. I thought I had dealt with this on page 17 [above p. 85], but I see I have not made it clear enough. I am now making the relevant sentence there run as follows:

> Since the national currencies of the member states will be given fixed exchange values in terms of bancor, it follows that they would have a defined gold content which would also be their official buying price for gold above which they must not pay.

That meets the point—doesn't it? I agree it would be a great help and convenience if the United States were to go on having a selling price for gold. But it would be difficult to put this into the charter of the system for the reason you give.

2. Your wording here is not quite exact I think. You do not mean the Clearing Bank would buy and sell the *currencies* of member countries but their bancor balances, for the Clearing Bank would never hold the currency of any member country. But I think I see the point you really have in mind and I am dealing with it by making a passage on page 4 [above p. 72] run:

> The central banks of all member states would keep accounts with the International Clearing Bank through which they would be entitled to settle their exchange balances with one another at their par value as defined in terms of bancor.

3. I am not quite sure here whether you want to have two stages, one corresponding to my 'deficiency country' and the other corresponding to your criterion of the debit substan-

tially exceeding the average debit.[12] I see no objection to strictness of the treatment of a 'deficiency country' depending on your criterion; indeed much to be said for it. But I do not like to substitute this for my definition of a 'deficiency country' on account of the uncertainty it involves.* I think it is important that countries should be able to discern by reference to the amount of their own debit how fast they were approaching the deficiency position. On your criterion this would depend on the actions of the rest of the system so that they would have no uncertainty in the matter. I prefer therefore to keep my definition of deficiency but would like to see something on your lines worked out when we come to details.

4. I am strongly in favour of interest charged on credit balances and, whilst this is not fundamental to the scheme as a whole, I should be sorry to see it go. It is an important part of the balancing system to provide some deterrent against the development of a credit position. It seems to me both theoretically and practically right. I cannot believe that a central bank would start speculating in commodities in order to avoid a one per cent bank charge. I am not so much wedded to the increase of the charge to two per cent on credits in excess of half the quota.

5. What is inserted here about the United States controlling movements of capital must depend on what conclusions are reached in the separate paper dealing with this subject in more detail. I put the passage in because I understood the Bank of England attach high importance to it and that it was likely to appear as part of the proposals in the paper dealing specifically with this subject. I am quite ready to leave it out if the decision is reached to leave it out in the other paper.

[12] Harrod, regretting that there was no special treatment in the scheme for countries whose debits exceeded the average of such countries, suggested that countries whose debits (adjusted for the volume of foreign trade) were abnormally large in terms of the average of debits be treated more severely.

* I have also failed, so far, to find a suitable way of drafting it. Have you? It's not very easy.

I regard it as a convenience of some importance rather than essential. Indeed I say in the text that I do not think it essential. Perhaps therefore you will argue this point in relation to the other document. My paper will then follow suit.

6. I inserted 'half' in relation to surplus conditions to meet your point of treating them more leniently than deficiency countries. And now you accuse me of want of symmetry. I think it is really important to retain a quarter for deficiency countries since a country so placed should assuredly be allowed the relaxation permitted to a deficiency country before it has got too deep in the mud. There is not really a want of symmetry here since no compulsory provisions affect a deficiency country until its debit reaches half its quota. But it leads to rather simpler drafting to put it in the way I now have. I dare say with further thought one could get it tidy on your lines. The essential thing to my mind is that a debit country should have a considerable range where it has increased discretion and is not subject to compulsion, namely the range of its debit between a quarter and a half its quota. All the rest is drafting.

7. This also seems a drafting point which might be considered in the next revision.[13] The whole of page 11 [above p. 79] could I think be drafted rather better.

8. This is a point of substance where I disagree. The 5 per cent depreciation is discretionary not compulsory. It seems to me it would often be preferable, if a change were necessary to make it by a single significant amount rather than by a series of small steps.[14] This would not prevent a central bank from moving 2 per cent. at a time, if this seemed to be the right process, but there might well be cases, I should have thought, where a single move of 5 per cent would be better

[13] Harrod referring to (5) on page 79 above, suggested that the wording seemed to contradict the essential feature of the scheme that a debit was the natural result of the transactions of many individuals coupled with an obligation to deal at par on the part of the Clearing Bank.

[14] Harrod had suggested that discretionary exchange depreciation be limited to 2 per cent.

than moves of 2 per cent, 2 per cent, and 1 per cent in three consecutive years, which would spin it out and prolong the uncertainty altogether too far.

9. I have taken this verbatim from the Board of Trade paper. If they are persuaded to alter this then I should follow suit.[15] At present I agree rather strongly with the Board of Trade.

10. I agree that this is open to misunderstanding and I have deleted it.[16]

Yours,
[copy initialled] J.M.K.

In sending the draft to Governor Norman, Keynes added his own short explanation of the scheme.

To M. NORMAN, *19 December 1941*

Dear Mr Governor,

Here is the latest revise of my International Bank Memorandum. It is (I hope) sufficiently near its final form to be worth your personal attention. Apologies for sending you so indigestible a Christmas present!

One or two points I would emphasise:–

(1) Considerable parts of the proposal are in the nature of trimmings and are not essential, at any rate in this form. They are capable of large modification in the light of discussion and to suit both legitimate criticisms and less legitimate prejudices. I put them in the substantive scheme because only in this way can I indicate the sort of purposes the Bank might be able to serve.

The *essence* of the scheme is very simple indeed. It is the extension to the international field of the essential principles of *banking* by which, when one chap wants to leave his re-

---

[15] Harrod had suggested deleting (v) on page 81 above.
[16] Keynes on page 90 had referred to 'the fissiary issue of the new system'.

sources idle, those resources are not therefore withdrawn from circulation but are made available to another chap who is prepared to use them—and to make this possible without the former losing his liquidity and his right to employ his own resources as soon as he chooses to do so. Just as the domestic situation was transmogrified in the eighteenth and nineteenth centuries by the discovery and adoption of the principles of local banking, so (I believe) it is only by extending these same principles to the international field that we can cure the manifest evils of the international economy as it existed between the two wars, after London had lost the position which had allowed her before 1914 to do much the same thing off her own bat.

I do not believe that there can be *any* scheme of value which does not embody this principle.

(2) My proposal is *multilateral*. We might be forced to fall back on bilateral arrangements as a very bad alternative if all else fails. But if we can get a multilateral system, I do not see how anyone in his senses could fail to prefer it. Therefore let us try for it.

(3) In particular, I believe that a multilateral plan is a necessary condition of the maintenance of the sterling area and the financial position of London. You will see what I have said about this on pp. 14–17 [above pp. 82–4] and p. 26 [above p. 94]. From what Lord Catto tells me, I think you may have got a wrong impression of my proposals in this respect. So far from their endangering the sterling area, I claim it as one of their chief merits that they offer us the best chance of maintaining it in the traditional sense—i.e. that the British Commonwealth make London their financial headquarters —which I, like you, deem of high importance. A multilateral system, by giving us something similar to the gold standard in its best nineteenth-century days, allows international banking (apart from capital controls) to go on just as before. A series of bilateral agreements, to which all the members of

the sterling area would have to be parties, seems to me quite impracticable—and very dangerous.

(4) Perhaps you will think the proposals too ambitious, too idealistic, altogether too grand. But isn't this a merit? The B.I.S. embodied a great, indeed a necessary, idea. Because it fell on evil days, partly because of its associations with reparations, partly because of the abstention of U.S.A., we must not turn cynical or disheartened—but, rather, brace ourselves up for another shot. This plan is a bold bid to combine the great historical advantages of the nineteenth-century gold standard with modern ideas and the requirements of the post-war world.

Vis-à-vis the Americans, I feel confident that a big *international* scheme, which does at least *try* to 'win the peace', has ten times the chance of acceptance compared with something which does not help the world at large and looks (to them) like no more than pulling *our* chestnuts out of the fire.

Even if it turns out too big for the Americans to swallow (which I don't expect), nevertheless it will have been wise and worth while to *start* by putting it forward. If they have rejected a world scheme, then we can, with much better grace, invite their help for something smaller and more particular to ourselves.

So I hope for your blessing and your approval. I have received more encouragement for this from all quarters in Whitehall than for anything I have ever suggested.

Yours sincerely,

[copy not initialled]

I shall be away from London next week.

On reading the third draft, Lord Catto commented.

THE ORIGINS OF THE CLEARING UNION

From LORD CATTO, *1 January 1942*

I have read with great interest the third draft of your proposals for an International Currency Union. I thank you for having tried to meet the points I raised in discussions on the previous two drafts. I like your new draft and I think the principles you put forward would bring us about as near a 'financial millennium' as you and I are likely to see in our lifetimes.

It is impossible to forecast post-war conditions. We may already see the drift of some things fairly clearly; in others the outline is very dim and may quickly change. It is not possible therefore to give a definite opinion as to what may be feasible or workable in the post-war period. But in any conditions which one may reasonably anticipate I see no reason why your proposals should not be entirely capable of practical application, although their success will depend upon the extent to which peoples of the countries of the post-war world realise their interdependence. Without such realisation your proposals or any other attempts to deal with the problem will be doomed to failure. It may be that remedies which are in no sense cures may be forced upon countries of the post-war world in the struggle for existence. Whether there will be sufficient common-sense to try something on the lines of your proposals without the lesson having to be learnt through the struggle for existence I do not know. One would think that the pre-war lesson would be enough. But however long the way may be to financial and economic sanity in international affairs, we must all work towards that good end: and I, for one, am grateful to you for showing the light at the end of the tunnel, even if the way be long and dark.

My congratulations.

CATTO

1 January 1942

As Keynes's re-drafted paper moved through further departmental discussions and inter-departmental committees as a part of a larger document from the Treasury on post-war policy, Harrod continued to bombard Keynes with suggestions. His main points concerned the status of bancor for he was still concerned about its possible depreciation vis-à-vis gold, the provision charging interest on surplus deposits, the absence of sanctions against what might be called ultra-debtors and the lack of a proposal for the initial, experimental period concerning exchange rates.[17]

[17] On this last point, Keynes commented on 9 January 1942: 'I will give thought to the question of a transitional period. But I would much prefer to deal with it by some general clause, that during the first five years the representatives of the founder states on the governing board, acting in agreement shall have power to

He also emphasised to Keynes and Sir Richard Hopkins that Keynes's scheme should go forward with full Treasury blessing, rather than as a personal statement, with a full appreciation of its strengths and weaknesses, a point which both accepted, and that there should be accompanying proposals for an International Investment Board (plans for which he had drafted and pushed forward repeatedly during this period).

After this draft, Keynes also attempted to deal with Mr Cobbold's worries concerning the sterling area and to meet D. H. Robertson's points on the need to compel the continuation of purchasing power in circulation and to be stricter with deficiency countries. He also commented on observations by Sir Richard Hopkins, who was preparing the general appreciations and introductions to various papers in the Treasury bundle.

When Hopkins set out his 'Critical Observations' on Keynes's plan, Keynes replied with a long, detailed series of comments and rejoinders, plus a covering letter of interest.

To SIR RICHARD HOPKINS, *22 January 1942*

Dear Hoppy,

My notes on your 'Critical Observations' are set out on a separate paper. But before you proceed to read these comments and rejoinders, I should like to say how much I appreciate the fairness and thoroughness of your criticism. I do not disagree that most of the points are well taken. My indictment, if I was to dare to draw one up, would be not intellectual but *moral*!

You make me feel again what I felt so often in the last twenty-five years: how fearfully and dangerously rash you cautious people are! Time after time during my active years

relax any particular provision. I am not at all keen on definitely encouraging exchange chaos in the early years. Any change by one party would react inconveniently on others. I rate very low the amount of relief to be got from quick changes of this kind, and it might be all the more difficult to keep the wages situation in control if labour was able to make the rejoinder that all one had got to do, *if* the higher wages proved troublesome, was to depreciate the exchange. I am almost keener on aiming at stable exchange rates during the transitional period than I am later on. Many changes might be made on highly temporary grounds. I have not yet met anyone who was in favour of exchange chaos in the early years on its merits, and I should like to wait until there really is strong pressure in this direction before yielding to the imagination of it. So, as I have said, I would prefer a general covering clause, elastic enough to cover the situation in the event of unforeseen developments'.

the authorities have gone bald-headed straight into (what have seemed to me) plainly evident perils, because (so they have argued) it would have been incautious to adopt constructive measures or to do anything worth mentioning until after we knew for certain what we were in for. Time after time what I wanted to see done has happened in the end, but only *after* great misfortunes. Must this always be so? And must you use your gifts and your influence in this direction?

I agree with the passage I have marked in this week's *National News-letter* attached (the preceding passages are also interesting). And in this connection I emphasise, what you have indeed mentioned in passing, that 'the new organisation could be one round which other international agencies for dealing with particular economic problems might be gathered'. This is of first-rate importance because it allows us to put up a scheme which may seem in its entirety to make the beginning of an entirely new stage in the economic organisation of the world. The *psychological* importance of something which *looks* significant can scarcely be over-stated. Yet you are arguing just the opposite!

Yours ever,
[copy initialled] J. M. K.

As some of Keynes's comments on Hopkins' 'Critical Observations' are useful in showing the way Keynes's mind was moving, they appear below.

From Notes on 'Critical Observations on the Clearing Bank Plan', 22 January 1942

3. *Page 3. 'Position of the United States'*. I do not feel it is quite correct to emphasise as much as this the special position of the United States. It is unsafe to predict more than a short time ahead which countries are going to be in the creditor position. Very likely there will be surprises and, whilst most probably the United States will be the largest creditor, she may be far from the only one. I would rather see it expressed

that, so far as there is a bill, the creditor countries, *whoever they may turn out to be*, will have to foot it and that the U.S.A. will doubtless contemplate the probability of herself, amongst others, being in that position. But one could go on to point out that she and the others would not foot the bill any more than they would have to in the absence of the Clearing Bank, assuming they had an equally large favourable balance. In terms of real resources the country with the favourable balance has to foot the bill in the sense of allowing the real consumption of the rest of the world to increase at its expense, whether that favourable balance is liquidated by lending or by receiving gold or through accumulating a credit balance at the International Bank. Moreover, in this context, the compensating advantage which the U.S. would receive deserves equal emphasis. They will need time in which to re-order their economy in such a manner as to produce an international balance which, when attained, will be beneficial not less to themselves than to the rest of the world. Without the Clearing Bank they would be faced by a much more awkward problem and the necessity to make hastier arrangements than with the assistance of the Bank. Just as the debtor countries need time to adjust themselves to the conditions of the post-war world, so, hardly less, do the creditor countries...

6. *Page 7*: The important question of timing is here raised. It is a defect in my draft plan that I have not dealt with this, and I should like to add a clause covering it.

The dilemma between the importance of starting in the first flush of enthusiasm and giving the plan a long-term expansionist bias, and, on the other hand, the risk of inflationary conditions in the immediate post-war period is a real one. I should like to give fresh thought to the question what protection against this can be introduced in the very early years.

But, whilst this is fair criticism, it is also important to

emphasise the fact that it is particularly in this early period that *we ourselves* shall require a margin of reserves and assistance towards achieving a balance. We certainly do not want the deflationary pressure to be primarily on ourselves during the initial period: although we shall certainly have to limit the extent of our demand on the outside world by the continuance of rationing and other controls. Thus it might be better to run some inflationary risks than to find ourselves quite at the mercy of others. The European countries requiring relief will be more easily attended to on philanthropic lines than our triumphant selves. We may reasonably hope that lend lease arrangements will not be cut off too suddenly or too completely. But it is particularly in the transitional period that we ourselves will require what the Prime Minister would call the 'easements' of the Clearing Bank plan. As I have said, I should like to think again as to the best compromise between these alternative dangers.

In the longer run our interest in an expansionist organisation is, it seems to me, overwhelming. I do not see how the expansion of exports which we shall require for solvency can be expected under any other conditions. We must not jeopardise this through over-caution. The avoidance of inflationary conditions in the immediate post-war period will have to be provided, in my judgment, not by credit deflation or currency pressures, but by the continuance of the sort of controls over raw materials and other supplies which have been developed during the war itself...

8. *Page 12*: This view of the importance of allowing exchange fluctuations is one which is held by some authorities. I myself greatly doubt the utility of sudden exchange depreciations to meet sudden developments. Broadly speaking, the factor governing the exchanges in the long run is the level of money wages relatively to efficiency in one country as compared with another. This is not as a rule anything which changes very suddenly. The causes of sudden difficulties are

very rarely, I should have thought, properly dealt with by exchange depreciation, which may easily do more harm than good. On the particular point that nothing can be done for a whole year an amendment could easily be made giving discretion to the governing board and to the country itself, acting in agreement, to take action at any time. This would be an improvement. I do not believe it will be as difficult as is expected to start off with reasonably appropriate exchange rates, since, up-to-date at any rate, there have not been in any country those large changes in wage rates which happened last time.

But my main point here is that there should be some comparison with the practicable alternatives. The Bank of England's notions on exchange rates were more rigid than mine. It is difficult to envisage any form of international agreement relating to the currencies which allows much more fluidity in this respect than the Clearing Bank scheme. It is quite true, as stated on page 13, that in some quarters the feeling might prevail that freedom to manipulate the value of currency is an important instrument of government. But clearly, if this view is pressed, it stands in the way of all currency agreements whatever. I should have claimed for the Clearing Bank plan that it went a little further in meeting this attitude of mind than most alternatives would.

I should be reluctant, apart from the small change suggested above, to give much more fluidity, because the atmosphere of settled exchange rates seems to me to be an important ingredient in achieving post-war stability. If money wage rates in a particular country have got thoroughly out of gear, there is nothing to be done but to alter the exchanges. In other contingencies the possible benefit to be gained is, I am sure, greatly exaggerated, and it would be exceedingly easy to do more harm than good. This is the lesson of nearly all the depreciations which took place after the last war. Perhaps the best case which could be cited to the contrary would be our own experience when we went off the gold standard. I think the change then made was helpful, but it was only one of a number of reliefs. Even such advantage as used to exist in depreciating the exchange has been greatly diminished by the growing practice of linking money wage rates to the cost of living. If money wages in this country always go up when the cost of imported food stuffs rises, the power of exchange depreciation to help us begins to evaporate. Apart from this, it is only when a reduction in the price of our exports by 10 per cent increases the demand for them by more than 10 per cent that we benefit in the slightest degree. We always stand to lose through depreciation from the fact that a large part of our invisible exports is fixed in terms of sterling. To sell 10 per cent more textiles at a price 10 per cent less is simply giving the stuff away without a ha'porth of advantage. This does not mean that there is not an optimum level for the exchange, but if we can find a level, though not necessarily the optimum, which we and our markets and our competitors have settled down to, it is only in exceptional circumstances that we could gain much by disturbing it.

At any rate, there is this much to be said on the other side against anyone who complains that the plan would introduce an undue fixity of the exchange.

9. *Page 14*: I do not agree with the criticism which, of course, for what it is worth, cancels out with the criticism just considered, that the possibility which the scheme allows for changes in exchange rates in circumstances which may be foreseen is conducive to a flight of capital. I disagree because of the difference in kind in these cases between the expectation of small changes and the expectation of large changes. The expense and trouble of all speculative operations is such that they are never called into being on any significant scale except by the expectation of very large changes. No one will speculate in a commodity because he thinks its price may rise

or fall 5 per cent (or even 10 per cent, for that matter). Nor will the expectation of a change which may be as much as 5 per cent at a date which cannot be accurately foreseen make a flight of capital attractive to any rationally calculating person. To move capital resources from one country to another and then back again, together with a possible loss of interest meanwhile, costs more than 5 per cent, or, at the very best, such a large proportion of 5 per cent that the thing is not worth while. At any rate, it should be pointed out that a critic cannot have it both ways. A scheme which allowed unlimited currency depreciations would be clearly more conducive to a flight of capital than the plan under discussion.

Over the weekend of 24 and 25 January 1942, Keynes re-drafted some sections of his proposals for the discussions then proceeding. With these revised sections, plus other drafting changes, the proposals went into print for the War Cabinet's Reconstruction Problems Committee, as paragraphs 61 to 134 of a memorandum by the Treasury on External Monetary and Economic Problems.[18]

PLAN FOR AN INTERNATIONAL CURRENCY
(OR CLEARING) UNION

A

61. The practical difficulties in the way of Anglo–American economic co-operation after the war should not dissuade us from attaching the highest importance to it. We must do our utmost to find common ground, and much will depend on the method of our approach.

62. It would be a mistake merely to put forward the extent and extremity of our post-war difficulties and follow up this

[18] The whole document ran to 84 pages of foolscap of which the first 6 were a concise summary. The other documents in the 'sandwich' were a first attempt at estimating the post-war balance of payments deficit, a discussion of Keynes's proposals, a discussion of the International Economic Board and Development Corporation proposed by Professors Hansen and Gulick, a discussion of trade policy, and a proposal for an international investment scheme.

complaint with a plea that there is nothing to be done except to leave us a free hand to use all those expedients which we may find useful and necessary in our self-regarding interests. Any statement on these lines should be introduced only in the shape of a warning that we must not be asked to abandon possible safeguards until something better is definitely in sight, or a hint of the unsatisfactory outcome to which the failure of a constructive plan might drive us.

63. It would also be a mistake to invite, of our own motion, direct financial assistance after the war from the United States to ourselves, whether as a gift or a loan without interest or a gratuitous redistribution of gold reserves, though we may reasonably hope that lend lease supplies of food and raw materials will not cease immediately after the end of hostilities. The United States will consider that we have had our whack in the shape of lend lease and a generous settlement of 'consideration'. If the British Commonwealth stands astride the world with the vast prestige of victors, though shared with Russia and the United States herself, some natural jealousy will not be absent. We, in particular, in a distressed and ruined continent, will not bear the guise of the most suitable claimant for a dole, however real and heavy our difficulties. The assistance for which we can hope must be *indirect* and a consequence of setting the world as a whole on its feet and of laying the foundations of a sounder political economy between all nations.

64. Finally, it would be a mistake in approaching the United States to put in the forefront proposals for an increased solidarity and significance for the British Commonwealth or the sterling area in isolation from the rest of the world, which would arouse both prejudice and suspicion. Such proposals must be ancillary to, and part of, a more general international scheme.

65. On the contrary. If we are to attract the interest and enthusiasm of the Americans, we must come with an am-

bitious plan of an international complexion, suitable to serve the interests of others besides ourselves, which to a hopeful spirit may carry a chance of making the post-war economy of the world more reasonable and promising than it was before—something capable of wide and various application. We can feel confidence that Americans will be brought to a sympathetic understanding of our difficulties. But, however hard-up we may be for the time being, we—on the assumption which underlies all our post-war plans—shall be standing on the top of the world, one of the two or three masters of the future. It is not with *our* problems of ways and means that idealistic and internationally-minded Americans will be particularly concerned.

66. Should we not share these purposes and interests with our American friends? Why should we confine ourselves to trying to patch up something which is as like as possible to what we are doing now and may with luck and skill just serve our turn? If we sincerely wish to collaborate with them to larger ends, they will soon discover it—and they would soon discover the opposite, if that were to be true. This, therefore, is the first criterion on which our proposals must be judged.

67. But further, it is not as if we had another plan which was, from our point of view, just right. Nothing of the kind. The more we look at the alternatives, the less we like them. They are neither one thing nor the other, but a patched-up contrivance, mainly based on abnormal war experience, which might do well enough to carry us through a transitional period, but is not very likely to evolve into a satisfactory permanent system or one which will fit in with (or help) what may be happening in the rest of the world. The most attractive version assumes a high degree of economic solidarity within the British Commonwealth. With so broad a bottom we might (perhaps) safely stand on it without support from outside. But we should run the risk of isolating ourselves from the United States and the rest of the world without real security that we had constructed a reliable economic union within the Empire.

68. It is, therefore, an ambitious and far-reaching scheme that is proposed in what follows. Certain elements in it are fundamental. Others are not, and are capable of being treated this way or that without impairing the main purpose. It would obscure the character and possibilities of the scheme if we start off with too much modification and compromise before we have heard the American point of view; and would very likely result in spoiling it in advance with unnecessary and unwanted concessions. But that must not lead anyone to suppose that the details are put forward dogmatically. The detailed plan is to afford a basis for discussion, as one variant of a central idea which is capable of being worked out in various ways. It is put forward, not as a cut-and-dried scheme to be formally adopted by the British Government, but for discussion and amendment between all those represented at the conversations as a constructive suggestion which might be found capable of contributing to the solution of the main economic problem which will face, not only us, but all the world.

B

69. The proposal is to establish a Currency Union, here designated an *International Clearing Union*, based on international bank money, called (let us say) bancor, fixed (but not unalterably) in terms of gold and accepted as the equivalent of gold by the British Commonwealth and the United States and all members of the Union for the purpose of settling international balances. The central banks of all member states (and also of non-members) would keep accounts with the International Clearing Union through which they would be entitled to settle their exchange balances with one another at their par value as defined in terms of bancor. Countries having a favourable balance of payments with the rest of the world as a whole would find themselves in possession of a credit account with the Clearing Union, and those having an unfavourable balance would have a debit account. Measures

would be necessary (see below) to prevent the piling up of credit and debit balances without limit, and the system would have failed in the long run if it did not possess sufficient capacity for self-equilibrium to prevent this.

70. The idea underlying such a Currency Union is simple, namely, to generalise the essential principle of banking, as it is exhibited within any closed system. This principle is the necessary equality of credits and debits, of assets and liabilities. If no credits can be removed outside the clearing system but only transferred within it, the Union *itself* can never be in difficulties. It can with safety make what advances it wishes to any of its members with the assurance that the proceeds can only be transferred to the clearing account of another member. Its problem is solely to see to it that its members keep the rules and that the advances made to each of them are prudent and advisable for the Union as a whole.

71. It is proposed that the Currency Union should be founded by the United States and the United Kingdom, which would be designated founder states and given a special position. Their representatives, and those of other members, on the Governing Board of the Clearing Bank would be appointed by the Governments of the several member states; the daily business and technical arrangements being carried out, as at present, by their central banks.

C

72. The plan aims at the substitution of an expansionist, in place of a contractionist, pressure on world trade.

73. It would effect this by allowing to each member state overdraft facilities of a defined amount, proportionate to the importance of its foreign trade and subject to certain regulative provisions. That is to say, each country is allowed a certain margin of resources and a certain interval of time within which to effect a balance in its economic relations with

the rest of the world. These facilities are made possible by the nature of the system itself and do not involve particular indebtedness between one member state and another. A country is in credit or debit with the Clearing Union as a whole. This means that the overdraft facilities, whilst a relief to some, are not a real burden to others. For credit balances, just like the importation of actual gold, represent those resources which a country voluntarily chooses to leave idle. They represent a potentiality of purchasing power, which it is entitled to use at any time. Meanwhile, the fact that the creditor country is not choosing to employ this purchasing power would not necessarily mean, as it does at present, that it is withdrawn from circulation and exerting a deflationary and contractionist pressure on the whole world including the creditor country itself. No country need be in possession of a credit balance unless it deliberately prefers to sell more than it buys (or lends); no country loses its liquidity or is prevented from employing its credit balance whenever it chooses to do so; and no country suffers injury (but on the contrary) by the fact that the balance, which it does not choose to employ for the time being, is not withdrawn from circulation. In short, the analogy with a national banking system is complete. No depositor in a local bank suffers because the balances, which he leaves idle, are employed to finance the business, of someone else. Just as the development of national banking systems served to offset a deflationary pressure which would have prevented otherwise the development of modern industry, so by extending the same principle into the international field we may hope to offset the contractionist pressure which might otherwise overwhelm in social disorder and disappointment the good hopes of our modern world.

74. These facilities will be of particular importance as soon as the initial shortages of supply have been overcome. Many countries, including ourselves, will find a difficulty in paying for their imports, and will need time and resources before they

can establish a readjustment. The efforts of each of these debtor countries to preserve its own equilibrium, by forcing its exports and by cutting of all imports which are not strictly necessary, will aggravate the problem of all the others. On the other hand, if each feels free from undue pressure, the volume of international exchange will be increased and everyone will find it easier to re-establish equilibrium without injury to the standard of life anywhere. The creditor countries will benefit, hardly less than the debtors, by being given an interval of *time* in which to adjust their economies, during which they can safely move at their own pace without the result of exercising deflationary pressure on the rest of the world, and, by repercussion, on themselves.

75. Now this can only be accomplished by the countries whoever they may turn out to be, which are for the time being in the creditor position, showing themselves ready to remain so without exercising a pressure towards contraction, pending the establishment of a new equilibrium. The fact that this costs them nothing deserves emphasising. The accumulation of a bancor credit, instead of accumulating gold, does not curtail in the least their capacity or their inducement either to produce or to consume. The substitution of a credit mechanism in place of hoarding would have repeated in the international field the same miracle already performed in the domestic field of turning a stone into bread.

76. There might be one or two other ways of effecting this temporarily or in part. For example, U.S.A. might redistribute her gold. Or there might be a number of bilateral arrangements having the effect of providing international overdrafts, as for example an agreement by the Federal Reserve Board to accumulate, if necessary, a large sterling balance at the Bank of England.

77. The objection to particular arrangements of this kind is that they are likely to be influenced by extraneous, political reasons and put individual countries into a position of par-

ticular obligation towards others; and also that the distribution of the assistance between different countries may not correspond to need and to the actual requirements as they ultimately develop. Moreover, for reasons already given, we are not likely to be specially eligible applicants for bounty of this kind. If, for example, the problem were to be met by a redistribution of America's gold, it is unlikely that we should get any of it, partly because we should have so lately received assistance under lend lease, partly because the British Commonwealth are the largest producers of gold, which output would be regarded, rightly or wrongly, as ours at one remove.

78. It should be much easier, and surely more satisfactory both for them and for us, to persuade the United States to enter into a general and collective responsibility, applying to all countries alike, that a country finding itself in a creditor position *against the rest of the world as a whole* should enter into an arrangement not to allow this credit balance so long as it chooses to hold it, to exercise a contractionist pressure against world economy and, by repercussion, against the economy of the creditor country itself. This would give us, and all others, the great assistance of multilateral clearing, whereby (for example) we could offset favourable balances arising out of our exports to Europe against unfavourable balances due to the United States or South America or elsewhere. How, indeed, can we hope to afford to start up trade with Europe (which will be of vast importance to us) during the relief and reconstruction period on any other terms?

79. These advantages of the proposed International Clearing Union are so great that they surely overshadow most reasons of objection on lesser grounds.

80. If, indeed, we lack the productive capacity to maintain our standard of life, then a reduction in this standard is not avoidable. If our wage and price levels are hopelessly wrong, a change in the rate of exchange is inevitable. But if we possess the productive capacity and the difficulty is the lack

of markets as a result of restrictive policies throughout the world, then the remedy lies in expanding opportunities for export by removal of restrictive pressure. There is great force in the contention that, if active employment and ample purchasing power can be sustained in the main centres of world trade, the problem of surpluses and unwanted exports will largely disappear, even though under the most prosperous conditions there may remain some disturbances of trade and unforeseen situations requiring special remedies.

D

82. The arrangement by which the members of the Clearing Union start with substantial overdraft facilities in hand will be mainly useful, just as the possession of any kind of reserve is useful, to allow time and method for necessary adjustments and a comfortable safeguard behind which the unforeseen and the unexpected can be faced with equanimity. Obviously, it does not by itself provide any long-term solution against a continuing disequilibrium, for in due course the more improvident and the more impecunious, left to themselves, would have run through their resources. But if the purpose of the overdraft facilities is mainly to give time for adjustments, we have to make sure, so far as possible, that they *will* be made. We must have, therefore, some rules and some machinery to provide that equilibrium is restored.

83. Perhaps the most difficult question to determine is how much to decide by rule and how much to leave to discretion. If rule prevails, the liabilities attaching to membership of the system are definite, whilst the responsibilities of central management are reduced to a minimum. On the other hand, liabilities which would require the surrender by legislation of too much of the discretion, normally inherent in a government, will not be readily undertaken by ourselves or by the United States. If discretion prevails, how far can the ultimate decision be left to the individual members and how far to the

central management? If the individual members are too free, indiscipline may result and unwarrantable liberties be taken. But if it is to the central management that the discretions are given, too heavy a weight of responsibility may rest on it, and it may be assuming the exercise of powers which it has not the strength to implement. If rule prevails, the scheme can be made more water-tight theoretically. But if discretion prevails, it may work better in practice. All this is the typical problem of any super-national authority. An earlier draft of this proposal was criticised for leaning too much to the side of rule. In the provisions below the bias is in the other direction. For it may be better not to attempt to settle too much beforehand and to provide that the plan shall be re-considered after an initial experimental period of (say) five years. Only by collective wisdom and discussion can the right compromise be reached between law and licence.

84. The proposal put forward below differs in one important respect from the pre-war system because it aims at putting some part of the responsibility for adjustment on the creditor country as well as on the debtor. This is an attempt to recover the advantages which were enjoyed in the nineteenth century when a favourable balance in favour of London and Paris, which were the main creditor centres, immediately produced an expansionist pressure in those markets, but which have been lost since New York succeeded to the position of main creditor, the effect of this change being aggravated by the breakdown of international borrowing credit and by the flight of loose funds from one depository to another. The object is that the creditor should not be allowed to remain entirely passive. For if he is, an intolerably heavy task may be laid on the debtor country, which is already for that very reason in the weaker position.

85. The detailed provisions proposed (the particular proportions, &c., suggested being merely tentative as a basis of discussion) are the following:–

(1) The two founder states will agree between themselves

the initial values of their own currencies in terms of bancor and the value of bancor in terms of gold; and the initial values of the currencies of other members will be fixed on their joining the system in agreement with them. A member state may not subsequently alter the value of its currency in terms of bancor without the permission of the Governing Board except under the conditions dealt with below; but during the first five years after the inception of the system the Governing Board shall give special consideration to appeals for adjustments in the exchange value of a national currency on the ground of unforeseen circumstances.

(2) The amount of the maximum debit balance allowed to any member state shall be determined by reference to the amount of its foreign trade, and shall be designated its *quota*. There need be no limit to the amount of a credit balance.

The initial quotas might be fixed by reference to the sum of each country's exports and imports on the average of (say) the three pre-war years, being either equal or in a determined *lesser* proportion to this amount, a special assessment being substituted in cases where this formula would be, for any reason, inappropriate. Subsequently, after the elapse of the transitional period, the quotas might be revised annually in accordance with the actual volume of trade in the three preceding years.

(3) A charge of 1 per cent per annum will be payable to the Reserve Fund of the Clearing Union on the average balance of a member state, whether credit or debit, in excess of a quarter of its quota; and a further charge of 1 per cent on the average balance, whether credit or debit, in excess of half its quota. Thus only a country which keeps as nearly as possible in a state of international balance on the average of the year will escape this contribution. These particular charges are, clearly, not essential to the scheme. But if they are found acceptable, they would be valuable inducements towards keeping a level balance, and a significant indication

that the system looks on excessive credit balances with as critical an eye as on excessive debit balances, each being, indeed, the inevitable concomitant of the other. Any member state in debit may, however, borrow from the balances of any member state in credit on such terms as may be mutually agreed, by which means each would avoid these contributions.

(4)—(a) A member state may not increase its debit balance by more than a *quarter* of its quota within a year without the permission of the Governing Board. If its debit balance has exceeded a quarter of its quota on the average for at least a year, it shall be entitled to reduce the value of its currency in terms of bancor, provided that the reduction shall not exceed 5 per cent within a year without the permission of the Governing Board.

(b) As a condition of allowing a member state to increase its debit balance in excess of a *half* of its quota, the Governing Board may require (i) a stated reduction in the value of the member's currency, if it deems that to be the suitable remedy, (ii) the control of outward capital transactions if not already in force, and (iii) the surrender of a suitable proportion of any separate gold reserve it may hold in reduction of its debit balance.

(c) If a member state's debit balance has exceeded *three-quarters* of its quota on the average for at least a year (or is excessive, as measured by some formula laid down by the Governing Board, in relation to the total debit balances outstanding on the books of the Clearing Union), it may be asked by the Governing Board to take measures to improve its position and, in the event of its failing to reduce its debit balance below the figure in question within two years, the Governing Board may declare that it is in default and no longer entitled to draw against its account except with the permission of the Governing Board. Each member state, on joining the system, shall agree to pay to the Clearing Union any payments due from it to a country in default towards the discharge of the latter's debit balance and to accept this arrangement in the event of falling into default itself. A member state which resigns from the Clearing Union without making approved arrangements for the discharge of any debit balance shall also be treated as in default.

(5) A member state whose credit balance has exceeded a *half* of its quota on the average of at least a year shall discuss with the Governing Board (but shall retain the ultimate decision in its own hands) what measures would be appropriate to restore the equilibrium of its international balances, including—

(*a*) measures for the expansion of domestic credit and domestic demand;

(*b*) the appreciation of its local currency in terms of bancor, or, alternatively, an increase in money wages;

(*c*) the reduction of excessive tariffs and other discouragements against imports;

(*d*) international loans for the development of backward countries.

E

86. The special protective expedients which were developed between the two wars were sometimes due to political, social or industrial reasons. But frequently they were nothing more than forced and undesired dodges to protect an unbalanced position of a country's overseas payments. The new system, by providing an automatic register of the size and whereabouts of the aggregate debtor and creditor positions respectively, will give a clear indication whether it is reasonable for a particular country to adopt special expedients as a temporary measure to assist in regaining equilibrium in its balance of payments, in spite of a general rule *not* to adopt them.

87. It is not proposed to incorporate any specific arrangements for such relaxations in the constitution of the Clearing

Union itself. But the existence of the Clearing Union would make it possible for member states contracting commercial treaties to use their respective debit and credit positions with the Clearing Union as a test. Thus, the contracting parties, whilst agreeing to clauses in a commercial treaty forbidding, in general, the use of certain measures or expedients in their mutual trade relations, might make this agreement subject to special relaxations if the state of their respective clearing accounts satisfied an agreed criterion. For example, a treaty might provide that, in the event of one of the contracting states having a debit balance with the Clearing Union exceeding a specified proportion of its quota on the average of a period and the other having a credit balance of a specified amount, the former should be free to resort to import quotas or to barter trade agreements or to higher import duties of a type which was not permitted under the treaty in normal circumstances. It might even provide that such exceptions should only be allowed subject to the approval of the Governing Board of the Clearing Union, and in that case the possible grounds for exceptional action might cover a wider field and other contingencies.

88. Apart from such temporary indulgence, the members of the Clearing Union should feel sufficiently free from anxiety to contemplate the ultimate removal of the more dislocating forms of protection and discrimination and expect the prohibition of some of the worst of them from the outset. In any case, members of the Currency Union would not allow or suffer among themselves any restrictions on the disposal of receipts arising out of current trade or 'invisible' income. It might also be possible to obtain recognition of the general principle that commercial treaties between members of the Union should, subject to any necessary safeguards and exceptions, exclude—

(i) import restrictions, whether quantitative or in the form of 'duty-quotas' (excluding, however, prohibitions genuinely designed to safeguard, e.g., public health or morals or revenue collection);

(ii) barter arrangements;

(iii) export quotas and discriminatory export taxes; and

(iv) excessive tariffs.

89. The question of preferences and of other relaxations from most-favoured-nation treatment, which would be of a normal and continuing character, does not fall within the scope of this paper, and must be settled on principles outside the sphere of the Clearing Union.

90. The above provisions might enable us to give some satisfaction to Mr Cordell Hull over a wide field, since we should be accepting a non-discriminatory international system as the normal and desirable régime.

F

91. It is a great advantage of the proposed Currency Union that it restores unfettered multilateral clearing between its members; so that no action is necessary, except where a country is out of balance with the system as a whole.

92. Compare this with the difficulties and complications of a large number of bilateral agreements. Compare, above all, the provisions by which a country, taking improper advantage of a payments agreement (for the system is, in fact a *generalised* payments agreement) as Germany did before the war, is dealt with not by a single country (which may not be strong enough to act effectively in isolation or cannot afford to incur the diplomatic odium of isolated action) but by the system as a whole. If the argument is used that the Currency Union may have difficulty in disciplining a misbehaving country and in avoiding consequential loss, with what much greater force can we urge this objection against a multiplicity of separate bilateral payments agreements.

93. Thus we should not only return to the advantages of

an international gold currency, but we might enjoy them more widely than was ever possible in practice with the old system under which at any given time only a minority of countries were actually working with free exchanges.

94. The advantages of multilateral clearing are of particular importance to London. It is not too much to say that this is an essential condition of the continued maintenance of London as the banking centre of the sterling area. Under a system of bilateral agreements it would seem inevitable that the sterling area, in the form in which it has been historically developed and as it has been understood and accepted by the Dominions and India, must fall to pieces.

95. In conditions of multilateral clearing everything would go on exactly as before without our having to ask anyone to accept special or onerous conditions. We should, in this respect, be back again in the best days of the gold standard. The traditional advantages of banking in London would be retained, precisely because London has been built up on the basis of an international currency having universal validity. But if we try to make of the sterling area a compact currency union as against the rest of the world, we shall be putting a greater strain on arrangements, which have been essentially (even in time of war) *informal*, than they can be expected to bear.

96. It is possible to combine countries, some of which will be in a debtor and some in a creditor position, into a currency union which, substantially, covers the world. But surely, it is impossible, unless they have a common banking and economic system also, to combine them into a currency union not with, but against, the world as a whole. If other members of the sterling area have a favourable balance against the world as a whole, they will lose nothing by keeping them in sterling, which will be interchangeable with bancor and hence with any other currency, until they have occasion to use them. But if the sterling area is turned into a currency union, the

members in credit would have to make a forced and *non-liquid* loan of their favourable balances to the members in debit. Incidentally, they might find themselves involved in making between them an involuntary loan to London at the rate, perhaps, of £100 million a year cumulative. They would have to impose import regulations and restraints on capital movements according as the area as a whole was in debit or credit, irrespective of their own positions. They would have to be bound by numerous bilateral agreements negotiated primarily (at least so they would believe) in the interests of London. The sterling resources of creditor Dominions might come to be represented by nothing but blocked balances in a number of doubtfully solvent countries with whom it suited *us* to trade. Moreover, it is difficult to see how the system could work without a pooling of gold reserves.

97. It is improbable that South Africa or India would accept such arrangements even if other Dominions were more complying. We should soon find ourselves, therefore, linked up only with those constituents which were running at a debit, apart from the Crown Colonies, which, perhaps, we could insist on keeping.

98. Is it not a delusion to suppose that the *de facto*, but somewhat flimsy and unsatisfactory, arrangements, which are carrying us through the war, on the basis that we do our best to find the other members of the area a limited amount of dollars provided that they lend us a very much larger sum in sterling, can be carried over into the peace and formalised into a working system based on a series of bilateral agreements with the rest of the world, accompanied by a strict control of capital movements outside the area?

99. The sterling area, if we mean by this the system under which the members of the British Commonwealth do their international banking through London, grew up under conditions of freedom. It lives and breathes by being a voluntary system. It is only in that same atmosphere of the City of

London as Liberty Hall dealing in a currency of general acceptability that we can expect to preserve it. The notion that a multilateral plan, based on an international standard, jeopardises the position of the sterling area must be based on a rigid and (one would think) politically impracticable version of the sterling area concept and not on its historical and actual significance. A multilateral plan would, therefore, be of great assistance in maintaining the position of London in relation both to the British Commonwealth and to many other countries which like our way of doing business and would give up most reluctantly the facilities we have given them.

G

100. It may be convenient at this point to note in more detail the position contemplated for centres of international banking such as London, New York or Paris, and for currency groups within the membership of the Clearing Union covering more than one country, such as the existing sterling area or groups, like the Latin Union of former days, which may come into existence covering, for example, the countries of North America or those of South America or the groups now under active discussion covering Poland and Czechoslovakia or certain of the Balkan States.

101. The governing principles should be: first, that the Clearing Union is set up, not for the transaction of daily business between individual traders or banks, but for the clearing and settlement of the ultimate outstanding balances between central banks (and certain other super-national institutions), such as would have been settled under the old gold standard by the shipment or the earmarking of gold, and should not trespass unnecessarily beyond this field; and, secondly, that its purpose is to increase *freedom* in international commerce and not to multiply interferences or compulsions.

102. Thus the fabric of international banking organisation, built up by long experience to satisfy practical needs, should be left as undisturbed as possible. Except as regards a provision, explained below, concerning the balances of central banks themselves, there should be no obstacle in the way of the existing practices of international banking except those which necessarily arise through measures which individual central banks may choose to adopt for the control of movements of capital.

103. Nor should it be necessary to interfere with the discretion of central banks which desire to maintain a special intimacy within a particular group of countries associated by geographical or political ties. There is no reason why such central banks should not be allowed a double position, both as members of the Clearing Union in their own right with their proper quota, and also as making use of another financial centre along traditional lines, as for example, Australia and India with London or certain American countries with New York. In this case their accounts with the Clearing Union would be in exactly the same position as the independent gold reserves which they now maintain, and they would have no occasion to modify in any way their present practices in the conduct of daily business.

104. There would be other cases, however, in which a dependency or a member of a federal union would merge its currency identity in that of a mother central bank, with a quota appropriate to the merged currency unit as a whole, and *not* enjoy a separate individual membership of the Clearing Union, as, for example, the French colonies, the federated states of the American Union or of Australia, and possibly the British Crown Colonies.

105. At the same time there should be a general encouragement to central banks, which do not belong to a special geographical or political group, to keep their reserve balances with the Clearing Union and not with one another, except

in the case of a specific loan from a member state in credit with the Clearing Union to a member state in debit. It should, therefore, be laid down that overseas balances may not be held in another country except with the approval of the central bank of that country; and, in order that sterling and dollars might not appear to compete with bancor for the purpose of central bank reserve balances, the founder states might agree together that they would not accept the reserve balances of other central banks in excess of normal working balances except in the case of banks definitely belonging to a sterling area or dollar area group.

H

106. The position of gold would be left substantially unchanged. What, in the long run, the world may decide to do with gold is another matter. The establishment of an International Clearing Union does not require any significant or immediate change. Indeed, by providing an automatic means by which some part of the favourable balances of the creditor countries can be settled, the current gold production of the world and the remnant of gold reserves held outside the United States may yet have a useful part to play. Moreover, gold still possesses great psychological value which will not have been diminished by recent events; for the desire to possess a gold reserve against unforeseen contingencies is likely to remain. Gold also has the merit of providing in point of form whatever the underlying realities may be, an uncontroversial standard of value for international purposes, for which it would not yet be easy to find a serviceable substitute.

107. It is conceived, therefore, that the international bank-money which we have designated *bancor* would be defined in terms of a weight of gold. Since the national currencies of the member states would also be given a defined exchange value

in terms of bancor, it follows that they would have a defined gold equivalent which would also be their official buying price for gold above which they must not pay. Any central bank would be entitled to obtain a credit in terms of bancor by paying actual gold to the credit of its Clearing Account, thus securing a steady and ascertained purchaser for the output of the gold-producing countries and for countries holding a large reserve of gold.

108. Central banks would be entitled to retain their separate gold reserves and ship gold to one another against a clearance between them in the books of the Clearing Union, provided they did not pay a price above parity; they could coin gold and put it into circulation, and, generally speaking, do what they liked with it.

109. One restriction only would be, for obvious reasons, essential. No central bank would be entitled to demand gold from the Clearing Union against its balance of bancor; for bancor would be available only for transfer to the Clearing Account of another central bank. Thus between gold and bancor itself there would be a one-way convertibility only, such as ruled frequently before the war with national currencies which were on what was usually called a 'gold exchange standard'. This need not mean that the Clearing Union would only receive gold and never pay it out. If the Clearing Union found itself in possession of a stock of gold, the Governors of the Bank should have the discretion to distribute the surplus between all central banks possessing a credit balance with it, proportionately to such balances, in reduction of their amount.

110. The question has been raised whether these arrangements are compatible with the retention by individual member states of a full gold standard with two-way convertibility, so that, for example, any foreign bank acquiring dollars through the Clearing Union could use them to obtain gold for export. It is not evident that a good purpose would

be served by this. But if any member state should prefer to maintain full convertibility for internal purposes, it could protect itself from any abuse of the system or inconvenient consequences by providing that gold could only be exported under licence.

111. The value of bancor in terms of gold should be fixed but not unalterably. The two founder states, the United States and the United Kingdom, acting in agreement, should have the power to change it. Clearly, they should exercise this power if the stocks of gold tendered to the bank were to be super-abundant for their legitimate purposes. No object would be served by attempting further to peer into the future or to prophesy the ultimate policy of the founder states in this respect.

112. Changes in the value of the national currencies of member states stand in a different category. For the real significance of such changes is to be found not in relation to gold itself but in relation to the values of national currencies amongst themselves. The general principles by which such changes should be governed have been discussed in a previous section. It would be undesirable, if it can be avoided, to lay down more precise rules in advance, since it is difficult to distinguish by means of a rigid formula the cases, in which a change in the rate of exchange will assist the restoration of equilibrium and is the right remedy, from those cases where some other type of measure is more appropriate.

J

113. It is widely held that control of capital movements, both inward and outward, should be a permanent feature of the post-war system—at least so far as we are concerned. If control is to be effective, it probably involves the *machinery* of exchange control for *all* transactions, even though a general open licence is given to all remittances in respect of current

trade. But such control will be more difficult to work, especially in the absence of a postal censorship, by unilateral action than if movements of capital can be controlled *at both ends*. It would therefore be of great advantage if the United States and all other members of the Currency Union would adopt machinery similar to that which we have now gone a long way towards perfecting in this country; though this cannot be regarded as *essential* to the proposed Union.

114. This does not mean that the era of international investment should be brought to an end. On the contrary, the system contemplated should facilitate the restoration of international credit for loan purposes in such ways as those mentioned in 122 (5) below. The object, and it is a vital object, is to have a means of distinguishing—

(*a*) Between movements of floating funds and genuine new investment for developing the world's resources; and

(*b*) Between movements, which will help to maintain equilibrium, from surplus countries to deficiency countries and speculative movements or flights out of deficiency countries or from one surplus country to another.

115. There is no country which can, in future, safely allow the flight of funds for political reasons or to evade domestic taxation or in anticipation of the owner turning refugee. Equally, there is no country that can safely receive fugitive funds which cannot safely be used for fixed investment and might turn it into a surplus country against its will and contrary to the real facts.

116. The general principles of the control of capital movements need not be discussed here. It is evident that the existence of an International Clearing Union would make such control easier.

K

117. It has been suggested that so ambitious a proposal is open to criticism on the ground that it requires from the members of the Currency Union a greater surrender of their sovereign rights than they will readily concede.

118. But, in the present version of the plan, no greater surrender is required than in any commercial treaty—certainly not greater than in the binding undertakings against discrimination which the United States is inviting us to make. The obligations will be entered into voluntarily and can be terminated on certain conditions by giving notice.

119. In the second place a greater readiness to accept super-national arrangements must be required in the post-war world than hitherto. The arrangements proposed could be described as a measure of financial disarmament. They are very mild in comparison with the measures of military disarmament, which it is to be hoped the world may be asked to accept.

120. Surely it is an advantage, rather than a disadvantage, of the scheme that it invites the member states and groups to abandon that licence to promote indiscipline, disorder and bad-neighbourliness which, to the general disadvantage, they have been free to exercise hitherto.

121. There is nothing here which we need be reluctant to accept ourselves or to ask of others. Or if there be anything such, let it be amended.

L

122. An International Currency Union might become the instrument and the support of international policies apart from those which it is its primary purpose to promote. The following suggestions are not a necessary part of the plan. But they are illustrations of the additional purposes of high

importance and value which the Union, once established, might be able to serve:–

(1) The Union might set up a Clearing Account in favour of the international body charged with post-war relief and reconstruction. If necessary, it might supplement contributions received from other sources by granting overdraft facilities in favour of this body, this overdraft being discharged over a period of years out of the Reserve Fund of the Union, or, if necessary, out of a levy on credit clearing balances. By this means it is possible to avoid asking any country to assume a burdensome commitment for relief and reconstruction, since the resources would be provided in the first instance by those countries having credit Clearing Accounts for which they have no immediate use and are voluntarily leaving idle, and in the long run by those countries which have a chronic international surplus for which they have no beneficial employment.

(2) If the United States were to wish to effect a redistribution of gold reserves, the Clearing Union would provide a suitable channel for the purpose, the gold so re-distributed being credited (e.g.) to the account of the Relief and Reconstruction Authority.

(3) The Union might set up an account in favour of the super-national policing body charged with the duty of preserving the peace and maintaining international order. If any country were to infringe its properly authorised orders, the policing body might be entitled to request the Governors of the Clearing Union to hold the Clearing Account of the central bank of the delinquent country to its order and permit no further transactions on the account except by its authority. This would provide an excellent machinery for enforcing a financial blockade.

(4) The Union might set up an account in favour of international bodies charged with the management of a Commodity Control, and might finance stocks of commodities

held by such bodies, allowing them overdraft facilities on their accounts up to an agreed maximum. By this means the financial problem of holding pools and 'ever-normal granaries' would be satisfactorily solved.

(5) The Union might be closely linked up with the Board for International Investment. It might act on behalf of this Board and collect for them the annual service of their loans by automatically debiting the Clearing Account of the country concerned. The statistics of the Clearing Accounts of the member states would give a reliable indication as to which countries were in a position to finance the Investment Board, with the advantage of shifting the whole system of clearing credits and debits nearer to equilibrium. This important question is the subject of separate papers. (Appendices 2 and 3).

(6) There are various methods by which the Clearing Union could use its influence and its powers to maintain stability of prices and to control the trade cycle. If an International Economic Board is established, this Board and the Clearing Union might be expected to work in close collaboration to their mutual great advantage. If an International Investment or Development Corporation is also set up together with a scheme of Commodity Controls for the control of stocks of the staple raw materials, we might come to possess in these four institutions a powerful means of combating the evils of the trade cycle, by exercising contractionist or expansionist influence on the system as a whole or on particular sections. This, again, is a large and important question which cannot be discussed adequately in this paper; and need not be examined at length in this place because it does not raise any important issues affecting the fundamental constitution of the proposed Union. It is mentioned here to complete the picture of the large purposes which the foundation of the Currency Union might be made to serve.

M

123. Our post-war currency and exchange system should be one which is capable of wide, indeed of universal, extension as further countries become ready for it. Nevertheless it would be an advantage if the proposed Union could be brought into existence by the United States and the United Kingdom as joint founder states, covering the United States and its possessions and the members of the British Commonwealth. The position of Russia, which might be a third founder, if she can be a party to this kind of international institution, would need special consideration. Other members would then be brought in—some from the outset, some as soon as they had established an internal organisation capable of sustaining the obligations of membership. This approach would have the great advantage that the United States and the United Kingdom (the former in consultation with the Pan-American countries and the latter with the other members of the British Commonwealth) could settle the charter and the main details of the new body without being subjected to the delays and confused counsels of an international conference. It would also mean that considerable progress could be made irrespective of the nature of the European political settlement and before the conditions of adherence of the European members could be finally determined. Moreover, membership would be thus established as a privilege only open to those who conformed to certain general principles and standards of international economic conduct. The management and the effective voting power might inhere permanently in the founder states.

124. In view of our experience and of our geographical and political position in relation to Europe, the United States and the British Commonwealth, we could justifiably ask that the head office should be situated in London with the Board of Managers meeting alternately here and in Washington.

125. Members of the Board would be appointed by the governments of the member states, each of which would have a vote in proportion to its quota. But there might be a provision, at any rate for the first five years, by which the British and American members when acting in agreement could outvote the rest of the Board.

126. There is no reason why the central banks of non-member states should not keep Credit Clearing Accounts with the Union; and indeed it would be advisable for them to do so for the conduct of their trade with member states. But they would have no say in the management.

127. Members should be entitled to withdraw from the Union on a year's notice, subject to their making satisfactory arrangements to discharge any debit balance. They would not, of course, be able to employ any credit balance except by making transfers from it, either before or after their withdrawal, to the Clearing Accounts of other central banks. Similarly it should be within the power of the Governing Board to require the withdrawal of a member subject to the same notice.

128. The principles and governing rules of the Union should be the subject of general reconsideration after five years' experience, if a majority of the Governing Board desire it.

129. It would be of great advantage if the general principles of the International Clearing Union could be agreed beforehand, with a view to bringing it into operation at an early date after the termination of hostilities. Such a proposal presents, however, something of a dilemma. On the one hand, many countries, ourselves not least, will be in particular need of reserves of overseas resources in the period immediately after the war. On the other hand, goods will be in short supply and the prevention of inflationary international conditions of the first importance. The expansionist tendency of the proposed system, which is a leading recommendation of it as

soon as peace-time output is restored and the productive capacity of the world is in running order, might easily be a danger in the early days of a sellers' market and a super-abundance of demand over supply.

130. A reconciliation in detail of these divergent purposes is not easily found until we know more than is known at present about the means to be adopted to finance post-war relief and reconstruction and particularly as to the intentions of the United States regarding a temporary continuance of lease lend arrangements for food and raw materials after the termination of hostilities. If these intentions are on liberal and comprehensive lines, it might be better for relief and lend lease arrangements to take the place of the proposed quotas during the 'relief' period of (say) two years. The immediate establishment of the Clearing Union would be compatible with provisional arrangements regarding the overdraft quotas which could take alternative forms according to the character of the other 'relief' arrangements.

131. If the finance of relief is actually furnished through the Clearing Union, which has been suggested above as one possibility, and if that, combined with some continuance of lend-leasing by the United States, appears likely to provide the world with as much purchasing power as is desirable in the early days, the coming into force of the overdraft quotas might be postponed until the founder members are agreed that the need for them is impending. In this case credit clearing balances would be limited to the amount of gold delivered to the Union, and the overdraft facilities created by the Union in favour of the Relief Council, the International Investment Board or the Commodity Controls. Alternatively overdraft quotas might be allowed on a reduced scale during the transitional period. At any rate, it might be proper to provide that countries in receipt of relief or lend lease assistance should not have access at the same time to overdraft facilities, and that the latter should only become available when the former had come to an end.

132. If, on the other hand, relief and lend lease facilities look like being inadequate from the outset, the overdraft quotas may be even more necessary at the outset than later on.

133. We must not be over-cautious. A rapid economic restoration may lighten the tasks of the diplomatists and the politicians in the resettlement of the world and the restoration of social order. In our case the possibility of exports sufficiently expanded to sustain our standard of life and our solvency is bound up with good and expanding markets. We cannot afford to wait too long for this and we must not allow excessive caution to condemn us to perdition. Unless the Union is a going concern, the problem of proper 'timing' will be almost insoluble. It is sufficient at this stage to point out that the problem of timing must not be overlooked, but that the Union is capable of being used so as to aid rather than impede its solution.

N

134. In most of its objectives and in many of its methods this paper is in fundamental accord with alternative proposals which have been or could be put forward. The special merits claimed for this particular version include the following:–

For ourselves

(1) Our British problem of gaining enough receipts overseas to balance our import requirements is so acute that we can scarcely hope to solve it except through a scheme which—

(a) by a strong expansionist stimulus throughout the world provides willing markets for a largely expanded volume of our exports;

(b) offers facilities for the multilateral clearing of international payments, since we cannot afford to have any of the credit balances, which we may acquire overseas, to be blocked and unavailable as a set-off against our debit balances elsewhere;

(*c*) provides us with a margin, during the period before we can re-establish equilibrium, by an international scheme which does not require us to ask particular favours or accommodations from the United States but merely gives us, and requires of us, the same facilities for the expansion of international trade and maintenance of international equilibrium which all the countries will be asked to receive and to allow;

(*d*) affords us the possibility of subsequent rectifications of the rate of exchange against the rest of the world without the risk of competitive depreciations or of complaints by other countries in the event of the initial value of sterling proving to be higher than the level at which we can balance our overseas trade.

(2) A multilateral system preserves, to the full extent compatible with the control of capital movements, the traditional freedom of London as a financial centre. Above all it allows the historical continuity of the sterling area in the same form and with the same absence of restraint as heretofore. For it is evident that any system of numerous bilateral agreements would put in great jeopardy not only the sterling area but the whole position of London as an international centre.

For the United States and the world at large

(1) It provides a general framework by the aid of which *all* countries can hope to rehabilitate their currencies.

(2) It offers a criterion by the help of which we can satisfy American aspirations, which we ourselves share with Mr Hull and Mr Sumner Welles, for the greater freedom of international trade supported by firm undertakings.

(3) It is a plan which can be used to further such general world purposes as—

(*a*) post-war relief and reconstruction;

(*b*) international T.V.A.;

(*c*) the finance of commodity agreements;

(*d*) the preservation of peace;

(*e*) the control of the trade cycle and the stabilisation of prices; and, generally,

(*f*) the maintenance of active employment everywhere.

(4) It is capable of arousing enthusiasm because it makes a beginning at the future economic ordering of the world between nations and 'the winning of the peace', and might help to create the conditions and the atmosphere in which much else would be made easier.

The full Treasury memorandum came up for discussion at the meeting of the Committee on Reconstruction Problems on 31 March 1942. At the committee, the memorandum's proposals were the subject of criticism on several grounds, particularly by Mr Bevin. The criticisms included their exclusion of Russia, their return to the rigidity of the Bank Act of 1844 and their restoration of an Anglo-American gold standard condominium over the rest of the world. As well, the overdrafts were held to be too small and the scheme held to emphasise external finance too extensively.

After this preliminary discussion, Keynes and Sir Richard Hopkins took part in the meeting.

From Minutes of a Meeting of the War Cabinet Committee on Reconstruction Problems, 31 March 1942

SIR RICHARD HOPKINS replied that nothing was further from the minds of the authors of the memorandum than to create conditions such as those described in the objections stated. If the history of the last twenty years was surveyed there had been no greater difficulty for this country than that of obtaining adequate resources to buy from abroad and so to maintain the standard of living. At the end of this war our position would be even more difficult. One of the first things needed was to get a new system not dependent on gold and an investment system which was also international. In consequence Mr. Keynes had developed a plan which had the object of getting rid of the contractionist system. It was true that this plan aimed at a recognised relationship of currencies one to another, but uncontrolled variations as between currencies had been one of the most definite elements in unsettlement of commerce and industry. The whole object of the proposals was expansionist and not contractionist. During the last twenty years the relationship of currencies had been under no central control with the result that each currency had been dealt with on an individualist basis producing much involution in the treatment of currency and trade, leading eventually to the German methods which had brought the system of currency control into extreme disrepute. Proper control of the world currency problems would have to be under a restricted number of countries, obviously the United Kingdom and the United States and, if possible, Russia in due course. The latter part of the memorandum dealt with the problem of multilateral versus bilateral trade arrangements and the memorandum was strongly in favour of getting rid of the complications which had existed before the war in international trade. On this point the American outlook as expressed by Mr Cordell Hull and his followers, was Victorianism and was far too loose and indefinite for present circumstances. The proposals in the memorandum were in fact a halfway house between extreme control and complete absence of control and the primary object had been to find the conditions under which the greatest multiplication of trade could occur. So far from the proposals in the memorandum requiring unemployment and under-consumption in order to support the exchanges he felt that they were measures under the shelter of which proper steps could be taken for dealing with unemployment in individual countries with the greatest prospect of success.

MR KEYNES, in reply to a question as to how these proposals differed from the old theory of the gold standard, remarked that he did not think that he personally would be suspected of tenderness towards the gold standard. In fact these proposals completely dethroned gold in polite language. They were the exact opposite of the provisions of the Bank Act of 1844 because the volume of currency was not fixed in relation to gold. 'Bancor' could be acquired in return for gold, but gold could not be acquired in return for bancor. The quantity of bancor was absolutely elastic and in fact the proposals substituted bank money for gold, which would not in future limit the amount of money there would be. As regards this country there was no doubt that it would end the war with a very adverse balance and in fact in order to supply itself sufficiently from overseas it might well require an increase of 50 per cent or more of its export trade. This would be impossible unless other countries were to be in a position to buy and provision were made for a sound multilateral system. He could see no way of our obtaining the necessary export markets except by proposals such as these. We could not get what we all wanted, namely, good trade and full employment, except by dethroning gold and creating a system of international credits so that trade was not limited by the amount of gold available. In his view these proposals were the most 'anti 1844 Bank Act' proposals that could be devised. As regards the question whether the prices of primary commodities would be sufficiently high, in his view the danger before this country was that they might be too high. There would be no difficulty in persuading producing countries to charge high prices. What, however, was essential to any proper system of international trade was a system of suitable prices at the right level. Under these proposals the producing countries would be able to put the burden of sudden fluctuations on the international board. In present circumstances an industrial slump now led to an agricultural slump. We might not be able to prevent the former, but it was hoped to prevent the latter by placing the burden of surplus production on the shoulders of the stabilisation board.

As regards the suggestion that these proposals maintained the system of extracting from producing countries interest on loans of far greater amount than the loans themselves so that the producer paid for the loan first in the price, then in the rate of interest, and then in amortisation, Mr. Keynes replied that the plan was for loans for construction purposes with very low interest. In fact the international body could lend for one half or one third of the usual rates. As regards the unemployment point, the one way of avoiding unemployment in this country was by developing exports and the clue to exports was the ability to get payment for them. As regards Russia, there had been no intention in the minds of the authors of the memorandum that she should be excluded from these proposals. In fact, reference was made in paragraph 123 to Russia becoming a 'third founder'.

Some further discussion on the memorandum took place, reference being made to

(i) the possibility of declaring countries in default;

(ii) the practicability of a censorship which would be necessary for complete exchange control; and

(iii) the desirability of bearing in mind the relationship of imperial preference to these proposals and the necessity of early consultation with the Dominions and India.

The Treasury memorandum went to the War Cabinet in a paper, dated 10 April 1942 which included the various recommendations of the Reconstruction Problems Committee, in particular its recommendation that it serve as the basis for conversations with the Americans under Article VII. Before the Cabinet meeting, Keynes met Mr Bevin.

To SIR RICHARD HOPKINS *and* H. WILSON SMITH

My interview with Mr Bevin this afternoon about the Clearing Union served, I think, a useful purpose. In particular, I discovered wherein lay the basis of his opposition. He is afraid that the new scheme, though giving a certain amount of leeway, might result in the last resort, in a return to the evils of the old automatic gold standard, and he remembers that that, in the last analysis, was what drove him, against his natural inclinations, to fight the General Strike. I told him that I thought few or no responsible persons today contemplated the use of the old weapons, deflation enforced by dear money, resulting in unemployment, as a means of restoring international equilibrium, and that, if the new scheme was to break down, this would not be the remedy which anyone would seek to adopt. He replied that, if this was made perfectly clear, he would feel very much happier about it all.

I then suggested that I should draft for him a passage,

which would clear up any doubt there is on this matter. I think he had in mind, not so much an amendment of the document itself as a rider, which could be attached to the instructions given to the British representatives. I enclose in a letter to his secretary a formula which I think might meet the case and then satisfy Mr. Bevin. Perhaps this could be sent round to Mr Gee after the Chancellor has seen and approved it.

J. M. K.

22.4.42

In putting forward these proposals, the British representatives should make it clear that the measures under para. 85(4) (*c*) which the Governing Board can ask a country to take 'to improve its position', if it has a substantial debit balance, do *not* include a deflationary policy, enforced by dear money and similar measures, having the effect of causing unemployment; for this would amount to restoring, subject to insufficient safeguards, the evils of the old automatic gold standard.

The proposed amendment was approved by the War Cabinet, as was a suggestion by Sir Stafford Cripps that Russia be included in the scheme from the outset.

At this stage, Keynes wrote to Richard Kahn.

From a letter to R. F. KAHN, *11 May 1942*

We spend more and more time on post-war questions. So far as external affairs are concerned, I think we have really made some progress. My currency schemes, which you saw in an early version, have gone through a vast number of drafts without, in truth, substantial change. It has been somewhat of a business getting them through all stages, but successfully achieved at last. After getting through official Whitehall, they then had to be got through Ministers of various sorts and kinds, and, finally, last week they were considered at a special meeting of the War Cabinet, which gave them a general blessing. Now it is a question of capturing American sympathy. Winant is doing his best to get a deputation of important American officials over next month. We cannot be certain if he will succeed. If, in due course, they do arrive, everything will depend on their reactions. As you may suppose, it has been rather a *tour de force* getting the thing so far as it has got. It is still a tender plant, which can be easily blasted by a harsh word from any quarter. What keeps it alive is the singular unattractiveness of all alternatives. The only strenuous advocate of a bilateral post-war world on merits is Hubert [Henderson]. I see what he has in mind and cannot deny much force to many of his arguments. All the same, it will, I am sure, be a great misfortune if, as a *pis aller*, we are driven along that alternative route. That is, indeed, the general opinion, and that, as I have said, is why a radically new contraption is more favourably regarded than one might have expected.

I have also prepared a general scheme for the international control of commodities with buffer stocks and price stabilisation. At present this is at an earlier stage of pilgrimage through Whitehall, but seems to be going fairly well.[19]

[19] On this, see *JMK*, vol. XXVII.

Chapter 2

FROM CABINET AGREEMENT TO WHITE PAPER, 1942–1943

During the period in which the Clearing Union made its way through the War Cabinet and its Reconstruction Committee, following the Anglo-American agreement on Article VII, the British began preparing the ground for conversations on post-war planning. Initially, the preferred channel of communication was through the American Ambassador, whom Keynes saw on 3 and 16 February.[1]

At that stage, the Americans were far from ready for conversations and it was the spring before extensive discussion on the form of the conversations began in London. The initial impetus, as far as Keynes was concerned, seems to have come from a memorandum R. F. Harrod sent to Keynes on 15 April. In his memorandum Harrod emphasised the need to be forthcoming and open with the Americans, if only to overcome previous suspicions, to accept the necessity of a liberal trading world as a goal of post-war policy and to leave discussions of Britain's post-war difficulties to one side until the shape of the post-war economic order became clearer. He then proposed the establishment of an Anglo-American Economic Service which would take the initiative in organising the post-war world and to which other members of the Allies could associate themselves, as and when convenient and desirable. The Service, with the Clearing Union as its financial cornerstone, would also initiate a buffer stock scheme, an investment board to control the international flow of capital and therefore align the development of backward regions to the needs of contra-cyclical policy, and an agency for post-war relief and reconstruction. Harrod's memorandum also advocated the abolition of controls on capital movements in the Clearing Union and continued to press for stronger penalties on debtors in the scheme.

On receiving the memorandum, Keynes replied.

[1] Keynes's contacts with Winant and Penrose were relatively frequent. In the course of 1942, his appointments diary lists five meetings with Winant, often for long evening discussions, as well as eighteen meetings with Penrose. In addition, he often saw other American officials in London, plus, of course, visitors such as Herbert Feis and Walter Lippmann.

Herbert Feis (b. 1893); economic adviser, Department of State, 1931–7, adviser on international economic affairs, 1937–43; Special Consultant to Secretary of War, 1944–6.

To R. F. HARROD, *19 April 1942*

Dear Roy,

YOUR MEMORANDUM ON FORTHCOMING U.S. CONVERSATIONS

I find this very interesting, and it brings to a head a number of issues on which we have got to make up our minds. With a very large part, particularly of the earlier portion, I am in agreement. The comments which seem worth recording are the following:–

1. I agree with you that we should not bring forward our own troubles at too early a stage in the discussion. That would not be the appropriate introduction to the constructive schemes, and until we have some notion how sympathetic the Americans are to the schemes we shall have no means of measuring how serious our troubles are likely to be. This applies, not only to the nature of our troubles, but also to the possible protective means we might have to adopt to deal with them.

2. To your Anglo-American Service I have no objection of principle. On the contrary. But it seems to me to raise considerable diplomatic and practical difficulties, the seriousness of which I cannot easily judge. These relate particularly to the position (*a*) of Russia, (*b*) of the Dominions and (*c*) of the rest of Europe. You bring in Russia, though rather perfunctorily towards the end, saying that they can presumably participate at a later stage if they want. But it seems to me that you are essentially thinking of it as a new version of what you previously called the Anglo-American Condominium. Your idea is that it should be worked out by ourselves and the Americans alone, and only at a later stage should others be brought in. The same difficulty applies to some extent to the Clearing Union and the Commodity Scheme, and at the Ministerial Committee it was raised prominently in connection with the former. But it seems to me to arise more

146

decidedly in relation to your proposed Anglo-American Service. If the Americans themselves seem disposed to this method of operation, it would certainly deserve to be considered very seriously. But, even so, on merits I am not clear how far it is right or prudent for us to distinguish ourselves too sharply from Russia and the Dominions, whatever we may feel about Europe. These difficulties about the position of other countries arise more particularly because you conceive this Service as dealing with relief and reconstruction, which I mention separately below.

3. You are quite right in arguing that the initial work of such an Anglo-American Service will be primarily concerned with relief and reconstruction. In view of what has happened in the Pacific and the Indian Ocean, this is more clearly so than it was even a short time ago. The damage effected there means that all over the world relief and reconstruction is likely to absorb all outside aid available for such general purposes for a considerable time to come. But this seems to me to make it more difficult to give to this country such a special position as you claim. How can you justify this for a country which, particularly in the early days, whatever may happen later on, so far from having any surplus resources available to help other people, may herself come very near to being one of the applicants for assistance? When one was thinking of a long-term programme applicable to undeveloped countries rather than to Europe, a special position to ourselves was easier to justify. It still is perhaps, so far as Asia is concerned; not so easily in regard to Europe.

4. It is not clear in your memorandum how conscious you are of the extent to which your proposal cuts across the preliminary scheme which Leith-Ross has been drawing up for relief and reconstruction. The position of that is that he is working hand in glove with the European Allies. There are also semi-separate conversations between ourselves and Russia. So far, not particularly through any fault of our own,

the United States is completely aloof. Indeed I have felt in the last week that the plans were in danger of going a good deal further than was wise without bringing the Americans in. The Russians have appealed to us on the subject in a document in which even the name of the United States never appears. I am not saying that Leith-Ross is necessarily on the right lines. But obviously you are going to the opposite extreme, and the possibility of going to that extreme is already somewhat prejudiced by what has already happened.

5. I agree with you in thinking that the question of capital control should not be put in the forefront of the programme but should emerge at a later stage out of other discussions. On the other hand, I disagree most strongly with your view that the control of capital movements may very possibly be unnecessary, especially if a Clearing Union comes into existence. My points of difference can be listed as follows:–

(a) I do not agree that the question of the precise nature of the control we exercise over such surplus for investment as may be developed in course of time is more fundamental than that of hot money and, therefore, due for prior discussion. The majority of the countries concerned, and certainly ourselves, will have no such surplus in the immediate future. On the other hand, we shall end the war with somewhere approaching £m2,000 of overseas liquid funds in London to which we cannot possibly afford to allow immediate freedom of movement. This is a subject about which we must speak as little as possible at the present stage for fear of increasing the tendency, which is already showing itself, towards an unwillingness to hold sterling balances. But for us some system for the control of capital movements is absolutely indispensable the moment the war is over.

(b) I am exceedingly averse to the idea that the Clearing Union should facilitate speculative movements by estimating their amount and then apparently behaving as though money which had gone abroad and been turned into a foreign currency still remained as part of the effective reserve of the country from which it has fled. In my opinion, this would tear to pieces the reliability of the Clearing Union Scheme and makes no sense to me whatever.

(c) I see no reason to feel confidence that the more stable conditions, e.g. the partial remedy of the trade cycle and the prevention of sharp movements in exchange rates, will remove the more dangerous movements. These are likely to be caused by political issues. Surely in the post-war years there is hardly a country in which we ought not to expect keen political discussions affecting the position of the wealthier classes and the treatment of private property. If so, there will be a number of people constantly taking fright because they think that the degree of leftism in one country looks for the time being likely to be greater than somewhere else.

(d) You overlook the most fundamental long-run theoretical reason. Freedom of capital movements is an essential part of the old *laissez-faire* system and assumes that it is right and desirable to have an equalisation of interest rates in all parts of the world. It assumes, that is to say, that if the rate of interest which promotes full employment in Great Britain is lower than the appropriate rate in Australia, there is no reason why this should not be allowed to lead to a situation in which the whole of British savings are invested in Australia, subject only to different estimations of risk, until the equilibrium rate in Australia has been brought down to the British rate. In my view the whole management of the domestic economy depends upon being free to have the appropriate rate of interest without reference to the rates prevailing elsewhere in the world. Capital control is a corollary to this. Both for this reason and for the political reasons given above, my own belief is that the Americans will be wise in their own interest to accept this conception, even though its immediate applicability in their case is not so clear.

(e) In my opinion you are grossly over-estimating the

amount of our speculative profits through the pre-war freedom to remit money in any direction. The figure of £m200, if that is the correct estimate, is the aggregate of all gains during the period of a capital description, which Leak's balance of trade figures deliberately leave out of account, since they only pretend to cover current transactions. They include, for example, the fortunes of American heiresses, capital funds transmitted to this country for charitable or similar purposes, such as the Pilgrim Trust, the Rockefeller money, the Dartington Hall Trust, etc. They include the fortunes accumulated by Englishmen abroad as, for example, our merchants in India, subsequently repatriated, if the maker of the fortune or his heirs return to residence in this country. They include the profits of our merchants, acting not merely as agents but as principals. I have myself stressed the importance of the item of actual capital profits through investment, but I have never supposed that these could be responsible for anything approaching the whole of the £m200 arising from capital gains and increments of every sort and description.

(f) As you know, I have no objection in principle to some formula, if one can think of a sensible one, on the lines of your Annex II. This seems to me a detail which we can discuss when we get down to details. Meanwhile I have not been able to understand just how your new proposal would work out in practice, so I am unable to judge whether it would lead to reasonable or to unreasonable consequences.

Let us suppose that a country has a debit index of ¼ and that the world debit index is ½. If the world debit index increases to ⅝, does this entitle the individual country's debit index to increase to ⅜ or to ⁵⁄₁₆? I cannot work out practical examples without knowing the answer to this question. But there is a further difficulty, whatever the answer may be, namely, that your formula deprives a country of any security as to the potential amount of its overdraft unless it is made, not alternative to mine, but as capable of giving a different higher limit. Otherwise a country, without having changed its debit balance at all, may suddenly find itself breaking the rules simply because other people's debit balances have gone down. There remains the objection that, so far at any rate, the formula is unintelligible to the ordinary man, and no one can see what it means in practice. Whatever embroideries one may feel strong enough to pin on at a later stage, I think it undesirable at this stage to make so essential a feature of the scheme unintelligible to the average reader.

[copy not signed or initialled]

Harrod replied with two letters commenting that he had always thought that the Dominions would be full members of the Service, as soon as the two great powers had settled their common ground. On the other hand, he regarded Russia as having no special claims for membership over many other allies and likely to confuse the discussions if she did participate. He also made a distinction between schemes requiring an international agency for their initiation and those requiring national action. In the former case, he argued that his proposed Service could form the agency and leave others to join in. If too many were involved in the early stages of the discussions, the schemes would never get off the ground.

To these letters and Harrod's request for a talk, Keynes replied.

To R. F. HARROD, *8 May 1942*

Dear Roy,

If you are to be in town next Thursday, I will keep a free time for a talk about your paper of May 4th and associated topics. I cannot manage the morning, and would prefer to keep the early afternoon free, though I could manage that if necessary. Would 5 o'clock on the 14th suit you?

On the merits of the case, and above all from the standpoint of practical convenience, I think there is everything to be said for the lay-out you advocate and the distinction between the two types of topics. I do not think that anything has happened seriously to prejudice this, if later on the arrangement seems to be the right one. The reference introduced by the Cabinet

151

to Russssia is to be regarded, I think, more as an attempt to prevent the matter being prejudiced the other way than as a positive injunction that Russia must be brought in on the ground-floor.

But how far in practice things will work out that way can only be discovered *ambulando*.

I do not know how far the Americans will welcome special Anglo-American relations as distinct from a more international set-up. We do not know, even if those with whom we first discussed the matter incline that way, whether it lies within the power of anyone to commit U.S. so deeply.

On the other side we are equally in the dark about the possibilities of collaboration with Russia.

Moreover, even if the Americans were to be of one mind with ourselves, it is a question whether it would be wise to present the rest of the world with what looked like an Anglo-American bloc. If there is anyone more unpopular than ourselves it is the United States; and if there is anyone more unpopular than the United States, it is Russia; and if there is anyone more unpopular than Russia, it is ourselves.

So I think it is altogether too early to take up a definite stand as between a predominantly Anglo-American set-up and one which, from the start, has a more international character.

Where I unreservedly agree with you is that the actual constitution of particular plans must be agreed and established by as few cooks as possible, with others invited to the dinner table after they have smelt the broth.

I submit to what you say in your two last paragraphs. I agree that that is how we ought to behave. But in the matter of post-war relief I remain sceptical how far we can get away with it when in fact it becomes clear that we shall not be providers of any significant part of the funds. However, that is no reason why we should not put a brave face on it.

Yours,
[copy initialled] J. M. K.

Keynes saw Harrod on 14 May.

In response to a critical note by H. D. Henderson on the liberal Keynesian proposals of subjects for the conversations, Keynes showed more of his thinking.

To SIR HUBERT HENDERSON, *9 May 1942*

YOUR NOTES ON THE ANGLO-AMERICAN DISCUSSIONS

I feel that you have done us a most valuable service in preparing this paper. The sort of thing you envisage may quite likely happen, at least in part. In fact, failing something to the contrary, these are the lines along which natural evolution will take place. It is, therefore, most important for us to see it all clearly and also to have such a moderate and persuasive brief from this point of view with which, if occasion arises, to meet the Americans.

Moreover, from our strictly selfish point of view, I should agree that this sort of thing might be safer and, in conceivable circumstances, more advantageous, but only subject to the two conditions (*a*) that we alone practise it and (*b*) that U.S. can be brought to acquiesce in it.

If I prefer, nevertheless, to start off along another course, my fundamental reasons are the three following:–

(1) I think it unlikely that the two conditions just mentioned above will be fulfilled in practice.

(2) There are two theoretical points to which I think you have not done sufficient justice:–

(*a*) You exaggerate the extent to which payments agreements are, as such, self-righting or productive of automatic equilibrium. Under a regime of government trading which covered exports as well as imports I should agree that payments agreements provide the opportunity for what you want. But, in the absence of government trading, both ways, it is far from being the case that they are self-righting. For one thing, the initiative to make them so lies with the creditor rather than with the debtor country; yet the potential importer in the creditor country has no particular motive to discriminate in favour of the goods of the debtor country. The fact that our purchase of cereal exports from the Argentine leads to a surplus of sterling in favour of the Argentine does nothing of itself to stimulate Argentine importers to purchase our cotton goods. In the absence of state trading, it is difficult to find ways of implementing a clause in a barter agreement which provides that cotton purchases from ourselves shall reach a minimum figure. And, in any case, a payments agreement is not the same thing as a barter agreement.

Pre-war experience of payments agreements showed precisely this difficulty, that they are not self-righting. That is what led to arrangements known as 'compensation agreements'. A compensation agreement is self-righting because the Argentine exporter who possesses surplus sterling can only get rid of it by parting with it to an Argentine importer at a sufficient discount to make it attractive to the Argentine importer to divert his purchases to Great Britain. Compensation arrangements of this kind have rather dropped out of sight in recent discussions, though I recently saw a proposal for multilateral compensation agreements, prepared by Sir Osborne Mance, whose mind was led in this direction by the fact that he was responsible for working a compensation agreement with Turkey which, I believe, existed before the war. But, of course, compensation agreements, and more particularly multilateral compensation agreements, are merely a complicated form of allowing the exchanges to reach their own level, which is a solution all of us agree in disliking for sufficiently good reasons.

I point out, therefore, that it is a fallacy to regard payments agreements as essentially self-righting. This is only true of compensation agreements, to which there are other grave objections, and to barter agreements which are difficult to implement except by a great extension of state trading.

(*b*) You are, I think too much inclined to speak as if equilibrium could only be restored by changing our respective shares in a fixed volume of trade. To argue in this way ignores the major part of the gain to be got from expansionism. If there is sufficient expansion, we may obtain a sufficient market for our exports without the United States having to contract any part of hers. That is why expansionism is the most hopeful line of solution.

In general, as I pointed out before, you seem to me to have reacted too strongly against the old doctrine. If effective demand throughout the world is adequate, the demand for exports will always be equal to the supply of them, and gluts will not occur. The more closely we approximate to conditions of adequate effective demand, the more completely this condition is fulfilled. For the problem to disappear altogether we have no doubt to assume an ideal state of affairs most unlikely to occur. But every increase of effective demand reduces the severity of the problem. Every increase of effective demand in an individual country, such as U.S., reduces the available surplus they have for exporting and increases their demand for imports. The old theory, which assumed Say's law and the adequacy of effective demand, led to the conclusion that the problem which is bothering us could not exist. On the assumptions made, this was and remains correct. I counsel more faith in the practical working out of measures to improve effective demand, even in face of appearances to the contrary.

(3) An initial approach along your lines will not fit in with the trend of public sentiment in this country any more than in the United States. No post-war plan has much chance of success which is not crystallising and attempting to carry into practice certain broad hopes which have come to be the

possession of the ordinary man. Adversity may well drive us to barter agreements and the like. But to start off on so pessimistic a hypothesis will lose us that support from general outside opinion without which nothing can be done. It is not as if there was one bias of opinion amongst well-disposed persons in the United States and another bias here. The bias here is exactly the same as in the United States. If I thought that those better hopes were necessarily doomed to failure, I would try to change the bias of opinion. But I do not think they are necessarily doomed to failure. All I would concede is that they are not certain of success, which is quite another matter.

Moreover, if we are driven back on more discriminatory arrangements, I should have expected that it would take the form of barter agreements under state auspices much more on Russian lines. There is the American bias and the Russian bias. I doubt if there is much between which is likely to be practical politics. And whether or not we end up with the Russian bias, is there not much to be said for having a good try with the American bias first of all?

(4) I am not at all attracted to your proposals for quantitative planning. These would be frightfully difficult to arrange for manufactured goods as distinct from staple raw materials— endless wrangling, and every country in the world would be involved. We should be in the gravest danger of quotas being fixed on a pre-war or other unsuitable basis. I do not know how the price would be fixed. Indeed, the more I contemplate what the details would look like, the greater is my aversion.

So much for criticism. More constructively, I believe that a good deal of the safeguards for which you are anxious can be grafted on to the Clearing Union scheme.

(i) There should be more emphasis on your point that the Clearing Union by itself does not ensure equilibrium, and that there must be room for special provisions, if, in practice, equilibrium is not secured.

(ii) There is already in the scheme provision for barter arrangements for the benefit of debtor countries. When we come down to details, there is room for the strengthening of all such escape provisions, subject always to this not provoking too much American hostility. To ensure this, they must be no more than escape provisions. In each case we have to bide our time and wait until the difficulties which are foreseen have actually arisen.

(iii) Further explanation is required of the position of non-members of the Clearing Union and defaulting or ex-members, trade relations with whom will have to be of a different character from that envisaged in general.

(iv) We must do our utmost to preserve latitude for state trading.

[copy initialled] J. M. K.

Throughout the rest of the spring and early summer discussions continued on the appropriate agenda for the Article VII discussions and on the possibility of American officials coming to London to begin informal discussions. On neither front was there much progress.

However, on 8 July, Sir Frederick Phillips sent Hopkins a 'summary' of a draft of a paper on post-war financial arrangements prepared in the American Treasury, with instructions that it should not be known that the British had seen it or knew of its existence and that Keynes should be the only other person to see it. The next day, Sir Frederick Leith-Ross sent London a copy of the scheme, which he had received from its author, H. D. White.

Keynes acknowledged receiving the draft from Phillips on 22 July, stating that he intended to look at it more closely during the ten days leave he proposed to take at Tilton from 24 July.[2]

On 3 August, his first day back from leave, Keynes wrote to Hopkins and Phillips, enclosing a discussion of the White scheme and a draft of the Clearing Union that might be suitable for circulation to the Americans. As

2 While Keynes was at Tilton, he received a further letter from Harrod once again pressing for stronger sanctions on excessive debtors. Harrod emphasised the need for such a sanction, because he did not believe that the United States would achieve equilibrium between savings and internal investment at full employment for one to two decades after the war.

the draft of the Clearing Union follows that one actually passed over to the Americans later in the month in most respects, we do not print it here. Rather we print the revised version below (p. 168) with a guide to the changes that occurred from the holiday draft appearing as Appendix 1.

To SIR RICHARD HOPKINS, *3 August 1942*

Dear Hoppy,

I enclose herewith my holiday task in the hope, however, that it will not mean any serious holiday task for you.

The first document is an analysis of the Harry White scheme, which it is a tremendous labour to read and digest in full. It obviously won't work. But nothing could be more encouraging than the general attitude shown and the line of approach indicated. I am, of course, not communicating any hints of our possession of this paper to anyone but yourself. It is, however, so important that it must surely, in due course, have a somewhat wider circulation. It may even be a little difficult if I am called on to explain the underlying reason for some of the changes I have made in the Clearing Union draft. The fact that I cannot discuss this document with anybody but you is part of my excuse for bothering you with this packet whilst you are away.

The second document is a revised version of the Clearing Union memorandum. You will see from the top paper what circulation I am giving it. I am asking for comments in writing. Perhaps these may be to hand just about the time you are returning.

I am sending copies of both these documents to Phillips, and also enclose for you a copy of my covering letter to him.

I am going back to the Treasury tomorrow, having had a very good time here and feeling extremely well, but having done enough work, I hope, not to have got into arrears. I have a project of absenting myself for a further spell of days some part at least of next week and the week after.

Yours ever,
KEYNES

To SIR FREDERICK PHILLIPS, *3 August 1942*

Dear Phillips,

I enclose an advance copy of the revised version which I have prepared for the Clearing Union plan in a shape suitable to be handed to the Americans and others outside Whitehall. You will notice that this has not yet received any criticisms either inside or outside the Treasury. I send it you at once, partly because I shall be grateful for any comments you may have, and partly because circumstances may conceivably arise in which it is useful to have a version in your hands to which we could conveniently refer by cable.

I have also been making a study of the Harry White document. Seldom have I been simultaneously so much bored and so much interested. I have prepared a fairly substantial note on it for Hoppy and enclose a copy of this for you. The general attitude of mind seems to me most helpful and also enlightening. But the actual technical solution strikes me as quite hopeless. He has not seen how to get round the gold standard difficulties and has forgotten all about the useful concept of bank money. But is there any reason why, when once the advantages of bank money have been pointed out to him, he should not collect and re-arrange his other basic ideas round this technique?

In preparing the revised version of the Clearing Union I have been careful not to introduce any passage from which acquaintance with the other document could be inferred. But you will notice that I have amended it in two or three important passages so as to give a ready opening for the introduction of ideas on the Harry White model.

It is, I think, more than clear that, as you put it in one of your letters to Hoppy, 'it is about time we weighed in'. I wonder how you have been getting on with the communications made so far.

Yours ever,

[copy initialled] K

NOTES ON THE MEMORANDUM FOR POST-WAR
CURRENCY ARRANGEMENTS TRANSMITTED
BY SIR F. PHILLIPS

I

(1) Since the proposed Stabilisation Fund is to perform clearing functions for its members, it might seem, at first sight, to have a closer resemblance to the Clearing Union than is the case. In fact the principles underlying it are fundamentally different. For it makes no attempt to use the banking principle and one-way gold convertibility and is in fact not much more than a version of the gold standard, which simply aims at multiplying the effective volume of the gold base. Nearly all the consequences aimed at could be equally well attained by halving prices in every country, or, more simply still, by devaluing all exchanges in terms of gold, so that they would maintain their relative values, but everyone's gold reserve would go twice as far as before in meeting adverse international balances. This is the basic mistake of the plan. Put this way, one sees how inadequate it is to solve the real problem. The scheme is only helpful to those countries which have a gold reserve already and is only helpful to them in proportion to the amount of such gold reserve. If, however, a country has only a little gold and, therefore, needs much support, the scheme provides on the contrary that it shall receive only a little support. To him that hath it is given. No adequate provision is offered for what happens when the resources provided, which in some cases would be exceedingly moderate, have been used up.

(2) The close adherence to the principles of the gold standard with two-way convertibility at every stage, means that the volume of international currency is not adjusted to need, but remains as before mainly dependent on the volume of gold mining and the policy of those countries which already have large gold reserves. As pointed out above, it

merely provides that a given quantity of gold shall go farther than before.

Phillips reports that the President has turned down the plan on the ground that it does not go far enough and that what he wants is a genuine international currency. Presumably someone has pointed out to him that this is simply the gold standard over again. Phillips reports, by the way, that the President would like to call his version of bancor Demos or, perhaps, Victor. No one apparently has suggested Pluto.

(3) The plan provides for two institutions, called the Fund and the Bank. The relationship between them is obscure, especially in connection with gold and the position of the notes which the Bank is free to issue. But, broadly speaking, the objects of the Fund correspond to the objects of the Clearing Union; whilst the objects of the Bank correspond to those of the International Investment Board and the Commodity Controls.

(4) Turning to details, the memorandum is very complicated, discursive and diffuse; difficult to understand and almost impossible to read. There are several points of detail of which I have not found it possible to make consistent sense. It is loaded with details which are unnecessary in so early a stage of the discussion. It would seem to be quite unworkable in practice and involves many difficulties. with which there is no attempt to deal and which are not even mentioned. Nevertheless, it is striking and encouraging that the general objects are the same as those which we have been pursuing. The concessions of national sovereignty recommended are the same or greater. The aid offered by the United States is far-reaching, though rather obscure. The attitude towards *laissez-faire* and the regulation of foreign trade is not materially different from ours. Finally, there are several subsidiary proposals which are of the highest interest and importance to us. Attention is called to these below.

(5) Before returning to these features, it is worth while to

mention the rather peculiar proposals for fixing what correspond to quotas in the Clearing Union and to the voting power on the management. In the case of the Bank voting power and subscriptions seem to be fixed as a minimum at 2 per cent of the national income, and not to be related to any other criterion; and voting power, but not subscriptions, at a maximum of 5 per cent of the total. In the case of the Fund, which is on the whole the more important of the two, a complicated weighted index is proposed for subscriptions (II, 66) depending largely on the country's gold holdings and gold production, substantially on its foreign trade and foreign investments and less importantly on its national income and population. Voting power, on the other hand, depends partly on subscriptions, but partly on an equal weighting for each member state as such. Apparently the British Empire counts as one, Russia counts as one, China counts as one. But each Central American State, e.g. Costa Rica and the rest, also count as one. Thus, in the final result, the minor states of Latin America, excluding Argentina and Chile, have nearly twice as many votes as the British Empire and more than ten times as many votes as Russia. These minor South American states can heavily outvote the British Empire, Russia and China taken together. Under this formula the United States, which also counts for one, does not, of course, come out particularly well. But not so badly as the rest, owing to the weight given to its subscriptions, in fixing which its gold holdings play an important part. Thus, although the minor Latin American states can outvote the United States, the United States can outvote the British Empire, the Dutch Empire, Russia and China added together. All of this seems very odd. But it is expounded in so confused a manner that I may have misunderstood it. I have, however, thought it advisable in revising the Clearing Union plan to be less dogmatic on the proposal that the quotas must be fixed primarily by reference to foreign trade. This still seems to me the most relevant criterion and it is still proposed. But it is emphasised that the formula for fixing quotas, which is obviously a detail, is open to discussion without prejudice to the rest of the plan.

II

I call particular attention to the following parts of the memorandum which seem to contain helpful or suggestive proposals:–

(1) There is an exceedingly generous proposal, which would be most helpful to us (II, 20 *et seq.*), for dealing with liquid balances, which may be wholly or partly blocked, existing in any centre at the end of the war prior to the inception of the new scheme. This is so important that the introductory passage is worth quoting in full:

The situation with respect to blocked balances in England is quite different. The gold and foreign exchange reserves which England will have at the close of the war are certain to be far too small relative to the sterling balances blocked there to permit England to remove restrictions on the withdrawal of funds by foreign owners. England may end the war with more than 5 billion dollars of deposits belonging to residents of other countries, while her liquid foreign exchange resources are likely to be much less than that. Moreover, England will need whatever gold she will be able to accumulate, and indeed should have more foreign exchange available than she is likely to have, in order to operate properly even were the total of foreign balances in England much smaller. Most of these balances belong to the Dominions who would wish to keep substantial sums in England in any case—unless there was imminent danger of sterling depreciation. Against some of the remainder there are offsetting blocked currencies. Nonetheless, the drain on British foreign liquid exchange reserves could easily be greater than England could safely permit.

The unblocking of these sterling funds is highly to be desired. Probably, no single action would do more to stimulate world trade, prevent pressure on numerous exchanges, and reduce the probability of widespread depreciation of currencies. The restoration of confidence in the soundness of British currency, the assurance that international monetary problems are to be intelligently handled, and renewed hope that currency stability will be achieved after the war that would follow a successful unfreezing of sterling, would alone justify every effort to solve through international action the problem of blocked balances in Britain.

A proposal then follows, by which in effect the balances in question are made entirely liquid through the Fund for the purposes of the holder, whilst Great Britain would have to clear them off at a rate which works out approximately to 4 per cent per annum. It is not clear whether the amount of the debt not cleared off carries interest. Apparently the Fund would hold a corresponding amount of sterling, which it would be free to invest in British Government securities. Thus in effect it might be that we should be paying (say) Treasury bill rate, though possibly more, on the part of the sterling balances which were being dealt with in this way and had not been repaid.

In the original version of the Clearing Union this particular nettle was not grasped, because it was thought inadvisable to call attention to the magnitude of the problem. In the revised version a tentative passage has been introduced, which does not embody the proposed solution, but would provide a peg on which such a proposal could be hung.

Willingness on the part of the Americans to contemplate arrangements along these lines is clearly of the very first importance. It is noticeable that the amount of liquid resources which would be made available under this proposal is very much greater than that which would be made available by the normal operation of the Fund. In fact, this part of the plan, though brought in as a sort of after-thought, seems to be on a much ampler scale than any other part of it.

(2) A further useful proposal is made (II, 48), which might help to get over the difficulty of some countries' restricting capital movements, whilst others were unwilling to do so. The proposal is as follows:–

Each country agrees (a) not to accept or permit deposits or investments from any member country except with the permission of that country, and (b) to make available to the government of any member country at its request all property in form of deposits, investments, securities, of the nationals of member countries, under such terms and conditions as will not impose an unreasonable burden on the country of whom the request is made.

Clearly, in order to operate this proposal, a record would have to be kept of inward movements of capital and the country from which they came. If this record were kept and were made available to the government of the country from which the capital was flowing, and if these powers of what are in effect confiscation were put at the disposal of the government of the country losing the capital, the difficulties in the way of making unilateral control effective would surely be solved. In the revised version of the Clearing Union I have made no reference to this way out, but have provided an opening where it can easily be brought in.

(3) It is interesting to notice that there is a proposal for stabilising the prices of primary products, which closely resembles the very earliest version of the Buffer Stocks Pool, in which no element of restriction appears. The idea put about in some quarters that pressure will come from the Americans for restriction and that they would not look at a Buffer Stock scheme otherwise, is not borne out by this paper. There are several references to this proposal *passim*, but what Sir F. Phillips rightly describes as a concise version of the scheme is given in the following passage (1, 15).

The Bank can organize and finance an International Commodity Stabilization Corporation for the purpose of stabilizing the price of important commodities, provided:

a. At least five governments participate directly in the management and operation of the corporation and subscribe to part of the capital of the corporation.

b. The corporation will undertake to stabilize the price of any specific commodity only with the consent of the Bank.

c. The policy governing the operations of the Corporation gives, in the opinion of the Board, proper weight to the interests of world consumers as well as producers.

(4) The line taken towards Hullism is extremely moderate, as is indicated by the following quotations:–

The theoretical bases for the belief still so widely held, that interference with trade and with capital and gold movements, etc., are harmful, are hangovers from a Nineteenth Century economic creed, which held that international economic adjustments, if left alone, would work themselves out toward an 'equilibrium' with a minimum of harm to world trade and prosperity. (II, 41)

The requirement that there be accepted the general policy of foreign exchange trading in open, free and legal markets, and the abandonment as rapidly as conditions permit of restrictions on exchange controls, should be taken to mean that there shall be acceptance of the principle that controls and restrictions will be employed only when they are clearly justified by the economic circumstances, and only to the extent necessary to carry out a purpose contributing the general prosperity. (II, 42)

The belief that reduction in all import duties increases trade and yields a higher standard of living for all countries under all circumstances and in all stages of their economic evolution assumes that countries are usually utilizing virtually all their capital and labour; that a country chiefly agricultural in its economy has as many economic, political and social advantages as a country whose economy is chiefly industrial, or as a country which has a balanced economy; that there are no gains to be achieved by greater diversification of output. These assumptions, essential to the belief that 'Free Trade' policy is ideal, are not valid. They are unreal and unsound. 'Free Trade' policy grossly underestimates the extent to which a country can virtually lift itself by its bootstraps in one generation from a lower to a higher standard of living, from a backward agricultural to an advanced industrialised country, provided always it is willing to pay the price. The view further overlooks the very important fact that political relationships among countries being what they are, vital considerations exist in the shaping of the economic structure of a country other than that of producing goods with the least labour. (II, 55)

The actual principles which members are asked to accept are correspondingly mild and do not differ substantially from those which we ourselves are putting forward. There is no reference whatever to preferences as such. The main clause runs as follows:–

The member countries agree (a) to embark within a year after joining upon a program of gradual reduction of existing trade barriers—import duties, import quotas, administrative devices—and further agree (b) not to adopt any increase in tariff schedules, or other devices having as their purpose higher obstacles to imports, without giving reasonable opportunity for the Fund to study the effects of the contemplated change on exchange rates and to register its opinion. In rendering an opinion the Fund will make recommendations to which member governments agree to give serious consideration. (II, 53)

But there is also the following undertaking about export subsidies:–

Not to subsidize—directly or indirectly—the exportation of any commodity or service to member countries without consent of the Fund. (II, 58)

This, however, is followed by a passage suggesting that subsidies to shipping and air travel will probably have to be · allowed. The discussion concludes with a suggestion that 'it were probably better to exclude "services" altogether from the prohibition of subsidies'.

(5) There is no suggested surrender of sovereignty in the Clearing Union plan which would not be covered by the principles laid down in this document, which definitely advocates a reasonable measure of surrender of sovereignty. The discussion of this particular point concludes as follows:–

All members would be surrendering their 'rights' to an equal extent. Unless nations are willing to sacrifice some of their power to take unilateral action in matters of international economic relations, there is very little hope of any significant international cooperation—let alone collaboration.

III

Phillips reports, but not as a matter of certainty, that the Memo. was mainly the work of Harry White and was adopted by the U.S. Treasury, and that copies were circulated to various people, including the President, who was unfavourable on the ground that it did not go far enough. He adds that the document reached him by an indirect route and that we must not let anyone know that we have seen it or even that we know of its existence. It appears that Leith-Ross knows about it and has discussed it with Phillips. He promises further explanation and comment later on.

KEYNES

Before the Clearing Union scheme went to the Americans, it underwent more criticism and redrafting. Harrod continued to press Keynes to improve the position of the Dominions, which he thought should have a more important place than, say Brazil, unless the Americans put up extreme pressure. He also continued to press for stricter treatment of large debtors, again without success. Other drafting suggestions came from D. H. Robertson, Sir Frederick Phillips and others before a set of printed copies of a revised version went off to Washington. Sir Frederick Phillips sent a copy from this set to Mr White on 28 August.

PROPOSALS FOR AN INTERNATIONAL CLEARING UNION

I. *Preface*

About the primary objects of an improved system of International Currency there is, today, a wide measure of agreement:–

(*a*) We need an instrument of international currency having general acceptability between nations, so that blocked balances and bilateral clearings are unnecessary; that is to say, an instrument of currency used by each nation in its transactions with other nations, operating through whatever national organ, such as a Treasury or a central bank, is most appropriate, private individuals, businesses and banks other than central banks, each continuing to use their own national currency as heretofore.

(*b*) We need an orderly and agreed method of determining the relative exchange values of national currency units, so that unilateral action and competitive exchange depreciations are prevented.

(*c*) We need a quantum of international currency, which is neither determined in an unpredictable and irrelevant manner as, for example, by the technical progress of the gold industry, nor subject to large variations depending on the gold reserve policies of individual countries; but is governed by the actual current requirements of world commerce, and is also capable of deliberate expansion and contraction to offset deflationary and inflationary tendencies in effective world demand.

(*d*) We need a system possessed of an internal stabilising mechanism, by which pressure is exercised on any country whose balance of payments with the rest of the world is departing from equilibrium in either direction, so as to prevent movements which must create for its neighbours an equal but opposite want of balance.

(*e*) We need an agreed plan for starting off every country after the war with a stock of reserves appropriate to its importance in world commerce, so that without due anxiety it can set its house in order during the transitional period to full peace-time conditions.

(*f*) We need a method by which the surplus credit balances arising from international trade, which the recipient does not wish to employ for the time being, can be set to work in the interests of international planning and relief and economic health, without detriment to the liquidity of these balances and to their holder's faculty to employ them himself when he desires to do so.

(*g*) We need a central institution, of a purely technical and non-political character, to aid and support other international institutions concerned with the planning and regulation of the world's economic life.

(*h*) More generally, we need a means of reassurance to a troubled world, by which any country whose own affairs are conducted with due prudence is relieved of anxiety, for causes which are not of its own making, concerning its ability to meet its international liabilities; and which will, therefore, make unnecessary those methods of restriction and discrimination which countries have adopted hitherto, not on their merits, but as measures of self-protection from disruptive outside forces.

2. There is also a growing measure of agreement about the

general character of any solution of the problem likely to be successful. The particular proposals set forth below lay no claim to originality. They are an attempt to reduce to practical shape certain general ideas belonging to the contemporary climate of economic opinion, which have been given publicity in recent months by writers of several different nationalities. It is difficult to see how any plan can be successful which does not use these general ideas, which are born of the spirit of the age. The actual details put forward below are offered, in no dogmatic spirit, as the basis of discussion for criticism and improvement. For we cannot make progress without embodying the general underlying idea in a frame of actual working, which will bring out the practical and political difficulties to be faced and met if the breath of life is to inform it.

3. In one respect this particular plan will be found to be more ambitious and yet, at the same time, perhaps more workable than some of the variant versions of the same basic idea, in that it is fully international, being based on one general agreement and not on a multiplicity of bilateral arrangements. Doubtless proposals might be made by which bilateral arrangements could be fitted together so as to obtain some of the advantages of a multilateral scheme. But there will be many difficulties attendant on such adjustments. It may be doubted whether a comprehensive scheme will ever in fact be worked out, unless it can come into existence through a single act of creation made possible by the unity of purpose and energy of hope for better things to come, springing from the victory of the United Nations, when they have attained it, over immediate evil. That these proposals are ambitious is claimed, therefore to be not a drawback but an advantage.

4. The proposal is to establish a Currency Union, here designated an *International Clearing Union*, based on international bank money, called (let us say) *bancor*, fixed (but not unalterably) in terms of gold and accepted as the equivalent

of gold by the British Commonwealth and the United States and all the other members of the Union for the purpose of settling international balances. The central banks of all member states (and also of non-members) would keep accounts with the International Clearing Union through which they would be entitled to settle their exchange balances with one another at their par value as defined in terms of bancor. Countries having a favourable balance of payments with the rest of the world as a whole would find themselves in possession of a credit account with the Clearing Union, and those having an unfavourable balance would have a debit account. Measures would be necessary (see below) to prevent the piling up of credit and debit balances without limit, and the system would have failed in the long run if it did not possess sufficient capacity for self-equilibrium to prevent this.

5. The idea underlying such a Union is simple, namely, to generalise the essential principle of banking as it is exhibited within any closed system. This principle is the necessary equality of credits and debits. If no credits can be removed outside the clearing system, but only transferred within it, the Union can never be in any difficulty as regards the honouring of cheques drawn upon it. It can make what advances it wishes to any of its members with the assurance that the proceeds can only be transferred to the clearing account of another member. Its sole task is to see to it that its members keep the rules and that the advances made on each of them are prudent and advisable for the Union as a whole.

6. It is proposed that the Clearing Union should be designed and initiated by the United States and the United Kingdom and that Russia and perhaps one or more other members of the United Nations should then be invited to join them as founder states. Other members would then be brought in—some from the outset, some as soon as they had established an internal organisation capable of sustaining the obligations of membership. This approach would have the

great advantage that the charter and the main details of the new body could be drafted without being subjected to the delays and confused counsels of an international conference, though this need not stand in the way of informal consultation with those concerned. It would also mean that considerable progress could be made irrespective of the nature of the European political settlement and before the conditions of adherence of the European members could be finally determined. Moreover, membership would be thus established as a privilege only open to those who conformed to certain general principles and standards of international economic conduct.

II. *The provisions of the plan*

7. The provisions proposed (the particular proportions and other details suggested being tentative as a basis of discussion) are the following:–

(1) The Governing Board of the Clearing Union will be appointed by the governments of the several member states; the daily business with the Union and the technical arrangements being carried out, as at present, through their central banks.

(2) The founder states will agree between themselves the initial values of their own currencies in terms of bancor and also the value of bancor in terms of gold, which will not be varied subsequently except with their approval; and the initial values of the currencies of other members will be agreed with them on their joining the system. A member state may not subsequently alter the value of its currency in terms of bancor without the permission of the Governing Board except under the conditions stated below; but during the first five years after the inception of the system the Governing Board shall give special consideration to appeals for an adjustment in the exchange value of a national currency unit on the ground of unforeseen circumstances.

(3) The amount of the maximum debit balance allowed to

any member state shall be designated its *quota*. The initial quotas might be fixed by reference to the sum of each country's exports and imports on the average of (say) the [last] three pre-war years, being either equal or in a determined *lesser* proportion to this amount, a special assessment being substituted in cases (of which there might be several) where this formula would be, for any reason, inappropriate. Subsequently, after the elapse of the transitional period, the quotas should be revised annually in accordance with the running average of each country's actual volume of trade in the three preceding years. The determination of a country's quota primarily by reference to the value of its foreign trade seems to offer the criterion most relevant to a plan which is chiefly concerned with the regulation of the foreign exchanges and of a country's international trade balance. It is, however, a matter for discussion whether the formula for fixing quotas should also take account of other factors.

(4) A charge of 1 per cent per annum shall be payable to the Reserve Fund of the Clearing Union on the amount of the excess of the average balance of a member state, whether it is a credit or a debit balance, above a quarter of its quota; and a further charge of 1 per cent on the excess of the average balance, whether credit or debit, above a half of its quota. Thus, only a country which keeps as nearly as possible in a state of international balance on the average of the year will escape this contribution. These charges are not absolutely essential to the scheme. But if they are found acceptable, they would be valuable and important inducements towards keeping a level balance, and a significant indication that the system looks on excessive credit balances with as critical an eye as on excessive debit balances, each being, indeed, the inevitable concomitant of the other. Any member state in debit may, however, borrow from the balances of any member state in credit on such terms as may be mutually agreed, by which means each would avoid these contributions.

(5) (*a*) A member state may not increase its debit balance

by more than a *quarter* of its quota within a year without the permission of the Governing Board. If its debit balance has exceeded a quarter of its quota on the average of at least a year, it shall be entitled to reduce the value of its currency in terms of bancor, provided that the reduction shall not exceed 5 per cent within a year without the permission of the Governing Board.

(*b*) As a condition of allowing a member state to increase its debit balance to a figure in excess of a *half* of its quota, the Governing Board may require (i) a stated reduction in the value of the member's currency, if it deems that to be the suitable remedy, (ii) the control of outward capital transactions if not already in force, and (iii) the surrender of a suitable proportion of any separate gold or other liquid reserve in reduction of its debit balance. Furthermore, the Governing Board may recommend to the government of the member state any internal measures affecting its domestic economy which may appear to be appropriate to restore the equilibrium of its international balance.

(*c*) If a member state's debit balance has exceeded *three-quarters* of its quota on the average of at least a year (or is excessive, as measured by some formula laid down by the Governing Board in relation to the total debit balances outstanding on the books of the Clearing Union), it may be asked by the Governing Board to take measures to improve its position and, in the event of its failing to reduce its debit balance below the figure in question within two years, the Governing Board may declare that it is in default and no longer entitled to draw against its account except with the permission of the Governing Board. Each member state, on joining the system, shall agree to pay to the Clearing Union any payments due from it to a country in default towards the discharge of the latter's debit balance and to accept this arrangement in the event of falling into default itself. A member state which resigns from the Clearing Union without making approved arrangements for the discharge of any debit balance shall also be treated as in default.

(6) A member state whose credit balance has exceeded a *half* of its quota on the average of at least a year shall discuss with the Governing Board (but shall retain the ultimate decision in its own hands) what measures would be appropriate to restore the equilibrium of its international balances, including—

(*a*) Measures for the expansion of domestic credit and domestic demand;

(*b*) The appreciation of its local currency in terms of bancor, or, alternatively, an increase in money wages;

(*c*) The reduction of tariffs and other discouragements against imports;

(*d*) International loans for the development of backward countries.

(7) A member state shall be entitled to obtain a credit in terms of bancor by paying in gold to the Clearing Union for the credit of its clearing account. But no-one is entitled to demand gold from the Union against a balance of bancor, since such balance is available only for transfer to another clearing account. The Governing Board of the Union should, however, have the discretion to distribute any gold in the possession of the Union between the members possessing credit balances, proportionately to such balances, in reduction of their amount.

(8) Members of the Governing Board would be appointed by the governments of the founder states and of the other member states, the lesser states appointing in groups, so that the members would not exceed (say) 12 in number, each member having a vote in proportion to the quotas of the state (or states) appointing him. But there might be a provision, at any rate for the first five years, by which the representatives of the founder states could outvote the rest of the Board.

(9) The executive offices of the Union should be situated

in London and New York with the Board of Managers meeting alternatively in London and Washington.

(10) Members would be entitled to withdraw from the Union on a year's notice, subject to their making satisfactory arrangements to discharge any debit balance. They would not, of course, be able to employ any credit balance except by making transfers from it, either before or after their withdrawal, to the Clearing Accounts of other central banks. Similarly, it should be within the power of the Governing Board to require the withdrawal of a member subject to the same notice.

(11) The central banks of non-member states would be allowed to keep credit clearing accounts with the Union; and, indeed, it would be advisable for them to do so for the conduct of their trade with member states. But they would have no right to overdrafts and no say in the management.

(12) The principles and governing rules of the Union should be the subject of reconsideration after five years' experience, if a majority of the Governing Board desire it.

III. *Some advantages of the plan*

8. The plan aims at the substitution of an expansionist, in place of a contractionist, pressure on world trade.

9. It effects this by allowing to each member state overdraft facilities of a defined amount. Thus each country is allowed a certain margin of resources and a certain interval of time within which to effect a balance in its economic relations with the rest of the world. These facilities are made possible by the constitution of the system itself and do not involve particular indebtedness between one member state and another. A country is in credit or debit with the Clearing Union as a whole. This means that the overdraft facilities, whilst a relief to some, are not a real burden to others. For the accumulation of a credit balance with the Clearing Union

would resemble the importation of gold in signifying that the country holding it is abstaining voluntarily from the immediate use of purchasing power. But it would not involve, as would the importation of gold, the withdrawal of this purchasing power from circulation or the exercise of a deflationary and contractionist pressure on the whole world, including in the end the creditor country itself. Under the proposed plan, therefore, no country suffers injury (but on the contrary) by the fact that the command over resources, which it does not itself choose to employ for the time being, is not withdrawn from use. The accumulation of bancor credit does not curtail in the least its capacity or inducement either to produce or to consume.

10. In short, the analogy with a national banking system is complete. No depositor in a local bank suffers because the balances, which he leaves idle, are employed to finance the business of someone else. Just as the development of national banking systems served to offset a deflationary pressure which would have prevented otherwise the development of modern industry, so by extending the same principle into the international field we may hope to offset the contractionist pressure which might otherwise overwhelm in social disorder and disappointment the good hopes of our modern world. The substitution of a credit mechanism in place of hoarding would have repeated in the international field the same miracle, already performed in the domestic field, of turning a stone into bread.

11. There might be other ways of effecting the same objects temporarily or in part. For example, the United States might redistribute her gold. Or there might be a number of bilateral arrangements having the effect of providing international overdrafts, as, for example, an agreement by the Federal Reserve Board to accumulate, if necessary, a large sterling balance at the Bank of England, accompanied by a great number of similar bilateral arrangements, amounting to some

hundreds altogether, between these and all the other banks in the world. The objection to particular arrangements of this kind, in addition to their greater complexity, is that they are likely to be influenced by extraneous, political reasons; that they put individual countries in a position of particular obligation towards others; and that the distribution of the assistance between different countries may not correspond to need and to the real requirements, which are extremely difficult to foresee.

12. It should be much easier, and surely more satisfactory for all of us, to enter into a general and collective responsibility, applying to all countries alike, that a country finding itself in a creditor position *against the rest of the world as a whole* should enter into an arrangement not to allow this credit balance to exercise a contractionist pressure against world economy and, by repercussion, against the economy of the creditor country itself. This would give everyone the great assistance of multilateral clearing, whereby (for example) Great Britain could offset favourable balances arising out of her exports to Europe against unfavourable balance due to the United States or South America or elsewhere. How, indeed, can any country hope to start up trade with Europe during the relief and reconstruction period on any other terms?

13. The facilities offered will be of particular importance in the transitional period after the war, as soon as the initial shortages of supply have been overcome. Many countries will find a difficulty in paying for their imports, and will need time and resources before they can establish a readjustment. The efforts of each of these debtor countries to preserve its own equilibrium, by forcing its exports and by cutting off all imports which are not strictly necessary, will aggravate the problem of all the others. On the other hand, if each feels free from undue pressure, the volume of international exchange will be increased and everyone will find it easier to

re-establish equilibrium without injury to the standard of life anywhere. The creditor countries will benefit, hardly less than the debtors, by being given an interval of *time* in which to adjust their economies, during which they can safely move at their own pace without the result of exercising deflationary pressure on the rest of the world, and, by repercussion, on themselves.

14. It must, however, be emphasised that the provision by which the members of the Clearing Union start with substantial overdraft facilities in hand will be mainly useful, just as the possession of any kind of reserve is useful, to allow time and method for necessary adjustments and a comfortable safeguard behind which the unforeseen and the unexpected can be faced with equanimity. Obviously, it does not by itself provide any long-term solution against a continuing disequilibrium, for in due course the more improvident and the more impecunious, left to themselves, would have run through their resources. But, if the purpose of the overdraft facilities is mainly to give time for adjustments, we have to make sure, so far as possible, that they *will* be made. We must have, therefore, some rules and some machinery to secure that equilibrium is restored. A tentative attempt to provide for this has been made above. Perhaps it might be strengthened and improved.

15. The provisions suggested differ in one important respect from the pre-war system because they aim at putting some part of the responsibility for adjustment on the creditor country as well as on the debtor. This is an attempt to recover one of the advantages which were enjoyed in the nineteenth century, when a flow of gold due to a favourable balance in favour of London and Paris, which were then the main creditor centres, immediately produced an expansionist pressure and increased foreign lending in those markets, but which has been lost since New York succeeded to the position of main creditor, as a result of gold movements failing in their

effect, of the breakdown of international borrowing and of the frequent flight of loose funds from one depository to another. The object is that the creditor should not be allowed to remain entirely passive. For if he is, an intolerably heavy task may be laid on the debtor country, which is already for that very reason in the weaker position.

16. If, indeed, a country lacks the productive capacity to maintain its standard of life, then a reduction in this standard is not avoidable. If its wage and price levels in terms of money are out of line with those elsewhere, a change in the rate of its foreign exchange is inevitable. But if, possessing the productive capacity, it lacks markets because of restrictive policies throughout the world, then the remedy lies in expanding its opportunities for export by removal of the restrictive pressure. We are too ready to-day to assume the inevitability of unbalanced trade positions, thus making the opposite error to those who assumed the tendency of exports and imports to equality. It used to be supposed, without sufficient reason, that effective demand is always properly adjusted throughout the world; we tend to assume, equally without sufficient reason that it never can be. On the contrary, there is great force in the contention that, if active employment and ample purchasing power can be sustained in the main centres of the world trade, the problem of surpluses and unwanted exports will largely disappear, even though, under the most prosperous conditions, there may remain some disturbances of trade and unforeseen situations requiring special remedies.

IV. *The daily management of the exchanges under the plan*

17. The Clearing Union restores unfettered multilateral clearing between its members. Compare this with the difficulties and complications of a large number of bilateral

agreements. Compare, above all, the provisions by which a country, taking improper advantage of a payments agreement (for the system is, in fact, a *generalised* payments agreement), as Germany did before the war, is dealt with not by a single country (which may not be strong enough to act effectively in isolation or cannot afford to incur the diplomatic odium of isolated action), but by the system as a whole. If the argument is used that the Clearing Union may have difficulty in disciplining a misbehaving country and in avoiding consequential loss, with what much greater force can we urge this objection against a multiplicity of separate bilateral payments agreements.

18. Thus we should not only obtain the advantages, without the disadvantages, of an international gold currency, but we might enjoy these advantages more widely than was ever possible in practice with the old system under which at any given time only a minority of countries were actually working with free exchanges. In conditions of multilateral clearing, exchange dealings would be carried on as freely as in the best days of the gold standard, without its being necessary to ask anyone to accept special or onerous conditions.

19. The principles governing transactions are: first, that the Clearing Union is set up, not for the transaction of daily business between individual traders or banks, but for the clearing and settlement of the ultimate outstanding balances between central banks (and certain other super-national institutions), such as would have been settled under the old gold standard by the shipment or the earmarking of gold, and should not trespass unnecessarily beyond this field; and, second, that its purpose is to increase *freedom* in international commerce and not to multiply interferences or compulsions.

20. Thus the fabric of international banking organisation, built up by long experience to satisfy practical needs, should be left as undisturbed as possible. Except as regards a provision, explained below, concerning the balances of central

banks themselves, there should be no obstacle in the way of the existing practices of international banking except those which necessarily arise through measures which individual central banks may choose to adopt for the control of movements of capital.

21. It is not necessary to interfere with the discretion of central banks which desire to maintain a special intimacy within a particular group of countries associated by geographical or political ties, such as the existing sterling area, or groups, like the Latin Union of former days, which may come into existence covering, for example, the countries of North America or those of South America, or the groups now under active discussion, including Poland and Czechoslovakia or certain of the Balkan States. There is no reason why such central banks should not be allowed a double position, both as members of the Clearing Union in their own right with their proper quota, and also as making use of another financial centre along traditional lines, as, for example, Australia and India with London, or certain American countries with New York. In this case, their accounts with the Clearing Union would be in exactly the same position as the independent gold reserves which they now maintain, and they would have no occasion to modify in any way their present practices in the conduct of daily business.

22. There might be other cases, however, in which a dependency or a member of a federal union would merge its currency identity in that of a mother central bank, with a quota appropriately adjusted to the merged currency area as a whole, and *not* enjoy a separate individual membership of the Clearing Union, as, for example, the states of a federal union, the French colonies or the British Crown Colonies.

23. At the same time central banks, which do not belong to a special geographical or political group, would be expected to keep their reserve balances with the Clearing Union and not with one another. It should, therefore, be laid down

that central bank balances may not be held in another country except with the approval of the central bank of that country; and, in order that sterling and dollars might not appear to compete with bancor for the purpose of central bank reserve balances, the founder states might agree together that they would not accept the reserve balances of other central banks in excess of normal working balances except in the case of banks definitely belonging to a sterling area or dollar area group.

V. *The position of gold under the plan*

24. Gold still possesses great psychological value which is not being diminished by current events; and the desire to possess a gold reserve against unforeseen contingencies is likely to remain. Gold also has the merit of providing in point of form (whatever the underlying realities may be) an uncontroversial standard of value for international purposes, for which it would not yet be easy to find a serviceable substitute. Moreover, by supplying an automatic means for settling some part of the favourable balances of the creditor countries, the current gold production of the world and the remnant of gold reserves held outside the United States may still have a useful part to play. Nor is it reasonable to ask the United States to demonetise the stock of gold which is the basis of its impregnable liquidity. What, in the long run, the world may decide to do with gold is another matter. The purpose of the Clearing Union is to supplant gold as a governing factor, but not to dispense with it.

25. The international bank money which we have designated *bancor* is defined in terms of a weight of gold. Since the national currencies of the member states are given a defined exchange value in terms of bancor, it follows that they would each have a defined gold content which would be their official buying price for gold, above which they must not pay. The fact that a member state is entitled to obtain a credit in terms

of bancor by paying actual gold to the credit of its clearing account, secures a steady and ascertained purchaser for the output of the gold-producing countries, and for countries holding a large reserve of gold. Thus the position of producers and holders of gold is substantially unaffected.

26. Central banks would be entitled to retain their separate gold reserves and ship gold to one another, provided they did not pay a price above parity; they could coin gold and put it into circulation, and, generally speaking, do what they liked with it.

27. One restriction only would be, for obvious reasons, essential. No member state would be entitled to demand gold from the Clearing Union against its balance of bancor; for bancor is available only for transfer to another clearing account. Thus between gold and bancor itself there would be a one-way convertibility, such as ruled frequently before the war with national currencies which were on what was called a 'gold exchange standard'. This need not mean that the Clearing Union would only receive gold and never pay it out. It has been provided above that, if the Clearing Union finds itself in possession of a stock of gold, the Governing Board shall have discretion to distribute the surplus between those possessing a credit balance with it, proportionately to such balances, in reduction of their amount.

28. The question has been raised whether these arrangements are compatible with the retention by individual member states of a full gold standard with two-way convertibility, so that, for example, any foreign central bank acquiring dollars could use them to obtain gold for export. It is not evident that a good purpose would be served by this. But it need not be prohibited, and if any member state should prefer to maintain full convertibility for internal purposes it could protect itself from any abuse of the system or inconvenient consequences by providing that gold could only be exported under licence.

29. The value of bancor in terms of gold is fixed but not unalterably. It is proposed above that the founder states should have the power to change it. Clearly, they might exercise this power if the stocks of gold tendered to the Union were to be excessive. No object would be served by attempting further to peer into the future or to prophesy the ultimate policy.

VI. *The control of capital movements*

30. There is no country which can, in future, safely allow the flight of funds for political reasons or to evade domestic taxation or in anticipation of the owner turning refugee. Equally, there is no country that can safely receive fugitive funds, which constitute an unwanted import of capital, yet cannot safely be used for fixed investment.

31. For these reasons it is widely held that control of capital movements, both inward and outward, should be a permanent feature of the post-war system. It is an objection to this that control, if it is to be effective, probably requires the machinery of exchange control for *all* transactions, even though a general open licence is given to remittances in respect of current trade. Thus those countries which have for the time being no reason to fear, and may indeed welcome, outward capital movements, may be reluctant to impose this machinery, even though general licensing for capital, as well as trade, transactions reduces it to being no more than a machinery of record. On the other hand, such control will be more difficult to work by unilateral action on the part of those countries which cannot afford to dispense with it, especially in the absence of a postal censorship, if movements of capital cannot be controlled *at both ends.* It would, therefore, be of great advantage if the United States, as well as other members of the Clearing Union, would adopt machinery similar to that which the British Exchange Control has now gone a long way towards perfecting. Nevertheless, the uni-

versal establishment of a control of capital movements cannot be regarded as essential to the operation of the Clearing Union; and the method and degree of such control should therefore be left to the decision of each member state. Some less drastic way might be found by which countries, not themselves controlling actual capital movements can deter inward movements not approved by the countries from which they originate.

32. The position of balances in overseas ownership held in various countries at the end of the war presents a problem of considerable importance and special difficulty. A country in which a large volume of such balances is held could not, unless it is in a creditor position, afford the risk of having to redeem them in bancor on a substantial scale, if this would have the effect of depleting its bancor resources at the outset. At the same time, it is very desirable that the countries owning these balances should be able to regard them as liquid, at any rate over and above the amounts which they can afford to lock up under an agreed programme of funding or long-term expenditure. Perhaps there should be some special over-riding provision for dealing with the transitional period only by which, through the aid of the Clearing Union, such balances would remain liquid and convertible into bancor by the creditor country whilst there would be no corresponding strain on the bancor resources of the debtor country, or, at any rate, the resulting strain would be spread over a period.

33. The advocacy of a control of capital movements must not be taken to mean that the era of international investment should be brought to an end. On the contrary, the system contemplated should greatly facilitate the restoration of international credit for loan purposes in ways to be discussed below. The object, and it is a vital object, is to have a means of distinguishing—

(a) Between movements of floating funds and genuine new investment for developing the world's resources; and (*b*) Between movements, which will help to maintain equilibrium, from surplus countries to deficiency countries, and speculative movements or flights out of deficiency countries or from one surplus country to another.

VII. *The prevention of discriminatory practices*

34. The special protective expedients which were developed between the two wars were sometimes due to political, social or industrial reasons. But frequently they were nothing more than forced and undesirable dodges to protect an unbalanced position of a country's overseas payments. The new system, by providing an automatic register of the size and whereabouts of the aggregate debtor and creditor positions respectively, and thus giving a clear indication whether it is reasonable for a particular country to adopt special expedients as a temporary measure to assist in regaining equilibrium in its balance of payments, would make it possible to establish a general rule *not* to adopt them, subject to the indicated exceptions.

35. Whilst it may be possible to adopt a general pattern for commercial treaties, their detailed provisions would necessarily vary according to the ground to be covered in each case, so that such agreements would have to remain bilateral in character. On this assumption it would not be appropriate to incorporate specific arrangements for such general rules in the constitution of the Clearing Union itself. But the existence of the Clearing Union would make it possible for member states contracting commercial treaties to use their respective debit and credit positions with the Clearing Union as a test. Thus, the contracting parties, whilst agreeing to clauses in a commercial treaty forbidding, in general, the use of certain measures or expedients in their mutual trade relations, might make this agreement subject to special relaxations if the state of their respective Clearing Accounts satisfied an agreed

criterion. For example, a treaty might provide that, in the event of one of the contracting states having a debit balance with the Clearing Union exceeding a specified proportion of its quota on the average of a period and the other having a credit balance of a specified amount, the former should be free to resort to import quotas or to barter trade agreements or to higher import duties of a type which was not permitted under the treaty in normal circumstances. It might even provide that such exceptions should only be allowed subject to the approval of the governing Board of the Clearing Union, and in that case the possible grounds for exceptional action might cover a wider field and other contingencies. Protected by the possibility of such temporary indulgences, the members of the Clearing Union should feel much more confidence in moving towards the withdrawal of the more dislocating forms of protection and discrimination and in accepting the prohibition of the worst of them from the outset.

36. In any case, it should be laid down that members of the Union would not allow or suffer among themselves any restrictions on the disposal of receipts arising out of current trade or 'invisible' income. It might also be possible to obtain recognition of the general principle that commercial treaties between members of the Union should, subject to any necessary safeguards and exceptions, exclude—

(i) Import restrictions, whether quantitative or in the form of 'duty-quotas' (excluding, however, prohibitions genuinely designed to safeguard, e.g., public health or morals or revenue collection);

(ii) Barter arrangements;

(iii) Export quotas and discriminatory export taxes;

(iv) Export subsidies either furnished directly by the state or indirectly under schemes supported or encouraged by the state; and

(v) Tariffs in excess of a moderate level.

37. Subsidies in favour of domestic producers for domestic consumption, with a countervailing levy when such subsidised goods are exported, would not be excluded. This is a necessary safety-valve which provides for protective expedients called for on political, social and industrial grounds. Such subsidies (and the same applies to moderate tariffs) would be a permitted way of giving purely domestic protection to an industry which for special reasons ought to be maintained for domestic purposes only. The question of preferences and of other relaxations from most-favoured-nation treatment, which would be of a normal and continuing character, does not fall within the scope of this paper.

VIII. *The use of the Clearing Union for other international purposes*

38. The Clearing Union might become the instrument and the support of international policies in addition to those which it is its primary purpose to promote. This deserves the greatest possible emphasis. The Union might become the pivot of the future economic government of the world. Without it, other more desirable developments will find themselves impeded and unsupported. With it, they will fall into their place as parts of an ordered scheme. No one of the following suggestions is a necessary part of the plan. But they are illustrations of the additional purposes of high importance and value which the Union, once established, might be able to serve:–

(1) The Union might set up a Clearing Account in favour of international bodies charged with post-war relief, rehabilitation and reconstruction. But it could go much further than this. For it might supplement contributions received from other sources by granting overdraft facilities in favour of these bodies, the overdraft being discharged over a period of years out of the Reserve Fund of the Union, or, if necessary,

out of a levy on surplus credit balances. By this means it is possible to avoid asking any country to assume a burdensome commitment for relief and reconstruction, since the resources would be provided in the first instance by those countries having credit clearing accounts for which they have no immediate use and are voluntarily leaving idle, and in the long run by those countries which have a chronic international surplus for which they have no beneficial employment.

(2) The Union might set up an account in favour of the super-national policing body charged with the duty of preserving the peace and maintaining international order. If any country were to infringe its properly authorised orders, the policing body might be entitled to request the Governors of the Clearing Union to hold the Clearing Account of the delinquent country to its order and permit no further transactions on the account except by its authority. This would provide an excellent machinery for enforcing a financial blockade.

(3) The Union might set up an account in favour of international bodies charged with the management of a Commodity Control, and might finance stocks of commodities held by such bodies, allowing them overdraft facilities on their accounts up to an agreed maximum. By this means the financial problem of buffer stocks and 'ever-normal granaries' could be effectively attacked.

(4) The Union might be linked up with a Board for International Investment. It might act on behalf of such a Board and collect for them the annual service of their loans by automatically debiting the Clearing Account of the country concerned. The statistics of the Clearing Accounts of the member-states would give a reliable indication as to which countries were in a position to finance the Investment Board, with the advantage of shifting the whole system of clearing credits and debits nearer to equilibrium.

(5) There are various methods by which the Clearing

Union could use its influence and its powers to maintain stability of prices and to control the trade cycle. If an International Economic Board is established, this Board and the Clearing Union might be expected to work in close collaboration to their mutual advantage. If an International Investment or Development Corporation is also set up together with a scheme of Commodity Controls for the control of stocks of the staple primary products, we might come to possess in these three institutions a powerful means of combating the evils of the trade cycle, by exercising contractionist or expansionist influence on the system as a whole or on particular sections. This is a large and important question which cannot be discussed adequately in this paper; and need not be examined at length in this place because it does not raise any important issues affecting the fundamental constitution of the proposed Union. It is mentioned here to complete the picture of the wider purposes which the foundation of the Clearing Union might be made to serve.

39. The facility of applying the Clearing Union plan to these several purposes arises out of a fundamental characteristic which is worth pointing out, since it distinguishes the plan from those proposals which try to develop the same basic principle along bilateral lines and is one of the grounds on which the plan can claim superior merit. This might be described as its 'anonymous' or 'impersonal' quality. No particular member states have to engage their own resources as such to the support of other particular states or any of the international projects or policies adopted. They have only to agree in general that, if they find themselves with surplus resources which for the time being they do not themselves wish to employ, these resources may go into the general pool and be put to work on approved purposes. This costs the surplus country nothing because it is not asked to part permanently, or even for any specified period, with such resources, which it remains free to expand and employ for its

own purposes whenever it chooses; in which case the burden of finance is passed on to the next recipient, again for only so long as the recipient has no use for the money. As pointed out above, this merely amounts to extending to the international sphere the methods of any domestic banking system, which are in the same sense 'impersonal' inasmuch as there is no call on the particular depositor either to support as such the purposes for which his banker makes advances or to forgo permanently the use of his deposit. There is no countervailing objection except that which applies equally to the technique of domestic banking, namely that it is capable of the abuse of creating excessive purchasing power and hence an inflation of prices. In our efforts to avoid the opposite evil, we must not lose sight of this risk, to which there is an allusion in 38(5) above. But it is no more reason for refusing the advantages of international banking than the similar risk in the domestic field is a reason for returning to the practices of the seventeenth century goldsmiths (which are what we are still following in the international field) and forgoing the vast expansion of production which banking principles have made possible.

40. Apply this impersonal quality to the finance of relief and reconstruction after the war. It is one thing to ask the Parliaments and the Congresses of the various countries of the world to make contributions which they may or may not be able to afford in the unpredictable circumstances of the post-war transition, and which will be in any case a charge on their tax-payers and a permanent reduction of their own resources, arousing therefore political difficulties and competing with the claims of domestic social reforms. It is quite another thing to ask them to join in a general system which, without cost to their tax-payers and without prejudice to their own expenditure, requires of them to allow the temporary employment of surplus resources only so long as they themselves do not choose to use them. Or take again the finance

of buffer stocks. It is great facility not to have to ask for specific contributions from any named country, but to depend rather on the anonymous and impersonal aid of the system as a whole. We have here a genuine organ of truly international government.

IX. *The transitional arrangements*

41. It would be of great advantage to agree the general principles of the Clearing Union before the end of the war, with a view to bringing it into operation at an early date after the termination of hostilities. Major plans will be more easily brought to birth in the first energy of victory and whilst the active spirit of united action still persists, than in the days of exhaustion and reaction from so much effort which may well follow a little later. Such a proposal presents, however, something of a dilemma. On the one hand, many countries will be in particular need of reserves of overseas resources in the period immediately after the war. On the other hand, goods will be in short supply and the prevention of inflationary international conditions of much more importance for the time being than the opposite. The expansionist tendency of the plan, which is a leading recommendation of it as soon as peace-time output is restored and the productive capacity of the world is in running order, might be a danger in the early days of a sellers' market and an excess of demand over supply.

42. A reconciliation of these divergent purposes is not easily found until we know more than is known at present about the means to be adopted to finance post-war relief and reconstruction. If the intention is to provide resources on liberal and comprehensive lines outside the resources made available by the Clearing Union and additional to them, it might be better for such specific aid to take the place of the proposed overdrafts during the 'relief' period of (say) two

years. Nevertheless, the immediate establishment of the Clearing Union would not be incompatible with provisional arrangements, which could take alternative forms according to the character of the other 'relief' arrangements, qualifying and limiting the overdraft quotas.

43. If, however, the finance of relief is actually furnished, in part at least, through the Clearing Union, as has been suggested above, and if that, combined, perhaps, with a temporary continuance of lend-leasing by the United States or other aid from outside the Clearing Union, appears likely to provide the world with as much purchasing power as is desirable in the early days the coming into force of the overdraft quotas might be postponed until the founder members were agreed that the need for them was impending. In this case credit clearing balances would be limited to the amount of gold delivered to the Union, and the overdraft facilities created by the Union in favour of the Relief Council, the International Investment Board or the Commodity Controls. Alternatively, overdraft quotas might be allowed on a reduced scale during the transitional period. At any rate, it might be proper to provide that countries in receipt of relief or lend lease assistance should not have access at the same time to overdraft facilities, and that the latter should only become available when the former had come to an end.

44. If, on the other hand, relief from outside sources looks like being inadequate from the outset, the overdraft quotas may be even more necessary at the outset than later on.

45. We must not be over-cautious. A rapid economic restoration may lighten the tasks of the diplomatists and the politicians in the resettlement of the world and the restoration of social order. For Great Britain and other countries outside the 'relief' areas the possibility of exports sufficient to sustain their standard of life is bound up with good and expanding markets. We cannot afford to wait too long for this, and we must not allow excessive caution to condemn us to perdition.

Unless the Union is a going concern, the problem of proper 'timing' will be nearly insoluble. It is sufficient at this stage to point out that the problem of timing must not be over-looked, but that the Union is capable of being used so as to aid rather than impede its solution.

X. *Conclusion*

46. It has been suggested that so ambitious a proposal is open to criticism on the ground that it requires from the members of the Union a greater surrender of their sovereign rights than they will readily concede. But no greater surrender is required than in a commercial treaty. The obligations will be entered into voluntarily and can be terminated on certain conditions by giving notice.

47. A greater readiness to accept super-national arrangements must be required in the post-war world. If the arrangements proposed can be described as a measure of financial disarmament, they are mild in comparison with the measures of military disarmament which the world may be asked to accept. There is nothing here which we need be reluctant to accept ourselves or to ask of others. It is an advantage, and not a disadvantage, of the scheme that it invites the member states to abandon that licence to promote indiscipline, disorder and bad-neighbourliness which, to the general disadvantage, they have been free to exercise hitherto.

48. The plan makes a beginning at the future economic ordering of the world between nations and 'the winning of the peace'. It might help to create the conditions and the atmosphere in which much else would be made easier.

During the rest of August, September and early October, a good part of Keynes's time on Clearing Union matters was taken up with a paper by Harrod entitled 'Foreign Investment, Industrialisation and the Clearing

Union'; successive drafts of which reached Keynes in both August and September. Keynes discussed both drafts with Harrod both in correspondence and in person, but they did not come to anything, largely one suspects, as Keynes 'did not find it helpful as a guide to immediate policy' and recommended to Sir Alfred Hurst[3] and his Treasury colleagues that the ideas not be pursued, especially, given that Britain was unlikely to be a creditor for some time after the war, as the Americans should be the source of proposals on international investment.

During the same period, discussions on the Clearing Union itself moved forward. Sir Frederick Phillips met Messrs Berle,[4] Pasvolsky and White for a preliminary discussion of the plan and on 6 October received from Berle a series of questions on the scheme. Keynes himself discussed it with Mr Winant on 23 September and Mr Riefler who had come to London to represent the Bureau of Economic Warfare in the American Embassy. Also, during the visits of Morgenthau and White to London, Keynes managed to have a long discussion on 23 October with White on their two plans, as well as seeing him on other occasions. Finally, when representatives of the Dominions came to London to discuss post-war planning at the end of October, Keynes explained the Clearing Union and Sir Frederick Phillips reported on his American conversations.

The upshot of these discussions with the Dominions and the Americans was another draft of the Clearing Union scheme, dated 9 November. Sir Frederick Phillips returned to Washington, taking the revised draft with him for presentation to the Americans. A list of the changes incorporated in this draft appears as Appendix 2.

During the period after the Dominions discussions, conversations with the Americans continued in a rather desultory way which rather alarmed London, as other documents on commercial policy and commodity policy[5] were coming forward through the Whitehall machine.

As a result, Keynes, after consultations within the Treasury and with the Foreign Office, wrote to Sir Frederick Phillips.

To SIR FREDERICK PHILLIPS, *16 December 1942*

My dear Phillips,

I take the opportunity of Eddy Playfair's leaving tomorrow to send you this rambling letter, which may be the best way

[3] Sir Alfred Hurst (b. 1884); entered Treasury, 1907; Under-Secretary for Mines, 1940–2; in charge of Reconstruction Secretariat of War Cabinet, 1942–4.
[4] Adolf August Berle, Jr. (b. 1895); Professor of Law, Columbia University; Assistant Secretary of State, U.S.A., 1938–44; U.S. Ambassador to Brazil, 1945–6.
[5] On these, in so far as Keynes was involved, see *JMK*, vols. XXVI and XXVII.

of conveying to you our rather confused state of thought over here and getting your counsel on it.

Let me take first of all the present position of the various documents.

1. *The Clearing Union.* Your report of the meeting at the State Department on 26th November to consider our replies, suggests a very harmless, indeed, almost too harmless an atmosphere. Nothing difficult or dangerous seems to arise there. Indeed, apart from the questions you have reserved, there are only the statement you promise on Questions 1 and 2[6]—which is an entirely imaginary issue—and the more substantial matter whether there is an assurance we could give the U.S. Treasury on the matter raised under Question 8.[7] This report gives me the impression that Feis is an advocate on our side, that Pasvolsky understands it all only to a limited extent, and that Berle, though friendly, is extremely on the cautious side. Perhaps this will all be elucidated when we have the further document with alleged counter-suggestions promised in your telegram 6005.

Unless these counter-suggestions contain a surprise, either favourable or unfavourable, the question arises 'what next?'. I will take this up again after mentioning the state of the other papers. But, as you know, there is a feeling that we should hand the paper as soon as possible to Maisky,—that is, unless the 'counter-suggestions' indicate otherwise; and there is also something to be said for showing it to T. V. Soong[8] if, as we still rather expect (though without certainty), he turns up here in a month or so's time.

2. *Primary products.* You will have had my drastic redraft

---

[6] Questions 1 and 2 concerned the gold points and consistent cross rates of exchange under the scheme.

[7] Question 8 concerned the disposable assets held by the Union to ensure liquidation of credits in the event of the Union's dissolution or war, as well as the withdrawal of a member in credit.

[8] T. V. Soong (Sung Tzu-Wen) (b. 1891); Minister of Finance and Vice-President of Executive Yuan, 1928–31, 1945–7; Governor, Central Bank of China, 1930–3, Chairman of Board of Directors, 1935–43; Chinese Minister of Foreign Affairs, 1942–5.

of this. It has been circulated to most of those concerned. So far there are no indications of substantial criticism. The D.O. and C.O. are producing numerous drafting amendments, but nothing which I have seen so far which goes to the root of the proposals. It is, therefore, reasonable to hope the revised version of this will be through the official Hurst Committee in the reasonably near future, and personally I do not see any reason to suppose that Ministers will withhold that mild degree of blessing with which they are accustomed to allow us to take the next step,—in this case of showing it to the Americans. Whether we shall continue the piece-meal policy and let them have this document semi-officially, in the same way as the Clearing Union, as soon as it is ready, is quite another matter.

3. *Commercial policy.* I believe that Eady is writing to you about this. I am not in close touch with it. Here, of course, there may be much more controversy and delay on the part of the Ministers. But whether that need take an enormous amount of time I am not sure. If there is not too much trouble, something will go through. On the other hand, if there is trouble, I should expect that they would take the obvious way out of deciding that it is not advisable for us to take the initiative.

Whether the official document, when we get it, will be in the most advisable form for submission to the Americans I personally am far from sure. On the positive side I am in considerable sympathy with Hubert Henderson that the technique of import restriction has many advantages over tariffs, particularly for this country, and that we should not willingly relinquish it. On the other hand, it is not easy to devise a method or formula which is entirely clear of the charge of lending itself to discriminatory methods. Efforts are being made now to produce a non-discriminatory technique. At any rate it would, I hope, be made clear that, if we ask for the continuance of import restrictions, we shall put it forward as merely an alternative way of attaining the same result as tariffs and will promise to provide that import restrictions will be used only on occasions when it is possible to apply them in an entirely non-discriminatory manner. On the question of preferences it would be interesting to know what you think of the politics of the matter. In theory the Americans may claim that we have agreed to get rid of preferences altogether if the rest of the settlement is on satisfactory lines. Do they in practice really expect this, or would they be content with substantial reductions? According to some authorities, they would be so content. In this case, is it advisable for us to make some concrete suggestion, such as a reduction of 50 per cent? It seems to me that, assuming a reasonably satisfactory settlement in other directions, there is not likely to be very much left of preferences, and, therefore, we shall do far better to be handsome about it at the beginning and not make too much of it as a bargaining point.

Generally speaking on the matter of safeguards, I should like to see us put our case in a positive, and not in a negative, form. That is to say, we propose so-and-so on the general understanding that this proposal is part and parcel of the economic negotiations as a whole, and that we hold ourselves at liberty to change our minds in the contingency (which we hope is improbable) of any serious collapse in regard to the other issues. We should not introduce too many *specific* safeguards, qualifying each concession with an escape clause by which we need not really apply it unless we want.

Finally, do you think it wise to suggest a ceiling or any other specific quantitative reduction of tariffs? It seems to me that, if something of that sort gets out in Republican circles, it might easily produce dangerous repercussions. In regard to the concessions for which we ask, I should like to be as vague as possible. Would it not be better to say that we would accept any proposals for the reduction of tariffs and for a ceiling to tariffs which the Americans are prepared to propose; leaving ourselves entirely in their hands in this matter; and, as regards preferences, say that we would provide for *pari passu* reduction on a more generous scale than any formula applicable to tariffs,—(say) that the reduction or the ceiling in the case of preferences should be twice as great and half as high as what may be agreed to in the case of tariffs. Then we could follow these general remarks up with a schematism on the lines which the Overton Committee are now considering, but without the specific figures of the latter. As I mentioned above, I am writing without real acquaintance with what that Committee is after and am thinking on very general lines.

4. *International investment.* Is Harry White giving any sign of life here? I still remain of the opinion that, in this matter at any rate, it is better for the Americans to take the initiative. I am wondering, however, whether it would be helpful to take that half of Harry White's draft which relates to international investment and try to lick it into shape. Would Harry resent this, or would he appreciate it?

Well, one way or another, it seems to me that we ought within three months, and perhaps a little sooner, to have advanced as far as we can in Whitehall without further contact with Washington. And that brings me to the question of what sort of procedure we ought to be aiming at. It seems to me that there are three alternatives:–

(1) The first is to jog along by the same sort of very informal procedure used in the case of the Clearing Union; handing over any document as soon as it is ready; proceeding piece-meal by very tentative measures and gingerly steps. I expect you will agree that that will be rather hopeless. I cannot imagine you wanting to face the same sort of desultory proceedings on all the other documents. Moreover, at the end of it all, we should only have dealt with a few young gentlemen at the State Department and will have failed to reach any sort of definitive conclusions.

(2) The second alternative is that, as soon as we are ready

here, we should send out a small deputation to join you with
the object of having a continuous, more or less formal
conference with some corresponding American body, occupying at least a month. On our side, that would not present
any particular difficulty. But is there a sufficient prospect of
the Americans setting up a similar body for us to deal with?
The two essential conditions seem to me to be (a) that the State
Department should be prepared to discuss, though, of course,
without any prior commitments, nevertheless on an authoritative basis, with the intention that any results which are
reached would be submitted to the two Governments in a
perfectly formal manner, and (b) that the body in question
should be really representative of the Administration as a
whole, and not merely a private tea party of the State Department. If the President deliberately hands over the whole of
post-war matters to the State Department, perhaps with some
assessors from the Treasury and elsewhere, well and good.
But it should be clear that we are dealing with the Administration as a whole and are not open to subsequent attack by
some other Department in Washington which was not represented and thinks it ought to have been. If this procedure
is adopted, perhaps there should be two stages—a preliminary conference in Washington (since it now seems hopeless
to get them to come to London, though otherwise London
would be much better); then a reference back to the Governments; and then perhaps a further meeting in London at
which other powers would be brought in. (Again, of course,
it would be much better that the wider conference should be
in Washington and the narrower one in London, if only they
would agree to that.) Meanwhile it might be helpful if
ministers on this side as well as on your side of the Atlantic
were free to be somewhat more open about the whole matter
and fly a kite or two in Parliament or elsewhere. On these
post-war economic questions it is plain that public opinion has
to be captured and that not much can be done in a hole and

corner way. On this side, anyhow, criticisms are becoming frequent. I attach a paper giving an extract from a recent article in the *New Statesman*.[9]

(3) Perhaps this second alternative is not too bad, if it can really come about, subject to the conditions suggested. But I do not feel confident that it is the right way and, therefore, want to try on you a possible third alternative. You may remember a despatch from Halifax dated 21st April, 1941, in which he reported a conversation with the President in which the President had argued that the best way of preparing for post-war matters on the economic side would be to appoint a joint Anglo-American Commission of small numbers to prepare some ideas for the consideration of the two Governments. This was the paper which was known at the time, I think, as 'The Three Wise Men Proposal'. Now, what about reviving something on those lines today? The idea would be that the Prime Minister and the President would appoint a small joint Anglo-American Commission to report to the two Governments on proposals for the post-war economic settlement. The Governments would, of course, be in no way committed to the Commission. The fact of the Commission's appointment would be public. They would treat the job as a wholetime one carried out partly in Washington and partly in London, occupying them from three to six months. There might be four or five members on each side and a Chairman. They would perhaps be partly official and partly unofficial, or semi-official,—at any rate, sufficiently official for the Governments to be kept in touch and to make sure that the Commission did not report anything seriously contrary to what was likely to be acceptable to either of the appointing Governments. When the Commission had reported, then its conclusions would, if the two Governments so decided, be put before a wider body of powers for their consideration. The

---

[9] The article 'First Essentials of Economic Reconstruction' appeared in the issue of 14 November 1942.

advantage of such a body would be that a common draft could be prepared under Anglo-American auspices without being open to the charge of being either a British draft or an American draft. Progress could be made to a fairly high degree of finality without the Governments having to take premature responsibility. Yet the existence of the body would provide them with a good explanation to the public, if they were charged with not getting anything done. This procedure would perhaps lift the whole matter out of the rut, prevent it from getting bogged down and give it a more authoritative position. The countervailing disadvantages are obvious.

I believe that the F.O. would probably welcome something on these lines and would very likely advise the Foreign Secretary to approach the Prime Minister with such a suggestion, if the Chancellor of the Exchequer was ready to be associated with him. When the original proposal came up I was in Washington. I believe that at that time it received a good deal of support from the F.O., but was turned down by the Chancellor, largely on the advice of [Sir] H.J. [Wilson]. But at that time there were, of course, good reasons for holding back from such an enterprise which may no longer exist. We had not even begun to clear our minds, and it might have been dangerous to let loose a Commission which would necessarily be most ill-instructed about the attitudes, or probable attitudes, of Whitehall. On the other hand, it would now be free from some at least of these objections.

On the American side, if this were to appeal to them, the President would be given an opportunity of bringing in names which might have influence in circles outside purely official Washington. Clearly in the long run the real trouble is going to be Congress. Would it be possible to find a member or two of such a body on the American side who would carry weight with Congress and make a real difference from that point of view?

I have probably said enough to let you see pretty clearly

what the points are on either side. Eady and Waley know I am writing to you, but this is a purely personal effort to get your reactions.

We have to bear it constantly in mind that, in the long run, large economic projects cannot possibly come into existence except with the aid of an instructed and educated public opinion. The form of presentation is going to be of the first importance. The public will not, of course, be able to pass judgment on any of the details. But they will be influenced by the general atmosphere. The preparation of the right atmosphere must not be overlooked; and we must not think that we can get very far merely by drafting fairly sensible details.

Well, I promised you a rambling letter and have duly delivered it. No other particular news. Lubin[10] is here, but no one quite knows why. He seems to be interested in social questions such as Citrine and Beveridge. However, he is going in about a fortnight's time to North Africa, I suppose to report to the President on the economic and financial set-up there. We may, therefore, try to get an opportunity to indoctrinate him with sensible ideas.

Yours,
[copy initialled] K.

Phillips replied to the letter as follows:

From SIR FREDERICK PHILLIPS, *8 January 1943*

My dear Keynes,

The following replies to your letter of the 16th ulto. from paragraph 4 onwards. I will deal with the other points shortly.

I agree that it should be left to the Americans to take the initiative on International Investment. Harry White is showing few signs of life. I think a wholesale recasting of his memorandum would not please him. But if it

[10] Isadore Lubin (b. 1896); economist; U.S. Commissioner, Bureau of Labour Statistics, 1933–46; Economic Adviser in the White House, 1940–5; legal adviser to U.S. delegation, Bretton Woods Conference, 1944.

were possible to produce a small number of amendments, or a number of short amendments, indicating closeness of study, he might be flattered. It is wonderful what can be done to alter the sense of a document sometimes by a few amendments.

The three alternatives have been closely studied and I have discussed the position with Campbell and Opie. The third alternative deserves attention first. I can conceive political chiefs finding other methods blocked, attacked on the one side by charges of inactivity and blindness to great problems, attacked on the other side by charges of rash and secret negotiations with foreigners coming with almost relief to such a solution as a temporary way out from their troubles. But further reflection does not strengthen the case. The proposal may have had good points in 1941 but we are not in 1941. Very natural then for the main democratic belligerent and the main democratic non-belligerent to put their heads together on the future. But events, and Roosevelt with or ahead of them, have moved a very long way since. If there is to be publicity (and the good explanation to the public is the heart of the thing) never shall we see a joint Anglo-American Commission of this kind. There would be an official or unofficial or semi-official Russian wise man, ditto Chinese wiseman, with Canada squawking across the Border, and London insisting that Van Zeeland[11] shall be on to represent Europe, and why should the I.L.O. and the League be ignored? By this time the idea has lost its attraction for me. The dilemma is that you must have a team from each country for no one man can cover the ground. But it is hardly a workable idea to have a team from each of several countries to draft plans.

This, as we do not like the first alternative and cannot think of a fourth, throws us back on the second. I doubt if a private tea party of the State Department now fairly describes the American side. They have a pretty elaborate hierarchy of committees on which nearly all the important departments are, I fancy, well represented.

The proposal for the despatch to Washington of a small mission will not be popular with the Administration, but as we can see no better alternative this is what we shall have to peg away at.

Yours sincerely,

F. PHILLIPS

With progress in Washington towards Anglo-American discussions on post-war monetary proposals so slow and with the prospect of the Americans widening discussions of the White Plan for a stabilisation fund to

[11] Paul van Zeeland (b. 1893), sometime Prime Minister of Belgium.

involve other countries, Whitehall also turned to discuss the Clearing Union with countries outside the Commonwealth, passing copies to the Russians, the Chinese and the European Allies. In the Russian and Chinese cases, Keynes prepared simplified summaries of the scheme for the guidance of the officials directly involved, drawing particular attention to points in which the two countries might be interested.

On 26 February, Keynes opened a discussion on the Clearing Union, before passing the European Allies copies of the November 1942 draft of the scheme.

Speech to a meeting of the European Allies, 26 February 1943

Financial Secretary, Your Excellencies and Gentlemen, we are very glad after a rather abnormal period of gestation at last to produce our long promised baby. I hope it is the first of a family because while the monetary side of matters may be logically prior, it certainly will not by itself carry us all the way. In contemplating the long-term economic arrangements for the world as distinct from short-term problems of relief and so forth, we have thought of it as falling into four main chapters. There is the monetary chapter; there is another chapter dealing with primary products, stabilisation of their prices, regulation of their supply and so forth; there are the questions of commercial policy, tariffs, subsidies, import regulation and the like. And there is the question of whether there should be some sort of new institution for international investment by which those unbalanced credits which come into existence hereafter can be distributed to the general advantage of the world.

We have been working more particularly in this country at the first of the two, though we have also got thoughts about the others. It may be we shall be able to distribute at no very distant date a paper on primary products because that is rather well on. If I may say so we were rather hoping the United States would take the initiative over international investment because they are so very directly concerned with that. Commercial policy affects all of us. There have been already conversations in which some of you have taken part with the D.O.T. That is evidently a chapter which has also got to be very carefully considered. When we have the whole thing in front of us we can form a picture of the kind of post-war world we are aiming at, but I think there is no harm in starting with the monetary arrangements, the external monetary arrangements, because as soon as one gets down to details it is clear you cannot get very far with the other bits of the programme until you first of all have formed an idea of the monetary set-up.

Now so far as the internal problem goes we have this very useful first report of the sub-committee of the experts. The paper we shall be handing you today, while it will affect that indirectly, is essentially concerned with the external problem. As the Financial Secretary has said it is on lines which are not original and which many other thinkers have been following. In detail plans can differ from one another but I venture to say there is really only one plan in essence. In substantial matters whatever is satisfactory will embrace certain fundamentals. So far as the details go it will scarcely be useful for me to go into that much until you have the paper in writing. These matters are not so easy particularly in a language which is foreign to many of you that one can get very far in purely oral discussion without having seen the proposals in black and white, but it might perhaps help to say a few words about the general conception of the thing.

First of all there are the problems which have not arisen merely out of the war but were menacing every country in the decade before the war, aggravated the great slump, provoked world wide unemployment and, generally speaking, perhaps impoverished the world very nearly as much as the war itself has impoverished the world. I believe we should all like if we could to get back to multilateral clearing, if that is the right expression, that is to say, a system in which the currency of one country was available for making purchases everywhere else indiscriminately. Not easy but, if attainable, desirable. We should like to have some agreed system to prevent competitive exchange depreciations. Exchanges have to be altered from time to time because the social and wages policy of different countries do not keep step with one another necessarily but there should be no exchange depreciations which are merely passing on one country's perplexities to its neighbours. Some provision should be made against that.

Then a very fundamental point: where there is a want of balance in trade dealings so that the imports of some countries are much greater than their exports and the exports of other countries much greater than their imports, when that happens, and it may happen for perfectly good reasons, the pressure of adjustment should not fall, as it has in the past, almost wholly on the weaker country, the debtor. The creditor may be equally to blame, he may be less to blame, he may also be more to blame. We should like to have a set-up which made it as much the duty of the creditor country as of the debtor country to ensure a proper balance. If he can just insist on gold which perhaps the debtor has not got, he makes the only alternative the pressure of deflation and contraction of trade so as to get an export equilibrium on a lower basis. If we could have a system which would put pressure on the creditor as much as the debtor we might be a great step forward to removing the other consequential difficulties of want of balance. And along with that there should be we think an atmosphere of expansion rather than the contrary. We should look forward to world trade being much greater than it has been in the past, to the wealth of the world being much greater, the scale of things being larger and there should not be some pressure on all of us, some contractionist feeling, some elemental feature of the system which was forcing us in our own short-sighted policy to contract rather than expand. Those are our objects and I believe they will be the common objects of all here. It is when one comes to the technical methods for attaining those ends perhaps that more than one opinion can be held. There again, I should say things that look different, if they are satisfactory, will prove in the last resort not to be so different as they look. There are not so many remedies really.

This particular plan perhaps takes its most characteristic feature from the analogy of banking within a country, within a closed system. Up to the seventeenth century payments were largely made in coin and therefore if an individual was not using his receipts, if he did not use the coin which he received for what he had furnished, that coin became dead. It was not available to anyone else. In the course of the Middle Ages that had caused a most disastrous pressure through the continuous shortage of currency because it was going out of activity. Then came the great discovery of modern banking, starting so far as our immediate parent was concerned, I think one can say, in Holland, but there were some earlier ideas in Italy and elsewhere. But modern banking really started in Holland and London, I believe the Bank of England was literally the first institution quite of that kind that came into existence.

Now the point of this banking was that a man who accumulated a deposit, a man who was not using the receipts did not deprive the rest of the community of purchasing power because his bank would then lend out the deposits to somebody else so that purchasing power which was not being used by one party was placed at the disposal of another party. That, of course, was liable to danger in the opposite direction, that is to say of too much expansion and safeguards had to be gradually devised in the course of the centuries to prevent that. But the fundamental point was sound, that if for the time being one man was selling more than he was buying, that should not put a stop on things but should enable somebody else more or less automatically to buy more than he was selling. Modern banking has developed that to a very fine degree of perfection within a given country. But we have, broadly speaking continued with the uncivilised practices of the Middle Ages as between countries. Individual banks were beginning particularly in the period before the war to try to remedy this by special arrangements with those of their neighbours with whom they were in particularly intimate contact. The sterling area is a very striking example of trying to extend this system beyond the boundaries of a single country, but still, taking the world at large, we have not had any system by which in a regular and half automatic way that part of its receipts which one country does not choose to use is made available to others. Therefore the proposals we are making to you are embracing from one point of view the essential practices of internal banking.

We call the plan a clearing union because the purpose is to set off transactions against one another so far as you can clear and then to deal with the resulting credit and debit balances as still off-setting one another in the same way they do in internal banking. We have not adopted another possible feature of banking by which you have capital, subscribed capital, which you can then lend out. That is an alternative way of approach which our plan does not adopt. It is perplexing to some people at first that that should not be necessary. In the first days of banking great stress was laid on the possession of capital but we have learned as time goes on that that is of insignificant importance. You need the capital if you are not in a closed system and have to meet liabilities for credit outside your system, but in a closed system you can reach your conclusion by simply off-setting the deposits of some members against the overdrafts of others. The deposits on the one side are necessarily exactly equal to the overdrafts on the other, so that as there is no liability to pay outside the system it involves no risk and therefore requires no capital. I do not say you cannot attain our results by a system which introduces an element of capital, I only say it is a characteristic of ours that it springs from the further development of internal banking by which what matters is the off-setting of the deposits of some customers against the overdrafts of others.

Now in an internal system the banks exercise certain discipline over their customers. They do not allow overdrafts to an unlimited extent at will and one of the problems in an international system is to have a proper analogy to that by which the member states, the clients of the institution, can have overdrafts reasonably adequate to their purpose and yet are not undisciplined. Therefore your particular attention is invited to the proposals that are made to prevent the advantages of the system from being abused. It may be that is a part of the plan which is open to considerable improvement. It is a new development and it may have been approached with a little timidity. I am not sure. We shall be interested in having your opinion. But one feature of it, which is again perhaps put too timidly, is strikingly important, and that is that the discipline is not exercised solely on the debtor, on the country that wants overdrafts because, of course, it can only be in a position of wanting overdrafts because some country from which it has purchased is not using the proceeds of those purchases for corresponding purchases. Therefore the problems of the debtors can only arise if creditors are not choosing to make use of the purchasing power they have obtained. If you can get the creditors to aim at balance you will be correspondingly mitigating the problems of the debtor. We have been very gentle towards the creditors because we are a little scared of them. Possibly that is a part of the scheme that could be stiffened up, if those concerned are prepared to stiffen it. Anyhow the intention is in that direction. There is no provision by which the creditor is limited in his liability to accept a credit balance with the institution if he chooses not to use it. He need never have a credit balance. He is still left with every conceivable liberty he has now. But if he does not choose to use it, no maximum is set. That may be open to criticism. It may be possible to devise a compromise. On the other hand, on the overdraft side a limit clearly has to be set and the discipline has to get stricter as a country approaches it.

There have also to be provisions by which rates of exchange can be altered if circumstances indicate it to be necessary, but not altered by unilateral action, only altered in accordance with the general principles of the system. We also assume a system which in fact, I think, is applied in nearly all your parent countries, that is of centralising henceforward exchange dealings in a national institution, not allowing purely private enterprise dealings in exchange. I do not know that that is an essential feature; it is certainly one that greatly facilitates matters. We contemplate the central bank or similar institutions monopolising dealings in foreign exchange for its own nationals and an internal clearing with separate banks. Then it is left with a final balance for or against and that final balance would then be cleared with this international clearing union. That would get rid of the whole element of exchange speculation which caused so much trouble after the last war.

It would also make possible a further system of control to which we in this country attach great importance and that is the control of capital movements. We think it entirely impracticable that individual nationals of a country should be free to move assets abroad or invest abroad quite irrespective of whether their country had a favourable balance which made such transactions possible. We are very far from wanting to interrupt the historic course of foreign investment, but foreign investment of individuals that does not correspond to a favourable balance is clearly something which can only cause trouble and can do no good, in the same way as flights of capital for reasons of political fear or fluctuating ideas of where the 'better 'ole' is. All that we want to get rid of. Therefore we contemplate that there would be a system of control of exchange dealings which would make it possible to prevent capital transactions except where they were approved. On the other hand an open general licence would be given to all transactions in respect of current trade, and that would be an essential part of the conception of multilateral clearing so that if you sell goods to a given country you can be absolutely sure of the facility to use the proceeds in any other country whatsoever. We believe that a right system of exchange control, so far from leading to the abuses of bilateralism, could be a bulwark of multi-lateralism undisturbed by unwanted and injurious capital movements. There is also provision by which the general scale of operation of the whole system moves upwards and downwards with the size of world trade, that is to say the quotas, the over-draft facilities of individual members will be proportional to their foreign trade and will go up and down with that. So you are not fixing the quantity of international [money] irrespective of the amount of work which the international money has to do in the shape of financing trade; the two are connected together.

We do not take any action injurious to the position of gold. We think that gold still has an important part to play. But we think that the great fault of the pre-war system was that the quantity of international money was fixed by the accidental progress of the gold-mining industry; the quantity supplied was accidental and not related to requirements; therefore we are not allowing gold to determine henceforward the volume of international exchange. The world being what it is, it is likely the confidence gold gives can still play a useful part. We do, in fact, in a sense improve the position of gold beyond what it has been before, because we provide a secure market for it. The international institution will always be prepared to turn gold at a determined rate into the international money. There is a one-way convertibility into international money—we have given meanwhile the name of bancor to it, not a very good name, I hope you will think of a better one—there is one-way convertibility, you can turn gold into bancor, you cannot turn bancor into gold. That is a part of the scheme you will no doubt look at carefully. It means that those countries which have gold resources, those countries which produce gold, suffer no injury from this scheme, but, in fact, are provided with a secure market which one cannot say they will necessarily have in a world of monetary chaos after the war. In that sense, in that particular, this scheme is a conservative one.

We also throw out some suggestions of the way in which this system might become useful for wider international purposes. That is all very tentative. It is not essential to the scheme but it does show you how this scheme might become the linch-pin of a general international economic system of a far more ambitious kind than we ever contemplated before the war. Once you have settled these appalling difficulties of exchanges and multilateral clearing and controls and so forth, then the other international organisations become very much easier to set up and indications are given of the way in which this scheme might be worked into other schemes.

I doubt if it is worth while my attempting to go into more details than this until you have had a chance of looking at the paper. Our suggestion is that, as in the case of the documents which you have received earlier this morning, a sub-committee should be appointed to consider this document in detail. It might perhaps begin its meetings a fortnight hence and during that fortnight if any of you would like to clear up your minds by a conversation in the Treasury with myself or anybody else, we shall be at your disposal; just ring up and fix a time to have a talk. It might be we could save time by clearing up matters for you by answering questions. Then our idea is, at some such date as a fortnight hence, the sub-committee might meet. We should then sit down to the document in a series of sessions, perhaps fairly continuously, really to get our teeth into it and take it paragraph by paragraph, hear the criticism, hear also the suggestions, take it both in detail and in its larger implications. That is our suggestion of the future programme. Then, at a later time if we can add further documents to it, that can be done. But we have not anything in view at the moment except this. As the Financial Secretary has said there is also an American paper, we do not know at what moment that will be available. But we shall not have lost time, I think, if we start off with this one. There are some very important differences, there are also some very strong resemblances between both papers. I am sure we shall not have lost time by studying this in detail in the next few weeks.

Keynes's comments on page 211 led D. H. Robertson to minute to him on 3 March

'Are we to love, honour, cherish and thank or
To kick in the bottom the blokes who hold bancor.'

When the Treasury in London received another revision of White's Stabilisation Fund, the eighth re-draft of the proposals Keynes had first received from Sir Frederick Phillips the previous summer, Keynes turned to a comparison of the Clearing Union and the Stabilisation Fund, with a first draft dated 18 February and a revised version, printed below, that went into circulation on 1 March.

A COMPARATIVE ANALYSIS OF THE BRITISH PROJECT FOR A CLEARING UNION (C.U.) AND THE AMERICAN PROJECT FOR A STABILISATION FUND (S.F.)

1. *Interconvertibility of currencies*

In this respect the two schemes are identical in aim but the C.U. is stricter, since S.F. allows for exceptions both initially and subsequently. Cf. C.U. 39 with S.F. v, 2.

2. *Control over capital transfers*

Both schemes (C.U. VII and S.F. V, 2) provide for this. S.F. II, 5 may appear to be stricter than anything in C.U., but is, in fact, ineffective, because it confuses the gross remittances of a country and the net balance remaining to be cleared. S.F. II, 3(a) and 4 appear to mean that a country can never use its quota if it is making any capital payments whatever including settlement of its debts. How could this be worked in practice? The technique of control contemplated under S.F. is obscure. C.U. expects (C.U. 34) the submission of all exchange transactions to the prior scrutiny of an authority which is the only legal source and repository of foreign exchange. Does S.F. contemplate the same?

3. *Limits of financial assistance to debtor countries*

Both schemes establish a quota for each member country (C.U. 7(3) and S.F. I, 2). There is a suggestion (but no more) that the scale of quotas might be much smaller under S.F. than under C.U. Obviously this is a very fundamental matter. Under S.F. the aggregate of all quotas shall be 'the equivalent of at least $5 billion', of which the major part would probably belong to U.S.A., Russia, and United Kingdom. Under C.U. they might be more like $40 billion. In certain circumstances, however (S.F. II, 3(b)), a country may receive assistance in excess of its quota. Indeed it would seem that the quota under S.F. corresponds for most purposes to *half* the quota under C.U. It will be assumed below that this is the right comparison (e.g. in 8, 9 and 10 below).

4. *The formula for quotas*

C.U. (7(3)) fixes them by reference to the volume of foreign trade with special assessments where this is inappropriate, but adds that it is a matter for discussion whether the formula should also take account of other factors. S.F. (1, 3) is more indefinite—'the formula should give due weight to the important factors relevant to the determination of quotas, e.g. a country's holding of gold and foreign exchange, the magnitude of the fluctuations in its balance of international payments and its national income'. It is impossible to judge the effect of this until more details are filled in. *Prima facie* it would be proportionately not less favourable to Great Britain than the C.U. formula. The first criterion would work adversely to the other members of the sterling area unless they were allotted a notional share of the foreign exchange they have pooled with us, or unless their sterling balances are reckoned as a holding of foreign exchange. Generally speaking it would seem to give more assistance to those needing less and less assistance to those needing more. Nevertheless it would not be impossible to fill in the missing details in such a way that there might not be much to choose on balance between the two formulas. Certainly there is plenty of room for a compromise between the two as regards proportions, if the absolute amount under S.F. is substantially increased. Until the missing details are filled in none of the lesser powers will have sufficient means of estimating how they would stand under S.F.

5. *Provisions for changing quotas*

In S.F. (1, 3) the quotas appear to be fixed initially without any automatic provision for subsequent change, and the formula is of such a character that changing it would be difficult. Specific changes can be made by a four-fifths majority (S.F. 1, 6). In C.U. (7(3)) the quota changes *pari passu* with the volume of foreign trade. This has the great advantage that the volume of new international currency outstanding is a function of the volume of the trade which it is required to finance.

6. *Collateral against quotas*

C.U. requires no collateral except, at discretion, in the case of a member who has run heavily into debit (7(6)(*b*)). S.F. (1, 4) requires 50 per cent collateral for the start, but three-quarters of this (i.e. 87½ per cent of its quota) is in its own paper. 12½ per cent of its quota has to be covered by gold in the case of countries having substantial gold reserves, which may conceivably, but improbably, be increased subsequently to 25 per cent by a four-fifths majority (S.F. 1, 5). Most countries would have to put up only 5 to 7½ per cent of their quotas in gold. There would be no great difficulty in putting up these modest amounts. But there is no provision (not even in II, 7 as a means of acquiring a scarce currency or in S.F. IV, 8 to satisfy a member who withdraws) under which they serve any subsequent purpose of the scheme. These deposits appear to be flummery or fancy dress, to the wearing of which there could be no serious objection, if it is thought to look well. It might, however, be argued that to ape first the appearance of a gold standard and second the appearance of a capitalised bank will not be specially attractive to public opinion. What is the nature of the special reserve under S.F. II, 3(*c*)?

7. *The capacity of the schemes to satisfy the demands of members made against their quotas*

In C.U. there is no stipulated maximum to credit balances (C.U. 8) and therefore no limitation on the capacity of the Union to meet demands on it within the amount of members' quotas. Under S.F. the Fund is not necessarily in a position to honour its obligations, since its stock of the currency of a given country is limited to the amount of that country's quota. Indeed it is limited to *half* that country's quota unless *all* members agree hereafter to increase their contributions under S.F. 1, 5. The account of what happens, when a country's accumulated favourable balance, which has been financed through the Fund, exceeds its quota, is obscure (S.F. 11, 6 and 7). It is asked to give favourable consideration to proposals for remedying the situation. But there is no hint what form these proposals might take. On the other hand, the creditor country appears to be put into a hopeless position, and has but little choice except to make more of its currency available to the Fund by one means or another. For it is precluded, except with the approval of the other members of the Fund, from appreciating its exchange in terms of other currencies, or from making bilateral clearing arrangements (S.F. v, 4) or indeed from any other expedients which would enable it to continue exporting. Thus the only practical remedy available to a creditor country to prevent its assistance to the Fund from reaching its quota is to stop exporting or to lend otherwise than through the Fund or to withdraw from membership,—remedies, all of which are equally available to it under the C.U. The S.F. draft does not appear to realise that these difficulties all arise before the limit has been reached and as soon as the Fund imposes the rationing on the use of a scarce currency under S.F. 11, 7. The proposals for rationing seem unworkable. If, however, some sort of protection to a creditor country is thought to be sensible in itself or necessary for political reasons, we will reconsider suggestions hitherto rejected for limiting the liabilities of creditor countries to accept bancor.

8. *The rate at which quotas may be drawn upon*

The provisions of the two schemes (C.U. 7(6)(*a*) and S.F. 11, 3(*b*)) are substantially the same, but C.U. is somewhat stricter.

9. *The means of disciplining a debtor member*

The provisions of the two schemes (C.U. 7(6)(*b*) and S.F. 11, 3(*b*) and (*c*)) are substantially the same. The S.F. may seem stricter in that increases beyond the S.F. quota (corresponding to increases beyond half the C.U. quota) require the approval of the Board. But in effect this is also the case under C.U. 7(6)(*b*). The S.F. really is stricter in requiring the surrender of any new gold or foreign exchange (S.F. 11, 8) than C.U., which only requires it from heavily indebted countries (C.U. 7(6)(*b*)(iii)). The means of disciplining a creditor country is sadly lacking under S.F.

10. *Rates of interest charged under the schemes*

The charge on debtors under C.U. 7 comes into force sooner and more heavily than under S.F. 11, 3(*d*), being 1 per cent in excess of a quarter of the quota and 2 per cent in excess of a half, instead of what corresponds to 1 per cent in excess of a half under S.F. Under S.F. there are no provisions corresponding to the C.U. charges on credit balances (7(5)).

11. *The fixing of rates of exchange*

Under C.U. 7(2) these are fixed initially by agreement and cannot be changed subsequently except by agreement, with the qualifications that a debtor country is entitled to a 5 per cent depreciation (C.U. 7(6)(*a*)) and a creditor country is entitled to appreciate (C.U. 7(7)(*b*)). Under S.F. 11, 2, III, 2 and v, 1 the Fund fixes the rates unilaterally, and they can only be changed by a four-fifths majority. Thus in this respect there is a greater surrender of sovereignty under S.F. than under C.U., and the rigidity is very excessive.

12. *Exchange dealings*

The C.U. presumes that member countries will operate an official monopoly of exchange transactions. Under S.F. this seems to be implied in—

II, 8—returns of initial exchange holdings of members.

II, 7—rationing of currencies in short supply.

II, 2—pegged exchange rates.

II, 3—the prevention and (II, 5) the facilitation of capital transfers.

V, 4—bilateral foreign exchange clearing arrangements.

But remnants of a free exchange market appear to be implied by—

II, 2—'To fix the rates at which it will buy and sell one member's currency for another.'

II, 8—'agrees to discourage accumulation of foreign balances by its nationals', and 'privately held foreign balances'.

V, 1—fluctuation of exchange rates within certain limits.

The question what happens when a currency becomes scarce is much affected by the answer to the above.

13. *The position of gold*

C.U. 7(8) guarantees a market for gold. S.F. II (8) gives the Fund an option to reject an offer of gold. It does not require members to accept gold. Neither the Union nor the Fund is under an obligation to supply gold in any circumstances. Does S.F. II (8) apply to newly mined gold, compelling the producing country to offer this to the Fund? The above is qualified, however, by S.F. III, 3, which is obscure and appears to bear no relationship to any other part of the scheme.

14. *Blocked balances*

The approach of the C.U. (35) to the question of blocked or semi-blocked balances in overseas ownership at the end of the war is very tentative. S.F. (II, 9) deals with this question in a manner very liberal to the countries owing or owning such balances and makes its treatment of this a prominent part of its proposals. II, 9 of S.F. would be exceedingly helpful to Great Britain but could be grafted without difficulty on the C.U. Indeed these proposals fit the general framework of the C.U. much better than that of the S.F. For the size of the balances to be handled is disproportionate to the indicated size of the normal quotas, and the proposal to make them liquid would greatly increase the risk that the Fund would soon run short of scarce currencies. The definition of what is a blocked balance needs care since there would be an incentive to declare all balances to be blocked on these terms. Should not the phrase be abnormal war balances?

15. *Earning power*

The C.U.'s sources of income are the charges on excess debit and credit balances under 7(5) and 'a small commission' on transactions under 7(4). The S.F. has more extended powers of earning income, namely—

(*a*) the interest on the securities in which 25 per cent (and ultimately 50 per cent) of the quotas is paid under I, 4, which is a charge on all members alike in proportion to their quotas;

(*b*) the interest charges on excess quotas under II, 3(*d*);

(*c*) payments in respect of blocked balances under II, 9(*d*);

(*d*) interest on the investment of blocked balances under II, 9(i);

(*e*) interest on investments of currencies under II, 13;

(*f*) interest on loans under II, 14 (this is an obscure clause, the object of which is not clear);

(*g*) the service charge on transactions under II, 15.

There may also be other sources of earnings appropriate to a bank for the S.F. is authorised to function very much on the lines of a central bank. Half the profits in any year are then returned to the members in proportion to their quotas under IV, 9(*b*). Thus, for example, the interest payable in proportion to quotas under 1, 4 is, in all probability, handed back again under IV, 9(*b*).

16. *The position of non-members*

Under the C.U. non-members can hold credit balances (7(15)) but cannot receive overdraft facilities. Under the S.F. the currencies of non-members can be held for sixty days (II, 10) but not for longer except with a four-fifths approval. This is verbally inconsistent with II, 16, and it is not stated what happens to the currencies after sixty days if approval is refused.

17. *Voting power*

Voting power under the C.U. is governed by the same formula as quotas (7(10)). This is also the case under the S.F. except that the voting power is weighted to a certain extent in favour of the lesser powers (IV, 1). It is impossible to say how this would work out in practice under the S.F. until both the formula for quotas and the absolute amount of the quotas have been disclosed. There is a further qualification under the S.F. by which no one country shall have more than one-fourth of the voting power. Since most decisions of importance under the S.F. require a four-fifths favourable vote, this means that if the formula is so worked that one power, e.g. the U.S.A., reaches the maximum of one-quarter of the voting power, it will have a *liberum veto* over all significant decisions. On the other hand, it would not have any positive power corresponding to this negative authority, so that in most controversial matters the initial set-up would have

223

to remain unaltered, even though the dissenting minority is no more than one-fifth. Under the C.U., on the other hand, all action permissible under the charter is settled by a straight majority, subject only to a minor qualification under 7(10).

18. *Management*

Under the C.U. all member-States are represented individually in the Assembly (7(16)) and elect the Governing Board of 12 or 15 by proportional representation on the basis of their voting power. Under the S.F. (IV, 1) all member-States are represented individually on the Board of Directors and elect an Executive Committee of not less than 11 on the basis of their voting power. Under the S.F. the Board cannot establish regulations governing the operations of the Fund except by a four-fifths vote (IV, 6). The location of the Head Office under the C.U. is in London and New York. Under the S.F. this is not stated.

19. *Statistics*

C.U. 7(12) and S.F. V, 6 are substantially the same.

20. *The trade cycle and expansionism*

There are no provisions in the S.F. for handling the trade cycle and promoting expansionism corresponding to those which are to be found *passim* in the C.U. (see particularly 41(5)).

21. *Outside activities*

There are no facilities under the S.F. for the collaboration with other international bodies provided for in the C.U. in paragraph 41.

22. *More generally*

The most fundamental difference between the two schemes is rightly indicated in their titles. The American ideas take shape in a Stabilisation Fund with a 'limited liability' subscription, whereas the Bancor proposals aim at an International Clearing with a wide use of credit. The following consequences follow, amongst others:–

	Unitas		*Bancor*
1.	Initial quotas levied by way of a general subscription of capital.	1.	Initial quotas provided by a creation of international credit.
2.	Quotas represent a right to purchase the currencies of other members.	2.	Quotas represent a claim to overdraw on international account.
3.	Presumption that individuals remain free to deal in exchange with one another for 'current account' purposes.	3.	Requirement that exchange transactions be centralised with the Clearing Bank through national controls.
4.	Control over capital movements in principle, but in practice by *ex post facto* use of correctives.	4.	Control over capital movements implying prior scrutiny of all transactions and preventive action.
5.	Sanctions provided against the weaker party.	5.	Correctives deliberately applied (at least partially) to the stronger party.
6.	General intention to share a small part of existing foreign resources, but to stop short of expansion, whether general or particular.	6.	General intention to be 'expansionist'.

225

23. *Conclusion*

Nevertheless, when a conclusion has been reached which alternatives are preferable on the matters analysed above where there is a difference of substance between the two proposals, the final results can be dressed up in terms of the language and general set-up of either plan, according to taste. From the practical point of view the most important questions under the S.F. are the nature of the provisions for exchange control, the adequacy of the quotas and the workability of the proposed solution for dealing with scarce currencies.

On looking at these notes and the White scheme, R. F. Harrod wrote to Keynes.

From R. F. HARROD, *2 March 1943*

Dear Maynard,

I have been reading your notes on the S.F. with great interest. I have only just had the opportunity of seeing the two documents this evening. I agree with most of what you say save in your comment on 7 (on S.F. 7) and in your last sentence of 9.

Here I find myself in disagreement with your tone and nuance. You point out that S.F. 7 creates difficulties for the credit countries, are on the whole disparaging, but suggest we might in certain circumstances make concessions to the American point of view.

I submit on the other hand that S.F. 7 is most highly advantageous for us and gives us what we should never have dared to ask for or hoped to get.

It embraces two possibilities. One, only lightly touched on, is that the credit country would provide extra emergency credit when its quota was exhausted. This does not seem to be looked on with much favour by them. It might be argued that this is none the less how the thing would work out in practice. If that were so, we should be in exactly the same position as under the C.U.

The other possibility, the main one presented, is a rationing of the scarce currency (We need not bother about the proposals seeming 'unworkable'; something could no doubt be worked out). Under this there are two alternatives. Either free dealing in foreign exchange would be allowed and

226

the scarce currency would go to a premium in the free market. Or other countries would have to ration purchases from the scarce currency country. Either of these alternatives give us a more favorable solution than the proposals of the C.U. The wording of the last sentence of 7 indicates that it is the latter they have in mind.

The main objective of an expansionist policy aiming at the maximum of trade is to secure that the tendency of certain countries to build up large credit positions does not compel other countries to deflate or raise trade barriers. Either of the alternatives set out in the last paragraph would protect the debtor countries from this more adequately than the C.U. proposals. Either appreciation of the particular credit country's currency in the free market, if any, or the rationing of purchases from it would deflect purchasing power from the market of that country to the market of other foreign countries or the home market. No deflation or general protection in the debit countries would be required. There would, if purchases were rationed, be discrimination against a particular country, but this would be discrimination according to an orderly and agreed plan, and confined to the occasions where it was really justified.

The cardinal point is that the Americans offer us in this what we could never have asked of them in the negotiations especially after signing Article VII, namely that we (and other countries) should be allowed to discriminate against American goods if dollars are running short.

It is definitely better than the C.U. proposal. I think we agreed that under the proposal there was always the danger—in my judgement a very threatening one—that some countries would build up such large credit positions that the general run of debit countries would in due course exceed their quotas and that thus the general system would break down. Under the American system the check imposed on the countries tending to excess credit safeguards the debit countries. It means that the situation could not arise in which general run of debit countries tended to exceed their quotas. Some might of course do so—but to these we want in any case to apply special correctives. Indeed the American plan provides a mechanism, which we never succeeded in finding, for automatically sorting out what in some of my earlier notes I called 'excess' debit countries from the general run of debit countries. This is itself is an advantage in their scheme.

It is no discredit, if I may say so, to the author of the C.U. that he did not find this satisfactory solution. The Americans have happily played a card which according to the rules of the game we could not play.

I infer from all this that our main object from now on should be to hold the Americans to S.F. 7. How this had better be done, in terms of tact and tactics, I will not presume to say. Clearly we must not underline the difficulties (e.g. about rationing) but on the contrary do our utmost to find a way out of them. We must not raise objections to any part of S.F. which is logically linked to S.F. 7.

It seems to me that if we can hold Americans to S.F. 7, the main battle of long range economic planning is thereby won. This is the crucial point. All the other points are of comparatively small importance.

I should like to suggest that a cable ought to be sent to Phillips and anyone else involved in discussions formal or informal on this paper stating explicitly that from now on our main object should be to hold the Americans to the principles of S.F. 7.

Yours

ROY

Harrod's letter and the following notes from D. H. Robertson, led to further discussions.

From D. H. ROBERTSON, *3 March 1943*

C.U. and S.F.

Lord Keynes's comments dated 1.3.43.

(1) I agree in being unable to make sense of the para. in question.

(2) See (11) below.

(3) I do not follow this criticism. S.F. seems to me quite self-consistent. Suppose we want in a given month to cover a current adverse balance with U.S.A. of $20m. and also to repay $5m. of R.F.C. loan. S.F. 11, 3 (a) says we can get the $20m. from the Fund, and S.F. 11, 5 says we also stand a chance of getting the $5m. If the Fund refuses us the $5m., it is still open to us to find it out of any balances or gold we possess, without prejudicing our right to get the $20m. from the Fund.

(4) Surely it is not true that C.U. assumes either complete control of capital movements or a monopoly of exchange dealings on the part of every Member State. The penultimate sentence of §34 explicitly denies this.

Again surely it is not true that a Member State (whether or not exercising a monopoly of exchange dealings) can keep important holdings of foreign exchange outside the Clearing Union. The first section of §26 explicitly denies *this*!

(5) Yes.

(6) Not a *right*, but might, when scratching round for dollars (S.F. top of p. 3) find some country (e.g. India) which would sell it some dollars for gold.

(7) I think S.F. 11(8) makes better sense than is admitted. In the case supposed, i.e. if we had acquired some $ and wanted to keep them, we should be allowed to keep them if they were not 'scarce', but if they *were* scarce should have to turn them in and accept a ration. But it might quite well happen that we had acquired some $ but wanted Swiss francs. §8 then binds us to effect the exchange through the Fund instead of doing a direct deal with some country which has Swiss francs and wants dollars. This seems to me—given the whole scheme—as a reasonable and intelligible provision for encouraging 'multilaterability'.

(11) Last but not least

As Lord Keynes's suggestions bring out, it is really a technical flaw in both plans that they attempt to make the same 'quota', transmogrified in various ways, serve as a yardstick both for a country's borrowing rights and for its lending duties. There is no real logic about this, but it is probably too late to go back on it. This being so, the proposal to allow a country which thinks itself more likely to be a creditor than a debtor to opt for having a sub-standard quota may be the best way out.

It could be a great advantage if we could stop at this, avoiding both (*a*) the complexities (*b*) the pessimistic emphasis on withdrawal-rights–*alias* breakdown—contained in the draft amendment of C.U. §7(7). But I agree (*b*) may be necessary for Congressional reasons. As regards (*a*) everything of course depends on how far we can rely on American intentions as regards direct lending outside the Union. Can the reply in 909 to question (2) perhaps be regarded as sufficiently encouraging to warrant us in going a step backwards towards our original standpoint, which was one not of cajoling creditors into holding bancor balances but of actually rapping them on the knuckles for doing so? If so, we could dispense with the complexity of the credit-quota.

D. H. R.

To R. F. HARROD, *4 March 1943*

My dear Roy,

Your letter of March 2nd about S.F. and C.U. gives food for thought. I will take the points in order. To begin with, there is the first possibility you refer to, by which countries start with limited liability with the suggestion that perhaps they will provide extra emergency credit when their initial quota is exhausted. I have never been so strongly opposed to this method of approach as some others have. The argument raised against it, which is a strong one, is that it introduces from the outset an uncertainty concerning the value and convertibility of bancor which would prejudice confidence in the system. A good deal depends, of course, on how large the initial quota is. If it is large enough, I myself feel that I am not obdurately opposed to the principle of limited liability.

Take next the other possibility. Your first alternative here is, I think, ruled out by S.F. v, 1, whereby all members bind themselves to maintain the parity of exchange. There remains, therefore, the second alternative of your second possibility, namely, the one to which you attach importance and regard as playing into our hands.

I agree that, read literally, the interpretation you give to this is the only one which makes any sense. Perhaps I ought to have attached more importance to it. I interpreted it as a half-baked suggestion, not fully thought through, which was certain to be dropped as soon as its full consequences were appreciated. I cannot imagine that the State Department really would put forward as their own solution the rationing of purchases from a scarce currency country. You must remember that the evidence as to the extent to which the State Department have actually accepted this document of Harry White's is somewhat flimsy. I should expect that the moment emphatic attention was drawn to this alternative, it would be withdrawn.

Nonetheless, I agree with you that it needs careful consideration and good handling. I will see that this is brought to Phillips's attention. But I should hesitate, as at present advised, to make the assumption that this alternative is really open to us as the basis of our future policy and instruction to Phillips.

Yours,

K

From D. H. ROBERTSON, *5 March 1943*

C.U. & S.F.

Harrod's interesting letter says more lucidly and uncompromisingly what I was fumbling after, viz. that on the face of it the limitation of liability sought by S.F. is quite consistent with the original idea of C.U., which was *not* to find a way of unlimited borrowing on short term from the Americans (though Roy himself tried to pervert it in this direction!), but to find a way of pitching the Americans *off* short-term lending into long-term lending, important expansion, raising of money income etc. etc.

You may be right in suspecting that they don't quite realise what they have now said, but I think this line of thought is well worth following up.

D. H. R.

From R. F. HARROD, *6 March 1943*

Dear Maynard,

Many thanks for your letter of March 4. I appreciate your point about the probability that the Americans may run out if the State Department has yet not appreciated the full consequences of the proposal. I rather guessed it was what you would say!

On the other hand the State Department has in public utterances shown itself alive to the troubles caused to the rest of the world by the persistent U.S. credit position in the thirties. They must be well aware of the internal obstacles to radical tariff reduction. It is just possible that they are prepared to make an honest attempt to solve this problem on lines that they can get across at home. It would probably be easier for them to launch this rather complicated currency plan than a very drastic tariff reduction plan. Instead of having to present a highbrow economic argument to Congress in favour of free-er trade they could in the last resort use an honest to God type of argument—Well, they cannot buy our goods if they have not the money to pay for them, can they?

However,—even if that is too optimistic a view—I understand that this document has been or is being circulated to the United Nations. They cannot very well behave as though they had never made the proposal. If they show signs of running out, we can ask them what they intend to put in its place.

I suggest that the line we ought to take is that we assumed the rationing of scarce currency to be indissolubly linked to the limited credit quota proposal. We can point out that the latter is quite unworkable without the safety valve of rationing. We ought not to discuss limited credit as something which might stand on its own feet or can be considered on its own merits

231

apart from rationing (or something similar). Then if they are determined to wriggle out of rationing, they would be thrown back onto the unlimited credit of the C.U. But it is just possible that they will feel the rationing, though it really puts them into more of a pickle, easier to launch at home than unlimited liability. I think that the limited credit+rationing is vastly better for us than unlimited credit, unless you could also have unlimited debit, which we have not asked for, and has obvious objections.

We can argue that the scarce currency trouble is not likely to arise (*a*) if they make the initial quota large—this argument could be used as a leverage for getting them to enlarge it—and (*b*) if there are satisfactory arrangements for longer-term lending. Above all, anyhow, do not let us frighten them off rationing either by saying that it is almost bound to occur in practice or that we should find it hard to work.

I lay particular stress on the importance of linking limited credit quotas and rationing as two aspects of one proposal.

Yours,

ROY

P.S. Even if the Americans do retract I feel that we are in a stronger position than we were before. The door will be open to us later on, if we wish, to make our own proposals for discrimination (always provided that it is to proceed on agreed lines within the framework of a broad multilateral system) without being accused of ratting from Article 7. They have established the precedent.

To R. F. HARROD, *8 March 1943*

Dear Roy,

C.U. and S.F.

From the tactical point of view a lot to be said for what you put forward in your letter of March 6th. I am sending Phillips a copy of our correspondence.

Yours,

J. M. K.

Meanwhile, the Government had decided to issue the Clearing Union proposals as a White Paper and told the Americans this. Initially, the President declined Mr Morgenthau's suggestion that the Americans use the occasion to publish their proposals. However, after *The Financial News* in London carried a summary of the White Plan on 5 April, the President rescinded the decision not to publish. The same day, Mr Morgenthau communicated a slightly revised version of the draft, commented on by Keynes in March, to Congress. This was published in Washington on 7 April, the same day that Parliament received the Clearing Union White Paper.

The April 1943 Clearing Union White Paper, in addition to having a preface evolved from a Keynes suggestion of 22 February, contained several revisions of the November 1942 draft. These changes, where substantial, are dealt with in Appendix 3. The preface appears below.

From Cmd. 6437, Proposals for an International Clearing Union, 7 April 1943

PROPOSALS FOR AN INTERNATIONAL CLEARING UNION

Preface

Immediately after the war all countries who have been engaged will be concerned with the pressure of relief and urgent reconstruction. The transition out of this into the normal world of the future cannot be wisely effected unless we know into what we are moving. It is therefore not too soon to consider what is to come after. In the field of national activity occupied by production, trade and finance, both the nature of the problem and the experience of the period between the wars suggest four main lines of approach:

1. The mechanism of currency and exchange;

2. The framework of a commercial policy regulating the conditions for the exchange of goods, tariffs, preferences, subsidies, import regulations and the like;

3. The orderly conduct of production, distribution and price of primary products so as to protect both producers and consumers from the loss and risk for which the extravagant fluctuations of market conditions have been responsible in recent times;

233

4. Investment aid, both medium and long term, for the countries whose economic development needs assistance from outside.

If the principles of these measures and the form of the institutions to give effect to them can be settled in advance, in order that they may be in operation when the need arises, it is possible that taken together they may help the world to control the ebb and flow of the tides of economic activity which have, in the past, destroyed security of livelihood and endangered international peace.

All these matters will need to be handled in due course. The proposal that follows relates only to the mechanism of currency and exchange in international trading. It appears on the whole convenient to give it priority, because some general conclusions have to be reached under this head before much progress can be made with the other topics.

In preparing these proposals care has been taken to regard certain conditions, which the groundwork of an international economic system to be set up after the war should satisfy, if it is to prove durable:

(i) There should be the least possible interference with internal national policies, and the plan should not wander from the international *terrain*. Since such policies may have important repercussions on international relations, they cannot be left out of account. Nevertheless in the realm of internal policy the authority of the Governing Board of the proposed institution should be limited to recommendations, or at the most to imposing conditions for the more extended enjoyment of the facilities which the institution offers.

(ii) The technique of the plan must be capable of application, irrespective of the type and principle of government and economic policy existing in the prospective member states.

(iii) The management of the institution must be genuinely international without preponderant power of veto or enforcement to any country or group; and the rights and privileges of the smaller countries must be safeguarded.

(iv) Some qualification of the right to act at pleasure is required by any agreement or treaty between nations. But in order that such arrangements may be fully voluntary so long as they last and terminable when they have become irksome, provision must be made for voiding the obligation at due notice. If many member states were to take advantage of this, the plan would have broken down. But if they are free to escape from its provisions if necessary they may be the more willing to go on accepting them.

(v) The plan must operate not only to the general advantage but also to the individual advantage of each of the participants, and must not require a special economic or financial sacrifice from certain countries. No participant must be asked to do or offer anything which is not to his own true long-term interest.

It must be emphasised that it is not for the Clearing Union to assume the burden of long-term lending which is the proper task of some other institution. It is also necessary for it to have means of restraining improvident borrowers. But the Clearing Union must also seek to discourage creditor countries from leaving unused large liquid balances which ought to be devoted to some positive purpose. For excessive credit balances necessarily create excessive debit balances for some other party. In recognising that the creditor as well as the debtor may be responsible for a want of balance, the proposed institution would be breaking new ground.

Publication of the White Paper brought Keynes a large volume of correspondence. From this correspondence three letters are of interest. First Gerald Shove[12] wrote.

[12] Gerald Frank Shove (1888–1947) economist; Lecturer in Economics, Cambridge, 1923–45; Reader 1945–7; Fellow of King's College, 1926–47.

From G. SHOVE, *8 April 1943*

Dear Maynard,

The 'Keynes Plan' is masterly. It combines the clarity of Mill, the ingenuity of Ricardo and the wisdom of Marshall.

Yours,

GERALD

Second, Keynes received a letter from Sir Edward Peacock. On this Keynes noted, before passing it around the Treasury, 'There are not many opinions that I would rather have than Peacock's for wisdom and sageness on a matter of this kind'.

From a letter from SIR EDWARD PEACOCK, *21 April 1943*

Having read you and Harry White and the observations of various people upon the Plans, and having thought a little about it, I venture to say to you that your Report seems to me to be a great charter. If we could adopt it we should have put the coping stone upon our monetary machinery. No doubt we shall be prevented from going so far, but one day we shall have it all and the document will stand as a witness of your foresight and knowledge and skill.

Finally, Lord Catto added his views.

From LORD CATTO, *30 April 1943*

My dear Keynes,

Now that it has been published, I want to congratulate you on your Clearing Union.

I have avoided adding myself to the critics. I felt sure your basic principles were sound and unalterable. I was content to let others, with greater theoretical knowledge than I have, do the criticising. As I expected, the final document does not differ at all in essentials (nor much even in detail) from your very early drafts which I was privileged to see and, if I may say so, to encourage.

In my view, such changes as may be necessary in the future in order to reach international harmony, cannot materially affect the basic principles or your main outline of the needed structure. If such a plan can be started with goodwill and worked as designed by its architect, I see no reason why it should not be entirely practical in its operation. At this stage that is perhaps the only aspect of it on which I feel competent to venture an opinion.

But I have one anxiety! That is the timing. You seem to share this, judging by paragraphs 41 and 42 of the White Paper. Whilst the world is trying to right itself in the early period of changeover from war to peace, there will be vast and abnormal trade movements and great and quickly changing international monetary swings. Consideration will have to be given as to whether the automatic controls of the Clearing Union will be sufficient to guide these exceptional monetary changes of the early post-war period. It would be a tragedy if these put a strain on it which it was not designed to bear. It is likely, therefore, that, at the beginning, it will be essential to maintain much of the wartime methods of control of our international trade and monetary affairs; or at any rate some combinations of them and the Clearing Union. Much will depend upon conditions and relationships—particularly with America—when the time comes, but it will all require a lot of patient and tactful timing.

Yours ever,
CATTO

Chapter 3

FROM WHITE PAPER TO JOINT STATEMENT
APRIL 1943 TO APRIL 1944

With the publication of the proposals for the Clearing Union and the Stabilisation Fund, and the prospect of further talks, discussion centred to a considerable extent on the meaning of the American proposals. Soon after publication, D. D. Braham, a leader writer on *The Times* wrote to Keynes, thanking him for a briefing and stating that he had found the American proposals 'very difficult to disentangle'. 'From one passage', he continued, 'it looks as if they actually proposed in certain cases to limit and ration American exports. Surely they can hardly mean this, for it would provoke a storm of protest by American manufacturers and even from American labour.'

Keynes replied

To D. D. BRAHAM, *12 April 1943*

My dear Braham,

Thanks for your letter of April 9th, and particularly for your leader, which took just the right line, I thought.

In your letter you have, of course, touched the spot so far as the American proposals are concerned. The main question is whether that peculiar passage to which you refer is or is not to be believed and taken seriously. It is, of course, absolutely essential to the logic of the scheme. For under the American plan clearly a currency can become scarce, and some answer must be produced to the question what one then does about it. The answer actually given is the rationing proposal to which you call attention. Some people here believe that this is to be taken seriously and is far and away the most valuable and important part of their proposal, inasmuch as it throws the burden on the creditor country to the maximum extent. The other view, which I am a little inclined to share,

238

is that only the author of the scheme has perceived that passage, and that it has slipped through others concerned without their grasping its significance. But if it really is a proposal to limit and ration American exports, it is, of course, of the highest significance. But, as you rightly question, can it really mean this? Has the State Department appreciated the meaning of what they are putting forward? So far there is no comment from the American press indicating that anyone has tumbled to the importance of this passage. But, of course, as one might have supposed, the whole interest seems to be in the least significant issues, namely, the exact disposal of the voting power and the exact position of gold.

Yours sincerely,
[copy initialled] K.

The 'scarce currency clause' also came up frequently as Keynes and Sir Frederick Phillips kept each other informed of developments.

To SIR FREDERICK PHILLIPS, *16 April 1943*

My dear Phillips,

For some time I have been meaning to send you a substantial letter on Clearing Union and Stabilisation Fund. But the state of the mails is very discouraging to correspondence. That and a great deal of pressure over one thing or another has made me put off from day to day. Meanwhile you will be hearing the latest news from Dennis Robertson. But, all the same, I should like to try to put down on paper my own up-to-date state of mind. I do not feel I have a real clue to *your* general feeling about the present state of the negotiations. Is it all truly unsatisfactory and in danger of getting confused and utterly bogged down? Or is it just a case of the mills of God grind slowly?

1. *The European Allies.* Over here the principal new feature

239

is, of course, the attitude of the European Allies. It is fair to say that all of them without exception, not only prefer the Clearing Union, but prefer it very strongly, and for what I, at any rate, would regard as sound, fundamental reasons. After all, there are several reasons why S.F. in its present form cannot look too attractive to a smallish country. Moreover they appreciate the genuinely international and fundamental character of C.U. They are extremely perplexed how to tackle the Americans about it and several of them have been round to ask our advice. Our general suggestion to them has been that, whilst letting the American Treasury know quite definitely how much they prefer C.U., they should avoid controversy or advocacy at this stage, should probe the White plan with questions rather than objections, and should urge that it ought not to be too difficult to find a means of harmonising the plans if a general conference of experts could be called together for the purpose.

If only they can be brave enough, we feel that nothing could be better than for the Europeans to make the running for us for the next few weeks on the above lines. I wonder what attitude Gutt[1] and the Dutchman de Jongh,[2] who are, I think, already on your side, are actually taking. They went off full of good intentions from our point of view. The Dutch in particular are, of course, in a position to be highly independent in a matter of this kind. In two or three weeks Baranski[3] will be going across on behalf of the Poles, and Mládek[4] for the Czechs and also, I rather think, Varvaressos[5] for the

[1] Camille Gutt (1884–1971), Belgian Minister of Finance, 1934, 1939–45; Minister of National Defence, 1940–42, of Communications, 1940–42, of Economic Affairs, 1940–45; Minister of State and Managing Director of International Monetary Fund, 1946–51.

[2] D. Crene de Jongh, President of the Board for the Netherlands Indies, delegate at Bretton Woods Conference, 1944.

[3] Leon Baránski, Director-General, Bank of Poland; delegate at Bretton Woods, 1944.

[4] Jan Mládek, Ministry of Finance, Czechoslovakia; Deputy Chairman, Czech Delegation to Bretton Woods Conference, 1944.

[5] Kyriakos Varvaressos, Governor of the Bank of Greece; Ambassador Extraordinary for Economic and Financial Matters; Chairman, Greek Delegation to Bretton Woods Conference, 1944.

Greeks. I may be giving some or all of these letters of introduction to you, and you might find it worth while to keep
in touch with them. All those I have named are exceptionally
able and fully comprehending the issues. Old Baranski talks
in a voice and accent that makes one lose the thread unless
one attends carefully. But in fact he is well worth listening
to. There is no Allied representative, I think, whose observations go so deep as his. As you may have gathered, the Poles
and the Czechs are working in close collaboration, and
similarly the Belgians and the Dutch.

2. *Press comments.* You will be getting about the same time
as this letter our first batch of press cuttings, from which you
will see that there has been no significant criticism and almost
universal approval. No sign of hostility can be detected here
in any quarter. Our knowledge of American press comment
is so far rather scrappy. Nothing has reached us yet from any
critic whom one could describe as expert or influential. It is
depressing that so much attention has been concentrated on
voting. It never crossed my mind that we were under an
accusation of having tried to rig this. Indeed, so little attention
was paid to it that we had not even examined how it would
work out in practice. Some of the American press comments
dealing with this as a branch of power politics is, in its way,
an extraordinary exhibition of vulgarity. Fortunately this, as
I indicate in the enclosure, is a matter on which it ought to
be exceedingly easy, not only to compromise, but to accept
the American formula (I am speaking here of the proportionate voting power, not of the requirement for a four-fifths
majority).

3. *The immediate programme.* For the time being a certain
interval for opinions to crystallise will do no harm. There is
likely to be a debate in the House of Commons in the week
beginning May 10th, and a debate in the House of Lords in
the week following that. Is there, do you think, any good
purpose in further bilateral conversations between ourselves
and U.S. except to elucidate matters of doubtful interpret-

ation? So far, asking questions does not seem to have led to much in the crucial cases. Have they ever answered the question you asked them as to what interpretation we were to place on the proposal to ration scarce currencies? There are some other important points of doubt still outstanding, as indicated in the enclosed.

Should we not now aim at a general conference between all concerned to hammer things out and reach some compromise, say, in June? With the Europeans and the Dominions in sympathy with us, our position should be much stronger in a general than in a bilateral discussion. If only we could persuade the Americans that London is a better climate than Washington in summer! But I suppose that is hopeless.

4. *The underlying tactics.* Personally I have been quite conscious that we were in a sense propagating for the Harry White plan by pressing the Clearing Union in the way we have, but that there was no harm in that. Indeed quite the contrary. After all, the Harry White Plan is not a firm offer. The real risk is that there will be no plan at all and that Congress will run away from their own proposal. No harm, therefore, at least so it seems to me, if the Americans work up a certain amount of patriotic fervour for their own version. Much can be done in detail hereafter to improve it. The great thing at this stage is that they should get thoroughly committed to there being *some* plan; or, what is perhaps another way of saying the same thing, that their public should get thoroughly used to the idea that some such plan is inevitable.

Isn't it a very good thing, for the same kind of reason, that we have got to the point of publishing the two plans? If in fact we had managed to reach a compromise behind the scenes, isn't it about ten to one that Congress would have turned it down? The present tactics allow steam to be blown off at an early stage without injury to anyone. We must get over our teething troubles in public. We must know the worst, if there is a worst, about Congress at an early stage, and then gradually accustom everyone to the whole thing. So, in spite of grumbling, I do not really feel at all discontented at the general course things have been taking.

5. *The time and mode of compromise.* Our feeling here is that it is very important not to discuss compromises until the right time arrives, and that this decidedly is not yet. But, obviously, there is plenty of room for compromise in due course. The result of recent discussions and criticisms has been to make me at least rather clearer in my own mind what the substantial points are and where we could give way without serious injury. So, for your private eye, I attach to this letter an up-to-date analysis, as I see it, and would very much appreciate any comments from you on this.

6. *International investment.* Is there any news whatever about a possible American project on the subject of international investment? In your letter of 8 January you gave me very mild encouragement for the idea of producing for Harry White some amendments of the scheme he left with us last year. I have not in fact acted on this. Is he showing any sign of life in the matter? The other day I suggested to the Dutch that possibly they might like to take the initiative. I feel confident that we should not. But some of the European Allies are taking very strongly the line that neither C.U. nor S.F. is complete without an international investment organisation, and they are a little reluctant to pass finally on the currency proposals until they know a little more about what is intended on the investment field.

Yours ever,
[copy initialled] K.

P.S. I attach a cutting from last night's *Evening Standard*. Send it to Morgy with your (or my) compliments—if you dare!

Keynes's enclosure ran as follows.

NOTES ON C.U. AND S.F.

1. *Voting power.* It would be of no importance if we were to be reduced to (say) 10 per cent voting rights, if that is what it would come to under their formula, instead of 15 per cent or whatever it works out at under our formula. Indeed, we were so little interested in this that we never calculated just what it would work out at. The important question is whether four-fifths majority should be required for all major matters. I do not see why we should not give way completely to the American point of view on the question of the formula covering our proportionate vote, if they yield on the provision requiring a four-fifths majority.

The compromise might take the following form. There is no reason of principle against the quotas for voting being different from the overdraft quotas or, under S.F., the subscription quotas. We do not yet know what the U.S. formula is. When we do know what it is, I should have thought it exceedingly likely that we could accept it out of hand as governing quotas for voting purposes. This is an issue on which we can be handsome and accept whatever proportion they think it right to suggest.

On the four-fifths majority issue we might compromise by requiring (say) a three-quarters majority (I hope not as much as four-fifths) for certain specified questions, whilst allowing all usual matters within the charter of the institution to be settled by a plain majority.

2. *Gold.* Criticisms in the press seem greatly to exaggerate the distinction between the two schemes in their treatment of gold. I do not see much significant difference except that under S.F. there is no provision for changing the gold value of unitas. Possibly this is one of the matters where a decision by a three-quarters majority might be conceded. Indeed, I rather think that our own original draft required the agreement of all the founder states to a change in the gold

value of bancor. On the other hand, if a change in the gold value of bancor can only be effected by a large majority, there should be a power to the institution to refuse to accept gold if the gold holdings come to exceed some specified amount.

There is, of course, the distinction that there is a two-way convertibility between unitas and gold. As it is, this has no significance, since unitas seems to serve no purpose. If unitas were brought to life as is suggested below, then this might become a significant difference between the two schemes. But, in that event, it is difficult to see how the gold-convertibility of unitas could be maintained.

3. *Multilateral clearing.* I mean by this, speaking in S.F. terms, that any one currency can be used to purchase from the Fund any other currency at the par of exchange. All sorts of difficulties obviously arise if this is not permitted. For there is no security of multilateral clearing. Is it intentional or accidental that S.F. is drafted so as not to provide a certainty of multilateral clearing? S.F. III, 4 is so drafted that a member can only purchase foreign exchange from the Fund *with its local currency.* In 8 it can offer the Fund foreign currencies in exchange for other foreign currencies it requires, but the Fund is under no obligation to agree to the transaction. It would be quite easy to re-write 4 so as to provide that a country can purchase any one currency with any other. In fact it is not so drafted. In our early comments we did not sufficiently stress this peculiarity of S.F. It goes very deep and is perhaps not so easily met by a re-draft as would appear on the surface.

4. *The scale of quotas.* Loveday's table here is interesting. It suggests that our 75 per cent of imports *plus* exports is a bit on the high side. Two-thirds might perhaps be nearer the right figure than three-quarters. In a comparison between this and the $5 billion of S.F. a good deal depends on whether the $5 billion is intended to cover the whole world or only the United Nations. It also depends on the inter-

pretation of S.F. III, 3 B. The Fund starts off with an amount of a country's currency equal to 12·5 per cent of its quota. It also has 25 per cent of that country's quota in that country's securities. Does 3 B mean that in the first year a country can sell to the Fund an amount of its own currency equal to 87½ per cent of its quota (i.e. its quota diminished by the 12·5 per cent which the Fund already holds in that country's currency), the uncalled portion of the quota being left out of account and also that part which is subscribed in bonds and not currency. If so, the effective borrowing quota of a member is very nearly double its so-called quota. So that $5 billion, from the debtor's point of view, is equivalent to nearly $10 billion under C.U. It will be helpful to know if this is the right calculation. If so, $10 billion of S.F. quota might be not inadequate from the debtor's point of view. On the other hand, though from the debtor's point of view the effective quota may be double the nominal quota, this is not the case in regard to the creditor. This makes a straightforward comparison difficult. An S.F. quota of $10 billion would give a very narrow margin for creditors compared with C.U., which is unlimited in this respect, or even if C.U. were modified to limit a creditor's liability to his quota. Nevertheless, I should hesitate to say that an increase of S.F. to $10 billion might not be enough for a start, even if the U.S. share of this remained at $2 billion. The fundamental difficulty would be with the S.F. set-up that the rights of debtor countries to acquire particular creditor currencies might be far in excess of the capacity of the Fund to furnish such currencies.

All this part of S.F. is very confusing and difficult to understand until it is further elucidated.

5. *Abnormal war balances.* The obscurity here is the answer to the question what the country selling abnormal war balances sells them for. If it is allowed to sell them for any currency it chooses, it will naturally select those most likely

to become scarce. Therefore, unless the safeguard in J is introduced, there might be a terrific drain from the very outset on the Fund's stock of potentially scarce currencies. The right way of drafting all this would seem to be that, when a country owning an abnormal war balance in foreign currency needs to use some of it to meet a current deficit in another currency, it should be allowed to release and use the currency in question after the manner proposed before making use of its own quota rights to acquire the currency it needs. This, I think, would be a considerable improvement.

On the other hand, is it possible that the abnormal war balances are sold for unitas? The draft has an appearance as though originally this was the intention, but when some such provision disappeared, nothing was put in its place. This would be impracticable, of course, if the provision is retained by which unitas is exchangeable for gold. But, if unitas was given a one-way convertibility only, this would seem to be the right solution. As soon as members can acquire unitas other than for gold and the unitas so acquired is not convertible into gold, we are moving half way towards C.U.

6. *The rationing of scarce currencies.* We are still in the dark as to what this really means. There are those (e.g. Roy Harrod) who argue that this is a splendid, comprehending gesture by U.S.A. to throw the whole burden on the shoulders of the creditor where it should properly lie, and that it is deliberately intended to bring Congress and exporters right up against it, as soon as more than a modest favourable balance of trade has developed. I find it difficult to take up so buoyant an attitude. It seems to me that at the most Harry White has put a quick one across the State Department and that the real significance of this provision has escaped notice. I have not heard of any American press comment on the matter. But over here I have had a letter from the leader-writer of *The Times* enquiring whether he can safely trust his eyes when he

reads this passage which is on the face of it contrary to all that the State Department holds dear.

What is the true interpretation? Without this provision the logic of the whole scheme breaks down, and it would be very difficult to concoct a working alternative.

7. *Subscribed capital versus banking principle.* Further reflection convinces me that this is the most fundamental issue and the one on which we should be slowest to compromise. *In practice*, no doubt, S.F. could be brought to work very much like C.U. if the quota were large enough. Nevertheless, the difference here goes very deep when one looks to the future; and the disadvantages of a change-over more dangerous and far-reaching than may appear at first sight. This is also the view of the Europeans. If we could hold firm on the banking principle, we might compromise freely on everything else. For one thing, the linking up with other international institutions would be difficult, if not impossible, on the subscribed capital basis.

KEYNES

16.4.43

From SIR FREDERICK PHILLIPS, *22 April 1943*

My dear Keynes,

In reply to your letter of the 16th it is difficult to be optimistic at present as to the future of post-war planning. As I have warned London half-a-dozen times, the control of the Administration over Congress has become feeble. If that meant only that Congress had to be separately convinced, after the Administration had been convinced, it would be a considerable handicap since in the very nature of things a legislative body must always find it difficult to reach a common view on technical and detailed proposals. But if the situation has gone past this stage so that prejudice is aroused against a plan because it is pressed by the Administration the difficulty in making progress becomes very great.

Quite recently the Treasury introduced a purely routine bill to obtain statutory sanction for an increase in the total of the national debt beyond the limit previously established by law. This necessary legislation, by the addition of a rider, was made the opportunity of Congress over-ruling the President's decision on a totally different subject, viz. the limitation of individual incomes. Another routine bill introduced by the Treasury to extend for two years the present Stabilisation Fund and the power of the President, within certain limits, to alter the gold value of the dollar is faring no better. As soon as it got to the Senate Committee strong objection was taken to extending the President's power to alter the value of the dollar and that part of the bill was cut out. The Administration seem to have accepted this rebuff but the policy of turning the other cheek was not a success. As soon as the bill got before the House of Representatives Committee they proceeded to cut out the power to extend the life of the Stabilisation Fund. As the House is now at variance with the Senate there will be another opportunity of bringing up this matter, but the incident is significant. The one victory which the Administration has gained was the defeat of what is known as the 'Ruml Tax Plan' by a narrow majority on fairly strict party lines. This, however, was a case where the Administration wished to defeat proposals obnoxious to them, and it has helped them not at all in getting forward their own tax programme. It will be interesting to see whether the State Department have better success in carrying their bill for extending the period of the trade agreements. Cordell Hull and his whole department have made tremendous efforts but even so it seems a little unlikely that they will get the bill in the form in which they introduced it.

The dilemma is that without cordial acceptance by the Administration post-war plans would be stillborn but the fact of that cordial acceptance may itself prove something of a handicap. It is to be hoped that the divorce of the legislative and executive functions prescribed by the American Constitution may not prove a decisive obstacle to a reasonable post-war settlement.

2. These remarks refer to post-war planning generally, and not to monetary plans alone. So far as the press and the public are concerned, I believe that on the whole no harm, and possibly some good, was done by the publication of the two divergent plans. It encourages people to believe that there is something in the idea and that there should be a plan of some sort. I am taking on all occasions the line that the two plans are different versions of one alternative, the other alternative being the absence of a plan at all, and a return to the chaos which prevailed in monetary relations during the period between the two wars.

It is very difficult to make out any definite Congressional reaction to the two plans. It is unlikely that Congress would show any special love for the Harry White plan because it is put up by the U.S. Treasury. Their instinctive reaction to that would be a desire to rewrite the whole thing themselves. Nevertheless, the fact that Morgenthau has praised the principle of the American veto will, of course, make it more difficult to get through Congress a plan which does not contain that feature.

As I say the public reaction to the two plans has not been unfavourable; it might easily have been much worse. But I do not see the prospect of so strong a public feeling as to influence the actions of Congress. In this connection the position taken by the Federal Reserve Board is of some importance. I hear from all sides that they do not like the C.U. plan and I suspect that their attitude to the S.F. plan is not really different. What their own ideas may be has not been revealed.

The first steps being to secure agreement with the Administration and then with the United Nations, these reflections on what Congress might do may seem to you premature. However, doubts and fears as to Congressional reactions will very much colour the attitude of the Administration.

3. I have seen Crene de Jongh but not Gutt, and will talk to the other European Allies as they come. Crene de Jongh will, I think, do very well though he is a bit too much inclined to grumble at the fact that the United Nations were not presented with a joint scheme.

I am seeing the Canadian experts (Rasminsky and Mackintosh) tomorrow. The Australians have sent over Coombs,[6] whom I have also seen. Under the influence of Dr. Evatt[7] they are taking the line that, before any plan at all is considered, it must be laid down in advance that the primary duty of every country is to raise its own employment and production to the maximum by its own efforts. They will not get far with the Americans on this. Close has told me privately that Smuts[8] will be mainly influenced by the consideration—which plan seems to offer the more secure future for gold?

4. As regards our own contacts with the Americans the position has changed considerably. There was an official announcement that the Treasury, though consulting others, would be expected to 'carry the ball', and the State Department are lying very low.

I think, therefore, I shall go to Morgenthau in future, and not to Berle.

[6] Herbert Cole Coombs (b. 1906); Assistant Economist, Commonwealth Bank of Australia, 1935; Economist to Commonwealth Treasury, 1939; Director-General, Post-War Reconstruction, 1943; delegate, Bretton Woods Conference, 1944; Governor, Commonwealth Bank of Australia, 1949–60, Chairman, 1951–60; Governor and Chairman, Reserve Bank of Australia, 1960–68.
[7] Herbert Vere Evatt (1894–1965); Attorney-General and Minister for External Affairs, Australia, 1941–9; Prime Minister of Australia, 1946–9.
[8] Jan Christian Smuts (1870–1950); Prime Minister of South Africa, 1919–24, 1939–48.

The decision when we should go and put further questions presents some little difficulty. I am inclined to wait to ascertain how the Canadians get on but shall probably be asking for instructions before long.

5. There is no news whatever about a possible American project on the subject of international investment and I doubt if we shall hear more until they have got further with the S.F. plan. There is, of course, no harm in the European Allies pressing the point.

6. You speak of a general conference between all concerned, say in June. I feel quite sure there will not be a general conference before the fall when the weather in Washington is excellent. A conference summoned at the present juncture might last as long as the Council of Trent, without arriving at the degree of unanimity among the majority faction which the Council of Trent succeeded in obtaining.

The real question is, how we arrive at some adjustment between our views and the American views, which is an essential preliminary to any conference. I do not think it will be much use raising this before the Americans have gauged the weather from their discussions with the itinerant experts. I have reason to believe that Ilsley did make some tentative suggestion to Morgenthau for private tripartite talks between British, American and Canadian experts, but that this idea did not find favour. However, something of this kind seems to me likely to prove the least inconvenient method of proceeding, and the attempt might be renewed somewhat later.

7. As regards the nature of a compromise, my tentative observations are as follows:-

(a) *Quotas.* I should be reluctant to say that we will accept the American view because we do not know what that view really is and there is no assurance that, even if we did accept it, other countries would not object. It seems to me the simplest solution is this: that the quotas and voting power should be based on (i) foreign trade statistics and (ii) gold holdings. Since foreign trade statistics would give a ratio, roughly; U.K. 5—U.S. 4, and gold holding statistics would give a ratio of, roughly: U.K. 1—U.S. 20, any desired result can be produced from these criteria. It may even be that voting power could be divorced from quotas, though I am not too sure this would be very acceptable.

(b) As regards gold, I cannot make out that the S.F. plan would produce any change in the *status quo*. The danger of the *status quo* is that there is only one ultimate buyer for new gold. No doubt a number of countries would very much like to accumulate large stocks of gold, but they cannot do that with any satisfaction to themselves unless they have a sufficiently large and persistent favourable balance of payments. The situation has been saved so far by the fact that the one country with a persistently large and stable favourable balance of payments has been willing to buy any gold offered. The danger is that a unilateral decision by that country against buying more gold would upset the whole system in the absence of alternative buyers.

The Clearing Union plan does not make much change in the *status quo*, but it does make a little. The Clearing Union itself comes in as an additional buyer under an obligation to buy gold from member states. It also has the right to distribute its gold holding if it become excessive, among countries with creditor balances, so that none of them could shirk an obligation to buy some of the gold. It would not be in the power of any single country to upset the system unless it were willing at the same time to break up the Clearing Union.

(*c*) As regards multilateral clearing, I think it is of the essence of the S.F. plan that the fund cannot be *compelled* to supply France, say, with dollars against sterling even though it is compelled to supply France with dollars against francs.

(*d*) I will write further on scale of quotas, abnormal war balances, and the rationing of scarce currencies.

(*e*) As regards subscribed capital versus the bank principle, all that you say is very true, but you do not meet the point of the simple-minded American citizen who has gathered vaguely that it is a question of issuing more international currency and who is shocked at the idea of a currency without any gold backing at all. It occurs to me that if we were to make a ruling that all countries must keep X per cent of their gold reserve in the Central Fund, the Central Fund would then have at its disposal X per cent of 25 billions of gold. Also, it would have this amount at its disposal for good, since gold payments between members would not affect the total. The difficulty is to think what on earth the Central Body could do with such a fund other than putting it in a new hole in the ground. However, if we think hard enough, perhaps some use may occur to us.

Yours sincerely,

F. PHILLIPS

P.S. I enclose the debate on the question of discontinuing the present Stabilisation Fund which you will find very interesting. They were not expressing hostility to international plans; they were expressing very decided hostility to the President and Morgenthau committing the United States to plans without specific Congressional assent.

From SIR FREDERICK PHILLIPS, *29 April 1943*

My dear Keynes,

I meant to have sent you a lengthy supplement to mine of the 22nd but find that after all I have not very much to write about.

Reverting, however, to the passage in the enclosure to your letter of the 16th about *multilateral clearing*, the fact is that the Americans have always regarded it as an essential feature of their plan that a country requiring foreign currency must buy that currency with its own.

I do not, however, agree with your criticism that this means that there is no security of multilateral clearing. It seems to me merely silly. Suppose there are three countries—the United States, Canada, and the United Kingdom—and that Canada has a favourable balance of 150 with the United Kingdom, but an unfavourable balance of 50 with the United States. It is open to the United Kingdom to demand 150 Canadian dollars from the fund for sterling and it is open to Canada to demand 50 United States dollars from the fund for Canadian dollars. Thus Canada has in fact used 50 of her favourable balance with the United Kingdom to discharge her unfavourable balance with the United States. This is multilateral clearing. The criticism of the suggested American rule is then that it is pointless.

As regards the scale of quotas, the Canadians were putting some questions on this but I have not heard the result. I will let you know shortly if they got anything of value on this or on the rationing of scarce currencies. I propose to raise the question of abnormal war balances myself when I see the Treasury.

As I have reported by cable it appears that the U.S. Treasury had in mind the possibility that bonds subscribed in payment of initial capital might be made salable in any country. This whole part of the subject seems to have got into a mess and I think it is not unlikely they will drop the idea of subscriptions in the form of securities.

The Canadian experts told me that one of the difficulties they anticipated as regards acceptance of the Clearing Union, is that financing by overdraft is 'not regarded as respectable' in the United States, it being the practice of banks to demand and businesses to give securities when seeking loans.

Yours sincerely,

F. PHILLIPS

To SIR FREDERICK PHILLIPS, *4 May 1943*

My dear Phillips,

By a miracle your letter of 22 April arrived here on the 28th, so that I got a reply to mine of the 16th within 12 days. If only it was always so!

I enclose a further analysis of the Stabilisation Fund, which I made over the Easter holiday, and also a covering note, for eventual rather than immediate use, of the principal change which seems to me will be necessary to bring the ideas of C.U. and S.F. into reasonable harmony. You will see that I have deliberately had the questions set out on a separate sheet from the covering note. At the same time Waley was working at the same subject, and I enclose a copy of his note.[9] To a small extent the two overlap, but he to a larger extent than I is aiming at criticism and not merely analysis. Broadly speaking, there is nothing important in his note with which I do not agree.

Here, at any rate, is some material for questions or for criticism, whichever it is you are doing, if and when you do resume the conversations with Morgenthau. There still remains a good deal to elucidate merely on the basis of questions.

Turning to the observations in paragraph 7 of your letter:–

(*a*) *Quotas.* I do not see any serious objection to the quotas for voting power being different from the quotas for overdraft, accepting the American formula for the former and trying to get as near as possible to our formula for the latter. The Chancellor will be saying in the House next week that he attaches no particular importance to voting power and has no reason to suppose that the American formula, when he knows it, will not be reasonably acceptable to us, if it is to other people.

(*b*) My own feeling is that the difference between the two schemes in their treatment of gold is rather exaggerated. At

[9] Not printed [Ed.].

255

any rate, it would not be very difficult to bring them into harmony on this point. I cannot believe that the Americans really attach importance to an immutable value of gold, since their own legislation contemplates the contrary. I anticipate that in the debate in the House this is a point which will be fixed on. The Labour people are likely to attack S.F. as being a gold-bug scheme. No harm perhaps in our showing a certain amount of political feeling on the subject. But I find it difficult to believe that this is really going to be one of the ultimate difficulties.

(c) I am much interested that you regard the failure of S.F. to establish multilateral clearing as being of the essence of that plan. Surely that is a fatal objection. On the other hand, it does not seem to me to be of the essence in the sense that it could not be altered fairly easily without upsetting other features too much. However, I am not quite sure about that and would be interested to know your view.

(d) We are particularly anxious for some news about the rationing of scarce currencies.

(e) I very much like your suggested treatment of the gold reserve question. I see no objection to a formula on the line you indicate.

There is to be a debate on the Clearing Union in the House of Commons on May 12th occupying the whole day, and in the House of Lords on May 18th. On May 12th, the Chancellor opens the debate. I am seeing today in batches a number of Members who are likely to take part in the debate so as to see how far it is necessary or possible to influence the tone of the debate. What we shall try and impress on those taking part is that this is of high importance as the first step towards post-war international arrangements on the international scale and that everyone should emphasise the necessity of some plan securing the main objectives of the two alternatives at present before the House.

I have read the Congressional Record of April 21st with a very great deal of interest. This seems to me exceedingly

satisfactory. Not only were none of the Congressmen op-
posing the idea of there being some such international
scheme, but the whole debate seemed to be on the assumption
that, in due course, some such plan was desirable. All they
were doing was to emphasise the fact that it was Congress that
must have the last word so far as American participation is
concerned,—which, after all, is quite reasonable. Nor was
there any sign of encouraging any unduly competitive atmosphere in considering the two plans.

As you will have gathered from recent telegrams, our main
immediate perplexity is as to the future course of the
negotiations. We seem to have got into the sort of fluffy
muddle, of which only Morgy is capable. You will find that
the remaining Allies will be drifting across gradually. I fancy
Gutt may go any time. Tonight I am seeing Mládek, who is
leaving this week. I have not yet heard about Baranski's latest
plans. Dimovic, the Yugoslav, will probably be putting off for
two or three weeks. (Their available staff on the economic and
financial side is very small, and it is most difficult for him to
get away for more than a brief period. He is a highly
intelligent young man, who knows S.F. and C.U. inside out
better than anyone perhaps, though too often concentrated
on minor details.) Now the point, of course, is at what stage
and in what manner are S.F. and C.U. going to be brought
face to face? Phillimore's telegram from Rio, which was repeated to you as Washington No. 424, is a further confirmation that the rest of the world is likely to prefer C.U. to S.F.
I still favour the notion, as I think you do, that at some point
we should try to go into a huddle with Harry White in Ottawa,
in the hope of getting to grips. My ideal order of procedure
would be the following:–

(1) The completion of the present bilateral conversations
in Washington, coupled with the hope that the American
Treasury 'will gradually come to perceive the weight of
preference amongst the other participants.

(2) A huddle with Harry White in Ottawa, at which perhaps

I might join you, with a view to preparing for a more general conference,—something which could be represented as preparing the agenda and might, with luck, amount to something rather more constructive than that.

(3) A general conference on the expert level, on the basis of no Governments being committed, but aiming at preparing a report which the experts would submit to their various Governments.

(4) Assuming a sufficient measure of agreement has been reached, a meeting of Ministers to o.k. the results.

Before you get this letter you will have heard from Robbins the latest position about the Commodity Scheme and the discretion given you as to how and when this is transmitted to the Americans. It remains to be seen whether it will be convenient or possible to keep this in a completely separate compartment.

Yours,
[copy initialled] K.

Keynes's 'Easter holidays' note ran as follows.

THE STABILISATION FUND

The following is intended to be a more or less complete list of the questions which have to be answered before the working of the S.F. is intelligible.

The analysis involved in making this list brings out the three points following:

1. S.F., as it stands, makes no coherent sense.

2. The provision for a four-fifths majority does not turn out as serious as appears at first sight. A compromise here should not be difficult.

3. The great majority of the difficulties arise from not making unitas an effective international unit in the sense that

bancor is. If the Fund dealt only in terms of unitas, instead of dealing in dozens of different currencies, many of these difficulties would be resolved. Provisions such as the following would go a long way towards making intelligible sense of S.F., and without something of the sort it is difficult to see how to turn it into a consistent and significant plan—

(i) A country can obtain a deposit in terms of unitas in the following ways

(*a*) in exchange for the instalments of its quota subscription on the lines of S.F. II;

(*b*) by selling additional amounts of its currency to the Fund within the limitations of S.F. III, 3;

(*c*) in exchange for gold;

(*d*) by transfer from the unitas deposits of other members in exchange for the currencies of those members;

(*e*) under those provisions of S.F. which allow the Fund to conduct sundry banking operations.

(ii) A country holding the currency of another member can require that member to buy it back with unitas, so long as the latter has a unitas deposit or is in a position to obtain one unconditionally under S.F. III, 3.

(iii) A country cannot be required to accept unitas to an amount in excess of its quota, *plus* any unredeemed portion of its original subscription. (This provision is not strictly required, since a country is never *required* to accept unitas—it can always, if it prefers, retain the local currency it finds itself with.)

(iv) So long as a country has, or is entitled under S.F. III, 3 to, a unitas deposit, it shall agree to purchase its currency with unitas at a fixed parity of exchange which may not be altered without the approval of the Fund.

(v) The undertakings of S.F. VI about maintaining exchange stability and refraining from exchange restrictions cease to apply if a country's stock of unitas (actual and potential) is exhausted or if its stock exceeds its outstanding subscription by more than its quota.

It would not be difficult to modify S.F. in a way which would answer reasonably the other conundrums.

KEYNES

27.4.43

QUESTIONS RELATING TO THE STABILISATION FUND

II, 2 Can the formula now be supplied?

III, 1 In terms of what accounting unit are deposits accepted? If local currency is deposited, what can be done with it? How can the depositor use it? If foreign currency is deposited, can this only be withdrawn in terms of that same currency? If so, what is the point of depositing it? Presumably this clause is subject to VI, 2.

III, 2 Is the initial fixing of rates a unilateral act by the Fund? Does it require the assent of the member concerned? Is it correct that the initial rates require only a bare majority, but all subsequent changes a four-fifths majority? Does this mean in practice that we can never again change the dollar value of sterling without the assent of the U.S.? And that the U.S. can never change the value of the dollar in terms of sterling without our approval?

III, 3 This appears to apply, not if a country has an adverse balance with the members as a whole, but if it has an adverse balance on current account with the particular country whose currency is demanded. Is this intended? How is it ascertained? How are re-exports regarded? Cf. the wording in III, 4.

III, 3 B Do 'holdings' include (i) initial subscriptions under II, 4, (ii) subsequent subscriptions under II, 5, (iii) deposits under III, 1 made by the country in question or by other countries, (iv) currency acquired under III

(8), (v) currency acquired under III, 12, (vi) additional deliveries of currency under IV, 4, as well as deliveries under III, 4? Does 'currency' include or exclude securities expressed in that currency?

III, 3B If a country comes to an end of its drawing power on the Fund, does its undertaking under VI, 1 to maintain a stable rate of exchange lapse? If not, how does it implement this undertaking?

III, 3C Of what will this special reserve consist?

III, 4 What is the meaning of 'local currency'? Is it a central bank deposit?

III, 4 and 5 Do these clauses mean that a country which is repaying indebtedness, e.g. by a normal sinking fund, cannot use the Fund at all except by a four-fifths approval? I.e. a country can use the Fund normally, only if it would have an adverse balance on the assumption that it was not repaying any debt? In other words, is it a normal condition of using the facilities of the Fund that a country shall have defaulted on its sinking funds? In the absence of full exchange control, how is the existence of an adverse *current* balance ascertained? What is the period over which 'current' is calculated? Is the repayment of a three months' credit, a two years' credit, a five years' credit a 'current' transaction?

III, 6(*a*) Does this mean that a country is not under an obligation to supply its currency in exchange for gold except to the extent of its own initial contribution? Cf. IV, 3 below.

III, 7 What is the position of the exporters of a country whose currency is scarce? Does the undertaking to maintain stable rates of exchange lapse when a currency has become scarce?

III, 8 What happens if the offer is rejected? What, in this event, can the holder of an unwanted foreign currency do with it? Has multilateral clearing broken down?

III, 9 When the Fund buys blocked foreign balances, in terms of what does it pay for them?

III, 12 When the Fund sells obligations, in terms of what are they paid for?

IV, 3 Is there any means except the deposit of gold by which a unitas deposit can be created? What can the holder of a unitas deposit do with it? Can he buy with it any currency he desires? If not, is there any secured outlet for gold? There seems no provision except under this clause by which a country has a right to dispose of gold.

V, 1 A bare majority is enough except where otherwise provided. Is the following a correct summary of the effect of this?

The following matters are settled by a bare majority:
  (i)   initial exchange rates under III, 2;
  (ii)   recommendations to a debtor country under III, 3 (*b*) (i);
  (iii) recommendations to a debtor country under III, 6;
  (iv)   the apportionment of a scarce currency under III, 7;
  (v)   transactions under III, 8;
  (vi)   transactions under II, 1, 3, 12, 15;
  (vii) changes in the gold value of currencies under IV (2);
  (viii) declarations of default under V (8);
  (ix)   permission to a country to impose exchange restrictions under VI, 2;
  (x)   recommendations of measures to facilitate control over capital movements under VI, 3;
  (xi)   permission for bilateral exchange arrangements under VI, 4;

The following matters require a four-fifths majority:
  (i)   subsequent quota calls after the initial payment under II, 5;
  (ii)   changes in quotas under II, 6;
  (iii) subsequent changes in exchange rates under III (2);
  (iv)   the use of the Fund to facilitate capital transactions under III, 5;

    (v)   to hold non-member currencies under III, 10;

   (vi) transactions under III, 11, 13, 14;

  (vii) to make regulations under V, 6. (Thus, if there is a failure to make a general regulation because a four-fifths majority is not obtainable, nevertheless the same policy can be followed in any particular case by a bare majority.)

VI, 1 The maintenance of a stable exchange rate is a bilateral, not a unilateral, act. To what 'appropriate action' does the undertaking to maintain a stable dollar–sterling rate commit the U.S. and the U.K. respectively? Clearly it does not require gold convertibility. Presumably it does not require each country to hold the currency of the other without limit. Does it commit, e.g., U.K. to turn surplus sterling owned by U.S. into dollars, whenever the latter requests it, by buying dollars from the Fund? If so, what happens if the U.K. is not entitled to draw dollars from the Fund—as may happen for a variety of reasons, particularly because it is financing capital transactions or because dollars are scarce in the Fund?

VI, 1 Is it intended that fluctuations should be within such a range as the old gold-points? Or narrower? Or wider?

VI, 7 Does the undertaking 'to accept appropriate legislation to facilitate the activities of the Fund' involve accepting the Fund's recommendations, e.g. under II, 6? If the intention is more limited, could it be further defined?

To SIR FREDERICK PHILLIPS, *5 May 1943*

My dear Phillips,

Your letter of April 29th arrived just as my letter of May 4th was being sealed up. I thought it best not to delay that letter, in the hope that it might catch an earlier bag, and to reply to yours separately.

(1) I daresay you are right that the American provision

about multilateral clearing is pointless rather than objectionable. But it is not, I think, quite as simple as you suggest in
the third paragraph of your letter. Suppose Canada's favourable balance with the U.K. results in her holding sterling,
she cannot use that sterling to demand Canadian dollars from
the Fund. If she can compel us to demand it on her behalf,
then it comes to the same thing as you are saying. But there
is no clear provision in the Fund to that effect, unless it comes
under the general undertaking to preserve stable exchanges.
If instead of Canada you write Brazil, it seems to us that the
position of our owning Brazilian currency and having
ourselves the right to proffer them to the Fund, puts us in
a clear position, whereas the actual draft does not. If,
however, you are right as to its effect, clearly, as a matter of
drafting, it would be much simpler to require the Fund to
sell any currency for payment in any other. But why then
did you say in your letter of 22 April that you thought the
failure to provide for multilateral clearing was an essential
feature of S.F.?

(2) I am amused by your last paragraph about security
being necessary to make lending respectable. Of course, it is
exactly the opposite over here. But when, for the sake of
respectability, American business men give security, does it
take the form of their own I.O.U.? I should have thought not.
For that is what it amounts to under S.F.

(3) Mládek is expecting to leave to take part in the talks on
behalf of Czechoslovakia in the course of this week. I have
given him a letter of introduction, of which I enclose a carbon.
I rather think, though I am not sure, that Baranski for Poland
intends to turn up about the same time. In currency matters
the Poles and the Czechs are working in double harness and
have an agreement behind the scenes to say the same thing.
I understand that Gutt no longer intends to go to Washington
for Belgium and that Belgium will be represented by Boel,[10]

[10] Baron René Boel, Counsellor of the Belgian Government; delegate, Bretton
Woods Conference, 1944.

who does not intend to go over for about a fortnight. As I mentioned in my previous letter, the Yugoslav also is not leaving for about a fortnight. Thus, it will clearly be well into June before the bilateral conversations are complete, quite apart from South America. Is there any indication of Russia participating in them?

(4) I had a series of meetings yesterday with various M.P.'s of all parties, who are likely to take part in next week's debate. They showed, on the whole, a remarkable knowledge of the schemes, which they had been studying pretty closely. The danger is, I think that they might express too much open hostility to the American scheme, which is extremely unpopular in all quarters, more unpopular perhaps than it really deserves. I tried to impress on all of them the risk of excessive criticism leading to the whole thing being dropped, and I am hopeful that, when the debate comes, they will all take a tactful line. I was rather astonished at the strength of the feeling in favour of C.U. as against S.F. All those I met were enthusiastic for C.U. except perhaps Pethick-Lawrence, who is inclined to take the line that even that tends to tie us up too much. Left to himself, I think the old chap would like us to keep a completely free hand. He made it plain, of course, that he vastly preferred C.U. to S.F., but wondered whether C.U. did not itself go too far in tying us to stable exchanges, etc.

(5) You may like to have an early copy of the enclosed analysis in this week's *Economist*. I do not know why they thought it necessary to print the misleading first paragraph. They could, by asking, have learnt enough about the real facts to have made them not wish to express it just in this way. I also enclose this month's *Socialist Commentary* to show you the way in which the rather left Left is approaching it.

I had lunch yesterday with a collection of bank managers brought together by Mr Sidney Parkes, General Manager of Lloyds. Their attitude was much the same as the M.P.s', liking C.U. and very strongly critical of S.F. I have also had a note from Peacock to the same effect. It is clear that, if one had wanted to get up a demonstration against S.F. in this country, nothing would have been easier.

Yours,

[copy not initialled]

P.S. I am seeing to-night Varvaressos, who is expecting to go over next week to represent Greece. He is a very able old chap. The Greeks work more or less with the Poles and Czechs, but more independently. Vavaressos is a strong C.U. adherent but very much scared of crossing the Americans.

I have just heard from Keilhau[11] that he will be going in a week or two as head of the Norwegian delegation. He is a very old friend of mine, but at heart an old-fashioned *laissez-faire* economist, who hates planning of any kind. I shall be seeing him before he goes, but have not yet discussed Clearing Union with him. I should expect him to dislike both C.U. and S.F. but to dislike S.F. more. However, we shall see.

I enclose our print of S.F. in case a copy has not reached you.

In mid-April, Keynes asked R. F. Harrod to speak on the two schemes at the Annual Meeting of the Royal Economic Society. Harrod replied.

From R. F. HARROD, *14 April 1943*

My dear Maynard,

I quite agree with what you say. I did not mean to press my idea, but only to offer it in case you get into a difficulty about speakers on the other subject and were in embarrassment.

I don't quite understand how you can want me to speak on the C.U. and the S.F. You do not presumably want a lot of pious generalities which would be unworthy of the Royal Economic Society. If I were to say what is really in my mind it would be as follows:–

[11] Wilhelm Keilhau (d. 1974); economist; Director, Bank of Norway; Chairman, Norwegian delegation, Bretton Woods Conference, 1944.

1. The C.U. is an admirable scheme as far as it goes, but it is not a complete scheme and would be liable to break down unless buttressed by a really effective scheme for getting sufficient foreign investment.

2. It would also be desirable to supplement S.F. by a foreign investment scheme. But, unlike ours, it is technically self-supporting and would continue to function even without such a supplement.

3. The reason why we did not and could not put up a technically complete scheme was that it would not have been tactful for us to put up something so awkward for credit countries and might have exposed us to the charge of ratting from Art. VII about which it was known that we were uneasy.

4. The American scheme would ease our problems much more effectively than our own.

5. It might appear to follow that we should close with the American scheme (while pressing for certain modifications such as more elastic foreign exchange relations and larger quotas). The reason for not doing so is that we are not yet sure if the Americans would stand by it or even appreciate its full implications. We are like a bridge player who does not double three hearts, tho' quite confident of victory in that suit, for fear of frightening his opponent into three spades.

Now really would that be suitable? You yourself said in an earlier letter that the situation required 'good handling'. It may be that the press will have already attained the above degree of lucidity before the meeting. But I doubt it.

That is why I don't think the subject a good one for the R.E.S. at all. I think that academic economists are bound to attain a higher degree of lucidity than the press, and in view of the need for 'good handling' the less public lucidity there is on this matter the better.

For me to speak would be particularly unfortunate—I hope I am not guilty of undue self importance. Suppose a U.S. press cutting agency presented a paragraph on these lines to the U.S. Treasury. They would probably know that in some obscure way I was 'advising' H.M.G.

Or again, suppose that the monetary conference was on and I was known to the P.M. to be fussing that some important telegram should be sent or stopped and that then his eye lit upon a newspaper in which I was reported making a speech so replete with indiscretion. What would he think of one?

That is, quite frankly, why I did not ask for leave to give the address. I could not ask for something which I myself felt to be so very wrong.

I do not know whether the five propositions listed above represent the views of the Treasury. I was rather disappointed the other day when I happened to fall into conversation with Bewley, whom I supposed to be fairly high up in the Treasury, and found that the idea that there was this favourable point in the American scheme was quite a new one to him.

Yours,
ROY

To R. F. HARROD, *27 April 1943*

My dear Roy,

I expect you are right not to take part in, or at any rate not to open, the C.U. discussion at the R.E.S.

Some of your points it would be very suitable to press, for example the importance of supplementing C.U. by a foreign investment scheme. But a good many of your other points seem to me more political than economic, and I think that those taking part in the discussion would find plenty of economic matters to raise without getting too much involved in political and diplomatic questions. However, we shall see. It will probably be much easier for someone who has been less immersed than you have been in the diplomatic side of the matter.

I fully expect that we shall do well to compromise with the American scheme and very likely accept their dress in the long run. But I am sure that it would be premature to do so at present. For one thing, their plan is very far from being a firm offer. The real risk, I always have thought, is that they will run away from their own plan, let alone ours. By continuing to press ours, there is at least a little chance that they may develop some patriotic fervour for their own. We have, by the way, no confirmation as yet from Phillips that it would be safe to take seriously the proposals for rationing scarce currencies, or that this part of the scheme has been understood or approved by the State Department.

Yours,
[copy initialled] J. M. K.

On 18 May Keynes made his maiden speech before the House of Lords.

From House of Lords Debates, *18 May 1943*

My Lords, I do not address you for the first time with any less trepidation because the subject of our discussion this afternoon is one with which I have become very familiar in recent months. But I rely on your Lordships' sustaining kindness to a newcomer. The proposals for an International Clearing Union have been brought before Parliament at an early but not too early a stage of their evolution. The procedure adopted is somewhat novel. I hope your Lordships will approve it for, if it is an innovation, it appears to me to be a happy one. This Paper has been the subject of long preparation. To associate it too closely with a particular name is, I venture to say, to do it an injustice. It has been the subject of intensive criticism, and progressive amendment and the final result is the embodiment of the collective wisdom of Whitehall and of experts and officials throughout the Commonwealth. At the same time, it has been brought to the judgment of Parliament and of the public opinion of the world before any final crystallization of ideas.

It seems to me to be far better that our own Treasury and the Treasury of the United States should have decided to seek wider counsels before concentrating on the preparation of an actual plan—much better that they should take this course than that, without open consultation with their Legislatures or with the other United Nations, they should have attempted to reach finality. The economic structure of the post-war world cannot be built in secret. Mrs Sidney Webb, whose recent loss we so greatly deplore, in my judgment the most remarkable woman of our time and generation, once defined democracy to me as a form of government the hall-mark of which was that it aimed to secure 'the consciousness of consent'. So in the new democracy of nations which after this war will come into existence, heaven helping, to conduct with amity and good sense the common concerns of mankind the instrumentalities we set up must first win for themselves a general consciousness of consent.

The first of these instrumentalities to be considered is before your Lordships' House this afternoon—at a season in our affairs on this day of national thanks-giving when we can feel entitled, and indeed are required, to look forward to what is to come after. It is, I hope, the first of several. Indeed, it cannot stand by itself. For it attempts to deal with one aspect only of the economic problem. Your Lordships will, I take it, this afternoon be concerned chiefly with the broad purpose and method of these proposals and not with technical details. The principal object can be explained in a single sentence: to provide that money earned by selling goods to one country can be spent on purchasing the products of any other country. In jargon, a system of multilateral clearing. In English, a universal currency valid for trade transactions in all the world. Everything else in the plan is ancillary to that. Serious tariff obstacles, though we may try to abate them, are likely to persist. But we may hope to get rid of the varied and complicated devices for blocking currencies and diverting or restricting trade which before the war were forced on many countries as a superimposed obstacle to commerce and prosperity.

Now this universal currency is essential to the healthy trade of any country, and not least to our own, for it is characteristic of our trade that the best markets for our goods are often different from our best sources of supply. We cannot hope to balance our trading account if the surpluses we earn in one country cannot be applied to meet our requirements in another country. We shall have a hard enough task to develop a sufficient volume of exports, but we shall have no hope of success if we cannot freely apply what we do earn from our exports wherever we may be selling them, to pay for whatever we buy wherever we may buy it. This plan provides for that facility without qualification. That is the main purpose. If, however, general facilities on these lines are to survive successfully for any length of time, it will be a necessary condition that there should be a supply of the new money proportional to the scale of the international trade which it has to carry; and, also, that every country in the world should stand possessed of a reasonable share of that currency proportional to its needs. The British plan proposes a formula intended to give effect to both those objects. There may be a better one, and we should keep an open mind, but the aim is clear.

It is not necessary in order to attain these ends that we should dispossess gold from its traditional use. It is enough to supplement and regulate the total supply of gold and of the new money taken together. The new money must not be freely convertible into gold, for that would require that gold reserves should be held against it, and we should be back where we were, but there is no reason why the new money should not be purchasable for gold. By such means we can avoid the many obvious difficulties and disadvantages of proposing that the old money, gold, should be demonetised. The plan proposes therefore what is conveniently described as a one-way convertibility. What shall we call the new money? Bancor? Unitas? Both of them in my opinion are rotten bad names but we racked our brains without success to find a better. A lover of compromise would suggest unitor, I suppose. Some of your Lordships are masters of language. I hope some noble Lord will have a better inspiration. What would your Lordships say to dolphin? A dolphin swims, like trade, from shore to shore. But the handsome beast also, I am afraid, also goes up and down, fluctuates, and that is not at all what we require. Or bezant? The name, as the Financial Secretary to the Treasury recently recalled in another place, of the last international coin we had—the gold unit of Byzantium. In the same line of thought Professor Brogan has recently suggested talent, named after a place which perhaps we shall soon be in a position to regard as at our service. So far every bright idea in turn has been turned down. I fancy that our Prime Minister and President Roosevelt could between them do better than most of us at this game, as at most other games, if they had the time to turn their minds to writing a new dictionary as well as a new geography.

The plan, as I have said, allots to every country an initial reserve. That is a once-for-all endowment. There is, therefore, a risk that the arrangements will break down because some improvident country runs through its stock of bancor and gold and has none left to meet its engagements. To provide against that is a very delicate matter, for it may seem to involve interference with a country's domestic policy. The plan provides in such case for consultation and advice. The country may be required to take certain specific measures. There remains in the background, if eventually unavoidable, the severe penalty of depriving the improvident country of any further facilities, which, after all, is the only effective remedy the private banker has, unless his client is actually fraudulent. It is most important to understand that the initial reserve provided by the Clearing Union is not intended as a means by which a country can regularly live beyond its income and which it can use up to import capital goods for which it cannot otherwise pay. Nor will it be advisable to exhaust this provision in meeting the relief and rehabilitation of countries devastated by war, thus diverting it from its real, permanent purpose. These requirements must be met by special remedies and other instrumentalities.

The margin of resources provided by the Clearing Union must be substantial, not so much for actual use as to relieve anxiety and the deflationary pressure which results from anxiety. This margin, though substantial, must be regarded solely as a reserve with which to meet temporary emergencies and to allow a breathing space. But the world's trading difficulties in the past have not always been due to the improvidence of debtor countries. They may be caused in a most acute form if a creditor country is constantly withdrawing international money from circulation and hoarding it, instead of putting it back again into circulation, thus refusing to spend its income from abroad either on goods for home consumption or on investment overseas. We have lately come to understand more clearly than before how employment and the creation of new incomes out of new production can only be maintained through the expenditure on goods and services of the income previously earned. This is equally true of home trade and of foreign trade. A foreign country equally can be the ultimate cause of unemployment by hoarding beyond the reasonable requirements of precaution. Our plan, therefore, must address itself to this problem also—and it is an even more delicate task since a creditor country is likely to be even more unwilling than a debtor country to suffer gladly outside interference or advice. In attempting to tackle this problem the British plan breaks new ground. Perhaps its approach may be open to criticism for being too tentative and mild; but this, I am afraid, may be inevitable until these things are better understood.

But at this point I draw your Lordships' attention to a striking feature of the proposals. Under the former gold standard, gold absorbed by a creditor country was wholly withdrawn from circulation. The present proposals avoid this by profiting from the experience of domestic banking. If an individual hoards his income, not in the shape of gold coins in his pockets or in his safe, but by keeping a bank deposit, this bank deposit is not withdrawn from circulation but provides his banker with the means of making loans to those who need them. Thus every act of hoarding, if it takes this form, itself provides the offsetting facilities for some other party, so that production and trade can continue. This technique will not prevent excessive hoarding from doing harm in the long run, since this may cause other countries to suffer the anxiety of a growing debit account which would eventually reach its permitted maximum. But a country which tends to hoard bancor beyond all reason will at any rate be exhibited before itself and before the whole world as the make-mischief of the piece; and will be under every motive of reason and of benevolence and of self-interest to take corrective measures. Nor, I fancy, will the hoarding of bancor prove as attractive or as plausible as the burying of gold seems to have been, if recent experience is a guide.

I turn now to an aspect of these proposals which has rightly caused considerable anxiety to well-judging critics. We set up a universal money; we make sure that its quantity shall be adequate; we share it out between the countries of the world in equitable amounts; we take what precaution we can against improvidence on the one hand and hoarding on the other. It is obvious that in this way we establish an immensely strong influence to expand the trade and wealth of the world, and to remove certain disastrous causes of inhibition and distress. But an obvious question arises. Are we doing this at the cost of returning, in effect, to the rigidity of the old gold standard, which fixed the external value of our national currency beyond our own control, perhaps at a figure which was out of proper relation to our wage policy and to our social policies generally?

The exchange value of sterling cannot remain constant, in terms of other currencies, unless our efficiency wages, and those other costs of production which depend on our social policy, are keeping strictly in step with the corresponding costs in other countries. And, obviously, to that we cannot pledge ourselves. I hope your Lordships will believe me when I say that there are few people less likely than I not to be on the look out against this danger. The British proposals nowhere envisage exchange rigidity. They provide that changes of more than a certain amount must not be made unless the actual state of trade demonstrates that they are required, and they provide further that changes, when made, must be made by agreement. Exchange rates necessarily affect two parties equally. Changes, therefore, should not be made by unilateral action. We do indeed commit ourselves to the assumption that the Governing Board of the Union will act reasonably in the general interest, and will adopt those courses which best preserve and restore the equilibrium of each country with the rest of the world. That is the least we can do, if any form of agreed international order is to be given a chance. But if, in the event, our trust should prove to be misplaced and our hopes mistaken, we can, nevertheless, escape from all obligations and recover our full freedom with a year's notice. I do not think that we can reasonably ask any completer safeguards than that.

There is another question which can very reasonably be asked: Are we winning one freedom at the cost of another? Shall we have to submit to exchange controls on individual transactions which would be unnecessary otherwise? In this respect the plan leaves each country to act as it thinks best in its own interests, and imposes nothing. Or, rather, the only condition which is imposed is that there shall be absolute freedom of exchange remittance for current trade transactions. In the control of capital movements, which is quite another matter, each country is left to be its own judge whether it deems this necessary. In our own case, I do not see how we can hope to avoid it. It is not merely a question of curbing exchange speculations and movements of hot money, or even of avoiding flights of capital due to political motives; though all these it is necessary to control. The need, in my judgment, is more fundamental. Unless the aggregate of the new investments which individuals are free to make overseas is kept within the amount which our favourable trade balance is capable of looking after, we lose control over the domestic rate of interest.

The Chancellor of the Exchequer has made it very clear

that the maintenance of a low rate of interest for gilt-edged loans is to be a vital part of our policy after the war as it has been during the war. For example, it is only if the rate of interest is kept down that the new housing we intend can be financed without excessive subsidy. But we cannot hope to control rates of interest at home if movements of capital moneys out of the country are unrestricted. If another country takes a different view of the necessities of the situation, it is free to do otherwise. The plan leaves each country to be the judge of its own needs. Those who are experienced in these matters advise that adequate control of capital movements should be possible without a postal censorship. I mention this to relieve a natural anxiety. Few of your Lordships, I expect, would stand for so gross as infringement on personal rights as a postal censorship in times of peace.

There is one important respect in which the British proposals seem to be gravely misunderstood in some quarters in the United States. There is no foundation whatever for the idea that the object of the proposals is to make the United States the milch cow of the world in general and of this country in particular. In fact the best hope for the lasting success of the plan is the precise contrary. The plan does not require the United States, or any other country, to put up a single dollar which they themselves choose or prefer to employ in any other way whatever. The essence of it is that if a country has a balance in its favour which it does not choose to use in buying goods or services or making overseas investment, this balance shall remain available to the Union —not permanently, but only for just so long as the country owning it chooses to leave it unemployed. That is not a burden on the creditor country. It is an extra facility to it, for it allows it to carry on its trade with the rest of the world unimpeded, whenever a time lag between earning and spending happens to suit its own convenience.

I cannot emphasise this too strongly. This is not a Red Cross philanthropic relief scheme, by which the rich countries come to the rescue of the poor. It is a piece of highly necessary business mechanism, which is at least as useful to the creditor as to the debtor. A man does not refuse to keep a banking account because his deposits will be employed by the banker to make advances to another person, provided always that he knows that his deposit is liquid, and that he can spend it himself whenever he wants to do so. Nor does he regard himself as a dispenser of charity whenever, to suit his own convenience, he refrains from drawing on his own bank balance. The United States of America, in my humble judgment, will have no excessive balance with the Clearing Union unless she has failed to solve her own problems by other means, and in this event the facilities of the Clearing Union will give her time to find other means, and meanwhile to carry on her export trade unhindered.

There are really only two contingences, in my opinion, which might lead the United States to accumulate a large balance of bancor—failure to maintain good employment at home, or a collapse of the enterprise and initiative required to invest her surplus resources abroad. Recent past history shows that in times of good employment in the United States her need for imports is so large, and her surplus of available exports so much reduced compared with other times, that a surplus in her favour does not develop; it is only if she ceases to require imports and is pressing her exports on the world that that situation arises. Why should our American friends start off by assuming so disastrous a breakdown of the economy of the United States? Moreover, if there are temporary difficulties which take time to solve, no one will gain more than a creditor if this maladjustment is prevented from starting a general slump, which eventually reaches, by repercussion, the creditor himself. I repeat that no one is asked to put up a single shilling except for so long as he has no other use for it. There is a significant difference, I suggest, between a liquid bank deposit which can be withdrawn at any time and a subscription to an institution's permanent capital.

The Motion of the noble Lord, Lord Barnby, relates to the proposals of the United States Treasury as well as to the British White Paper. Your Lordships will not expect me, nor would it be in place, to examine or criticise these proposals at any length, but there are a few remarks which I should like to make. The whole world owes to Mr Morgenthau and his chief assistant, Dr Harry White, a deep debt of gratitude for the initiative which they have taken. Public opinion on the other side of the Atlantic is not, I fancy, as well prepared as it is here for bold proposals of this kind, but that has not prevented the United States Treasury from putting forward proposals of great novelty and far-reaching importance. Most critics, in my judgment, have overstated the differences between the two plans, plans which are born of the same climate of opinion and which have identical purpose. It may be said with justice that the United States Treasury has tried to pour its new wine into what looks like an old bottle, whereas our bottle and its label are as contemporary as the contents; but the new wine is there all the same.

Some play, I notice, has been made with the idea that the voting power in the British proposal has been arranged in our own interest. Nothing, I can assure your Lordships, was further from our thoughts. The Chancellor of the Exchequer explained last week in the House of Commons that there is no reason to expect that the American formula, when it has been fully explained, will be unacceptable to us. Certainly to arrive at voting predominance by the use of a particular formula was neither an intention nor an essential part of our proposals. Again, the requirement in the American plan for a four-fifths majority will be found, if the paper is read carefully, to relate not to all matters by any means, but only to a few major issues. Whether on second thoughts any one would wish to allow a negative veto to any small group remains to be seen. For example, the American proposals might allow the gold-producing countries to prevent the United States from increasing the gold value of the dollar, even in circumstances where the deluge of gold was obviously becoming excessive; and in some ways, by reason of their greater rigidity, the American proposals would involve a somewhat greater surrender of national sovereignty than do our own.

The American plan requires the member states to provide so-called security against their overdrafts, a requirement which could certainly be met if it is thought useful; but the security in question only to a very small extent consists in an outside security in the shape of gold. It consists mainly of an I.O.U. engraved on superior notepaper, better than would be the case, perhaps, under our own scheme. I have said that, if that is thought useful and worth while, it does not involve any particular problem. The American scheme, again, sets a maximum to the liability of a creditor member to hold a credit balance, and there again that is a provision which is equally possible, if it is helpful, on either plan. But what happens when a creditor reaches his maximum is, in the American paper, somewhat obscure. I have not the slightest doubt in my own mind that a synthesis of the two schemes should be possible; but it does not seem advisable to atempt it until there has been time and opportunity to discover what the expert opinion of other nations and of all the world finds difficult or unacceptable in either scheme, and what it finds sensible and good. In the light of that opinion, the synthesis in due course should and must be attempted. I trust that your Lordships will wish the two Treasuries God-speed in their high enterprise. So ill did we fare in the years between the two wars for lack of such an instrument of international government as this that the resulting waste and dissipation of wealth was scarcely less than the economic cost of the wars themselves; whilst the frustration of men's efforts and the distortion of their life pattern have played no small part in preparing the soiled atmosphere in which the Nazis could thrive.

These Papers do not present a whole story, but only the first chapter. They do, however, make a start in framing a structure without which other measures cannot be well designed or fitted in. I would also suggest to those of your Lordships—and there are many—who have for years taken a particular interest in the evolution of international forms of government, that we here offer an essay of some importance in the new modes of international government in economic affairs, by means of which the future may be better ordered than the past. Neither plan conceals a selfish motive. The Treasuries of our two great nations have come before the world in these two Papers with a common purpose and with high hopes of a common plan. Here is a field where mere sound thinking may do something useful to ease the material burdens of the children of men.

When Sir Frederick Phillips, after a visit to Ottawa, reported to Keynes on Canadian views of the American plan, Keynes commented

To SIR FREDERICK PHILLIPS, *27 May 1943*

Dear Phillips,

THE CANADIAN VIEW OF S.F.

Your letter of May 20th arrived very promptly quite soon after your telegram. The general attitude of the Canadians seems not at all unsatisfactory,—much more to our liking than we feared it might be when we only had your telegram. Perhaps it would be useful for me to take your points in order:–

(1) I note that the Canadians are not at all disinclined to yield on the banking principle, though much preferring the

C.U. set-up. This seems to me rather a crucial question. One can yield on the question of asking security and on the question of limited liability to the creditor without yielding on the main structure. I should much prefer to make both the former concessions and yield on the main structure only in the last resort. While in a sense this is mainly a question of appearance, I fancy it comes to much more than that, if one looks forward into future developments and to the use of the Union for various general international purposes.

(2) The two proposals of the Canadians taken together about the size of the quota under S.F. seem to me to be adequate.[12]

(3) The Canadian interpretation of the scarce currency clause is most interesting. The reluctance of the Americans to discuss it seems to suggest that they are well aware of its implications but would like it to slip through with the least possible publicity. No reason why we should not conspire with them about this. But the question of what is meant by appropriate action by the other countries when a currency is scarce certainly needs clearing up. No doubt in practice the American intention will be that their own currency never should actually reach this position. And, if that is what they mean in practice, no harm perhaps in letting them have something in theory, if it helps them politically, even though it is, should it ever come into effect, impracticable and unsound.[13]

(4) The point about multilateral clearing: if the thing is to work out in practice as the Canadians say, why not draft it in this sense from the start? I am sure that this is a passage where a compromise should be extremely easy.[14]

[12] The suggested total was $68 billion, of which the U.S. share would be 30 per cent and the U.K. share 20 per cent.

[13] The Canadians took a view of the scarce currency clause approximating to R. F. Harrod's.

[14] The Canadians suggested that the drafting ambiguities in the American plan would not, except in the scarce currency case, affect multilateral clearing in practice.

(5) The question of limiting a country's right to demand Country X's currency to its adverse balance with X: Surely the Canadians are right about this. The American proposal is quite hopeless. But I do not see why they need hesitate to give it up.

(6) The same applies to the point about limiting the use of the Fund to adverse balance on income account. Surely this is impracticable.

(7) The Canadian view of exchange control seems only common sense.[15]

(8) I should not be surprised if the Canadians are right in thinking that the Americans will not persist too strongly in the four-fifths majority proposal. After all, this is double-edged and may have the effect of tying them up just as much as it ties up anyone else.

(9) The period of withdrawal under S.F. is two years; under C.U. it is one year. So we are already more liberal than the U.S. in this particular. Personally I do not dissent from the feeling of Towers and Rasminsky that there would be no practical objection to a much shorter period of notice than either of these periods.

(10) On the question of the gold element in the capital subscription, you do not say whether you tried on the Canadians your own proposal about bringing in the percentage of the country's gold reserve. I was rather attracted by that.

On all these, and also on various other points, I find it difficult to believe that a compromise is not fairly easy as soon as the softening process has gone on long enough and the Americans are prepared to compromise at all. But is it not necessary that the softening process should go on for quite a time yet and that they should become aware of the world-wide preference for C.U. before we begin to use up any of our compromise ammunition?

[15] The Canadians argued that scrutiny of all exchange dealings and controls on capital movements would be necessary from the start in both the U.S. and U.K. plans.

When the right time for a compromise really has arrived, my great perplexity is whether one should draft on the general S.F. model or on the C.U. model. Obviously it would be enormously easier to get it through if one drafts on the S.F. model and perhaps, therefore, one will come to this in the end. But my feeling is that this will in fact lose both practical advantage and the general good-will of the world, whilst being less educative and properly intelligible to the public to a greater extent than is easily calculated. Much may happen, of course, before we have to come to a final conclusion. Indeed, we may be dealing with different individuals. One of these days I will try my hand at drafts on both models. When one has actually made the draft it may be easier to judge how much one would lose by succumbing to the S.F. set-up.

Yours,
[copy initialled] K.

While further drafts of the White Plan (dated 8 May, 15 June, 26 June and 10 July) continued to reach London, the Americans began a long series of bilateral and group discussions in Washington with a number of countries including Britain. In addition, D. H. Robertson, then attached to the British Embassy in Washington, had a number of conversations with the American officials involved. As reports of these discussions reached London, Keynes commented to R. H. Brand.

From a letter to R. H. BRAND, *9 June 1943*

The future course of the discussion has two main aspects with which we are concerned. It does not seem possible to have very clear views about either of them. The first is the mode of procedure from now on. It is clear that practically the whole world, with only one or two insignificant exceptions, if there are any at all, prefers the general scheme of the Clearing Union to the Stabilisation Fund. We have now got the general reactions of the South Americans as well as of the

European Allies and the Dominions. If there were any means of reaching a democratic decision, there would, I think, be an overwhelming vote for proceeding to discuss a compromise on the general basis of C.U. Nearly all the countries concerned, however, are of course anxious that there should be some scheme and feel that the American is better than nothing, whilst, for obvious reasons, they are very timid about upsetting the American Treasury, from whom they have great expectations in more directions than one, by appearing critical. The Americans on their side are very cagey. They refuse to allow the Clearing Union to be mentioned even indirectly at any of the discussions which they are holding about S.F. The result is that the discussions which are taking place, if one is to judge by the reports which reach us, do not make much progress in getting to grips. Various desultory questions are asked, and unsatisfactory or inconclusive replies are given, and very often no reply at all, the question being reserved. So far as we can judge, the Canadians have been more successful than any other as interviewees in getting to grips, partly because they are not unduly nervous about how to handle the American Treasury and partly because they are exceptionally well informed on these matters.

The tactics of the American Treasury appear to be to avoid confronting S.F. with C.U. at any stage. Their idea is, I think, to pick up impressions and then produce a revised version of S.F. without ever allowing C.U. to come under serious discussion. I should doubt whether they can really be successful in that. It seems to me to be a tactic which only an inexperienced person could hope to bring to a satisfactory conclusion. At some time or other there will unavoidably have to be confrontation. That, of course, is what we want, but we are not inclined to hasten matters unduly. It looks as if it would be a good thing to allow the softening process to go on quite a bit longer, for however discreet the interviews of the various nations are, doubtless the real nature of the atmosphere will become clearly apparent in due course. When the time comes for a compromise or synthesis, it may be that it is the Canadians who, if they will work closely with us, will be in the best position to play a decisive part. But we should be extremely grateful to you, who are near the field of action, for any advice on these matters.

The second question will only arise when the confrontation takes place, namely, what the nature of the compromise ought to be. Our minds are, I think, getting a great deal clearer about this. For my own part I believe that the point I have emphasised on the first page of the enclosed memorandum is fundamental, namely, that we must have an effective international unit in terms of which transactions take place and which countries acquire the title to as a result of these transactions. If that is once established, the details can be better or worse, but the main character of the new institution will have been formed and established.

During the informal Washington discussions, Keynes carried on a discussion of the two plans with D. H. Robertson. This discussion had Keynes's notes of 27 April (above pp. 258–63) as its origin.

From D. H. ROBERTSON, *24 May 1943*

My dear Maynard,

C.U. and S.F.

I am confining this letter to three technical points.

(1) S.F. has been criticised as failing in multilaterality on the ground that it does not give (say) the Bank of England an unequivocal right to obtain dollars from the Fund in exchange for an excess holding of francs. Is not C.U., as it stands, open to an exactly analogous criticism? So far as I can discover, it contains no provision giving the Bank of England a right to turn francs into bancor.

As I understand it, under C.U. the Bank of England will be normally collecting francs from some of its nationals in exchange for sterling, and dishing out francs to others of them in exchange for sterling. The Bank of France will normally be acting in a corresponding manner towards its own nationals. Each of them will consequently be normally in possession of a working balance in the other's currency. Now suppose the balance of payments between England and France is favourable to England. Whether this situation shows itself in (1) a shrinkage of the B. of F.'s sterling balance or (2) a growth of the B. of E.'s franc balance depends on the nature of the transactions between the two countries, in particular on whether the goods which are the subject of trade are invoiced in (1) sterling or (2) francs. In case (1) the B. of F. will find itself short of sterling, and will presumably replenish its sterling balance by applying for bancor under its quota-rights and handing the bancor to the B. of E. in exchange for sterling. In case (2) the B. of E. will find itself with a surplus of francs. The B. of F., if it chooses to take the initiative, can apply for bancor and hand it to the B. of E. in discharge of its franc debt, thus substituting a bancor liability to the Union for a franc liability to the B. of E. But the B. of E., so far as I can see, cannot *compel* the B. of F. to act in this way; if the latter chooses to go on owing francs to the B. of E. rather than use up its rights under the quota scheme, the B. of E. has no recourse. It cannot convert francs into bancor in the way in which, under a gold standard, it could have converted francs into gold.

Thus S.F. and C.U. seem to me precisely on all fours in this respect. In both cases the smooth working of the scheme depends on the tacit assumption that a country will always be ready to use its rights under the general scheme rather than remain a debtor, in its own currency, to another individual country.

Do you agree with this analysis, please? If so does not C.U. 6 (11) need expansion to meet the point?

(2) I quite agree with the general view that, in the absence of exact statistical knowledge, the limitation, in S.F. III, 3, (a) of Fund-using rights to an adverse balance on income account would prove difficult to work in practice, and that even with such knowledge there would be difficulties of interpretation. But I think the suggestion in your note of 27.4.43 (and the same applies to the corresponding passage in Waley's note of 28.4.43) that the effect of this limitation is to debar a country in principle from use of the Fund altogether (except by special dispensation under III, 5) if it is making any capital payments at all (e.g. normal sinking-fund instalments) goes much too far and is indeed quite unwarranted. Suppose we can show that in the past quarter we have had an adverse balance of payments on income account with U.S. of x, and have made sinking-fund payments of y, the result of these two factors combined being a decline in our dollar

balance by xy, or an increase in America's sterling balance by xy or some mixture of the two. Then S.F. never says that we may not go to the Fund at all for dollars with which to replenish our dollar balance (or reduce America's sterling balance). All it says is that we can only go to the Fund for x dollars; if we want to restore the status quo completely as regards the balances mutually held by the two Treasuries or central banks, we must part with y in gold or in international securities. This seems to me a perfectly clear and logical provision; the only questions are (i) whether there will be sufficient information available to make it reasonably easy to interpret in practice: (ii) whether, even if there is sufficient information to work it, it is a *desirable* provision.

(3) How do you interpret C.U. 6 (10), third sentence (see also 29, last sentence)? In the event of the Board deciding to make such a distribution, is every nation with a bancor balance *compelled* to take some gold, or may it refuse? Phillips, in a correspondence with the South African minister here, has adopted the former interpretation, which has the advantage of giving an extra bit of security to the gold-producers. But this means in effect that, in respect of this particular wad of gold, the receiving country is being deprived for the occasion of its right to obtain bancor in exchange for gold; and I do not quite see how it could be enforced consistently with the general maintenance of that right. Have any of the Europeans raised the point with you, and if so what have you told them?

Yours ever,
DENNIS ROBERTSON

To D. H. ROBERTSON, *2 June 1943*

Dear Dennis,

C.U. and S.F.

Your letter of May 24th has arrived nice and promptly. I take your three points in order.

(1) I think you may be right that the actual drafting of C.U. is not as clear as it should be at this point. I had intended to give an absolute right to multilaterality. But I agree that some extra words are necessary to make this absolutely clear. The intention is there, and I think the implication is there, but there may be an error or insufficiency of drafting.

It is equally the case, I should agree, that S.F. can be

similarly amended without difficulty. All I ask is that it should be so amended. I do not consider that there is any essential difference between the two schemes on this ticket, provided we are agreed as to what we want and are prepared to adopt words which carry that into effect.

(2) I do not disagree with your elaboration of this. But I do not feel that it makes any real difference. I agree that if we take steps to provide for any capital payments we may be making by payment in gold or international securities, then we should be entitled to the use of the Fund. But, if we do not do this, the Fund does not provide us with a means of maintaining stability of the exchanges. In other words, the Fund is no good for its purpose in any case in which we are making any capital payments whatever unless these capital payments are not a net capital outgoing but are balanced by gold and net capital movements in the other direction. So I do not feel that your gloss makes the case any better. Moreover, the fact that the adverse balance has to be calculated with each country separately and does not relate to a net adverse balance with the world as a whole makes it still more unworkable and absurd. The result is that, even a country which has a favourable balance with the world as a whole cannot use the Fund for the purpose of multilateral clearing with any individual country with which, taken separately, it is out of balance. Since almost every country will be out of balance with some individual countries (indeed otherwise multilateral clearing would be entirely unnecessary), this clause reduces the utility of the whole set-up to the very least possible. Surely for a variety of reasons, this is quite outrageous rubbish and does not deserve even half-hearted defence.

(3) I had thought of this point, but it had not seemed to me worth while to complicate the exposition by going out of one's way to deal with it. My view is the same as Phillips's, namely that, when there is a gold distribution, every nation

with a bancor balance is compelled to take its share. On the other hand, I did not interpret this provision as taking away its right to re-deposit the gold. If several recipients of the gold were to exercise such a right, so that the Clearing Union still had more gold than it had a fancy for, then there would have to be a further, secondary distribution. If a point was reached where every country willing to take gold had had its credit balance discharged, so that any gold distributed always found its way back to the Union; and, if as a result of this the Union found itself unduly full of gold, then I conceived the remedy would be to alter the bancor price of gold. Indeed, it was precisely this contingency which I had in mind as likely to be the main justification for changing the price of gold, namely that every creditor country prepared to hold gold was already saturated and the Union was left to carry more than it cared about. Nevertheless, a situation where bancor was generally speaking preferred to gold seems a rather remote contingency for present consideration. If it was to be coming into sight, special provisions might be necessary, since one could not allow every central bank in the world to turn its gold into bancor in the expectation that the value of bancor in terms of gold was about to be reduced.

Yours ever,
[copy initialled] J. M. K.

From D. H. ROBERTSON *to* SIR WILFRID EADY, *3 June 1943*

My dear Eady,

I'll keep this letter to C.U. only. It is written after receipt of your telegram (CAMER 28) saying that Keynes is re-writing S.F. so as to make it make sense, but before receipt of the results. The news seems to fit in with a note on the general outlook which I wrote some time ago (A) to clear my own head. Meanwhile we have no intention of lowering the C.U. flag!

You will see from (B) that Phillips has written to White proposing the reopening of direct bilateral talks, with priority for questions on C.U. As regards that, I am a little disturbed to find on the record that there was talk of our providing a 'statement on the technical operations relating [to] the exchange transactions of central banks outside the Clearing Union to their operations within the Union.' If they renew the request, I don't feel very well equipped to meet it; but I am hopeful that Keynes will have got my letter of May 24 on this subject and found time to reply to it.*

With (B) was enclosed (C), a revised set of posers on S.F.

'...twenty-six† distinct damnations

One sure if another fails.'

This was based mainly on Keynes's note of April 27; I hope he will feel we have got in practically all his points. We thought it best to phrase the crucial question VII (3) on the innocent assumption that if our Sam is out of step with the rest of the battalion it is intended that it shall be up to him to do something about it; but we have also got the other side of the picture in under VII (2).

Meanwhile, White's individual tuition hours are understood to be in full swing,—mainly at the moment for Europeans, as the South Americans have not yet turned up in force, though there are believed to be a couple of Mexicans and one Paragueet knocking about somewhere. Watson has left us a 'Who's Who' which will be very useful when the flood sets in, as a pendant to Fraser's invaluable letter of May 10 about the Europeans. Of the said Europeans, Boel has been to see us, and De Jongh, and Keilhau (with Colbjörnsen the commercial attaché here). They are all evidently most anxious to keep in close touch with us, and we reciprocate. The Norwegians strike me as rather difficult; they don't think they will want short-term credits, and they profess not to be afraid of exchange depreciations by their neighbours, and so take rather a haughty line as to what an international scheme has to offer them. They are most emphatic that they would hate to be grouped with their traitorous fellow-Scandinavians for representation purposes; this, coupled with Watson's insistence that a similar hatred of one's nearest neighbours is universal in South America, makes us feel that that feature of C.U. will probably have to be dropped at the appropriate moment. I can't help feeling that the 'regional economic group' idea which the Dutch are working so hard might founder on a similar rock, unless the groups are so large as to be sub-worlds,—I suspect what they really want is a huge 'Atlantic' group comprising U.K. and the whole of Western Europe, as a make weight to Pan-America and Russianised-Europe. This has its attractions but raises very large issues. De Jongh has shown us the questions he has fired in on S.F.; they are largely devoted to exposition of the 'group' idea (though of course without giving any hint of my interpretation of it above), and otherwise strike me as rather

---

* Answered on June 2 so perhaps he has it by now. K.

† Please check. [Robertson's note.]

disappointing,—they display a pretty strong 'creditor mentality' and don't go to the heart of the scarce currency business.

White has invited Phillips to an 'informal' gathering on June 15 by such 'experts' as may then happen to be in Washington (no doubt however the Canadians could happen to be here that day). Phillips has thought it best to accept, making plain that he understands the subject of discussion will be the whole question of post-war international monetary policy, and not just the S.F. Plan. Of course it will be a ridiculous gathering, but it is evidently quite hopeless to get White to agree to a small hand-picked meeting which could really get down to it. So one can only hope that at least the party will do no harm, and (no doubt over-optimistically) that there may be something to drink.

Will you thank Eddie for his extracts from Cassel's gloomy letters of April 12 and April 28 about the Chinese? Does China's desire to 'stand on her own feet' extend to an unwillingness to receive any international loans, I wonder? Phillips does not think it is much good approaching T. V. Soong at present.

I see I have not yet mentioned Waley's note dated April 28, which we have also been studying carefully, especially the very pertinent passage on pp. 8 and 9 about the misconception of the nature of the problem of abnormal war balances shown in S.F. III, 9 (*e*). We have not put in a question about this at present; perhaps the moment for looking this particular gift-horse very firmly in the mouth will arrive if and when he is trotted out a propos of our ceiling for net balances,—see our REMAC 49. Meanwhile we should be glad to hear if you have had any further thoughts about him.

I will try to write a sequel before too long.

Yours sincerely,
DENNIS ROBERTSON

Last but not least—we found the Hansards of the debates in both Houses most interesting and encouraging. Alas! they had nothing of a press here, but the subsequent interest displayed by the Treasury is gratifying. I hope you have sent copies direct to Canada?

(A) NOTES ON C.U. AND S.F.*
I. *General appreciation of the situation*

I assume that C.U. and S.F. will retain their separate existence—the latter probably in highly amended form—until the 'general discussion by available experts' (stage 4, tel. 2151), but that before stage 5 (conference of Finance Ministers) can be reached, a single scheme must be hammered out. What are our present ideas as to the nature of this eventual scheme?

Three alternative objectives seem to be gradually crystallising.

(1) Relying largely on Continental support, to fight to the last for the *differentia* of C.U., viz. the overt committal of (limited) powers of money-creation to an international organ; but with concessions to the American desire to limit the extent to which they are prepared to commit themselves in advance to handling their inescapable problem through this particular (i.e. the 'impersonal') form of international lending:–

(2) to concede the *differentia* of S.F., viz. the ostensible retention of the money-creating power in the hands of individual states by means of the paraphernalia of 'capital' subscription, and to concentrate on securing

(*a*) quantitative approximation of the anti-contractionary potential of the scheme to that contemplated in C.U.,

(*b*) explicit recognition of the implications for exchange and commercial policy of the 'scarce currency' provisions:–

(3) while conceding the *differentia* of S.F. as under (2) to press not only for (*a*) and (*b*) but also for (*c*)—the preservation of some of the elegance of C.U. by turning unitas into a real medium of exchange instead of a mere unit of account,—a medium of exchange which would however only come into existence by way of exchange for existing media and not by way of *ex nihilo* creation (Lord Keynes's note of 27.4.43).

My own impression of the present situation is that the tide of events, especially as embodied in the outlook of the very compact and able Canadian team, is carrying us strongly in the direction of (2), that it might be deflected at a suitable moment towards (3), but that at some point objective (1) will in fact be found to have vanished quietly from the map. This impression *may* be modified after conversation with the Europeans, though I do not expect it to be. It does not of course mean for a moment that I think that at this stage we should abandon our efforts to expound and propagate C.U.; for it is only by an expert gathering impregnated with its atmosphere that the necessary modifications of S.F. could in the end be secured.

D. H. R.

* Written some weeks ago. D.H.R. 3.6.

From SIR FREDERICK PHILLIPS *to* H. D. WHITE, *2 June 1943*

(B)

My dear White,

I think you would agree that it is now desirable to push on to the completion of the 'elucidation' stage of the monetary plans. I have therefore gone through our files again to collect what points are outstanding.

As regards the Clearing Union plan, you will remember that a meeting took place at the State Department on November 26, 1942, at which Mr Bernstein was present for the U.S. Treasury, and at which we went through the written answers which I had given to the 11 questions I had been asked about the meaning of the Plan. The impression with which I came away was that many of these answers had been regarded as clearing up satisfactorily the points with which they dealt, but that there were some important points on which, partly because our paper had been recently redrafted and there had not been time for your experts to make a full study of the new text, further elucidation of the implications of our Plan would be desired. This refers, I think, particularly to the important questions numbered 7 and 10. If, in the period that has passed, further study of our Plan by your experts has revealed other aspects of it on which they would wish for further light, may I suggest that you should let me have a revised list of questions on any points you find doubtful?

We have been thinking over the oral answers which were given us at our meeting on 23 February to the questions which we had asked about various points in the Stabilisation Fund scheme. Several of these answers cleared up the points at issue, leaving nothing more to be said. Others, while we found them quite clear, revealed certain differences of approach which it would perhaps be premature to explore further at this stage until we have each of us heard more of what the representatives of other nations have got to say. But there were others again which left us still in doubt as to the meaning of certain provisions in the Stabilisation Fund plan.

I have combined these with some other points which have come up since in a new paper of which I enclose three copies. It looks rather long but is not really so and the object has been to make the enquiry complete.

Yours sincerely,

2 June 1943   F. PHILLIPS

I. *Quotas*

Can the formula for determining these now be supplied? (II, 2).

II. *Rates of exchange*

(1) Is the initial fixing of rates a unilateral act by the Fund, or does it require the assent of the country concerned? Are the initial rates determined by a bare majority, as compared with a change in rates, which requires a four-fifths majority? (III, 2).

(2) Are the fluctuations to be permitted of the same order of magnitude as the old spread between gold-points, or greater, or less? (VI, 1).

(3) Are differential rates of exchange for different classes of (visible and invisible) imports and exports to be permitted?

(4) Is the omission of any provision for changing the gold value of unitas, in the event of a world scarcity or redundancy of gold, intentional? (IV, 1).

III. *Deposits*

(1) Is the power of the Fund to accept deposits (III, 1) limited to a power to accept deposits *in gold* (IV, 3), or may it also accept deposits in (*a*) local currency (*b*) foreign currency? If so, what use can the depositor make of such deposits?

(2) Can unitas be acquired in any way except by the deposit of gold? (IV, 3).

(3) Can a unitas deposit be used for the purchase of any foreign currency the depositor pleases? (IV, 3). If so, does this mean that every member country is under obligation to deliver its own currency to the Fund without limit in exchange for unitas?

IV. *Facilitation of multilateral clearing* (III, 8)

(1) If a country's offer to sell to the Fund a given foreign currency A in exchange for another foreign currency B is declined, what can it do with its unwanted surplus of currency A? In order to obtain the supplies it needs of currency B, must it have recourse to its rights of resort to the Fund under III, 3 (*a*), even though its balance of payments with the world as a whole is favourable?

(2) Is the obligation to offer to sell to the Fund all foreign currencies and

gold acquired in excess of the amount held on joining the Fund subject to qualification in the case of countries whose stocks of foreign currencies and gold were, at the date they joined the Fund, abnormally low as the result of causes arising out of the war?

(3) In computing the excess holdings of foreign currency and gold liable to be offered for sale, what set-offs against a recorded increase in gross holdings by central banks or treasuries are to be allowed in the way of (i) an increase in the direct liabilities to foreigners of central banks and treasuries themselves (ii) an increase in the liabilities to foreigners of their commercial banks and other nationals?

(4) For purposes of the obligation to make an offer of sale to the Fund, is newly mined gold deemed to be 'acquired' by the producing country immediately on its production, or by such countries (including the producing country) as may be found in possession of it after a stated interval?

V. *Rights of recourse to the Fund* (III, 3 (*a*), 4 and 5)

(1) Can a country A only demand the currency of a country B if it has an adverse balance on income account *with country B*? Or may it demand it if, as a result of the operation of a free exchange market, it requires that particular currency in order to cover an adverse balance on income account with the world as a whole?

(2) How is it to be determined in practice how far a country's need for foreign exchange is caused by an adverse balance on income account and how far by the residual effect of capital movements in both directions? Does (*a*) the meeting of normal sinking-fund instalments (*b*) the repayment of a short-term (e.g. three months) credit, count as a capital movement? Is there any risk that a country will find itself debarred from recourse to the Fund altogether if it is known to be making any payments of a capital nature?

VI. *Quantitative limitation on rights of recourse to the Fund*

(1) In evaluating the Fund's 'holdings' of a country's currency at a given date (III, 3 (*b*) (*a*)) does 'currency' include or exclude securities expressed in that currency? (*b*) which of the following items are included in addition to currency handed to the Fund by the country in question for the purpose of covering its adverse balance of payments? (i) initial subscriptions (II, 4); (ii) supplementary subscriptions (II, 5); (iii) deposits made by the country itself or by other countries (III, 1); (iv) amounts handed over by other countries as excess foreign exchange (III, 8); (v) amounts obtained by the

Fund by the sale of its own or of other countries' securities (III, 1 and III, 12); (vi) additional deliveries consequent on devaluation (IV, 4).

(2) What will be the nature of the special reserve demanded from a country when the Fund's holdings of its currency exceed its quota? (III, 3 (c)).

(3) If a country has exhausted its rights of recourse to the Fund, does its undertaking (VI, 1) to maintain a stable rate of exchange lapse? If not, how does it implement this undertaking?

VII. *'Scarce' currencies*

(1) Are the prescribed purchases of scarce currency for gold (III, 6(a)) additional to such purchases of that currency as the Fund may be making for unitas in order to implement the right of the holder of a gold deposit to obtain for that deposit any currency he pleases (see question numbered III, 3 above)?

(2) When a country finds its demands for a scarce currency rationed (III, 7, third paragraph), is it entitled to restrict the demand of its nationals for the scarce currency by prohibiting or restricting imports from the country whose currency has become scarce?

(3) When a country's currency becomes scarce, and is tending therefore to appreciate in terms of all other currencies, does that country's obligation (VI, 1) to keep constant by 'appropriate action' its rate of exchange on the currencies of all other countries remain unaffected? Is such 'appropriate action' to be understood as including (i) the holding of unlimited amounts of the currencies of the other countries, (ii) the placing of limitations on the amount of foreign currencies which its exporters may offer for sale?

(4) Is the obligation resting on a country whose currency has become scarce to give 'immediate and careful attention' to the recommendations of the Fund (III, 6) to be understood as a qualification, or as an illustration, of the general obligation resting upon members 'to adopt appropriate legislation or decrees—to facilitate the activities of the Fund' (VI, 7)?

To D. H. ROBERTSON, *11 June 1943*

My dear Dennis,

Your letter of June 3rd to Eady arrived yesterday. As these questions are rather active just now, it may be convenient that I should let you have by return of post an interim reply on the points where I am particularly interested, and then hand the letter back to Eady.

(1) I hope you will have had by now my reply to your letter of May 24th. I answered it promptly on June 2nd, so I expect it has arrived.

(2) Your note (A) headed 'A General Appreciation of the Situation'. My own feeling is much the same. The chances of our getting (1) are not very good. The task is to develop (2), in spite of Canadian support, into (3). But I am sure the time for that is not yet. Our tactics at the moment should be, I suggest, to be as difficult and obstinate as possible. Only so shall we gain a real value for a more accommodating mood if and when the right time seems to have come for being accommodating.

(3) I have been much interested in paper (c) 'The Twenty-Six Distinct Damnations'. This is a faithful and satisfactory résumé of various points I have made, and in a good many of the ticklish cases it is expressed much better, and also more suitably. I have no positive criticisms on this. On second thoughts, however, there are one or two points which I should not have minded to see added, particularly the two following:–

(i) It seems to me that the full horrors under V—'Rights of Recourse to the Fund'—might have been still more developed. The more one looks at this clause, the more complete nonsense it seems to be. I offer you the following addition:–

'It would appear that

(1) If country A has a favourable balance with the world as a whole and so is in a position to lend abroad but an adverse balance with country B due to a capital transaction, country A cannot obtain country B's currency from the Fund; that is to say, a country cannot lend to a country with which it has an adverse balance, even though it is a creditor country towards the world as a whole.

(2) If country A has an unfavourable balance with the world as a whole as a result of lending beyond its capacity,

it can nevertheless obtain country B's currency from the Fund provided it is not B that it is lending to.'

(ii) The other point is the omission of any reference to the position of gold. There is an obscurity here in two respects. It is not clear whether a member country is under compulsion to furnish its currency in exchange for gold. (Indirectly this arises under your III (3) on the subject of 'deposits'.) But there is also an ambiguity as to the position of gold holders and producers. Einzig has pointed out that under S.F. IV, 3 the text says that deposits in terms of unitas *may* be accepted. It does not say *must*. Thus it is not certain that a gold producer can sell gold to the Fund under IV; nor does there seem to be any provision by which the holder of gold can be certain of turning it into the currency he wants under III.

(4) As you will have gathered from our telegram, we were much upset by the Canadian draft.[16] Fortunately I had just received a copy of that from Rasminsky before your telegram, 61 REMAC, arrived. It all seems a great misfortune. The Canadian re-draft is, of course, a great improvement so far as it goes. All the changes are for the better, and the drafting has been improved or made much clearer in many points of detail. But this makes one all the sorrier that it has been put in so definitely at this stage. For at a later date and with some further changes it might have been so easy for Canada to take the really decisive part of producing a mediated scheme. As it is they are wasting their ammunition. Really a most awful pity.

Whether, in addition to upsetting us, the document will please the Americans remains to be seen. There is such a large ingredient of copy-cat that, from that point of view, Harry White ought to be pleased and flattered. But whether he will be completely pleased by having all his skeletons dragged

---

[16] 'Tentative Draft Proposals of Canadian Experts for an International Exchange Union.' A first draft was sent to Keynes on 3 June. A slightly revised version was tabled in the House of Commons by the Minister of Finance on 12 July 1943.

out of their cupboards is not so obvious. In particular, the treatment of scarce currencies becomes horribly un-ambiguous.

(5) We have just had a visit from Dr Holloway,[17] the head of the South African Treasury and the chief adviser of Hof-meyr. We had been warned to expect him to be difficult and rather hostile. In the first interview at least there was not the slightest sign of that. He seemed to be a very delightful and extremely able fellow, with whom it is a great comfort to talk face to face. We gather that it is he who will be the principal adviser on these currency questions, and he is an out and out adherent of C.U. as against S.F. You will remember that we were rather given to expect that South Africa might take the other line. It is quite on the cards that he will be coming on to Washington later on to represent South Africa in these matters. His Minister has left him discretion whether or not to do this, and he had not yet quite made up his mind.

Yours ever,
[copy initialled] J. M. K.

From D. H. ROBERTSON, *14 June 1943*

Dear Maynard,

Clearing Union

The three points covered in your letter of June 2.

(1) I think the most logical place for the required amendment in C.U. would be after the first sentence of 6 (*b*). Something of this kind seems to be needed. 'Subject to special treatment for the abnormal war balances mentioned in paragraph 34 below, they shall also agree to redeem in bancor, at the request of any member state, any balances in their currency acquired by that state in excess of a normal working balance.'

(2) You will have received the revised version of S.F. and the dossier of questions and answers sent you a few days ago. The changes in III, 3 (*a*)

[17] John Edward Holloway (b. 1890); Economic Adviser to South African Treasury, 1934–7; Secretary for Finance, 1937–50; delegate, Bretton Woods Conference, 1944.

299

and III, 5 do, I think, go a good way towards meeting the difficulty about reasonable capital payments. Personally it seems to me quite arguable that, whether under an S.F. or C.U. set-up, there should be some attempt to limit the use of the pool for capital purposes from the start, however great the difficulty of definition in marginal cases. Under C.U. as it stands a country can, I think, exercise its 5% depreciation right even though its troubles are notoriously due to a flight of greed-capital or funk-capital. Is there not a case for stiffening this up?

The change in III, 3(a) also meets the point that a country A may need to buy B's currency to cover an adverse balance with the world as a whole even though A's balance with B is favourable. But I think if you look again you will see that it is not *this* clause which, in its original form, prevented a country with a *favourable* balance with the world as a whole from using an excess of one currency to purchase its deficiencies in another. The peccant clause in this respect is III, 8, which compels a country to offer surplus francs (say) to the Fund for dollars, but does not compel the Fund to accept the offer, even when dollars are not technically 'scarce'. It is therefore clause III, 8 which still needs altering.

(3) I must confess that the difference between (a) being permitted to refuse gold and (b) being compelled to accept it this morning but permitted to hand it back this afternoon, still seems to me a very thin one! I quite agree that a condition in which a great many countries were refusing or handing back gold would be the natural indication that the price of gold needed lowering. But if we contemplate that such a thing may happen (as I think we certainly ought to) we cannot claim that this 'share-out' provision gives much extra security to the gold producer. (Last word of your letter, for 'reduced' read 'raised' [above, p. 289]).

Yours ever,
D. H. R.

From D. H. ROBERTSON, *28 June 1943*

My dear Maynard,

C.U. and S.F.

I have made myself into an informal committee of two with Bernstein for the purpose of persecuting him as to what S.F. is really trying to say about the conditions under which a country can have recourse to the Fund. The result is two further changes of some importance in the very latest text just received and enclosed herewith.

1. A country can now buy any foreign currency the Fund possesses for the purpose of covering an adverse balance, predominantly on current account, with any member country.

This wording seems to cover satisfactorily both the 'hard cases' which had been raised, viz:

(i) That raised by the Canadians, where, owing to the existence of a free market in exchanges, England requires (say) gulden in order to cover an adverse balance with the world as a whole, though her balance with Holland is favourable;

(ii) that raised by me, where England requires gulden in order to cover an adverse balance with Holland, but is all square with the world as a whole (including Holland), and would therefore not be able to obtain gulden from the Fund if the right of recourse to the Fund were made to depend on having an adverse balance with the world as a whole.

2. In this last case, however, the clause as amended still leaves a gap. It permits England to buy for sterling the gulden she requires, but it does not give her any right to turn into sterling the foreign currencies—let us call them francs—of which she finds herself *ex hypothesi* with a surplus.

The Americans have taken a great deal of persuading that this gap needs filling. They have been thinking entirely in terms of a free exchange market, on to which the English Treasury or central bank would without scruple chuck its surplus francs, thus producing such a weakening of the market rate that the French Treasury or central bank would be obliged in self-defense to exercise its rights of recourse to the Fund in order to put the situation right. I have argued that as regards ourselves and Europe in general this picture may prove a very unrealistic picture, and that whatever scheme is adopted must contain some provision by which a country with a surplus of a particular foreign currency can normally get rid of it automatically, without recourse to an open market, in exchange for some other currency which it needs for predominantly current account purposes. They have accordingly now added a provision specifically obligating the Fund 'to purchase for local currency or needed foreign exchange any member currency in good standing acquired by another member country [in payment for current transactions],* when such currency cannot be disposed of in the foreign exchange markets within the spread established by the Fund'. The phrase 'in good standing' may need further definition, but some such qualification is, I think, reasonable, since, as pointed out in REMAC 99, paragraph 3, even under a C.U. set-up England (in my story) could not be confident that France would always be in a position to redeem England's surplus francs for bancor.

* These words seem to have vanished.

301

In the course of our conversations I have complained several times that the whole thing would look much simpler and more intelligible if the several rights and obligations were expressed in terms of Unicorn, and at one moment White seemed rather moved by the complaint. If you decide to surrender on the overdraft principle, but nevertheless attach importance to preserving Unicorn as a true international medium of exchange instead of a mere unit of account, I do not feel sure but that

'Now at the last when all have give him over
From death to life thou might'st him yet recover.'

As regards the phrase 'predominantly on current account', it is explained that that is intended to look after such things as regular amortisation payments, and no doubt one could argue for the extension of the list to include repayment of short-term credits, reasonable remittances for extension of business plants, etc. The Americans (and Canadians) are firm that, in spite of statistical and definitional difficulties, some attempt must be made to restrict the use of the Fund for capital purposes from the start, and I think myself they are right, i.e., that if the C.U. set-up were retained it would need stiffening up in this respect. As C.U. stands at present, a country could borrow bancor to finance a funk-flight or greed-flight of capital without let or hindrance until it has exhausted 50% of its quota.

Yours ever,

D. H. R.

P.S. May I add my own suggestion for the name of the international money, *Winfranks*—a compliment to the P.M. and the President, with a suggestion of victory, of the continuity of monetary history, and of the ancient unity of Europe under Charlemagne?

To D. H. ROBERTSON, *19 July 1943*

Dear Dennis,

C.U. and S.F.

1. I would have replied sooner to your letters of June 28th and July 5th[18] if I had not, owing to Phillips' illness,[19] had to turn aside entirely from C.U. during the last fortnight to

[18] Not printed.
[19] Phillips had collapsed soon after his return to London from Washington in July. He died early in August.

tackle the questions arising out of reciprocal aid and the new financial settlement with Stettinius.

2. Taking first of all your shorter letter of July 5th, the Belgians and Dutch having returned are so ashamed of themselves for having ratted that they are keeping out of my sight for the moment. Eady, however, has had an instructive conversation with Boel and has made an interesting note of which I enclose a copy.[20] Keilhau I am to see shortly. No news of the others.

3. I note the attitude of F.R.B. as reported by Walter Gardner.[21] I am sorry that Hansen uses such confusing language. If he said that the potential production was so great that, apart from a short transition, there is no reason why prices need rise more than what corresponds to the rise in efficiency wages, he would be less likely to be misunderstood. It would also lead up to the point that it is not F.R.B.'s cash position which will cause inflation. Business already has so much more liquid resources than it can conceivably use that the quantity aspect long ago ceased to be relevant. Moreover, *if* there is anything in the quantity argument, C.U. protects them from being flooded with the world's gold, whereas S.F. is deliberately designed to collect or re-collect gold; and there is no reason why they *need* alter their law to make bancor reserve money.

4. Turning to your letter of June 28th, your discussions with Bernstein are very interesting and fundamental. I agree very strongly with all your rejoinders and only hope that you are right in thinking that we can yet recover Unicorn as a true international medium of exchange. For that, we are still maintaining here, is the most fundamental condition of a satisfactory compromise.

5. Unfortunately we had only one brief conversation about

[20] Not printed.
[21] Walter N. Gardner; Chief, International Section, Board of Governors, Federal Reserve System; delegate to Bretton Woods Conference, 1944.

this with F.P. before he retired hurt, and we are not fully seized of his mind. He was questioning whether we could substantiate our conclusion that this is a matter on which we should stand pat. He did not, of course, object to our trying, but did not seem quite convinced that this issue, drily considered, mattered as much as all that. I think it does, and will try to reduce to a clear story why I think so. And I will then tackle the old bean again. (As I wrote to Waley, he does not look to me by any means too bad, but he is reconciled to four or five weeks in bed, and the intention is to leave him alone as much as possible for the first fortnight. He has been sending Miss Church to the London Library for volumes of Italian poetry and is resuming his studies of the Italian Renaissance. The truth is that he is utterly worn out by these three years in Washington and now that he has stopt trying to hold himself upright discovers immense relief in being prone.)

6. I suppose that we should decide in the next week or so what is to be our reply to White's suggestion that we, on our side, should now formulate what we regard as our essential conditions. That, I hope, we shall now turn to forthwith. The preparation of a full-scale Cabinet Paper by the Chancellor on the question of Reciprocal Aid and associated topics took all our time last week. We are by now reduced to infinitesimal numbers. This week Eddie is on leave every other day, since this is his wife's only leave opportunity. Your Edgar [Jones], though still in attendance, is not well, having a recurrence of his miner's coal dust on the lungs.

Yours ever,
[copy not initialled]

As the Washington discussions had continued, Sir Frederick Phillips had cabled London on the 'abnormal balances' proposals in the White Plan. On this Keynes commented.

To SIR DAVID WALEY, *22 June 1943*

ABNORMAL WAR BALANCES

(1) In paragraph 2 of REMAC 75 Phillips asks us whether we have given thorough consideration to the proposals in S.F. for dealing with abnormal war balances and warns us that they are again being called 'blocked balances'. This needs a reply.

(2) We have all of us, perhaps, been a bit lazy-minded (I am sure I have) in grappling with this subject owing to the unintelligibility of Section III, 9 of S.F., in which it is set forth. We have also been inclined, as a result, I now think, of not going into it in enough detail, to be unnecessarily ungrateful about the possible benefits of this clause. There is a general atmosphere about that we [do] not like the proposals. But I am not sure why. Is there any substantial reason why we should not welcome them?

(3) As an aid to finding an answer to this, I offer the following summary of what the clause appears to mean:–

(i) Under the provision of S.F. by which its resources are only available to meet deficits on current trade account (and the same point would hold substantially good *in general* even if, as will be necessary, some mitigation for the provisions of III, 3(*a*) are introduced), it follows that the pre-zero hour overseas sterling balances are frozen, or blocked in the sense that any use of them becomes a capital transaction subject to whatever the rules of capital control may be.

(ii) This may have serious consequences for those whose overseas reserves are thus blocked. Take India for example. It means that the greater part of her currency reserves become useless except to meet an Indian adverse balance of trade *with this country*. If S.F. comes into force, it would be utterly impracticable for us to make pre-zero hour sterling balances freely available (and, indeed, equally so if it doesn't).

(iii) White, therefore, offers a way out. The way out is

305

entirely optional and is only used if both we and India wish to use it. There is nothing compulsory about it. It is an extra facility to be available if both parties concerned would like to use it.

(iv) India, let us suppose, owns £100 million sterling in her currency reserves. She comes to us and asks to be allowed to liquidate an instalment of this, say £10 millions, under S.F. III, 9. If we and the Fund both agree, the Fund takes over the £10 million sterling from India and India's power of drawing on the Fund for any currency she wants is augmented to this extent, either at one remove by her selling the sterling for a currency she wants or at two removes by reducing the rupees held by the Fund and so increasing India's right to obtain desired currencies by replenishing the Fund's holding of rupees, as and when she wants foreign currency.

(v) The plan is so drafted as to make it appear that India has to agree to repurchase 40 per cent of the sterling from the Fund over a period of 20 years and that we have to repurchase another 40 per cent over the same period. But, in effect, it is *we* who have to repurchase 80 per cent, since the sterling repurchased by India is to be *free* sterling in her hands which she can immediately change into any other currency.

(vi) The upshot is that we have to repay £400,000 a year for 20 years. The balance of £200,000 is carried by the Fund for 23 years and is then dealt with by agreement between us and the Fund. India pays the Fund a commission of 1 per cent on the transaction and we pay the Fund another 1 per cent. India pays 1 per cent interest on £400,000 or on that part of it which is still outstanding. Similarly we pay 1 per cent interest on £400,000 or on that part of it which is still outstanding. In addition the Fund earns interest on the £10 million, or on that part of it which is outstanding, which it holds invested in some sterling Government security.

(vii) In short we pay a once-for-all commission of 1 per cent, a 4 per cent sinking fund, and ⅖ per cent per annum over and above the normal interest on the sterling Government security (⅖ per cent, because we pay 1 per cent on ⅖ of the total sum involved).

(viii) This seems very reasonable. India becomes liquid on easy terms. We fund on easy terms. Something of this kind seems to me to be an indispensable feature of S.F. I can see no reason why we should reject this optional facility. Clearly it would be very unfair to India for us to do so.

(4) In the Canadian revise of S.F. there is substituted for this a simpler but very much more limited proposal under which the Fund can acquire abnormal wartime balances during the first two years of its operation up to an amount not exceeding 5 per cent of the aggregate quotas of all countries. At the end of two years the Governing Board is to propose a plan for the gradual further liquidation. The Canadian proposal does not state that, e.g., sterling so acquired would not reckon towards the sterling quota, whereas this is specifically stated in the American version. Obviously, without this, the Canadian draft does not help at all.

(5) Subject to what may emerge in further discussion, I should like to tell Phillips that, on further consideration, we warmly welcome the proposal for dealing with the blocked balances and prefer the more definitive proposal of S.F. to the watering down in the Canadian revise. In any case, the Canadian version is no use unless it is made clear that abnormal wartime balances acquired by the Fund will be outside the regular quotas.

KEYNES

22.6.43

On reading Keynes's note, S.D. Waley commented that 'the idea of completely blocking all overseas sterling balances sends a good many shudders down my spine'. Keynes minuted in reply on 24 June, 'I had that shudder a long time ago and have got over it!'

In preparation for further discussions, at the end of June Keynes attempted yet another synthesis of the two plans, basing himself on the U.S. draft of 15 June and the essential conditions set out by Mr White at a meeting on 22 June.

THE SYNTHESIS OF C.U. AND S.F.

I

We accept the substance of White's essential conditions, namely:–

(i) We agree to the subscription principle;

(ii) We agree to the limitation of liability;

(iii) We agree that no country shall be required to change the gold value of its currency against its will.

We also accept the U.S. formula for quotas and voting power, and the general shape of S.F. We are prepared to agree, as a condition of the scheme, that the initial exchange rate between pound and dollar shall be £1 = $4.

II

Our own essential conditions are:–

(i) The Fund shall not deal in a mixed bag of currencies but only in unitas, holdings of which will be acquired by members in exchange for their subscriptions and which will not be redeemable in gold.

(ii) As regards the gold subscription, the original S.F. proposal, namely 12½ per cent of the quota, would be acceptable. If this is to be modified, it must be in such a way as not to give the scheme too pronounced a gold-standard appearance and, more particularly, must not unduly qualify its expansionist possibilities by draining gold from countries whose reserves are relatively deficient already.

(iii) The balance of the subscription must be in the shape of a non-negotiable government security.

(iv) The provisions for elasticity in changing the value of a member's currency and for preserving sovereignty in this respect shall be reconsidered.

(v) The greatest objection to S.F. in its revised version is that a creditor country can go on absorbing great quantities of gold as heretofore, before any real pressure is put upon it. For example, if U.S. puts up the whole of her subscription in gold (as, we understand, is intended), if the other gold subscriptions are on the latest formula, and if, under III, 8, a large part of the world's new gold production is forced to find its way to the Fund (as, we understand, is intended), a creditor country could absorb $m6,000 *in gold* before there is any pressure on it. Thus, in effect, *all* the proposals of C.U. intended to discourage such a development are dropped. It follows that we are left mainly dependent on a separate International Investment Scheme. Thus it is essential that the Plan be somewhat modified to meet the above criticism (see particularly clauses A4 and 5 and B9 below) and, if possible, that an International Investment Scheme is worked out *pari passu*.

III

The following provisions are suggested as satisfying both the above sets of essential conditions. They are based on the S.F. model. They do not attempt to cover the whole ground, but they do settle the more fundamental matters. The A clauses provide the essential constitution, the B clauses deal with the problems arising out of the new importance assigned to gold, the C clauses with exchange-flexibility, and the D clauses with sundry matters.

A1. A member shall subscribe in gold 12½ per cent of its quota or 20 per cent of its net gold holding (i.e. gold and foreign currencies convertible into gold *less* liabilities carrying a gold convertibility), and the balance in a government bond carrying interest at 1 per cent and non-negotiable except in the conditions specified below (A7). (But provisions for an additional subscription in gold might be worked out for any member whose initial gold holdings exceed its quota.)

A2. In return for this subscription a member will receive the equivalent of its quota in terms of unitas as a transferable credit on the books of the Fund, and will be free to transfer any part of its holding of unitas to another member; except that, if its holding is less than its quota, it shall not reduce its holding by more than a quarter in any year without the permission of the Fund.

A3. Every member engages to sell its currency to another member either for gold or for unitas, except that it may refuse to accept unitas if its holding of unitas *less* the Fund's holding of its bond exceeds its quota.

A4. Every member (M) engages to convert holdings of its currency belonging to another member (N) which arise out of current transactions into N's currency, unless the two conditions are *both* fulfilled that N is exercising its option under A3 not to accept unitas and the net gold holdings of M are less than its quota. If both these conditions are fulfilled, country N shall acquire from its exporters their holdings of M's currency at the par of exchange, so as to maintain the parity, and this currency shall only be available to pay for purchases of goods and services from M. (This, in conjunction with A5 below comes very near to solving the 'scarce currency' problem.)

A5. The Fund may at its option lend unitas to a member or borrow unitas from it on such terms and conditions as may be mutually agreed.

(This clause is more important than it looks. For it covers up the whole machinery of pressure by which the Fund can make mitigations to the problems both of excess-debtors and of excess-creditors conditional on the acceptance of its recommendations.)

A6. The obligation under A4 shall be suspended if a country's stock of unitas available to be transferred is exhausted and if its holding of gold and foreign exchange is less than half its quota. In this case the Fund shall be entitled to prescribe the conditions on which the country can remain a member of the Fund.

A 7. A country which is dropped or which withdraws from membership shall have its holding of unitas offset so far as possible against the Fund's holding of its bond. If the country is left with a net holding of unitas, any losses of the Fund may be deducted *pro rata* from this holding, and the country shall continue to be free to employ the balance of its holding of unitas to purchase the currencies of the remaining members as in clause 3 above. If, on the other hand, the Fund is left with a net holding of its bond, the rate of interest on the bond shall be raised to 5 per cent and shall carry a sinking fund of 2 per cent, and it shall be negotiable.

(This gives the creditor country, which leaves the Fund, very good security, namely the power to acquire (to pay for current transactions) the currency of any of the remaining members who are not themselves excess-creditors.)

B 8. A member whose holding of unitas is less than its quota may replenish its holding by selling gold to the Fund for unitas. A member may redeem in gold any part of its government bond outstanding with the Fund.

B 9. The Fund may at its option pay off any part of a member's holding of unitas in excess of its quota either in gold or in the government security originally subscribed by that member.

(It is of vital importance that action under B 9 should be *at the option* of the Fund. This goes a little way to meet our essential condition (v). The Fund might make the handing over of its gold to an excess creditor conditional on that member's taking some steps to right its position. If the Fund retains its gold, this remains as security for *all* net holders of unitas and is not sacrificed in the interests of the least deserving, namely the excess net holder.)

B 10. If a member's holding of unitas is less than its quota, it shall offer to sell to the Fund for unitas any excess of its net holding of gold over and above its quota. If its holding of unitas is less than 50 per cent of its quota, it shall offer to sell to the Fund any excess of its net holding of gold over and above 50 per cent of its quota.

(The first part of this is much better than a provision to sell an excess over its initial holding, since it may aid the more even distribution of gold and will prevent countries from using the Fund when they have substantial quantities of gold. Under the above a country must use any excess in its gold holding above its quota before calling on the Fund. The second part sufficiently safeguards the Fund from an accumulation of gold by an excess-debtor.)

C11. The initial value of unitas shall be fixed in terms of gold at the present gold equivalent of 1 dollar, but may be changed by a decision of the Fund.

C12. The par value of the currency of each member in terms of unitas shall be fixed by agreement between the member and the Fund, except that the initial value of the dollar in terms of unitas shall be 1 and the initial value of the £ sterling shall be 4.

C13. No subsequent changes shall be made by any member in the value of its currency in terms of unitas except after consultation with the Fund and by agreement with it, except that the Fund shall not refuse an application in the following cases:–

(i) If the gold value of unitas is changed by the Fund, a member shall be allowed to modify the value of its own currency in terms of unitas, so as to leave the gold value of its currency unchanged. (This preserves sovereignty over the gold-parity of its currency to all members and not only to those who command one-fifth of the votes.)

(ii) If a member desiring to reduce the value of its currency can show (*a*) that its holding of unitas has averaged less than half its quota on the average of the last year,

(*b*) that its holding of gold and foreign currencies is less than half its quota,

(*c*) that this is not the recent result of outward capital transactions other than those arising out of the contractual payment of its debts and obligations, and

(*d*) that this application in conjunction with previous changes does not involve an aggregate change at a rate exceeding an average of 1 per cent per annum since the date of the inception of the Fund or more than 10 per cent altogether.

(iii) If a member desiring to increase the value of its currency can show

(*a*) that its holding of unitas exceeded its quota by more than 50 per cent on the average of the last year,

(*b*) that its net holding of gold and foreign currencies is more than double its quota,

(*c*) that this is not the result of unnecessary obstacles in the way of outward capital transactions or of imports, or of subsidies to exports, and

(*d*) that this application in conjunction with previous changes does not involve an aggregate change at a rate exceeding an average of 1 per cent per annum since the date of the inception of the Fund or more than 10 per cent altogether.

((iii), which may look unnecessary, is partly for the sake of symmetry, but also to prevent weak countries from overvaluing their currencies,—a not impossible contingency.)

(iv) If during the initial period of five years a member, whose country has been in enemy occupation during the war, is able to show that conditions have developed which were unforeseen when the exchange rate was initially determined and would have been relevant to that determination in the sense requested if they had been foreseen.

C14. The obligation under 4 shall be temporarily suspended when an application is made under 13 pending its determination.

C15. A country whose application under 13 has been rejected shall be entitled to leave the Fund without being required to give the usual notice.

D16. The Governing and Executive Boards of the Fund shall settle all questions by a majority of the allotted voting powers, except that no country shall have its quota increased or decreased without its agreement and that a change in the Statutes shall require a four-fifths majority.

D17. The Fund shall be entitled to open an account in unitas in favour of a properly constituted international organisation or authority, which shall be entitled to lend or borrow unitas on terms which are mutually agreed.

D18. The Governing and Executive Boards shall bear it constantly in mind that the maintenance of employment and output at a satisfactory level throughout the world is their first and overriding duty. If there should be symptoms of falling employment in leading countries or of a general depression of prices and demand in international markets, they shall, therefore, exercise every discretion granted to them under these clauses to combat these developments, and should reserve decisions of caution and discipline to cases where individual countries appear to be getting themselves into difficulties of their own making and not forced on them by external conditions.

29.6.43

When he sent a copy of his synthesis to D. H. Robertson, the latter commented.

From D. H. ROBERTSON, *13 July 1943*

My dear Maynard,

Many thanks for your letter of July 1, enclosing what I will call for the sake of brevity the Whines Plan. I only got it yesterday, and on a first study there are a number of things that bother me about it. Some of them might disappear on further reflection, but the time-lag is already so long that I had better set them down and push them off for what they are worth.

I take the preamble to mean that you are prepared to agree to quotas (Q) on something like the following scale (billion dollars):

United States	3·0
United Kingdom	1·25
Rest of Empire	1·0
All other	4·75
Total	10·0

But we have to see what this means, under the Whines plan as compared with its predecessors, in terms of (A) maximum facilities open (without special arrangements) to a potential debtor, (B) maximum liability on a potential creditor.

Under the White Plan, latest revision, the formula for A varies between $A = Q$ (in the case when a country has no gold and is paying all its entrance fee in currency) and $A = \frac{3Q}{2}$ (in the case when a country's gold is greater than $3Q$, and it is therefore paying half its entrance fee in gold). Under the Whines plan, $A = Q$ throughout. The Whines Plan is thus less generous not only (as was to be expected) than the Keynes Plan, but (which will come as a shock) than the White Plan.

Under the Keynes Plan, B is so great that it is conceded it must be reduced. Under the White Plan $B = Q$, and when the Americans say that they are willing for their Q to be 3 billion, what they *mean* is that they are willing for their B to be 3 billion.

Under the Whines Plan, in the normal case when a country pays ⅛ of its entrance fee in gold, $B = Q + \frac{7Q}{8}$. B only becomes as little as Q if (under the special arrangements adumbrated in the last sentence of A 1) a country is permitted and elects to pay the whole of its entrance fee in gold. But in that case the country can refuse to accept unitas from its neighbours from the start, and the scheme breaks down. We seem therefore in a dilemma between asking the Americans to accept a B much larger than what we know them to be willing to accept and establishing a scheme under which the making of payments to the U.S. in unitas is (if the U.S. so chooses) impossible from the start.

Of course the Whines Plan could be made more generous, in absolute terms, to potential debtors by raising the absolute value of the quotas; and it could be made more acceptable to the Americans, in absolute terms, by lowering the absolute value of the quotas: but we are back on the old dilemma,—it cannot be amended in the two directions simultaneously!

In A 5 it is suggested that a stringency can be mitigated by the Fund borrowing unitas from an excess creditor. Now I see how, under the White Plan, the Fund can borrow dollars; but I do not see how, under the Whines Plan, the Fund can borrow unitas. Unitas is already a debt from the Fund to the country in question, and you cannot borrow your own debt. The utmost the Fund can do is to persuade the country to allow it to substitute a *deferred* liability to the country for a *sight* liability. But what would be the good of that? Surely the analogy, under the Whines Plan, to the borrowing of dollars under the White Plan, is simply the persuading of the country in question to hold more unitas than it is bound by the rules of the club to hold.

As regards the C group of rules, if the maximum depreciation permitted under C 13 (ii) is to be no more than 10 %, I feel there is a good deal to be said for throwing logic to the wind and permitting this margin unconditionally,—see REMAC 96, paragraph 2. On the other hand I do not see why a country which flouts the decision of the Board in this field of exchange-alteration should be given special indulgence in respect of the terms on which it can leave the club.

Yours ever,

D. H. ROBERTSON

Yet another draft of the White Plan, that of 10 July, drew another set of suggestions from Keynes.

To SIR WILFRID EADY, *19 July 1943*

1. I have now studied carefully the revised version of S.F. It is more logical and self-consistent than the previous draft. But in most other respects the substance has been changed for the worse. The revision shows no increase in political wisdom and not much in technical capacity. Some of its provisions are drafted with gross selfishness in the interests of a country possessing unlimited gold. In my judgment we must be prepared to face a complete breakdown unless important changes are made. Fortunately the necessary changes are not forbidden by any of Dr White's 'essential conditions'.

2. It is now urgent for us to reply to Dr White telling him

whether or not we accept the conditions which he has indicated to Sir F. Phillips as being, in his judgment, essential; and to respond to his invitation to state the conditions which we, on our side, regard as essential. Should our reply be considered by the interdepartmental meeting which originally considered the C.U.? Should our reply be approved by the meeting of Ministers and not merely by the Chancellor?

3. I recommend that we accept the substance of White's essential conditions, namely:–

  (i) We agree to the subscription principle;

  (ii) We agree to the limitation of liability;

  (iii) We agree that no country shall be required to change the gold value of its currency against its will.

Further, we had better also accept the U.S. formula for quotas and voting power, and the general shape of S.F.; and agree that the initial exchange rate between pound and dollar shall be $£1 = \$4$.

4. Our own essential conditions should be:–

(i) The provisions for changing the value of a member's currency and for preserving sovereignty in this respect must be drastically reconsidered and made much more elastic.

(ii) The Fund must not deal in a mixed bag of currencies but only in unitas, which will not be redeemable in gold and holdings of which will be acquired by members in exchange for their subscriptions and transferred between them by entries in the Fund's books.

(iii) The original S.F. proposal for the gold subscription, namely 12½ per cent of the quota, would be acceptable. If this is to be modified, it must be in such a way as not to give the scheme too pronounced a gold-standard appearance and, more particularly, must not unduly qualify its expansionist possibilities by draining gold from countries whose reserves are relatively deficient already. The balance of the subscription must be in the shape of a non-negotiable government security.

5. The entirely unacceptable features of the new draft which are inconsistent with the above conditions are the following:–

(i) The revised S.F. provides that, except during the initial three years when we are allowed a ten per cent change, sterling would be rigidly tied to gold, with complete surrender of Parliament's sovereignty, any change requiring a four-fifths majority of the voting power. We have reason to think that the Americans would not strongly resist an extension of the three years period to five years and the substitution of a simple for a four-fifths majority. But clearly this is not enough. The prospect that either the Cabinet or Parliament would agree to the above seems remote.

(ii) Our second condition is essential if the scheme is to be capable of intelligible exposition to Parliament and the public. It is also required unless we are to lose face altogether and appear to capitulate completely to dollar diplomacy. But there are also more fundamental technical reasons to which the Bank of England rightly attach primary importance. This condition means that, in return for their initial subscription in terms of gold and securities, members would be credited with corresponding amounts of unitas on the books of the Fund which they would be free to transfer to one another in exchange for needed foreign currencies. Thus the Fund would become passive so far as exchange dealings are concerned, just as the C.U. would be passive. Under the alternative proposed by Dr White, the Fund would possess a mixed bag of currencies in which it would deal at its discretion. It is true that it would only deal with central banks and not with the public. But it would exercise its discretion whether or not to accept or to supply particular currencies. It would purchase only those currencies which it decided (on no clear criterion) to be 'in good standing', and (also on no clear criterion) the sale of which 'is required to meet an adverse balance of payments predominantly on current account'; and it would ration scarce currencies. Moreover it would not assure multi-lateral clearing, since it would not undertake to buy any foreign currency and supply any other needed currency in exchange. The Bank of England maintain, and with reason, that such a system could be so worked as seriously to jeopadise the international position of sterling. There seems to be no serious argument on the other side why the Americans should decline this very great technical simplification. More turns on this than appears on the surface, since, otherwise, there are no clear limits to the active banking functions which the Fund might assume and its power to exercise a discriminatory discretion against certain currencies.

(iii) Our third condition is made necessary by the much larger gold subscriptions proposed in the revised draft. If we end the war with net gold and dollar reserves of (say) £400 million, we should be required to hand over £106 million of this to the Fund. If the U.S. ends the war with £4,700 million of net gold after deducting all their various liabilities (their present figure), they would be required to hand over £366 million to the Fund. It is not clear what this gold is to be used for—this remains an important obscurity to be cleared up. Either it is entirely immobilised or it is handed over to the U.S. as soon as they have a favourable balance of trade. Both these purposes are undesirable. It is entirely unreasonable that, with our large liabilities and responsibilities, we should hand over this high proportion of our total reserves to an untried institution. Moreover there is another new provision by which our right of recourse to the Fund would be severely limited whenever our gold reserves exceeded £160 million (i.e. half our quota). All this seems to be drafted partly to suit a country with unlimited gold reserves, partly to allow the scheme to be represented to Congress as essentially a gold standard scheme.

It is also essential that the security we give should be non-negotiable. At present the draft proposals take powers to use our securities, whether or not we are in a debtor position, as collateral if the Fund desire to borrow dollars from the U.S.

6. A draft which would meet the above points must be prepared shortly. For clearly our Delegation must have instructions what counter-proposal it is authorised to offer. But that is not immediately urgent. What is urgent is to communicate to the U.S. Treasury §§3 and 4 above, if these are agreed.

7. I submit that our delegation should be instructed to break off negotiations for the time being unless satisfactory concessions can be obtained on the three essentials above. There are certain other obscurities to be cleared up, and, of course, many other details which need amendment. But none of these are of the same importance as the above.

KEYNES

19.7.43

In May 1943 Professor Jacob Viner sent Keynes a copy of his article 'Two Plans for International Monetary Stabilisation'.[22] On reading the article, Keynes sent Viner a commentary which led to a reply from Viner. A final letter in the correspondence, from Keynes, came several months later, when the discussions had moved several stages further on.

To PROFESSOR J. VINER, *9 June 1943*

My dear Viner,

Thank you very much indeed for sending me an advance copy of the paper on international monetary stabilisation which is to appear in the *Yale Review*. We have read this over here with the greatest interest. It is one of the few important contributions to the discussion which have yet come to hand. I wish I could have a long talk with you about it all, but, as that for the time being is impossible, it may perhaps be useful

[22] *Yale Review*, Autumn 1943.

if I let you see the running commentary which I made for our purposes here as I read through your paper. I am also enclosing for you a copy of the speech on the matter which I made in the House of Lords, which is the only statement on the subject for publication over my own name which I have made.

1. On the top of page 6 you speak of unitas as having 'only book-keeping significance'. But has it even that in relation to the normal transactions of the Fund? Unitas comes in for the first time in Section IV and appears to have no relation to the normal transactions carried out under Section III. None of the transactions, as I understand the matter, in Section III will provide any country with a holding of unitas. The Fund itself will own a mixed bag of national currencies, and transactions will consist in exchanging one of the these for another. This is in some respects one of the most fundamental distinctions between S.F. and C.U. (the abbreviations for the two schemes which we over here are finding rather convenient). If members of the Fund were to acquire a holding of unitas in exchange for their initial contribution and then, as a result of clearing operations, exchange these holdings of unitas between one another, there would be very much less difference between the basic structures of the two schemes than there is at present.

2. I rather like your suggestion of *mondor*. Certainly we ought to be able to do better than either bancor or unitas. After I invited suggestions in my House of Lords speech, dozens of letters arrived, and I have received upwards of 100, most of them no good at all and no credit to the ingenuity of the human mind. They are mostly either made up terms, like bancor or mondor, or the names of ancient coins, such as staters or darics. In the first group I think your mondor is as good as any, and in the second group staters.

3. *Middle of page 8*. You here express the view that countries are not likely to accept an unlimited liability to be net creditors

321

under a scheme. I should think it extremely likely that you are right about this. I have always felt that the difficulty is to find a satisfactory alternative. I notice that you make no comment on the solution offered in S.F., namely, the rationing of scarce currencies under III, 7. Over here we find this feature of S.F. rather obscure. Are you clear how it would work? Do you think that is a satisfactory way out?

4. I should claim that C.U. keeps a tighter rein over the accumulation by debtor countries of acceptable assets than you have given it credit for. Under Clause 6(8)(b) a country is completely controlled in this respect as soon as it seeks to increase its debit above a half of its quota. Perhaps you mean that these provisions ought to come into force sooner in the rake's progress than when he has used half his quota. There is, of course, no point of principle in this being a half rather than some other figure.

5. *Voting quotas*. I hear from Dennis Robertson that he has already written to you about that. The voting quota you attribute to Great Britain is much higher than what we imagined we were suggesting. As perhaps you will have seen, the Chancellor of the Exchequer made it clear in the House of Commons debate that we attached no importance to our voting formula. I most strongly agree with you that in actual working voting power is not likely to prove important. If the organisation begins voting about everything, it will not be long before it breaks down.

6. More important than the voting provision is the four-fifths majority provision. I see that you point out elsewhere in your paper that this would mean that the United States equally with everyone else would have to suffer extreme exchange rigidity at the behest of a small minority. Do you also realise that the gold producing countries could block any proposal to alter the value of gold, however redundant gold might be? It is not obvious to us why the United States should wish to put itself at the mercy of a small minority on either

of these points. I expect, however, that there is nothing likely to prove a fundamental difficulty here, when we come down to settling details.

7. Personally I do not believe that the initial determination of exchange rates will be quite as difficult as you suggest on page 9. Conversations we have had here with the European Allies indicate that exchange depreciation is nothing like as fashionable as it used to be, and experience has taught many countries what a futile expedient it is except in quite special circumstances. My impression is that the European Allies will, in the interests of protecting pre-war savings in terms of money, have a bias towards over-valuing rather than towards under-valuing their currencies. In general I should have thought one would start from the *de facto* situation unless there was obvious reason to the contrary with special consideration obviously necessary in certain cases. And, as is indicated in C.U., the initial rates should be regarded as a little experimental during the first five years (6(3)) and changes should be allowed more freely than afterwards, if it looks as if a mistake had been made in the first instance. My own feeling about exchange rates is that we should aim at as great stability as possible and that exchange depreciation is not at all a good way of balancing trade unless the lack of balance is due to a particular cause. This particular cause is the movement of efficiency wages in one country out of step with what it is in others. One needs flexibility of rates to meet that contingency and, apart from that contingency one should generally speaking aim at stability.

8. For the same reason that I do not think it need be too difficult to fix exchange rates in the first instance, so also I do not put as high as you do on page 10 the difficulty of obtaining majority consent to the depreciation of a major currency should it be required later on. I should expect two criteria to be fulfilled,—first of all that the country in question was seriously in debit, and secondly that there was

satisfactory evidence that this position was caused, at least in part, by a tendency for its efficiency wages in terms of money to be out of step with efficiency wages elsewhere. At the same time I think you may very likely be right that both plans 'have unintentionally provided in effect for more rigidity of exchange rates than it will be wise to bind the post-war world to in advance'. All this needs a good deal of further thought.

9. *Page 11*. In dealing with the status of gold you write that 'in the White plan acceptability...is enforced indirectly by requiring the member countries, upon request by the Fund, to receive in exchange for their own currencies without limit gold deposits with the Fund made by other member countries'. Where do you find this provision in the plan? I have not been able to discover the clause you here have in mind.

10. As regards the position of gold holders and gold producers, do you not slightly overstate on page 12 the strength of their position under S.F.? There is, I think, no compulsion on the Fund to accept gold from anyone. I see no compulsion under Section III, where it is expressly provided in Clause 8 that the Fund may reject the offer of gold. Nor is there any compulsory provision in Section IV. Clause 3 of this Section states that 'deposits in terms of unitas may be accepted by the Fund from member countries upon delivery of gold to the Fund.' But the text says '*may*', not '*must*'.

11. *Top of page 14*. Not at all. Assuredly I share your concern about the possible menace of inflation, or rather, what is not quite the same, but is perhaps what you mean in this context, the possibility of redundancy of gold. Experience shows that what happens is always the thing against which one has not made provision in advance. These currency schemes are providing against the danger of an insufficiency of international money. For my own part, I should not be at all surprised if, in fact, the actual danger which meets us turns out to be just the opposite, namely, an excess of international

currency. Everyone seems to me to be assuming, without sufficient reason, that the United States is going to run after the war an enormous credit balance after having allowed for long-term capital movements. I regard this as quite uncertain. Suppose the opposite takes place, and the United States begins to export its gold holdings. Suppose at the same time Russia is using some part of her now quite gigantic hoards to pay for her imports of capital goods, and suppose simultaneously with this the normal gold output of the world is helped by scientific progress to increase. Nothing highly improbable in any of these possibilities. Between them they might certainly create the state of affairs about which you rightly feel concerned.

12. *Capital Export Controls.* As you will see from what I said in my House of Lords speech, we have no intention to use postal censorship after the war and do not think it necessary. In general on this question of exchange control I should be inclined to say that C.U. requires it with less compulsory necessity than S.F. Our view is that there is no adequate technique for capital control which does not involve a *pro forma* control over all exchange transactions, and that, I think, is what we are likely to set up in this country,—at any rate until someone instructs us as to an alternative technique for capital control. However this may be, C.U. does not enforce any such *pro forma* control on other countries. Each country is left to enforce capital control if it wants to or to leave all transactions free; and, if it does decide in favour of capital control, it is left to discover its own technique. S.F., on the other hand, seems to require the most meticulous exchange control. III, 3(*a*) provides that a member can only draw on the Fund 'to meet an adverse balance of payments on current account with a country whose currency is being demanded'. How is it possible to say whether any transaction is required to meet an adverse balance on current account unless there is complete capital control? And this section seems to require that

the statistics should relate in detail, not only to a country's position with the world at large, but to its position with each country in isolation. Now even a country which is a creditor on balance is certain to be a debtor with particular geographical areas,—otherwise multilateral clearing would not be necessary. Thus there would be very few countries which could ever make use of the Fund unless they had previously set up a meticulous exchange control which distinguished transactions, not only according to whether they were capital or current, but also according to the particular countries which would be the ultimate payers or receivers.

13. *Page 15.* I agree with you most sincerely as to the atmosphere in which the new organisation should start and the character of its personnel. It is of the first importance that it 'should be looked upon as an agency with predominantly routine peace-time functions to perform for a stable and ordinary world'.

Well, you will see from the above how much I should welcome a chance of conversation. But, meanwhile, the above must serve.

Yours sincerely,

KEYNES

From PROFESSOR J. VINER, *12 July 1943*

Dear Lord Keynes

May I take this opportunity of congratulating you both on the well-deserved honor which your country has conferred upon you, and upon the very effective and graceful—and ingratiating—speech with which you made your debut in the House of Lords. I thank you also for your very generous letter. I think we are not really far apart on any important issues, and I hope that the following comments will help to make it clear how far we are in agreement and whether any remaining points of disagreement are significant.

1. Re 'Book-keeping significance' of unitas. The White draft (IV, 1) states that: 'the accounts of the Fund shall be kept and published in terms of unitas'. I agree that except as a term for a specified quantity of gold,

'unitas' has no significance. I would also admit that even for bookkeeping purposes, the Fund accounts will have to be stated in terms of specific national currencies as well as in unitas. But I don't see that my text is inconsistent with any of this.

There is, I agree, an important difference in principle between balances with the Fund which retain their original form and credits in bancor terms with the Union. But there would be important difference in practice only if and as the Fund ran short of a particular currency in demand. The essential difference, therefore, is that under the Fund, but not under C.U., there are specific limits to the contribution which any country can be required to make, and therefore to the quantity of any currency which the agency can supply. I cannot see, however, how your suggestion that contributions to the Fund might be held in the form of unitas would alter this situation. Once a country's unitas credit balance had reached the limit of its contributory quota, debits to that country could not be liquidated as of right with unitas, i.e. unitas would no longer be 'legal-tender' for this purpose. Until that point was reached, exchange of currencies through the Fund without recourse to unitas would do the job of international settlement just as well, if not as elegantly, as would transfers of unitas balances.

2. I am glad that 'mondor' appeals somewhat to you. I have thought also of 'monda' as perhaps being more to the liking of those who want as little emphasis on gold as possible.

3. If a particular country's currency was scarce all-round, rationing should ameliorate the situation somewhat by preventing a disorderly scramble for the scarce currency, and by acting as a warning signal of a conspicuous kind to both the creditor country and the debtor countries to take equilibrating measures. I always find thinking in terms of the demand for a specific quantity of a specific foreign currency during a specific time-period rather unrealistic. If there are expectations of worsements in position, the amount demanded can expand indefinitely for both speculative and panic reasons. If expectations are neutral, immediate debt obligations are in the aggregate always to a large extent compressible or postponable, and acceptable means of payment always to some extent capable of expansion. Under S.F. the Fund itself can, if it wishes, and especially if its own credit status is good, come to the rescue in several ways.

The absence in the C.U. of a rigid limit to the creditor obligations is of course very attractive *per se* to those who are debtor-minded but it is literally terrifying to those who anticipate being creditors. Whether inherently desirable or not, I think that limits to credit obligations will absolutely without question have to be conceded to make the new agency

327

acceptable to all the essential countries. In my opinion, any creditor country will in all likelihood voluntarily agree to exceed these limits, or to take remedial steps such as funding of short-term indebtedness, if the governing board of the agency recommends such action strongly and the general situation makes such action appear reasonable. In any case, the scheme does not have to start out perfect in every respect, and it will not collapse merely because it does not provide in advance with full adequacy for every situation which can arise. The important thing is to get acceptance of a scheme with real possibilities and to rely on time and a good record to make possible its further development in directions which either experience or *a priori* analysis indicates to be desirable.

4. I did have in mind the freedom to borrow unconditionally until half the quota had been used. It is a difficulty under both plans that members have unconditional rights to borrow up to a point regardless of their degree of credit-worthiness. In this respect, I believe, neither plan has any historical counterpart whether in private or in public finance. I don't have any fully satisfactory solution, since I believe that the assured availability of credit upon demand is a most valuable feature of both plans. I would try to get the best of both worlds by limiting the unconditional quotas much more narrowly than you do, but making the conditional ones larger than the American draft does. I have elsewhere thrown out for consideration the suggestion that a distinction be made between active and inactive members, with members becoming active only as the agency's board by majority vote finds it ready to carry out its responsibilities under the plan. This fits in with my belief that the monetary agency should not be regarded as having an important operating role to play during the period—say one to three years—of post-war major adjustment, and that an agency of another—and less routine—kind is needed to meet the balance-of-payments difficulties of that period. On this see 13, below.

5. After Robertson raised the point, I found I had been guilty of a clerical error in my computations, and in a second batch of my preprints I made the correction called for. But I can't get the British figure down below 16½ per cent. However, I am in my final draft going to play down the voting issue still further.

6. I disapprove strongly, on non-economic grounds, of the individual country veto-power unless it is granted to all countries regardless of their quotas. I will see if I can't find space for pointing out that the 80 per cent majority rule would limit the power of the U.S. with respect to changes it may desire in an existing status as much as it would increase its power to stop undesired changes.

7. I agree with you with respect to exchange-rate problems during a fairly

stable period. I feel, however, that all rates will have to be regarded as highly experimental for several years after the end of hostilities. I want more flexibility than either the C.U. or the S.F. provides for the interim period. I want much less flexibility than, I presume, either you or White want for 'normal' times, but even for that period I think the results of the S.F. procedure would be to make rates in fact too rigid even for me. As to the criterion for permissible (or compulsory) changes in 'normal' times, I don't think relative trends of 'efficiency wages' would suffice, although they would be important. Exchange depreciations always have arbitrary differential effects as between foreign countries and internal economic groups, and, I think, are never a satisfactory means of adjustment of minor disequilibria. The wage criterion, moreover, accepts the business agent of the powerful trade unions as the ultimate and unlimited sovereign over monetary policy. Even an adjustment of exchange rates which seems called for by the situation as a whole will be likely to mean acute pressure for some important interests in some other countries, and these interests will not be easily assuaged by any general argument which does not fit their particular situation. Moreover, the common argument that the exchange rates of small countries [do not matter], seems to me to need qualification. For American wheat growers, Canada is the largest country in the world. Danish exchange matters for New Zealand, New Zealand exchange for Australia, the Argentine, Canada, etc. and Canadian and Argentine exchange matter for the U.S.

9. This mistake in my article has been pointed out to me by a number of correspondents. I will of course make appropriate changes in my final draft.

10. There is compulsion on the S.F. to accept gold to the full amount of the member country's quotas, II (4). I interpreted III (2), perhaps wrongly, as an obligation on the S.F. to have firm buying and selling prices for gold. I will try to find out whether White accepts this interpretation. In a letter (presumably confidential) White writes: 'As I read the text [of IV (3)] this commits the Fund to providing local currency for gold.' So that if I am misinterpreting this provision, so is its author!

11. I don't mean 'redundancy of gold' *here*, except as it would lead to inflation, which is what I have in mind. I am glad to find that we do not differ sharply here. I can't recall at the moment that either in the British White Paper or in the H. of Lds. or H. of C. debates the danger of inflation was anywhere as much as referred to, except for one reference in the White Paper which seems to imply that only during the immediate post-war period is it at all likely that an inflation problem would exist.

12. I obviously failed to distinguish between your specific proposals and

your apparent aspirations re exchange control. I will rewrite this section both to do justice to you and to qualify my own position somewhat.

Re the American III, 3(a), I think it is fantastic to think that it is possible, with or without exchange control, to ascertain accurately for periods as short as a month, let alone a week or a day, the state of the balance on 'current' account. Terms of payment are so variant and flexible that to determine the contribution to international debits and credits of the transactions of any month would require much more than a complete recording of all actual exchange transactions, for it would require also a complete recording of all transactions of that period which would involve exchange transactions later or which were financed in advance by earlier exchange transactions. I take it that in practice no attempt would be made strictly to enforce a provision of this sort. I agree wholly with you as to its impracticability.

13. Here I come to the most important point I want to raise with you. I think that discussion of both plans has been befogged by failure to distinguish between the international financial problems of the period immediately following the cessation of hostilities and those of the long-run more stable future. The expectation that the U.S. will be alone or almost alone as a creditor is plausible for the first period. Over the long pull, (with qualifications re the usability of the American gold accumulation) I think the U.S. is as likely to be short as to be long of foreign short-term funds. But the difficulties re size of voting quotas, size of borrowing quotas, motives of the [authors of] sections of the plans, etc. largely arise because the two plans are being interpreted primarily as plans to tide over the immediate post-war emergency period. It is being said, for instance, that England anticipates being short of dollars to amounts up to $1 million per annum and for a period extending up to three years or so during the immediate post-war period, and looks to the new agency to provide these funds 'anonymously', or as I would prefer to put it, in a 'denationalized' form. I don't question the need of England for such aid, or the urgency that the need be met by a dignified, non-political, and non-usurious procedure. But I don't think it would be a proper transaction for an equalization fund. What reason would there be to expect that in the third or fourth year England could liquidate such indebtedness? If she failed to do so, her status in the C.U. or S.F. at that time would be highly unsatisfactory. The British White Paper (36) says 'It should be emphasised that the purpose of the overdrafts of bancor permitted by the Clearing Union is, not to facilitate long-term, or even medium-term, credits'. So far, so good. But I have found nothing in the White Paper

330

which expressly disclaims intention to use the C.U. to tide over the dollar needs of the non-relief outside world during the transition period. I feel very strongly that these needs *should be met*, and as fully as possible, but by 'medium-term' credits. The Chancellor of the Exchequer in the House put it very well when he said: 'We must be very careful not to waterlog this scheme for handling current trading transactions with problems not directly related to ordinary current trade' (659). But he also put as one of the aims of the C.U. 'in order particularly, to meet the difficulties of the early period after the war, that countries whose economy has been gravely dislocated or damaged by the war, should have some temporary international monetary facilities to enable them to start up into national trading without undue delay' (651). And the Lord Chancellor, in the House of Lords, said: 'Heaps of people will find themselves in a position, as it were, of owning a battered motor car without any means of starting it. That is the reason why these plans—particularly thinking of the British plan—put in such an important place that part of the scheme which is designed to provide a restarter after the war for the trade of various countries' (558). Both statements seem to point to transactions which should properly be handled as medium-term—or even long-term— transactions.

I think it highly urgent that on both sides of the water it be made clear how much of the transition period problem the new monetary agency is intended to handle and what type of provision is to be made for the part of the problem to be handled otherwise. I believe such procedure would not only clarify thinking, but would also promote agreement. The U.S., I think, will have a very special role to play in the interim period—although limitations of supplies, if nothing else, will make it a much smaller role than some people contemplate—but in the long-run monetary stabilization field I don't think it especially likely that her role will be a very special one, and I think it will receive help as much and as often as it grants it. I put no stock in a 'chronic scarcity of dollars'. If the two fields were separated for discussion, I think many apparent conflicts of opinion would disappear, and that it would be much easier to ascertain—and enlarge—the area of agreement. Perhaps you would claim that your paragraphs 41–42 do make this distinction, but I read these paragraphs as relating only to countries receiving relief. In any case, they don't carry the examination of the problem far enough, and they fail to explain whether exclusion from overdraft because of receipt of relief brings with it also freedom from C.U. discipline with respect to exchange rates.

I should explain that I write in the happy role of a completely private citizen, and that what I write is totally without official significance.

Very sincerely yours,

JACOB VINER

P.S. You would do me a favor if you could send me a copy of the British print of the American plan to add to my private collection.

To PROFESSOR J. VINER, *17 October 1943*

My dear Viner,

I have long owed you an answer to your letter of 12 July, which was forwarded to me through Robertson. When it reached me in August we were preparing our minds for the conversations with the U.S. Treasury which have just been taking place, and the position was rather fluid. So I put off answering until our views had crystallised a little more. And then when I actually did come to Washington to carry on these conversations, I had been hoping to have a chance of talking to you personally. Now, however, I am at the end of my visit, and, to the great regret of all of us, you have not put in an appearance here during our stay.

No doubt you will hear in due course the main principles which emerged from these current conversations. In the opinion of all of us we have made really enormous progress towards a common view, and whilst there are still outstanding points of difference, my own expectation is that they will not be unduly difficult to settle after we have got back to London. The discussions have been most enjoyable, and the will to agreement very marked. Each group understands the other's point of view a great deal better than it did before.

Some of the points in your letter of 12 July have, of course, been put out-of-date by these conversations. But there are one or two of your central contentions about which I might say a word.

In your paragraph 4 you raise the question of the extent

332

of the freedom to borrow unconditionally. This is one of the matters on which we have not yet reached final accommodation. Our view has been very strongly that if countries are to be given sufficient confidence they must be able to rely in all normal circumstances on drawing a substantial part of their quota without policing or facing unforeseen obstacles. Indeed, we have been inclined to think, on second thoughts, that the Clearing Union may have been too strict on this, though this was actually balanced under the Clearing Union by the much greater size of the quotas. If the Clearing Union provisions were applied to the lower quotas now contemplated, we gravely doubt whether those concerned, particularly some of the smaller countries, would feel adequate confidence. And I regard the increase of confidence as perhaps one of the major contributions that the plans can make to future stability. This, therefore, is a point about which, after further reflection, I cannot agree with you. No doubt it is a difficult issue. But I am sure that it would be very unwise to try to make an untried institution too grandmotherly. When it has established traditions of action it might be easier. At the present stage it is confidence we want to confirm. What I say later, however, about the role of the monetary plans in the early post-war period may, perhaps, meet your feelings a little.

In paragraph 7 you raise the question of greater exchange elasticity. On this point we in London have come round entirely to your point of view. With some difficulty, we have persuaded White to come a good long way to meet us. I hope that you will find the new formula acceptable. My own feeling now is that it goes far enough.

Finally, there is the point you raise in your paragraph 13 about the relation of a monetary plan to the immediate post-war period. I am afraid that there was here, as you point out, some confusion between what the late Chancellor of the Exchequer said in the House of Commons, and what the Lord

Chancellor said in the House of Lords. It was, however, the Chancellor who was giving the authentic doctrine. The Lord Chancellor was making an improvisation and speaking off his brief. I was sitting near him in the House, but he spoke without giving me a chance of warning him off this particular statement. Nevertheless, you can feel assured that his remarks do not supersede the Chancellor's. We have not yet found the precise formula for defining the role of the plan in the early period. But you may feel confident that on this issue we are entirely of your mind.

Perhaps you will have noticed in the last *Economic Journal* a note about Sraffa's miraculous good luck in discovering, just in time, the missing papers of Ricardo. Since I have been in Washington I have had a report from Sraffa, who had visited Dublin, where the papers are, in order to inspect them. He reports that the scope of the find exceeds all expectations. The letters of Ricardo to Mill cover the whole period (1811 to 1823), and the set is pretty complete—more complete than that of the Mill to Ricardo letters (these were 49 in number, the Ricardo to Mill series are 57). In addition, there are two letters from Malthus, and one from McCulloch to Ricardo, which fill gaps in our collection. Also, there is a number of unpublished papers by Ricardo, some of them of great interest on the 'measure of value'.

As you will have seen from the note in the *Journal*, these have been discovered amongst Cairnes' papers. Apart from Cairnes' correspondence with J. S. Mill, and a few odd letters from Jevons, Tooke, and others, the rest of Cairnes' papers are not apparently of great interest. But they are very voluminous, and will provide material for a really good life of Cairnes. They contain no clue as to how or when the Ricardo papers passed from J. S. Mill (or from Helen Taylor) to Cairnes.

You may also be interested in the following extract from Sraffa's report to me:–

Incidentally, if someone in the future tried to understand how we got on the track of these Ricardo-Mill letters, he will find it equally mysterious. The fact is, it has all been based on a fortunate series of misunderstandings. I heard from Hayek that a Mr Mill of Dublin had the letters of Cairnes to J. S. Mill, as well as the replies. I assumed that he had inherited them, and it seemed plausible that he might have more of the Mill papers: so I enquired whether he had the Ricardo letters—and sure enough, he had.

It now turns out that the present Mr Mill enters the story purely in his capacity of husband of a granddaughter of Cairnes, that what he has is the Cairnes papers, and the supposed letters of Cairnes to Mill are merely copies supplied (as I believe), after his death, by Helen Taylor to the widow of Cairnes; that these do not contain a single scrap out of Mill's papers,— with the only exception of the Ricardo parcel; which has no business to be there. It is clear that, had my information been correct, I should never have dreamt of asking Mr Mill such an improbable question, as whether he had Ricardo's letters.

I enclose a copy of the London print of the United States proposal for your collection, and also a copy of the London print of the Canadian proposals.

Ever sincerely yours,

KEYNES

At the end of the summer series of Washington talks, H. D. White sent the following letter to Keynes.

From H. D. WHITE, *24 July 1943*

Dear Keynes,

We have almost completed our scheduled bilateral discussions on post-war monetary problems. Altogether we conferred with delegates of some 25 countries and also had several sessions of group discussions attended by delegates from about a score of countries. In the bilateral conferences the most of the provisions in the Fund draft were discussed, and in almost every case the more important provisions in the Clearing Union draft were also considered. In the larger group meetings, as your colleagues will doubtless inform you, both proposals were rather fully discussed though the American proposal was the point of departure in the agenda. In our bilateral

335

conferences with the British group I think the salient points in both proposals were fully discussed and compared.

I am enclosing a revised draft of the Fund proposal which you will recognize contains a number of significant changes. Some of the changes were recommended by the delegates of the various countries some are made to meet criticism of provisions in the original draft, and some are an attempt to include some of the ideas embodied in the Clearing Union draft. I believe that you will like most of the new and altered provisions, and will appreciate that we have tried to introduce as much flexibility as we dared.

We tried to explain to your colleagues that we feel that we must formulate the kind of proposal which has some chance of getting Congressional approval. Indeed, opinion in important financial and political groups seems for the moment to be moving away [from] rather than toward a policy of close international economic collaboration.

In our opinion, it would be a serious error to try to secure Congressional approval for a proposal which has little chance of being so approved. It would be far better to proceed more cautiously and be satisfied with a plan less ambitious but one for which there is at least a fighting chance of acceptance by Congress. As we indicated to your colleagues, there are certain requirements without which the chances of approval by Congress are, in our judgment, so slim as to warrant our not making the attempt. These requirements, to be sure, apply only a few aspects of the proposal, but they are basic.

The first requirement relates to the magnitude of the commitment. The technicians here are all in agreement that we would be fortunate if we were able to get Congress to commit itself to as much as $3 billion. Many believe that $2 billion is the maximum. We all believe it would be most unwise to have any provision which attempts a larger commitment. There is a better chance, we believe, for more dollars to be made available, if the commitment is not too high and the decision to make additional dollars available is left to administrative action, i.e., upon the decision made at the time by the Treasury and central bank.

The second point about which we feel there is no feasible alternative relates to the composition of the Fund. We believe that the Fund must have assets and that each country must participate in the contribution of those assets, and that gold must constitute some part of that contribution. Some of the technicians are strongly in favor of greater contribution of gold by countries having gold. We have tried to reach a compromise among our own technicians on this point and the provision dealing with gold in the appended draft constitutes such a compromise. I personally might have favored a lower percentage of gold for some of the countries but unless

336

we can get agreement on major issues among the interested administrative branches of the Government here there would be little chance of waging a successful fight for adoption in Congress.

Thirdly, we feel here that the votes accorded the members must bear some relation to contributions, i.e., countries with larger contributions must have more than those with smaller contributions.

Finally there has to be an understanding on the leading exchange rates before we can go much further in our discussions.

If we can get agreement on these four points we think the conference could work out a document that would have a good chance of getting general approval. We had hoped that if we can get agreement on these points, that an informal drafting committee composed possibly of men from four or five governments, could begin working on a draft for consideration by a formal conference to be held in the fall.

I am enclosing a pamphlet by B. M. Anderson,[23] a comment by Guaranty Trust Company, and a draft of a summary report of the A.B.A. Economic Policy Commission. Together with Williams' article in the July issue of *Foreign Affairs*,[24] they give some indication of the kind of opposition there is developing in the United States to efforts for any comprehensive scheme of post-war monetary proposals. Incidentally both Anderson's and Williams' articles appear to be having rather wide distribution.

Thank you for sending me the copies of the debate in the House of Commons and of your speech in the Lords. Your speech impressed me very favorably. You were more than fair in your comparison, and helped, I am sure, to allay some of the fears of your countrymen. In general, I thought that the discussion by the members was of a surprisingly high level, though, of course, there was evidence of considerable misunderstanding of both proposals as is to be expected at this early stage in discussions. The discussion seemed so good that I suggested to Phillips that he have the debates reprinted here and made available for distribution which he was kind enough to do.

I was disappointed that you weren't here to join in discussions that we had and hope if there are to be any further discussions that you will be able to find the time to participate.

The many discussions which we have been having leaves me with the impression that there will be no obstacle to securing agreement among most of the nations that participated in the informal bilateral discussions. If we

[23] *Post-war Stabilization of Foreign Exchange—the Keynes–Morgenthau Plan Condemned —Outline of a Fundamental Solution.*
[24] J. H. Williams, 'Economic Problems of the Peace: Currency Stabilisation: the Keynes and White Plans'.

can secure prior agreement on the basic points among the four major powers, I believe that a formal conference would have little difficulty formulating a document that had a good chance of being acceptable to Congress.

Sincerely yours,

HARRY D. WHITE

Between White's drafting of the letter, and its delivery to Keynes in London on 4 August, the British had suggested a formal set of Anglo-American talks covering the Article VII items of monetary policy, commercial policy and commodity policy in Washington beginning in the course of September. The Americans accepted the proposal. As a result, instructions were prepared for the British delegation to the discussions and approved at a meeting of the War Cabinet on 2 September.

The delegation's instructions centred on five points: each country should maintain the freedom to alter its own exchange rate, although there might be some form of objective test for guidance; gold subscriptions to the Fund should be limited to 12½ per cent of each nation's quota; the Fund should be passive in exchange markets and not buy or sell currencies (to achieve this, unitas, the unit of account for the Fund would become monetised); the Fund should be larger, about $10 billion in size; any attempt to deal with abnormal war balances should not be part of the scheme.

The British delegation[25] travelled by sea to New York. During the voyage members of the delegation spent the time preparing the ground for their discussions. In particular, they spent some time on Mr White's 'Proposal for a Bank for Reconstruction and Development of the United and Associated Nations', dated 4 August 1943, which Redvers Opie had communicated privately to the delegation. The delegation agreed on the desirability of such an institution, on the desirability of not publishing the plan at present 'since it would be heavily criticised and might bring contempt not only on the proposals in the document but also on the Stabilisation Fund' and on the importance of not indicating to the Americans that they had seen the plan. If the Americans brought the plan forward during the forthcoming discussions the chief criticisms raised would be that international invest-

---

[25] The delegation was led by Mr Richard Law; its members were Keynes, Waley, F. G. Lee, Robbins, N. B. Ronald, G. L. M. Clauson, P. Liesching, Meade, R. J. Shackle, and P W. Martin.

Sir Gerard Leslie Makins Clauson (1891–1974); orientalist; Assistant Under-Secretary of State, Colonial Office, 1940–51.

P. W. Martin, Head of Division, Ministry of Food, 1943–5.

ment on such a scale[26] could not yield returns in the long run and that, therefore, sanctions on defaulters must be less severe.[27] In addition, the plan should make the relationships between the Bank and the Fund clearer. If the document did not appear during the discussions, the delegation would press for a set of ground rules for international investment and an International Development Commission to examine proposals and recommend as to their timing.

On his arrival in Washington, Keynes had lunch with Mr Morgenthau on 14 September. At the lunch Keynes in reply to a question about his plans for the discussions said:[28]

> Keynes responded that he had been talking with White about it, and that there was to be a general meeting in which he was to bring his men and meet the Treasury and State Department people, and he thought that after that, if there had been some progress, that a drafting committee, to be selected among the United Nations, would begin work. He understood that this was our desire. He added that a promise had been made to his Parliament to debate the matter before it took final form and so he hoped there would be some statement of principles in a few pages that would be made public and which the Parliament could debate publicly before a final draft was published.[29]

Before the talks began, the delegation continued the discussions that it had had on the boat and in London on an objective test for exchange rate proposals. At this stage, Keynes favoured a test based on relative money costs of production, whereas James Meade favoured a test based on the level of a country's reserves.

On 15 September the American and British monetary groups[30] met to discuss the exchange rate issue. At the meeting the British suggested that exchange rate changes be initiated subject to the approval of the Fund to correct fundamental disequilibria in the balance of payments subject to several provisos: the Fund could not withhold its approval if the proposed changes, inclusive of previous changes, did not alter the rate by more than 10 per cent in a ten year period; the Fund, in giving or withholding approval to changes over 10 per cent would act so as to take account of

---

[26] Up to $10 billion per annum was the sum proposed.

[27] Keynes, who described White's proposals, according to one participant, 'as Bedlam and his drafting as positively Sumerian', thought that the Bank might get round the default problem by doing some of its investment in equity form.

[28] Morgenthau Diaries, Vol. 664. p. 29.

[29] At that time, Keynes was thinking in terms of a discussion in Parliament in late October.

[30] The U.K. group for the discussions was made up of Keynes, Professor Robertson, Professor Robbins, Mr Thompson-McCausland and Mr Opie. James Meade joined the group after 24 September.

changes in relative money costs of production (allowing changes if increased relative costs had led to overvaluation), the balance on current account position and the level of reserves. On all occasions the Fund would 'not be entitled to refuse a change on the ground of the social or political policies which may have led to the situation and shall approve a change which in the *de facto* situation would tend to restore equilibrium'. The Americans countered with their preference to leave discretion with the Fund beyond a margin of 10 per cent for the immediate post-war period and raised objections as to the form of the objective test in the shape of technical progress and non-traded goods. Keynes in reply raised the problem of discussing rate changes 'in full session and in "mixed company" before they were actually made'. After further exchanges of views, the meeting adjourned.

The next meeting, on 17 September, repeated the format of the first consisting of a general exchange of views on the changes in the gold value of unitas, the unit of account for the Fund, the size of the Fund and its disciplinary powers.

In the early stages of the discussions, it also became clear that White wished his, as yet unready, Bank scheme to go forward with the Stabilisation Fund proposals. The British pressed for delaying the publication of the scheme for a Bank until after the British had seen it and been able to react to it and asked for explicit instructions from London to that effect.

After these two meetings, Keynes expressed his reactions as follows

From a letter to L. RASMINSKY, *18 September 1943*

We are having most interesting and exciting discussions with Harry White and his associates in an atmosphere singularly free from unnecessary controversy or obstacle, and we all of us have high hopes that joint and common effort will emerge. White has the immense merit that he takes a high intellectual interest in these questions and approaches them on that plane and not on official or bureaucratic lines.

I hope I am not being too optimistic. But I think I can say for all concerned that the discussions are being thoroughly enjoyed.

On 21 September, there was the first plenary session covering all aspects of the discussions. Keynes's speech at this drew the following comment from one British observer.

Keynes's speech was absolutely in the first rank of speechifying. I have never heard him better—more brilliant, more persuasive, more witty or more truly moving in his appeal. His great appeal was that we should treat the whole economic [problem] as a unity and be prepared to present to the public a prospect of a radical solution of the problems of unemployment and of raising standards of living.

The same meeting also saw Keynes appointed chairman, with Meade and Robbins as members, of the Committee dealing with employment matters in the talks. On this Keynes commented

It is amusing that we who are in London not allowed to know anything on this subject should here be in charge of all international plans on the subject.

While the U.K. group continued informally to discuss an objective test for exchange rate changes and Keynes continued to hold his ground on his own proposal, Keynes raised the monetisation issue with White.

To H. D. WHITE, *21 September 1943*

My dear White,

I am now able to enclose my suggestions, which I promised, about the monetisation of unitas, for you and me to discuss amongst ourselves before passing them on for more general discussion. I suggest that the two of us might meet to have a further word about them some time on Wednesday [22 September] if you can spare the time.

I call your special attention to the hidden and unostentatious beauties of the provision that countries wishing to sell gold are expected to offer it first of all to the Fund if this serves their purpose equally well. This appears to me to get over the objection you raised the other day, whilst in course of time making the Fund the main central reserve of gold and steadily increasing the proportion of its assets represented by gold. Since gold obtained under this clause would be *free* gold it would be available to reduce excessive holdings of unitas, in other words, to deal with the scarce currency problem. I should expect this clause to increase the free gold assets of the Fund, perhaps a little slowly at first but in the end on a much larger scale than your present draft. It would mean, in particular, that if, for example, the United States was to lose, let us say, 2 billion of gold in the early period, most of this 2 billion would accrue to the Fund (unless it was on such a scale as to cause the recipients of it to become super-abundant holders of unitas) and be available to be released to the Fund to be returned to the United States in the event of the tide turning later on. I am hopeful that the more you consider this clause in conjunction with the extreme simplicity of the rest of the above the better pleased with it you will feel.

Yours sincerely,
[copy initialled] K.

SUGGESTIONS FOR THE MONETISATION OF UNITAS

Composition of the Fund

1. A member shall make a subscription to the Fund, equal to its quota, of which not less than 12½ per cent shall be in gold and the balance in securities carrying ½ per cent interest payable in unitas, receiving in return a corresponding balance expressed in unitas on the books of the Fund; and shall be entitled subsequently to subscribe up to a further 50 per cent of its quota on the same terms. The aggregate of the quotas of the member countries shall be the equivalent of at least $8 billion.

2. A member country may subscribe further gold in redemption of its securities at any time. If at the end of any year a member has a stock of gold and currencies freely convertible into gold in excess of its quota, it shall redeem its securities with gold to an amount equal to 2 per cent of its quota so long as any of its securities remain outstanding. The gold and securities initially subscribed and any gold subsequently subscribed under this clause shall remain as a pledge with the Fund, which may not part with it except when the member redeems it or withdraws from the Fund or on the Fund's liquidation. Gold so held shall be called *fixed* gold.

Provisions for exchange stability and multilateral clearing

3. A member shall undertake to sell its currency to another member in exchange for a transfer of unitas at parity on the books of the Fund unless it has given notice under 5 below.

4. A member shall undertake to buy its currency from another member in exchange for a transfer of unitas at parity on the books of the Fund so long as it has a balance of unitas or is in a position to obtain more unitas on the same terms as its original subscription.

Limitation of Commitment

5. A member whose holding of unitas has reached 120 per cent of its quota shall be entitled to apply further receipts of unitas to redeeming its original subscription—first the securities and then the gold. At any time after it has thus redeemed at least 80 per cent of its original subscription, it shall be entitled to give notice that it will only accept further unitas to the extent of 20 per cent of its quota. A member which has redeemed all or part of its original subscription for unitas shall be entitled to reverse its action at any time (on payment of the interest which it has saved) (e.g. If the U.S. quota is 2½ billion its maximum commitment is 3 billion.)

Gold

6. The Fund may buy gold from a member at its par value in exchange for a balance of unitas, the gold so acquired being *free* gold. A member may not buy gold at a price in excess of the par value of its currency. A member desiring to sell gold is expected to offer it to the Fund, directly or through another member, if this will serve its purpose in selling the gold equally well. The Fund may at its option, and with the approval of the member concerned, employ free gold to redeem any portion of a member's balance of unitas in excess of its quota.

343

7. If at the end of the year ending at any quarter a member, whose balance of unitas is less than its outstanding subscription, has increased its stock of gold and currencies freely convertible into gold and has reduced its balance of unitas during the period, it shall use this increase to replenish its stock of unitas.

21 September 1943

The monetary discussions continued, both in formal meetings on 21 and 28 September and in informal discussions. Amongst the issues discussed at the meetings were certainty of access to the Fund, the monetisation of unitas, borrowing quotas, limitations of the American lending commitment and the size of the gold subscription. To give some idea of the form discussions took, the minutes of the meeting of 24 September appear below.

DISCUSSIONS ON AGENDA UNDER ARTICLE VII
INTERNATIONAL MONETARY DISCUSSIONS

Note of a joint meeting of the U.K. and U.S. groups held on Friday 24 September 1943, at the U.S. Treasury

Present:

U.K. Group	U.S. Group
Lord Keynes	Mr Bernstein, Treasury
Professor D. H. Robertson	Mr Cassady, Treasury
Sir David Waley	Mr Luxford, Treasury
Professor L. Robbins	Miss Richardson, Treasury
Mr R. Opie	Mr Berle, State Department
Mr J. E. Meade	Mr Coe, O.E.W.
Mr L. P. Thompson-McCausland	Mr Currie
Mr A. S. J. Baster	Mr Goldenweiser, Federal Reserve System
	Mr Gardner, Federal Reserve System
	Mr Hansen
	Mr Livsey, State Department
	Mr Brown, State Department
	Mr Ben Cohen, White House

344

I. *The certainty of access to the Fund*

MR BERNSTEIN said that, under S.F., countries would have assurance of unconditional access to the Fund only up to the amounts of their gold subscription. He appreciated the need to give members a measure of certainty as to their drawing powers beyond that, and suggested that the Fund might make a firm commitment to supply a limited amount of foreign exchange within a given period, say, six months, renewed at the Fund's discretion half-way through each period. But the intention was that the Fund should have the power to refuse to renew if its resources were being abused, e.g. if used as cover for long-term capital movements.

LORD KEYNES doubted whether this proposal would meet his objections. The real function of reserves is to give confidence and Mr Bernstein's proposal seemed to cut at the root of confidence.

MR BERNSTEIN said he considered the primary function of the Fund was to cover periods of adjustment. It would be an abuse if the Fund were drawn on substantially by a member who was not attempting to adjust his position.

LORD KEYNES agreed that in the last resort rationing or policing was necessary, but it should be only in the last resort.

Several American representatives (MESSRS GARDNER, BERNSTEIN, and LUXFORD) then stressed the need to reserve the Fund's right to limit the use of the Fund to purposes for which it was intended.

MR BERLE said he thought it was generally desired that the resources of the Fund should:–

(*a*) be available with certainty for proper use;

(*b*) be denied by appropriate devices to countries requiring them for improper use.

MR GOLDENWEISER said it was largely a question of (*a*) the burden of proof, and (*b*) the stage at which the Fund should intervene. Lord Keynes's proposal was that we should agree on the proper uses for the Fund's resources, and, subject to a maximum rate of drawings, assume that members were keeping to the rules unless evidence to the contrary accumulated against them. Mr. Bernstein's proposal was to verify that members were keeping to the rules by maintaining a constant watch on them. Large countries would find this procedure intolerable, and he believed that Lord Keynes's thesis was the only one which could work in practice.

MR BERNSTEIN said that certain abuses would be prevented by limiting annual withdrawals to 25 per cent of the quota as the U.K. Group had suggested. But even within this allocation, a country might use the Fund's resources in a way that would upset its balance of payments position, and yet (under the United Kingdom proposal) be under no obligation to initiate correctives.

MR BERLE said that no great country would submit to this sort of scrutiny, and this was why there was a resort to arithmetical devices.

MR GOLDENWEISER asked whether abuses of the Fund could be defined.

LORD KEYNES agreed that capital flight could be defined sufficiently for this purpose, but not import of luxuries.

LORD KEYNES suggested that Mr Bernstein's point might be met if the *quantitative* restriction combined a maximum rate of drawing and a maximum total drawing beyond which a country should be obliged to take corrective measures.

PROFESSOR HANSEN asked if the contingency had been considered that a country which was getting out of adjustment might keep clear of the Fund's controlling power by exporting gold, and so the need to draw on the Fund would not arise until the maladjustment had gone far.

LORD KEYNES said that contingencies of this kind could only be covered by recommendations in the Fund's annual report. Special reports on particular countries might also be made with advantage at any time if the countries seemed likely to be involved in difficulties.

It was agreed:–

That the U.S. Group should produce a written version of Mr. Bernstein's proposals for discussion at a forthcoming meeting.

II. *Monetisation of unitas*

LORD KEYNES gave an exposition of the U.K. proposals to turn unitas into an international money. The questions of substance were:–

(1) *Borrowing power and size of lending commitments*

Our proposal was that voting power should be based on the quota, but lending commitments should be 20 per cent above it. As our suggestion was that quotas should be raised from $5 billions to $8 billions, aggregate borrowing powers would be $12 billions though it was not possible that everyone should be using their full powers at once. Any smaller figure, however, would mean that confidence in the scheme would be inadequate.

(2) *Subscriptions as a pledge*

The American plan allowed the gold subscriptions of members and their subscriptions in securities to be transferred to other members. This might involve such undesirable developments as gold flows from smaller to larger creditor countries and accumulations of sterling securities outside the United Kingdom callable at the discretion of another country. Our proposal was that the gold and securities subscribed should be a pledge, but not subject to current operations.

(3) *Size of gold subscription*

Our view was that no member should be *required* to subscribe more than 12½ per cent of its quota in gold. Our reasons for this were:–

(*a*) Partly *political*, e.g. our conservatives would be unwilling to part with so much gold to an untried institution, and our left-wingers would not want a scheme so near to the gold standard that it threatened to restrict the scope of internal social policy. There critics could, no doubt, be answered, but the answers would not be easy.

(*b*) Partly *on merits*. If gold subscriptions were large, countries with small reserves would find their position weakened for meeting calls not properly chargeable to the Fund, whereas the position of countries with large reserves would suffer little change. This was the opposite of what most people would agree would be a sensible trend in the redistribution of gold, and would encounter hostility among European countries.

(4) *The strength of the Fund*

We sympathised, however, with the view that the Fund must be strong and should ultimately concentrate in itself ample gold assets. We proposed:–

(*a*) If, at the end of any year, a member's gold holdings exceeded its quota, it should redeem its securities with gold equal to 2 per cent of its quota. The operation of this provision would gradually increase gold subscriptions to the high level required by the American draft of 10 July, 1943.

(*b*) Members should not use the Fund and increase their gold holdings simultaneously, i.e. countries gaining gold and reducing their unitas balances below their quota at the same time, should replenish the unitas balance with their new gold stocks—a similar provision was in the American draft.

347

(*c*) (Lord Keynes stressed the importance of this). A member desiring to sell gold would be expected to offer it to the Fund directly or indirectly if this would serve its purpose in selling the gold equally well. This would canalise free gold into the Fund from, e.g. the annual production of new gold and any gold outflow from the U.S. stock (which, of course, might find its way back to the U.S. later, if the dollar became a scarce currency). This device should help to make the principle of low gold subscriptions acceptable because the gold accretions to the Fund which it brought about would come from willing sellers as the result of a process of painless extraction.

(5) *Limitation of commitment*

We accepted this in principle, and our proposal was that when the 'ceiling' was approached, a member would have the right to give notice that it would refuse to accept further accretions of Unitas at any time up to the point when the ceiling was reached. A member might prefer not to exercise this right immediately, in which case things would drift quite comfortably. For a country which exercised its right, the Fund would be *functus officio* and new arrangements would have to be made, but no-one would be worse off for the Fund's having been in existence.

Thus, the 'scarce currencies' conception did not figure in our proposals.

Continuing, LORD KEYNES said that the above points of substance were translatable into S.F. terminology. Amongst the points not easily translatable were:–

(*a*) *Unqualified multilateral clearing*. This was our real purpose and the platform on which we must go to the general public and the trading world. The scheme must put this principle in the shop window in the plainest language. It was easy to express in unitas, but in S.F. looked too much like a charitable fund.

(*b*) *The duty of members to maintain exchange stability*. It was very difficult to express the idea of generalised exchange stability in terms of all other currencies, without using the concept of unitas. If all countries went back to gold, S.F. definitions would be easier. But that would not happen.

(*c*) *The passivity of the Fund*. Our proposals emphasised the principle of the Fund as the spare wheel of the financial coach, entirely passive until it was needed. In terms of S.F. drafting would be difficulty in any form which would not arouse hostility.

In conclusion, LORD KEYNES said that Britain wanted a system which looked different and was different from the pre-war system. He observed that the S.F. provision that the accounts of the Fund should be kept in unitas, contained the germ of agreement on the subject.

MR BERNSTEIN made a number of comments on Lord Keynes's proposals:–

(1) *Borrowing powers and size of commitment.* The S.F. draft itself allowed for inequalities between quota and lending or borrowing powers, and did not insist on precise equality. But the inequality should not be too great.

(2) *Size of gold subscriptions.* He appreciated the political difficulties raised by large subscriptions, and explained that the S.F. draft should be understood to mean a total gold subscription of 25 per cent of the quota.

(3) *Strength of the Fund.* There were no closed minds in the U.S. Group on this point. The provision for redemption of securities in gold by 2 per cent of the quota annually was probably sound. The provision for the preferential sale of gold to the Fund was weakened by the Fund's right to redeem excess unitas balances in gold, which could encourage countries to demand gold.

(4) *'Scarce currencies'.* It was true that this provision could be eliminated, but countries needing the scarce currency would object to early applicants for it being able to spend it perhaps on luxuries, whereas late-comers wanting necessities might find none left for them.

(5) No magic could disguise the fact that the Fund might be short or long of particular currencies even in unitas terms. The non-negotiable securities would be expressed in currency. LORD KEYNES said he did not dispute this as a matter of logic but he preferred the concept of a monetised unitas to express a generalised currency, or claim on the world at large.

MR BERNSTEIN said that the Treasury Group saw merit in all the points put forward by the United Kingdom Group, but would want to discuss them separately with the State Department. It might be difficult to persuade the bankers on several of the proposals.

MR BERLE said that what was wanted was a form of words which:–

(a) Freed the United Kingdom from the fear that it might have to subordinate its internal social policy to external financial policy summed up in the word 'gold'.

(b) Assured the United States that a share in their production was not claimable by tender of a new 'trick' currency, and that the economic power represented by the United States gold reserves would not be substantially diminished.

It was agreed:–

(1) That Messrs Bernstein, Thompson-McCausland, and Baster should arrange a provisional order of discussions for the next meeting.

(2) That the next meeting will be held in Dr. White's Room on Tuesday, 28 September, at 3.30 p.m.

29 September 1943

By the end of September, some members of the delegation were worried whether the monetisation of unitas issue might lead to the breakdown of the discussions on an issue that they thought of shadow rather then substance but which the Bank of England and some Ministers regarded as essential. As yet they proposed, however, to do nothing.

At this stage, however, Keynes was concerned with future procedure.

To H. D. WHITE, *30 September 1943*

My dear White,

Following on my conversation with you a week or two ago about subsequent procedure on the assumption that our present conversations end in success, I have had some cable correspondence with London. The procedure which would commend itself to them is, I think, very similar to what you were contemplating. But I had better report to you their views to make sure that these are exactly in line with Mr Morgenthau's.

The order of events as London conceives them would be as follows:–

(1) Any document emerging from the present Anglo-American conversations would be submitted to your Government and to mine, who would be asked to approve its communication for consideration and further discussion by representatives of Russia and China and the other members of the Drafting Committee when they have been chosen. This would have the effect, which was, I think, your idea, of giving more status to the proceedings without raising the difficulties of the extent of commitment by our Governments. That is to say, they would be approving it for further consideration and discussion without at this stage committing themselves in any way to the contents.

(2) The Drafting Committee would then be summoned with the least possible delay to examine and discuss the material put before them, which would be open to amendment by the Committee. The Drafting Committee would prepare a complete draft fit for publication.

(3) Copies of the draft would then be made available to all

interested governments; and be published immediately thereafter. In our case there would no doubt be a debate in Parliament and our Government might seek on this occasion a general expression of approval. Presumably Mr Morgenthau would be putting the draft before the Congressional Committees and seeking their reactions at about the same time.

(4) If the reception of the draft by Parliament and the Congressional Committees and other Governments concerned were deemed satisfactory, so that further progress on more formal lines appeared to be possible, then two possible alternatives would have to be considered. If the governments not represented on the Drafting Committee felt that there are important amendments which they could not refrain from pressing, it is possible that a further larger expert conference might be required to settle these differences. If, on the other hand, the Drafting Committee proved to have been so representative that agreement there carried with it agreement in all interested quarters, then it might be possible to proceed without any further expert discussion. That, I think, is the event that you were contemplating. But perhaps we have to provide for the less satisfactory alternative.

(5) If general endorsement of the plan has been obtained, then the appropriate formal procedure would have to be considered with a view to ratification.

In two respects the above conforms with what I understood to be in Mr Morgenthau's mind, namely, that nothing further would be published until after the Drafting Committee had reported, and that authoritative government approval of substance as distinct from procedure would not be sought until after this stage, there having been in our case a discussion in Parliament as a prior condition of approval, and in your case whatever is the corresponding procedure. And I hope that, in other respects also, it follows the general outline of events which he has in view.

In the telegram from London there were also observations

about procedure in relation to the international investment scheme, a copy of which we are hoping to receive in due course. I am afraid there is a risk of a little delay in discussing it, since London have expressed a desire to have a good look at it before discussion starts over here. But the particular point on which I have been instructed to express the very strong feeling of London is that no scheme should be published prematurely, or before we have had a chance of letting you know our reactions. I am asked to say that premature publication might cause very grave embarrassment indeed in London, and to express a strong hope that there will be no question of publication, at any rate until you have some impression as to how we are viewing it. I know this entirely conforms with your own ideas. But in view of the emphatic character of the telegram I have received I have felt that I ought to put the above on record with you.

Sincerely yours,
[copy initialled] K.

On 3 October, Keynes sent a series of letters to Sir Wilfrid Eady on the situation.

To SIR WILFRID EADY, *3 October 1943*

My dear Eady,

Sunday gives me a breathing space in which I can try to write you a letter, or series of letters, in reply to yours of the 23rd September, which I was very glad to get.

The Chancellor's death[31] was an extraordinary shock. It was one of the eventualities which one had not in the least contemplated, I don't quite know why, as possible. I heard the news quite casually on the 8 o'clock wireless when I tuned in to hear the beginning of Winston's speech in the House. The news was just dropped in as an incidental. Now that

[31] Kingsley Wood had died on 21 September of heart failure.

copies of *The Times* have arrived I find that almost every conceivable successor was tipped by the press except [Sir John] Anderson. For my own part I had no doubt at all that Anderson it would be. It did not seem to me that anything else was possible. As you may suppose, it has left Robbins and Meade greatly wondering whether or not they are to be separated from him. If it were to come about, it would upset them a good deal. So far we have had no indication whether he remains Chairman of his Committee. On the merits of the particular case it looks as if it will be extraordinarily difficult to replace him. From the more personal, constitutional point of view, I think it would be a great pity to upset the balance of power between the Chancellor and the President of the Economic Committee; and for the same reasons as Alan Barlow knows I have always thought it a mistake to link the Economic Section to the Treasury, where they would either be too powerful or not powerful enough.

All of us here were extremely pleased at Law's promotion.[32] He is making a perfect leader of the party, and our only anxiety is that this may involve him in further duties that might possibly mean his going home before we are finished. Do please use your influence against this. It is just at the last lap when things are beginning to crystallise that we shall most need him.

We have been a very happy party, with great concord all round. Our monetary group is working very well; both Dennis and Sigi have been extraordinarily helpful. Indeed, if we had been too contentious amongst ourselves I don't know how we could have managed, for we really are horribly over-worked and the pace is terrific. Several meetings every day and not nearly enough time to think out one's own policy or to read one's home work; all of which is much aggravated by the fact that I am lunching or dining out at least ten times a week. Fortunately, as I found on the previous occasion, the

[32] Mr Law became Minister of State at the Foreign Office.

climate of Washington, though not particularly aggreeable in itself, does agree with my heart. I got over-exhausted one day and had to take a day off to recoup, but apart from that I really have been remarkably well, in spite of talking and eating so much too much.

People in Washington are extraordinarily kind. It is immensely easier to get on than it was in those pre-Pearl Harbor days when I was here last. There was then a decided tension in the air that made everything very edgy. Today it is nothing but friendliness in every quarter. The (I suppose rather high-brow) group where Lydia and I are most comfortable are the Walter Lippmanns, Dean Achesons and the Archie MacLeishs (the Librarian of Congress and poet). We have really enjoyed ourselves extraordinarily on several occasions in their most hospitable company. I have seen quite a lot of Berle, who is a queer attractive, unattractive figure in disequilibrium with himself and the world. One never knows in what direction he will rush off. But he has been extremely helpful and generally tending to take our side in the discussions. I have also seen quite a lot of Pasvolsky, who is getting on like anything with all our Delegation, particularly Liesching's flock.

Our first fortnight was, as you may suppose, rather overshadowed by the rather extraordinary situation in the State Department. Remind me when I get back to tell you the full story of why Sumner Welles had to go. This is a most extraordinary country. It would corrupt the ink if I were to try to put it all down. No doubt Stettinius' is quite a good appointment, both from the general, and from our, point of view. All the same, it would in my judgment have been much better for us if Stettinius had been left where he was and Lou Douglas, who was the most likely alternative candidate, had gone to the State Department. How the new position will work out is pretty obscure. Crowley seems to be a figure who has made no definite impression on anyone. A good business executive, one gathers, but not particularly interested in policy or likely to impress his mark on it. This fact may mean that the best hopes of the State Department may be realised. I am informed they have lost all the economic departments concerned with foreign affairs which they had been laboriously collecting together during the last few months. OLLA, OFFRO, OFEC and OEW are all now under Crowley, who is a part of the Office of Emergency Management, that is to say, a part of the White House staff. The theory is that Crowley is in charge of operations but in matters of policy he is to work in strict conformity with the wishes of the State Department. Crowley being what he is, it may conceivably work out like this. If so, the State Department may really be gainers. They will get rid of the operation side, for which they are extremely unfitted and which does not interest them, and may conceivably keep the policy side. That is what Dean Acheson is hoping. Ostensibly he has had a large part of his job taken from him. But it may be that it is only the boring details he is losing and that he will still be in charge in effect of what really matters. Berle is hoping that there will be some re-organisation by which the responsibility of the Assistant Under-Secretaries will be more definite and they will be allowed to concentrate on particular groups of countries. Sumner Welles ostensibly took everything to himself in the first instance and then allowed items which did not interest him, and for which he had no time, to slop over at random into the hands of his subordinates, which meant that they had no sort of continuity of responsibility.

Under Crowley Laughlin Currie is Administrator, which means that he is, so to speak, the senior civil servant in charge of all the operations of the Department under Crowley, who has what we should regard as Ministerial responsibility. The staff of OLLA under Knollenberg is undisturbed and it is not yet clear to me which of the various matters in which he might take a preliminary interest Currie will in fact concentrate on.

Conceivably he will be content to leave OLLA mainly to Knollenberg. But conceivably he may not. If he does interest himself in it difficulties are likely to arise. Currie is an old friend of mine and I know him well, but there is no one more difficult to handle. He is extremely suspicious and jealous, very anti-British on such issues as India, and always inclined to assume the worst. He is not fundamentally unfriendly or unreasonable. But he is certainly one of the most difficult to be sure of. For example, if he were to take a strong line about the balances we might have a lot of trouble before he could be persuaded otherwise. I have not yet tried to tackle him either as to how he views his own position or what attitude he is likely to take up on current problems.

With Harry White, as you may suppose, we have been spending a vast amount of time. Any reserves we may have about him are a pale reflection of what his colleagues feel. He is over-bearing, a bad colleague, always trying to bounce you, with harsh rasping voice, aesthetically oppressive in mind and manner; he has not the faintest conception how to behave or observe the rules of civilised intercourse. At the same time, I have a very great respect and even liking for him. In many respects he is the best man here. A very able and devoted public servant, carrying an immense burden of responsibility and initiative, of high integrity and of clear sighted idealistic international purpose, genuinely intending to do his best for the world. Moreover, his over-powering will combined with the fact that he has constructive ideas mean that he does get things done, which few else here do. He is not open to flattery in any crude sense. The way to reach him is to respect his purpose, arouse his intellectual interest (it is a great softener to intercourse that it is easy to arouse his genuine interest in the merits of any issue) and to tell him off very frankly and firmly without finesse when he has gone off the rails of relevant argument or appropriate behaviour.

It is difficult to predict the course of events, or what stage it is any use our attempting to reach. In some separate letters, which may or may not get off at the same time as this one, I am trying to set forth the present position of the various ventures, but at the moment it looks to me that there is a reasonable chance of my getting off home somewhere about 31 October. A considerable hold-up will unfortunately arise out of the fact that, for reasons not known to me but which are said to be compelling, Harry White will be absent from Washington for a fortnight after the end of this coming week.

I should be grateful if you would let Hoppy and Catto see this and the other letters, and anyone else you think should.

Yours ever,
[copy initialled] K.

To SIR WILFRID EADY, *3 October 1943*

My dear Eady,

The monetary talks. As regards procedure, I sent Harry White a letter, a copy of which will have reached you before this. Since then I have had two conversations with him. He will be proposing certain changes, but these are, I think, likely to be acceptable to you. You will probably be informed by telegram in detail before this letter arrives.

The immediate practical upshot is that we gave up the idea of trying to collect the Drafting Committee to follow quickly after the end of the Anglo-American talks. The present suggestion is that these should follow, say, two months later and Harry White has expressed himself very benevolent to the suggestion that the Drafting Committee should meet in London.

What we shall aim at therefore in our talks is to produce an agreed directive to the Drafting Committee, not itself a detailed draft but a statement of principles covering some four or five pages. It is, of course, very far from certain that we can reach complete agreement, though I believe we can if we want to. It will not be essential that London should confirm what we eventually produce until after we have got back to explain it.

This directive to the Drafting Committee or statement of principles is of the highest importance, because that will be the operative document so far as the public is concerned. The present idea is that this statement of principles should be published, assuming that our two Governments have previously accepted it as appropriate at this stage, without, however, committing themselves finally to what might emerge from it. In our case it then will be the subject of a debate in Parliament. This, I think, is very much what the late Chancellor wanted, namely, that he should be able to go to the House with something comparatively simple and unencumbered by non-essential detail.

As regards bridging the gap between us, we shall know much more in the next few days and you will probably have learned much more before this letter arrives. The present indications are the following:–

(1) On elasticity of the exchanges, they will meet us to the extent of accepting broadly what we have proposed (but which you have not yet agreed) with the change that the second 10 per cent can only be made with the approval of the Committee, which must, however, take a vote on the matter, yes or no, within two days of the application being made.

(2) They will accept our formula for changing the gold value of unitas.

(3) They will increase the quotas to 10 billions plus the gold subscription, which is all but 12 billions.

(4) They will substantially accept our views on the amount of the gold subscription.

(5) They will agree to a system which is extremely severe on a currency which is in danger of being scarce. The latest proposal seems to mean that as soon as the Fund gives notice

that a currency is in danger of getting scarce all the members are entitled to prohibit all further imports from that country except under licence. I am absolutely astounded that the State Department should accept this, and still scarcely credit it. I have a much better solution which seems to me far easier for the Americans and still believe that this may come into the picture again. But if the above suits the Americans, not much need for us to dissent. It puts an enormous pressure on them, which is indeed Harry White's intention, never to allow such a situation to arise in practice.

(6) I think they will go a long way to meet us on the passivity of the Fund. They declare that what they intend is exactly what our draft says. But they will not agree to our draft and we cannot agree that their draft comes to the same thing in practice. However, there ought to be room for accommodation there.

On the other hand, the points of outstanding difficulty are the following:–

(1) They do not agree that the gold subscription shall be pledged and not freely available to the Fund to purchase a scarce currency.

(2) They want to give more discretion to the Fund to interfere with the members' freedom in using the Fund than we think advisable if anyone is to feel confidence that they really have reserves. But what exactly the minimum is with which they will be content is not yet sufficiently clear.

(3) They are adamant against the monetisation of unitas and hold out strongly for the mixed bag of currencies. They admit that our proposals are immeasurably better on merits, but declare that it is only by putting on this very peculiar fancy dress that they can get the thing through their own bankers. I do not believe a word of this and sometimes feel that the other departments are on our side, though with no strong convictions. Certainly this is the biggest snag so far as our Cabinet directive is concerned. In several respects their set-up

359

does far more violence to the natural mind of a banker than ours does. But there is nothing more difficult than to continue a controversy with people who admit that your proposal is immeasurably better than their own but nevertheless hold out on the ground that for obscure psychological reasons only theirs is practical politics.

By the end of this week we should know pretty clearly how we stand. During Harry White's absence we can try to draw up with Bernstein the agreed statement of principles. If all goes well and Harry on his return O.K.s what we have done in his absence, I can start straight home. All this may be too optimistic. But if it is, that may be all the more reason why I should start straight home.

Yours ever,
[copy initialled] K.

To SIR WILFRID EADY, *3 October 1943*

My dear Eady,

The International Investment Bank. As you will have gathered, Harry White's behaviour over this was most peculiar. During the first fortnight of our stay here he was engaged in getting it through at the interdepartmental level. In the course of this the document you have already seen received a good many minor improvements without changing its general smell and style. It appears that it then passed the President's desk with an unexpectedly short delay, though this may mean that Lubin passed it, without the President ever having cast even a side-long glance at it. Meanwhile, we had not heard anything except that matters were progressing.

At a meeting of the Plenary Conference on Thursday, from which I was absent as I was taking that day off, White suddenly announced that the scheme was being presented to Congress on Tuesday and would be simultaneously published. To the members of the State Department and the other departments affected who were present at the meeting this was as complete a surprise as it was to us. They had not had a word of warning about it, and the State Department in particular were, I am told, livid with annoyance. Why on earth Harry tried to bounce us all is a great mystery. Acheson told me that he was absolutely at a loss to fathom the motives of 'that man', as he called him.

Waley protested very strongly and had an interview with Harry afterwards. The line the latter took was that it was too late to do anything about it. 200 copies had gone out, with Mr Morgenthau pledged to inform Congress, and that in these circumstances publication was inevitable. I should add that shortly before this statement by White he had received my letter conveying your strong protest against premature publication. He subsequently pretended not to have read this letter, or at any rate to have read it so hastily as not to have imbibed its contents.

Next day I returned to the office and got White round to see me. I started off by telling him frankly and crudely exactly what we all thought about him. I said that this would be regarded at home as a very gross breach of the under-standing about premature publication between Mr Morgen-thau and the late Chancellor, and accused him of having systematically deceived me for the whole of the past week. All this produced a very good effect and entirely restored his good humour, and he began to cast round for ways out of the impasse which he had gratuitously created. He began by explaining that the 200 copies put into circulation were solely within the Government and that no copies had been com-municated outside. It merely meant that it had been fairly widely communicated on the interdepartmental level. In the second place, he allowed that communication to Congress would be in executive session and could therefore be in secret session without communication to the world, so that publication to the press was not inevitable.

The meeting ended, as you will have heard, by his agreeing that the document should be withheld from publication and should be communicated to the other United Nations with a reasonable time lag (though this part of the undertaking was not in very clear or reliable terms).

When I saw him yesterday he had travelled a further stage on the road of repentance and had decided that there was really no reason why the document as a document need be communicated to Congress on Tuesday. It would be sufficient if Mr Morgenthau were to give them the high lights, as he calls them, and to say that for the time being no document had been officially handed over to anybody.

I do not feel certain that this will actually happen. But if it does, then we shall have got as near to putting things as they were as possible.

There is now the question of the document itself. White asked us to let him know yesterday of any obvious points likely in our opinion to create a particular difficulty or misunderstanding. Waley and I had therefore a private talk in which quite unofficially, and after explaining that we had no authority to agree or disagree with anything, we made certain suggestions as to presentation which he received very amiably. The draft was obviously still in an unfinished form and several changes had been made since we had been given an advance copy on the previous day. We are not sending you the copy given us last week, since it seemed better to wait for the corrected version, which ought to be unofficially in our hands by Tuesday. This will go by bag as promptly as possible.

God knows what you will think of it when you see it, for it is an extremely odd document. In my opinon there are very genuine motives behind it. It is by no means what is wanted to do the trick, but it is capable in certain favourable circumstances of helping the situation.

The trouble is that in order to meet alleged American

feelings it has been wrapped up and camouflaged to look quite the opposite of its real intention. The result is, or so it seems to me, that an outside critic will regard it as the work of a near lunatic, or as some sort of a bad joke. What Waley and I did on Saturday was to try and persuade him to make the real purpose a little more obvious.

In my opinion, he is a perfect ass to approach the problem in this way. One cannot possibly attain useful results without facing the music, if there is music to face, and putting the scheme before the world for what it really is. You cannot humbug all the Continents simultaneously with a scheme intended to cover billions of dollars of trade. The thing must sail under its own proper colours.

Put shortly the camouflage adopted is the following. To all appearances the scheme makes no difference whatever between creditor and debtor countries. Debtor countries are called upon to play just as important a part in promoting overseas investment as creditor countries. There is no sort of linking up between responsibility for overseas investment and the possession of a favourable balance of trade. Indeed, everything is done to disassociate these ideas as much as possible. Now clearly that is plain loony. Harry admits that without the least wish to dissent. Having put these lunatic robes on his Frankenstein he then proceeds at various stages to introduce jokers, which might actually cause the scheme in practice to work out in a way exactly the opposite of what it appears to be on the surface.

How an intelligent and wise man like him can believe that this is the right way to approach a great issue, heaven knows. It is, of course exactly analogous to the mixed bag of currencies in the monetary scheme. Here also he has adopted an apparent set-up which is the exact opposite to the reality, for the purpose of ostensibly placating various prejudices. He may be right in thinking the United States is 25 years out of date, and that no American banker will accept anything unless you first of all make it look entirely imbecile, but are people really so silly, or if so silly, so easily deceived as all that?

It is rather a tragedy. For there are some very good ideas and immensely disinterested, fine international purpose in the scheme.

Both the currency scheme and the investment scheme are, I think, largely the fruit of the brain not of Harry but of his little attaché, Bernstein. It is with him rather than Harry that the pride of authorship lies. And when we seduce Harry from the true faith, little Bernstein wins him back again in the course of the night. Bernstein is a regular little rabbi, a reader out of the Talmud, to Harry's grand political high rabbidom. He is very clever and rather sweet, but knows absolutely nothing outside the turns and twists of his own mind. There is, as I have expressed it, a very high degree of endogamy between his ideas. The chap knows every rat run in his local ghetto, but it is difficult to persuade him to come out for a walk with us on the high ways of the world.

Much more about this through one channel or another in due course. This is just to give you the atmosphere.

Yours ever,
[copy initialled] K.

The next meeting on monetary matters took place on 4 October. One British participant described it as follows:

What absolute Bedlam these discussions are! Keynes and White sit next [to] each other, each flanked by a long row of his own supporters. Without any agenda or any prepared idea of what is going to be discussed they go for each other in a strident duet of discord, which after a crescendo of abuse on either side leads up to a chaotic adjournment of the meeting in time for us to return to the Willard for a delegation meeting.

The meeting discussed the limitation of drawing rights, the meaning of the scarce currency clause and the conditions limiting exchange rate variations within the range of 10–20 per cent from the initial par.

After the meeting, Keynes wrote to White.

To H. D. WHITE, *5 October 1943*

My dear White,

I promised to let you have in writing the suggestion which I scribbled down during the meeting yesterday. It runs as follows:–

'If by a three-fourths majority the Fund is of the opinion that a member country is flagrantly using the facilities of the Fund in a manner injurious to the maintenance of international stability, notice may be given to the offending member that it may not draw more than a further 25 per cent of its quota except with the approval of the Fund.'

What is your idea as to future procedure? As you know, we are very near the end of our visit here. I suggest that we should now concentrate on preparing the statement of principles which is to be the directive to the Drafting Committee. I am inclined to try my hand, on some part of it at any rate, in the near future.

We should also like to tell London the main points where we think we have cleared away matters of disagreement. In order to avoid misunderstanding, I am not sure that the best way might not be for us to prepare a summary of what we think we are in a position to tell London, and then get you to O.K. it.

Yours sincerely,
[copy initialled] K.

At the meeting on 6 October, as well as discussing the conditions surrounding changes in exchange rates, the participants agreed to prepare directives for the Drafting Committee that would meet to draw up finally the details of the Fund and to draft in terms of a Stabilisation Fund.

After the meeting, Keynes received further instructions from London. He therefore wrote White.

To H. D. WHITE, *7 October 1943*

My dear White,

When we got back from our meeting yesterday afternoon, I found a long telegram awaiting me. It will, perhaps, save time if I give you the substance of this by letter, without waiting for tomorrow's meeting.

The telegram is mainly concerned with provisions for the elasticity of the exchange. I am told that the question has been under further consideration by Ministers, and that I am to regard this telegram as conveying Ministerial instructions. Fortunately, the substance of the telegram is, on the whole, very helpful to our discussions. The telegram clearly expresses the preference of Ministers for a system under which an alteration in the exchanges requires only consultation and not formal approval by voting. Nevertheless, its tenor is not unfriendly to the compromise which we had been discussing with you. I have not yet had an opportunity of conveying to London your suggested modification. I am hopeful that the substitution of a decision after two days for a right to act merely after consultation with the Chairman may prove acceptable. On the other hand, what I told you yesterday on the question of a member whose application is refused being free to leave the Fund without further notice given is strongly confirmed. I believe that it will be very difficult to move London beyond the point I have indicated above.

Apart from this, the telegram raises a question of some importance which we have scarcely discussed, but which will not, I hope, present much difficulty. Although the present discussions are, and remain, non-committal so far as my Government (as well as yours) is concerned, Ministers feel that the circumstances out of which the present discussions arose put some responsibility upon us for taking the position of other countries into account. They are anxious that a situation should not develop where you or we seem to be expected to railroad an agreement through reluctant Allies. They feel that this relates particularly to the position in the immediate post-war period. For many countries the initial exchange rates will be experimental, and they are afraid that some of them may feel their discretion unduly fettered if they are asked to commit themselves to a rate which is necessarily adopted before future circumstances can be at all clearly foreseen. London is afraid that, to protect themselves from this, some of these countries may seek an initial rate which is unduly low. My own feeling, which I fancy you share, is that for various reasons they are much more likely to fix them too high. However that may be, there is clearly an exceptional risk arising out of the immediate post-war circumstances that the initial rate may prove inappropriate. It is to meet this point that (vii) of paragraph 6 has been added.

There are one or two observations in the telegram bearing on other points which we have had under discussion. You will see the covering note on the paper of principles which we are handing to you today, reserving our position as to the form in which the Fund is set up. London emphasises that they are not at present prepared to release us from our instructions to aim at the monetisation of unitas. In the second place, they emphasise their feeling that the gold subscription should not only be limited in amount but should be regarded as a reserve only transferable on the member's withdrawal or on the liquidation of the Fund. We have, therefore, thought it better to draft in accordance with this in the paper we are sending you, although we are well aware that you have not yet felt able to meet us on this.

As I said above, I consider the general tone of the telegram exceedingly helpful, and it considerably raises my hopes that London will support the line which the British group here have been taking in the discussions, in spite of the fact that this goes in some respects a little bit outside our instructions.

Yours sincerely,
[copy initialled] K

P.S. I have just heard that the *Daily Herald* in London is reporting a rumour that the British group has given way all along the line and has agreed to the gold standard being firmly re-rivetted on my poor country! Unquestionably, that is the most dangerous line of criticism, both in the Press and in Parliament, which we must put ourselves in a good position to rebut.

The next day he reported to Sir Wilfrid Eady on the Bank scheme's progress.

To SIR WILFRID EADY, *8 October 1943*

Dear Eady,

As you will have gathered from Law's cables, Morgenthau and White met us fairly handsomely at the last lap on the question of publication. After Law and I had both separately read the Riot Act, they seemed to become aware that there was something to be said in favour of not suddenly making these commitments without consultation. It was, I am convinced, sheer clumsiness of soul. The next day after I had with difficulty persuaded Harry White not to commit Morgenthau at this stage to the publication of the directive to the Drafting Committee, he told me that he was himself in two minds as to whether it would be wise to do so and wanted not to come to a firm conclusion until he actually had a draft of the directive in front of him. Clearly this is only commonsense. Why on earth, therefore, go plunging ahead without considering the consequences or consulting anyone? No answer whatever, so far as I am aware. Except, as I have said, just clumsiness of soul. In the Senate there was no reasonable discussion at all. After about five minutes, during which the Senators hopelessly mixed and combined in their minds the Bank and the Fund (which is not very surprising, since Harry has chosen to call his Bank a fund and his Fund a bank), they then discussed for an hour or two the problem of military currencies, for a Senator burst out 'What is the use of having a stabilisation fund when every description of unregulated military currency appears to be buzzing about the world.' As Morgy had not been at all prepared for discussion on this subject, the two of them, as usual, had a pretty rough ride.

In the Committee of the House, on the other hand, they seem to have had a fairly good and not too discouraging discussion. I understand that there was some criticism, but also a certain measure of support and sympathy.

The difficulty is, of course, that these plans are presented to Congress in just about the most unattractive manner and with just about the most unattractive faces and unattractive voices that human nature can compass. Not the slightest attempt to catch their imaginations or give them a picture of the problems of the post-war world. It is all made to look most unappetising, without any grand idea or purpose behind it. Yet I am sure that something quite the contrary of this might have a surprising success.

An experienced American told us the other day that during the ten years of Morgy's reign the U.S. Treasury has devoted its whole efforts to appeasing a non-existent public sentiment, and has invariably failed to be even dimly aware of the public sentiments which really exist.

There has been a good example of that this week in the presentation of the budget. Morgy made an enormous speech, demanding a vast and desirable increase of taxation. It could scarcely have been presented in a less attractive manner, or with a greater failure of persuasiveness. In today's papers Walter Lippman has a most excellent article pointing out how extremely advisable Morgy's programme is and how hopelessly he failed to introduce those arguments likely to commend and explain it to public opinion.

Returning to my muttons, I attach a collection of Press cuttings about the meeting of the Committees of Congress which Harry White gave me. You will see that apart from one or two gross errors, very little genuine news has reached the Press so far. If the U.S. Treasury can only have the sense to say no more about it I should expect the Press to forget the subject and allow us quite an appreciable respite of time.

After the end of this week, as you will have seen from the telegrams, White is leaving Washington. My private information is that he is visiting the European theatre. Obviously, therefore, not the slightest use for our hanging about for his return, since no one can predict just when that will be. All this is a deep, secret since, as usual in this country, White is trying to spring something over his colleagues, and the State Department and others concerned probably know nothing of his impending plans.

You will see that the arts of government as we understand them are not practised in this country. It may be that some other art, which we have difficulty in apprehending, is being employed. Indeed, if it were not so the final outcome must be a great deal worse than it actually is. Anyhow, it is important to bear in mind the total absence of the arts of government as we understand them. For otherwise we are led to impute to malice or unfriendliness what is in fact due to nothing of the kind.

Yours ever,
[copy initialled] K

The two days, 8 and 9 October, were full of continuous drafting which ended with amicable agreement on the directive for the Drafting Committee. However, one participant mentioned them as being 'full of explosions' and continued

Keynes has been storming and raging (When Bernstein in place of a short note of the Anglo-American interpretation to be placed on certain items in the directive produced another typically Bernstein document) 'This is intolerable. It is yet another Talmud. We had better simply break off negotiations.' Harry White has replied 'We will try to produce something which Your Highness *can* understand.' Negotiations were apparently broken off at lunch time.

However, a new American draft was available in the late afternoon and 'the scene ended with love, kisses and compliments all round' as the delegations agreed on the directive.

The next day, Keynes wrote to Eady and included his own report of the incident.

To SIR WILFRID EADY, *10 October 1943*

My dear Eady,

Perhaps I had better confirm by letter what I mentioned over the telephone about the probable date of my return. The currency talks finished yesterday, though there are some loose ends still to be tied up. We hope to exchange and initial on Monday four sets of documents:–

(1) The draft Directive of Principles, which will include both the U.K. version and the U.S. version on the points where we have decided to differ;

(2) Agreed Minutes which cover certain matters where we were agreed but which were too detailed for inclusion in the Directive. White is anxious that London's approval of these details, as well as of the Directive itself, should be the condition of further progress. Attached to these Minutes is also a clear summary of the points where we have failed to reach agreement;

(3) The substance of what we think might be issued to the Press, or in answer to Parliamentary questions, concerning the outcome of these talks;

(4) An exchange of letters establishing as precisely as possible what White and I have agreed between ourselves, subject to confirmation by others, as to future procedure.

It has been made abundantly clear that we have not committed you to any of these four papers. The whole of it is *ad referendum*. But we have thought it essential to get everything down in black and white, not least the question of future

371

procedure, which is to be dealt with in the exchange of letters.

The Chancellor will be particularly interested in the last named as it affects procedure in Parliament. I have made it clear that it is all subject to his approval. My hope and belief is, however, that what we are proposing is on the lines which are likely to be convenient to him. Probably some details will have reached you by telegram before you get this letter.

I feel that rather miraculous progress was made in the last few days of last week. I was doubtful up to the last moment whether they would accept a Directive which got so far away from the form of S.F. This was essential from our point of view, since it is the only clear way of disposing of points in S.F. which in detail may not be of the first importance, but are in the aggregate highly objectionable to us.

Fortunately the Federal Reserve Board, who have been extraordinarily helpful all through, and the State Department, as well as in fact Harry White himself, were not at all against this. The real trouble has been little Bernstein, whose heart, I am afraid, it has rather broken.

He made a last minute effort to win back the ground he had lost, by persuading White, at the end of our meeting on Saturday morning, to produce a document for us to sign on the dotted line as a supplementary agreement, in the light of which the Directive was to be interpreted, which brought about half of S.F. right back again [in] the exact words which the Talmudist wrote many months ago and has never been willing to alter, if he could help it, by an iota. It was evident that the Federal Reserve Board and the State Department had never seen this document before it was handed to us, and I much doubt if White himself had read it through. Time, however, was running very short and there seemed to be a danger of fatal obstacle. I, therefore, at the end of the morning meeting reacted rather violently, saying that it was really intolerable at the eleventh hour to have all these matters re-opened in exactly the same terms that we had started with before the discussions began. The other members of my Group thought I had overdone it, but after we had left the meeting a telephone message came along half an hour later that the paper was withdrawn, so that peace and progress were restored. It was one example, in my judgment, of how important it is in this country to react strenuously.

I am wondering, for example, whether we are reacting with sufficient violence against the statements of the five Senators, which have completely filled both the friendly and unfriendly Press for the last few days. I enclose an article by Lippmann on this matter, which you may like to see.

As his plans have actually worked out, White will still be available here on Monday morning. We shall, therefore, have a general talk with him on his Reconstruction Bank, and following that he will come to a final, private luncheon with me, from which I may get some useful guidance as to the remaining points of difference where he is really obdurate. My impression is that there are not many points on which in truth he would not be moderately willing to give way in the last resort. But that remains to be seen. I enclose some cuttings from the Press on the world bank scheme, which is described in one of the papers, as you will, as *my* brain child, which in all the circumstances is pretty bad luck. You will also see from the report in the Washington *Times-Herald* that White, after he had told me that they were quite satisfied, from internal evidence, that the draft which leaked in London was not a draft they had given to us, nevertheless fibbed to the journalists, saying that 'They might have leaked from some informal memoranda that might have been exchanged with British officials.' Yet all the same, I hold to the opinion which I have already expressed, that taking everything into account Harry White is probably just about the best man here, and the most serviceable to all concerned.

Yours ever,
[copy not initialled]

373

After a brief discussion of White's Bank proposal on 11 October, Keynes went on to New York for discussions with private bankers and representatives of the Federal Reserve Bank of New York to try and explain the plans afoot and prevent active opposition to and disruption of their future progress. He then returned to London, leaving S. D. Waley to carry on any remaining discussions. Before departing, he wrote his mother.

From a letter to F. A. KEYNES, *18 October 1943*

And we are very content indeed with what we have accomplished—greatly in excess of our best expectations. Everyone most kind, a great *will to agree*, and a remarkable comradeship growing up between the British and American civil servants with almost emotional scenes on parting. We all really are trying to make good economic bricks for the world after the war—however hopelessly difficult the political problems may be.

Keynes, on his return, reported on his discussions with the covering note and three documents printed below.

I. MONETARY POLICY

(I) *Covering report*

Three documents have emerged from the currency talks at the United States Treasury which finished on Saturday the 9th October.

The first is a letter which I handed to Dr White on the 11th October recording my understanding of the subsequent procedure as it had been discussed at the meeting of the two groups on the 9th October.

The second is a Draft Statement of Principles, prepared as a Directive to the Drafting Committee, which it is hoped to set up as a preliminary stage of a monetary conference at which all the United and Associated Nations will be represented. Certain passages of this document include alternative United States and United Kingdom provisions, where we agreed to differ for the time being, pending further consideration in London. The points of difference mainly arise out of matters where the British group were not in a position to go further towards agreement consistently with the Cabinet directive. The more important of them relate to the technical form of the Fund, and to the part to be played by gold. It will be seen that the American and British groups have been able to arrive at substantial agreement over a very considerable part of the field. I also attach a covering letter addressed to Dr White.

The third document is a short paper of agreed Minutes covering points where agreement was reached but which were too detailed to be embodied in the Draft Statement of Principles, and also a summary of the points of outstanding difference as exhibited in the main paper.

At the conclusion of the meeting on the 9th October Dr White proposed that we should exchange agreed versions of the first two papers initialled by him and by me, and should exchange correspondence on procedure. I have sent him initialled copies of the first two papers as being a faithful record of the stage at which our conversations stood on the 9th October, and I have also sent him the above letter on procedure. The letter he read in my presence and did not dissent from its accuracy as a record of what had passed on the 9th October. Nor is there any doubt that the first two papers, which have been prepared with the help of the Secretaries on both sides, are a faithful record. Nevertheless, owing to his early departure from Washington, Dr White has informed me that he prefers not to initial the record or confirm the letter until a later date when he has been able to study them at more leisure.

I also add, as a matter of interest, a version of the Statement of Principles translated into terms of a monetised unitas, which would bring it into conformity with our Cabinet directive.

To complete the record, I should add that Dr White informed me on the 11th October that the Congressional Committees have just decided to appoint a small confidential joint committee of both Houses to keep in close touch with the United States Treasury, both on the currency proposals and the Reconstruction Bank. This committee will either consist of four members, being one Administration member and one Opposition member from each House; or, alternatively, six members consisting of the Chairman of the three committees in each House which are interested. Dr White thinks that he may find it necessary to bring them into touch with what happened in the recent conversations, but he assures me that any proceedings in this committee will be strictly confidential and are quite free from any risk of leakage. Dr White expressed the opinion that the appointment of this committee, though somewhat alarming in appearance, might prove exceedingly helpful. The members of the Congress on the committee would be individuals of great authority and influence, and if by association with the conversations at an early stage they could be persuaded to give them at any rate some measure of their blessing, opposition in Congress would be greatly diminished. If, on the other hand, there were particular features of the plan which in the judgment of these experienced legislators would be likely to provoke opposition, we should be warned in good time and would be in a position to consider whether any modifications would be made to meet the case.

It is quite clearly understood between us that these conversations have been at the technical level and do not bind Ministers on either side. It is now for each group to communicate these papers to higher authority and take instructions as to what is acceptable and what is unacceptable.

KEYNES

(II) *Correspondence addressed by Lord Keynes to Dr White*

Dear White,

With reference to the explanatory conversations between American and British officials which have just been concluded on the subject of an international stabilisation and clearing scheme, I write to set out my understanding as to the documents which have been agreed between us and as to future procedure.

The two documents which you and I have initialled today* are, respectively, a Draft Statement of Principles and a Minute of more detailed points agreed and of points reserved for further consideration. The Draft Statement outlines certain principles which we both are prepared, as technical experts, to recommend to our respective Governments, subject to agreement being reached on outstanding points at issue. It is understood between us that, although for the purpose of our discussions the principles are set out and illustrated in terms of a fund which holds members' currencies, the British representatives are in no way committed to recommending such a form. The Minute is to be read in conjunction with the Draft Statement as amplifying certain points of agreement and defining certain points of disagreement.

It is intended that when agreement has been reached on the outstanding points of difference, and when our two Governments have agreed that the Draft Statement may properly be made the basis of further discussion, it shall be communicated in strict confidence to certain of the more important Governments of the United Nations. Unless there is sufficient agreement with the proposals among these nations, neither side will feel bound to carry it further. If, however, all goes well, the Statement will be communicated to all the United and Associated Nations, and shortly afterwards made public. But it is clearly understood by both sides

* No documents were initialled by Dr White.

377

that, unless and until this stage has been reached, no publication will take place. When and if publication is made, it will be simultaneous in Washington and London.

Procedure in Congress and in Parliament must, of course, be for Ministers to settle. On our part, if the Chancellor so decides, the Draft Statement of Principles may be the subject of a debate in Parliament shortly after publication; but final approval of the scheme will not be sought from Congress or Parliament until the Drafting Committee has reported to a Plenary Conference and this Conference has recommended the Plan for general adoption. There will be no further publication of any details prior to this. The Drafting Committee itself will be merely a preliminary stage in preparation for the Conference, and its recommendations to the Conference will not be made public.

Assuming that no serious obstacle to progress emerges from the preliminary debates, a Drafting Committee of (say) a dozen members representing a fairly wide range of Governments of the United Nations will be called together, we hope in London, at the earliest practicable date. The countries represented on the Committee might be United States, United Kingdom, U.S.S.R., China. Brazil, Mexico, Canada, Australia, France, Holland, Belgium and Greece.

These arrangements may be altered by agreement between us. I also reaffirm in conclusion that neither of our Governments are yet committed by anything that has passed between us in the recent discussions, all the conclusions of which are strictly *ad referendum.*

I should be grateful if you would confirm your concurrence in my understanding as expressed here.

Yours sincerely,

11 October 1943   KEYNES

Dear White,

In accordance with my undertaking last Saturday, I now enclose an initialled copy of the Draft Directive and of the Minutes as they emerged from our final conversation on Saturday. I shall hope for your confirmation, as well as an acknowledgement of my letter of the 11th October concerning procedure, in due course.

These two papers are, I think, a faithful record of the stage at which our discussions had then arrived subject to two additions which we understood Dr Bernstein wished to see included. The first of these is Clause 5 (ii)(*a*). We do not necessarily object to the addition of this clause, though this may not be the right place for it, but it was not actually discussed at our meeting. The other addition is 10 (i). This definitely carries out an addition on which we decided in principle, but the actual wording was not before the meeting. The new clause is agreeable to us, and I understand that Dr. Bernstein believes it will be agreeable to you.

It is as a faithful record that we shall present these papers to the Chancellor of the Exchequer and other Ministers interested in London. As I made clear in another letter, this does not mean that either party is not free to propose changes, either in substance or in drafting and arrangement.

Sincerely yours,
KEYNES

12 October 1943

(III) *Anglo-American Draft Statement of Principles*

Joint statement by experts of united and associated nations on the establishment of an international stabilisation fund

U.K. reservation (The following draft is intended to set out and illustrate certain principles. It is expressed in terms of a Fund which holds members' currencies. This form of

379

expression has been used to meet the convenience of the United States Treasury and in no way commits the British representatives to recommend acceptance of such a form.)

Sufficient discussion of the problems of international monetary co-operation has taken place at the technical level to justify a statement of principles. Governments will not be asked to give final approval to the principles until they have been embodied in the form of definitive proposals by the delegates of the United and Associated Nations meeting in a formal conference.

1. *Preamble*

The International Stabilisation Fund is designed as a permanent institution for international monetary co-operation. The Fund is intended to facilitate the balanced growth of international trade and to contribute in this way to the maintenance of a high level of employment. The Fund is expected to provide the machinery for consultation on international monetary problems. The resources of the Fund are to be available under adequate safeguards to help member countries to maintain currency stability while giving them time to correct maladjustments in their balance of payments without resorting to extreme measures destructive to international prosperity.

2. *Purposes of the Fund*

(i) To promote exchange stability, to maintain orderly exchange arrangements among member countries and to avoid competitive exchange depreciation.

(ii) To assure multilateral payments facilities on current transactions among member countries and to eliminate restrictions inconsistent with this objective.

(iii) To shorten the periods and lessen the degree of disequilibrium in the international balance of payments of member countries.

(iv) To give confidence to member countries by the provision of actual and potential support.

3. *Subscription to the Fund*

(i) Member countries shall subscribe in gold and in their local funds amounts determined by a formula to be agreed. Aggregate subscriptions (quotas) on the basis of the formula will amount to about $8·5 billion if all of the United Nations and the countries associated with them subscribe to the Fund, and to about $10 billion for the world as a whole.

U.S. statement

(ii) The obligatory gold subscription of a member country shall be related to its holdings of gold and free foreign exchange, and shall be fixed at 25 per cent of the subscription (quota) or 10 per cent of the gold and free foreign exchange holdings of the country, whichever is the smaller.

U.K. statement

(ii) The obligatory gold subscription of a member country shall not exceed 12½ per cent of the quota, and shall be retained by the Fund as a reserve security against the member country's liability to the Fund.

4. *Operations of the Fund*

(i) Members shall deal with the Fund only through their Treasury, central bank, stabilisation fund or other fiscal agencies. The Fund's account in a member's currency shall be kept at the central bank of the member country.

(ii) Subject to (iii) below, operations on the Fund's account will be limited to transactions for the purpose of supplying a member country, on the member's initiative, with a desired and 'available' currency or for gold.

(iii) But the Fund will also be entitled at its option, with a view to keeping a particular member's currency available,

(*a*) To borrow its currency from a member country;

(*b*) To offer gold to a member country in exchange for its currency.

5. *Availability and acceptability of members' currencies*

(i) A currency is available unless the Fund has given notice that its holdings of the currency have become scarce, in which case the provisions of 10 below come into force.

(ii) A currency is acceptable:

U.S. statement

(*a*) If at the time the currency is tendered to the Fund the member country represents that the currency demanded is presently needed for making payments in that currency which are consistent with the purposes of the Fund;

(*b*) If the Fund's total holdings of the currency of the member country have not increased by more than 25 per cent of the quota during the previous twelve months, and if they do not exceed 200 per cent of the quota; and

U.S. statement

(*c*) If the Fund has not previously given notice of 6 months to a year which has expired that a member country is making use of the Fund's resources in a manner that clearly has the effect of preventing or unduly delaying the establishment of a sound balance in its international accounts.

U.K. statement

[Add to the above.] The Fund will not give notice if its holdings of the member currency do not exceed 166 per cent of its quota.

(iii) The Fund may, in its discretion, make currencies available in exchange for a member currency that does not comply with the above tests on conditions that safeguard the interests of the Fund.

6. *Multilateral clearing*

(i) Subject to 13(iv) a member country agrees to buy back its own legally acquired currency from any other member with that member's currency or with gold, so long as its own currency is acceptable to the Fund and the other member's currency is available in the Fund.

U.S. statement

(ii) So long as a member's currency is acceptable, it is entitled to acquire any available currency in the

Fund, subject to half payment in gold or free foreign exchange from a member country whose official gold and free foreign exchange holdings exceed its quota.

U.K. statement

(ii) So long as a member's currency is acceptable, it is entitled to acquire any available currency in the Fund.

(iii) A member country desiring to obtain directly or indirectly the currency of another member country for gold is expected, provided it can do so with equal advantage, to acquire the currency if it is available, by the sale of gold to the Fund.

(iv) The local currency holdings of the Fund shall be freely transferable to any member country, subject to 4(ii) and the provisions of the plan.

7. *Par value of member currencies*

(i) The initial par value of a member's currency shall be agreed with the Fund when it is admitted to membership, and shall be expressed in terms of gold.

(ii) All transactions between the Fund and members, and all transactions in member currencies, shall be at rates within an agreed percentage of parity.

(iii) No change in the gold parity of a member's currency shall be made without its approval.

(iv) Members shall agree not to propose a change in the parity of their currency unless they consider it appropriate to the correction of fundamental disequilibrium, and changes shall be made only with the approval of the Fund, subject to the qualifications below.

(v) The Fund shall approve a requested change in the parity of a member's currency if it is essential to the correction of a fundamental disequilibrium. In particular, the Fund shall not reject, on the ground of domestic social or political policies which may have led to the application, a requested change which is required in the *de facto* situation to restore equilibrium.

U.S. statement

(vi) After consulting the Fund, a member country may change the established rate for its currency, providēd the proposed change, inclusive of any previous changes, does not exceed 10 per cent since the establishment of the Fund. In the case of application for a further change not covered by the above and not exceeding 10 per cent, the Fund shall give its decision within two days of receiving the application, if the applicant so desires.

U.K. statement

(vi) After consulting the Fund, a member country may change the established rate for its currency, provided the proposed change, inclusive of any previous changes, does not exceed 10 per cent within successive ten-year periods since the establishment of the Fund. In the case of application for a further change not covered by the above and not exceeding 10 per cent, the Fund shall give its decision within two days of receiving the application, if the applicant so desires.

(vii) Because of the extreme uncertainties of the immediate post-war period and recognising that rates established during such period will of necessity be tentative in many instances, during the first three years the Fund shall recognise that there will be need for many changes and adjustments and shall resolve cases of reasonable doubt in favour of the country requesting changes in rates.

(viii) Provision shall be made for an agreed uniform change in the gold value of currencies with the approval of the Fund and of all member countries with 10 per cent or more of aggregate quotas.

8. *Repurchase provisions*

(i) A member country may repurchase from the Fund for gold any part of the latter's holding of its currency.

U.S. statement

(ii) If at the end of stated periods, a member's official holdings of gold and free foreign exchange have increased, and those holdings are adequate, the Fund may require that half of the increase be used to repurchase any of the Fund's holdings of its currency in excess of its quota.

U.K. statement

(ii) If at the end of the Fund's financial year a

member's holding of gold and of gold-convertible currencies has increased, the rules of the Fund may require that it shall employ the whole or part of this increase to repurchase from the Fund any excess of the Fund's holding of its currency above its quota.

9. *Capital transactions*

(i) A member country may not use the Fund's resources to meet a large or sustained outflow of capital.

(ii) The Fund may require a member country purchasing foreign exchange from the Fund to control large or sustained outward movements of capital.

U.S. statement

(iii) These provisions are not intended to interfere with transactions which do not involve a substantial requirement of foreign exchange, or transactions required in trade, banking and other business.

(iv) Notwithstanding the above provisions, with the approval of the Fund, a member country may purchase foreign exchange to facilitate a transfer of capital.

(v) A member country may not use its control of capital movements to restrict payments for current transactions (except as provided in 10 and 13(iv)) or to delay unduly the transfer of funds in settlement of commitments.

U.K. statement

A member country may be asked by the Fund to exercise such control as is required to prevent large and sustained capital movements from being financed by recourse to the Fund. This provision is not intended to prevent the use of the Fund for capital transactions of reasonable amount approved by the member country's control as being required in the ordinary course of trade, banking and other business, or for the expansion of exports. Nor is it intended to prevent capital movements of other kinds which are met out of a member country's own resources of gold and foreign exchange.

10. *Apportionment of scarce currencies*

(i) When it becomes evident to the Fund that the anticipated demand for a currency may soon exhaust the Fund's holdings of that currency, the Fund shall inform the member countries and propose an equitable method of apportioning the scarce currency. When a currency is thus declared scarce the Fund shall issue a report embodying the causes of the scarcity and containing recommendations designed to bring it to an end.

(ii) A decision by the Fund to apportion a scarce currency shall operate as an authorisation to member countries after consultation with the Fund temporarily to restrict the freedom of exchange operations in the affected currency, and in determining the manner of restricting the demand and rationing the limited supply among its nationals the member country shall have complete jurisdiction.

11. *Management*

(i) The Fund shall be managed by a Board and Executive Committee representing the members.

(ii) The distribution of basic voting power shall be closely related to quotas, but no members shall be entitled to cast more than one-fifth of the aggregate votes.

(iii) All matters shall be settled by majority, except that a change in the basis for determining quotas shall require a four-fifths vote, and no member's quota shall be changed without its assent.

12. *Withdrawal*

(i) A member country may withdraw from the Fund by giving notice in writing.

(ii) Thereafter, the Fund may not sell the currency of that country if the Fund's holdings are less than the unliquidated portion of its quota, nor buy the currency of that country if the Fund's holdings are more than the unliquidated portion of its quota. After a country has given notice of withdrawal, its right to utilise the resources of the Fund is subject to the approval of the Fund.

(iii) The reciprocal obligations of the Fund and the country are to be liquidated within a reasonable time.

13. *Obligations of member countries*

(i) Not to buy gold at a price above the parity of its currency, nor to sell gold at a price below the parity of its currency.

(ii) Not to allow exchange transactions between its currency and the currencies of other members at rates outside a prescribed range based on the agreed cross parities.

(iii) To abandon as soon as possible, when the member country decides that conditions permit, all restrictions on payments for current international transactions with other member countries (other than those involving capital transfers), and not to impose any additional restrictions (except upon capital transfers, or in accordance with 10 above) without the approval of the Fund. The Fund may make representations that conditions are favourable to the abandonment of restrictions.

(iv) Not to engage in discriminatory currency arrangements or multiple currency practices without the approval of the Fund.

14. *The inauguration of the Fund*

Provisions shall be prepared to cover the transitional period and the definitive establishment of the Fund.

(IV) *Joint Minutes of Anglo-American meeting*

Joint Minutes of the meeting of United States and United Kingdom experts, United States Treasury, 9th October, 1943

At the final meeting of the experts of the United States and the United Kingdom, held in Washington on the 9th October, 1943, it was agreed that the following details not included in the directive to the Drafting Committee are also covered by the discussions on the same basis as the directive itself:–

3(i). The agreed formula is to give the United States a quota not to exceed $3 billion and the United Kingdom a quota of about $1·3. The formula will also provide for setting aside a special allotment of 10 per cent of the aggregate quotas to be used for the equitable adjustment of quotas.

3(i). 'Local funds' are to be a deposit account at the member country's central bank. In order to avoid an unnecessarily large working balance, the Fund would hold local funds in excess of a working balance in the form of non-negotiable, non-interest bearing government bills, payable at par on demand by crediting the Fund's deposit account at the central bank.

5(iii). When the provision of additional exchange to a member country is subject to special conditions, the Fund may as one of the conditions require the deposit of suitable collateral.

7. The unit of account shall be a given weight of gold. No change in the par value of the currency of member countries shall be permitted to alter the gold value of the assets of the Fund, except that in the case of a change under 7(viii) this provision may be waived by agreement.

The initial rates of exchange of member countries' currencies shall be based on the official dollar quotations of the 1st July, 1943. If this rate is inappropriate in the judgment of either the Fund or the member country, the initial par value of a member's currency shall be agreed between the member country and the Fund.

11. When the provision of exchange requires approval of the Fund, basic votes on such proposals shall be adjusted, notwithstanding 11(ii), by increasing the vote of creditor countries and decreasing the vote of debtor countries in the Fund. On the suspension or restoration of membership each country shall have one vote.

13(ii). Member countries shall not engage in exchange dealings in non-member countries or in non-member currencies that will undermine stability of exchange rates established by the Fund.

There is a difference of view on the following questions:–

3(ii). Whether the obligatory gold subscription should be of 25 per cent of the quota or 10 per cent of the gold holdings of a country, whichever is smaller; and whether the gold contributed to the Fund shall be held by the Fund as a reserve security.

5 (ii). Whether a currency should only be acceptable if it is tendered against another currency which that member can represent to be needed for payments due or shortly falling due.

5 (ii). Whether the qualitative controls should apply only after the Fund's holdings of local currency have reached a specified level, or whether such control may be applied at any time with notice of six months to a year.

6 (ii). Whether a member having holdings of gold and free foreign exchange in excess of its quota should be required to make payment as to 50 per cent in gold and foreign exchange for currency made available by the Fund.

7 (vi). Whether the right to change the established exchange rate of a member currency by a total of 10 per cent, should be renewed for each successive decade or not.

8 (ii). Whether the provision for the repurchase of local currency held by the Fund shall apply to part of the increase in the free *foreign exchange* holdings of a member country, or only to holdings of gold convertible currencies.

9. Whether the Fund may require a member country not to permit an outward movement of capital which is large and sustained (regardless of the source of the funds used to meet the flow) where a member country is significantly using the sources of the Fund.

In general whether the Fund, while established on the same fundamental principles as those set out in the Draft Directive, should not be set up and operated in terms of an international currency (monetised unitas).

(V) *The Draft Statement of Principles in terms of a monetised unitas*

In order to express the substance of the Draft Statement of Principles in terms of monetised unitas, the following paragraphs should be substituted for those carrying the same number in the Draft discussed with the American group:–

4. *Operations of the Fund*

(i) Members will receive a credit in the books of the Fund in terms of unitas equal to their subscription, which, subject to certain qualifications below, they will be free to transfer to the accounts of other members with the Fund.

(ii) A member whose currency is 'acceptable' shall undertake to buy its currency from another member in exchange for a transfer of unitas on the books of the Fund; and a member whose currency is 'available' shall undertake to sell its currency to another member in exchange for a transfer of unitas on the books of the Fund.

(iii) A member whose holding of unitas exceeds its quota shall be entitled to apply the excess to redeeming its original subscription, first the local funds and then the gold. A member which has redeemed all or part of its original subscription for unitas shall be entitled to reverse its action at any time.

5. *Availability and acceptability of members' currencies*

(i) A member's currency is available if its balance of unitas in excess of its outstanding subscription does not exceed its quota, and unless the Fund has given notice that the facilities for the purchase of currency by a transfer of unitas have become scarce, in which case the provisions of 10 below come into force.

(ii) A member's currency is acceptable:

(*a*) If the member has a balance of unitas with the Fund on which it is entitled to draw.

(iii) A member is entitled to draw on its balance of unitas with the Fund unless it has reduced its holding of unitas by more than 25 per cent of its quota during the previous twelve months; and if the Fund has not previously given notice of six months to a year which has expired, that a member country is making use of the Fund's resources in a manner that clearly has the effect of preventing or unduly delaying the establishment of a sound balance in its international accounts. The Fund will not give notice unless the member's holdings of unitas have fallen below 33 per cent of its quota.

(iv) The Fund may, in its discretion, make a further balance of unitas available to a member country that does not comply with the above tests, or in addition to its original subscription, on conditions that safeguard the interests of the Fund.

6. *Multilateral clearing*

((i), (ii) and (iv) are no longer necessary.)

(iii) The Fund may buy gold from a member at its par value in exchange for a balance of unitas, the gold so acquired being *free* gold. A member desiring to sell gold is expected to offer it to the Fund, directly or through another member, if this will serve its purpose in selling the gold equally well. The Fund may, at its option and with the approval of the member concerned, employ free gold to redeem any portion of a member's balance of unitas in excess of its outstanding subscription.

7. *Par value of member currencies*

(i) The value of unitas shall be expressed in terms of gold. The initial par value of a member's currency shall be agreed with the Fund when it is admitted to membership and shall be expressed in terms of unitas.

(ii) All transactions in member currencies shall be at rates within an agreed percentage of parity.

(iii) No change in the value of a member's currency in terms of unitas shall be made without its approval.

((iv) to (vii) unchanged.)

(viii) The gold value of unitas may be changed with the approval of the Fund and of all member countries with 10 per cent or more of the aggregate quotas.

8. *Repurchase provisions*

(i) A member may repurchase from the Fund for gold any part of the latter's holding of its local funds.

(ii) If at the end of the Fund's financial year a member's holding of gold and of gold-convertible currencies has increased, the rules of the Fund may require that it shall employ the whole or part of this increase to increase its holdings of unitas up to the amount of its quota.

10. *Apportionment of scarce currencies*

(i) When it becomes evident to the Fund that the anticipated demand for a currency may soon raise that member's holding of unitas to an amount exceeding its outstanding subscription by the amount of its quota, the Fund shall inform the member countries and propose an equitable method of apportioning the scarce currency. When a currency is thus declared scarce, the Fund shall issue a report embodying the causes of the scarcity and containing recommendations designed to bring it to an end.

(ii) Unchanged.

12. *Withdrawal*

(i) A member country may withdraw from the Fund by giving notice in writing.

(ii) Thereafter the member shall no longer be at liberty to operate on its account of unitas with the Fund, except that it may draw on any excess of its holdings above its outstanding subscription with the approval of the Fund.

(iii) The reciprocal obligations of the Fund and the country are to be liquidated within a reasonable time.

[The Clauses 1, 2, 3, 9, 11, 13 and 14 omitted above are identical in the two versions.]

13 October 1943

The version of the Joint Statement that existed at the end of the Washington negotiations in October 1943 was far from final. Between 9 October and the April 1944 publication of the Joint Statement by Experts on the Establishment of an International Monetary Fund as a White Paper, the October version went through seven drafts. Rather than follow all the drafting intricacies in detail, it is probably easiest to summarise the results.

(*a*) *Gold subscriptions.* The British accepted the American version of 3 (ii) in December 1943.

(*b*) *Sterilisation of Contributions.* The British accepted in December the American view that the Fund could use gold in its transactions.

(*c*) *Changes in Exchange Rates.* The British accepted the American view and 7 (vi) disappeared.

(*d*) *Gold Payments for Drawings.* The British accepted the American insistence that if a member's reserves equalled its quota, it should pay for half its purchases of foreign currency from the Fund in gold or gold convertible foreign exchange. However, the Americans accepted the British view that reserves for these purposes should consist of gold or gold convertible exchange.

(*e*) *Drawings for Capital Purposes.* The U.S. version was accepted in January with the adoption of the additional words 'provided such capital movements are in accordance with the purposes of the Fund'.

(*f*) *Repurchase Provisions.* The version agreed allowed that if at the end of the Fund's financial year a country's gold and gold convertible reserves had risen, the Fund could require that the country use one-half of the increase to repurchase its own currency provided the Fund's holdings were not below 75 per cent of its quota and reserves, defined net of liabilities, were not less than the country's quota.

(g) *Monetisation of Unitas.* The British made several attempts to get the United States to change the formulation at this point before accepting the non-unitas version in April.

The main outstanding issue was one of interpretation rather than drafting. It concerned a country's right to draw from the Fund. Despite Keynes's raising of the issue with Professor Viner in October (above p. 333), he accepted the American draft in December subject to 'a wider and less specific definition of the criterion on which the Fund is entitled to act'. With Keynes's acceptance came a readily accepted new draft which did not affect the original sense of the American proposals. However, he continued to argue, contrary to the draft, that drawings were unconditional within the criteria set down.[33] This was to cause problems later.

After his return to London, Keynes reported the mood to Redvers Opie.

From a letter to REDVERS OPIE, *7 December 1943*

Meanwhile, we are plodding along, none too fast, with the documents brought home and with Harry White's revised draft and the other papers which are reaching us through Sigi. Thank you for the note of your conversation with Bernstein, elucidating some of the reasons for some of the changes. Many of the U.S. Treasury revisions are, we agree with you, quite innocent. But, in some passages, particularly clause 7 and the formula relating to capital transactions, we shall probably want to stand firm on our original text.

The main points on which stress is being laid here are (1) the importance of adhering to the monetised unitas version, and (2) the need of being clearer about what happens during the transitional period, before we commit ourselves. The Bank of England people are taking the line that we should regard the monetised unitas version as being, from our point of view, an absolutely essential agreement. I take the line that it is so far preferable that it is well worth trying this on the U.S. Treasury again in the most emphatic manner. But, whilst

[33] See below pp. 404–6.

393

I have every natural reason for vastly preferring this set-up, I cannot persuade myself that the difference between the two versions is really such as to make it a justifiable reason for an ultimate breach. The emphasis on the transitional period, on the other hand, does seem to me justified and important. There is no prospect, of course, of our arriving at any clear-cut or definite plans in the near future, but it is essential that we should be sufficiently protected in the draft Statement of Principles, in the sense that our commitment to the scheme must be contingent on the satisfactory settlement of the transitional period and on our having an entirely free hand during this period. We have not yet got anything definite on paper about this, but we shall do so shortly, and you will see it in due course.

Generally speaking, we feel that the right policy is to try again on the U.S. Treasury any points where we feel confidently and clearly that our version is a real improvement or politically essential from our point of view, and you and Sigi must do your best to get as many of these points over as possible. This would leave a reasonably tidy document, even though there may be a passage or two here and there where alternative versions still remain. It will then be for Ministers to decide if any sticking points are still outstanding, and I personally, at any rate, hope that we shall have got to a point where real agreement can be reached.

In all this you have to bear it in mind that there were some quarters who confidently believed until recently that all these plans would die a natural death. Since it now seems possible that nature cannot be relied on to do the work, it is felt, not to put it more strongly, that there is no need officiously to keep alive any conception of any kind of an international scheme.

M. K.

To R. H. Brand he wrote on 16 December

It is not going to be plain sailing. There are quarters—perhaps you can guess which—not concerned officiously to keep alive any international currency scheme at all. At some later date, I expect a pretty difficult controversy.

He had not long to wait.

The reports on the various aspects of the Washington Discussions were circulated to the War Cabinet on 17 December. On 21 December the War Cabinet asked Mr Law to prepare a report focusing the issues arising from the Discussions for Ministerial decision.[34] The War Cabinet also asked Ministers to send Mr Law the questions they wished to raise on the subject.[35] All this was in preparation for subsequent discussions with the Dominions and in Parliament.

Keynes, other members of the Treasury and the Economic Section then became involved in drafting the relevant sections of Mr Law's report and answering the questions. In a note dated 19 January, 1944, Sir Wilfrid Eady, a not disinterested participant summarised the divisions that had developed, as he saw them.

From Article VII Summary of Present Strategic Position

3. *Currency Scheme*

White has substantially accepted the telegrams we sent especially about transitional period. But on examining some other suggestions he made we have found serious imperfections in existing text and further telegram must go to Washington. Keynes believes merely a matter of drafting, but personally I am not certain whether we have not brought to light two or three important differences of intention.

On the Chancellor's instructions I attended meeting of Law, Keynes, Robbins, last Friday to discuss Treasury note on Currency Scheme. The Treasury is riven on the subject and I was very unwilling to argue with Keynes in front of Law so told the Chancellor that we should prefer that the differences were reported to him and discussed with him and then on his general directive we would prepare a paper for Law.

Present position. Keynes fully engaged in pressing acceptability of Currency Scheme. Dennis Robertson equally emphatic but (*a*) Keynes has

[34] It implicitly rejected requests from Mr Hudson, the Minister of Agriculture, and Mr Amery, the Secretary of State for India, for an official committee to examine the Washington proposals.

[35] The most critical of the questions, which came from many sources, came from Mr Hudson, Mr Amery, and Mr Bevin.

approved cordially Henderson's essay on the International Economic History of the Inter-War Years,[36] and (b) Keynes has produced paper[37] on balance of payments position which suggests that the credits obtainable through Currency Scheme will be entirely inadequate and that we shall have to go cap in hand to Washington or New York for further accommodation. ? will we be embarrassed in this by acceptance of the S.F. credits which are mainly American.

Waley not enthusiastic for S.F. Thinks we ought to agree upon international monetary institution and that choice is between S.F. or nothing at all. On alternatives, see paragraph below. Henderson critical on merits of Currency Scheme especially of conflict of ideas between Currency scheme and Commercial Policy etc. Generally, I think, in favour of bilateralism.

Bank of England impressively critical of several technical issues. Still quite unconvinced that Fund is passive. Fund clearly deals in gold. Fund clearly deals in scarce currencies. Increases of gold of member countries to be paid into Fund thus making Fund larger dealer in gold. Possibility not yet resolved and arising out of present telegrams that Fund also wishes to have its own points for buying and selling a currency. Obviously impossible that sterling should be on offer at two differing rates by Bank of England and Fund.

Multilateral Clearing. Would be satisfied with transitional period arrangements provided that all countries with whom we would wish to make special payments agreements feel themselves equally free and certain that there would be no criticism from Americans or from Management if they did so. Finds great difficulty in believing that this will happen.

Sterling Balances. Keynes takes the view that all pre-zero-hour balances are capital and that therefore we may block them by Exchange Control on the authority of the text of S.F., Bank of England deride this. They feel we must make our own domestic arrangements with each of the holders of balances on the merits of the economic position and that so far from acquiring additional authority from the text of S.F. we shall be embarrassed by the obligation to move towards multilateral clearing in three years. E.g. how can we persuade India to fund our part of sterling balances for long period on nominal interest rates if India and we are signatories to agreement that sterling shall become freely convertible after short period. Bank of England also discern, with some plausibility, appearance of return to gold standard obligations without benefit of corrective obtained from old gold standard. Sterling has to be expressed in terms of gold. Parity rates have to be supported. In free markets, e.g. New York, Lisbon, Zurich,

[36] Reprinted in his *The Inter-war Years and Other Essays,* ed. H. Clay (Oxford, 1955).
[37] See *JMK*, vol. XXIV, pp. 1–18.

Stockholm, Tangier, Shanghai, we might be compelled to intervene with substantial loss of resources. Fund's holding of sterling can be sold to any member and any member holding sterling can exchange this for another currency through Fund. When multilateral clearing is in operation any member can require us to buy sterling holdings from them against their currency which we should have to get from the Fund or gold.

The argument is rather intricate but if any critics such as Einzig took it it cannot be disposed of very convincingly unless Keynes can produce the answer.

Management. This is connected with question of date at which the institution will be created and come into operation. Largest part of resources at disposal of the Fund coming from U.S.A. Notable, therefore, that immense American pressure will be exerted to have dominating position on Management. In present political atmosphere in Washington, and present 'power strength' of the two countries, Management might be either relatively experienced and very hostile, or political and possibly hostile, or a combination of both. Bank point out that the whole question of the principles under which a Management of an international exchange scheme with very wide executive powers should be created has not been discussed.

General framing of the scheme. Although very substantial modifications have been made, general structure of scheme is the same original American scheme. Attitude and technique is derived from Equalisation Fund technique, and whatever paper safeguards there are for passivity, development of the scheme must from its very nature be towards dealing exchanges. For their reputation the Management of the Fund would be unwilling to allow their holdings of currencies to be swollen by relatively high proportion of il-liquid sterling.

Scarce currencies. Keynes attaches great and political importance to this recognition that if a country, i.e. U.S.A., allows its currency to become scarce because it insists upon selling more than it is prepared to buy and refrains from investing abroad the difference, then all the signatory countries may apply exchange control to the dollar and limit imports. Bank of England point out that exchange control cannot be applied against the dollar only. It must be applied against all currencies or, which is very unlikely, simultaneously by all countries against all transactions in dollar. On limitation of imports they expressed a doubt whether it will be practicable for countries, on this ground only, to limit their receipts of e.g. American oil, lard, wheat, etc.

I confess that at the meeting here the Bank of England, Cobbold, Bolton and Clay, who have all been beautifully mannered have been impressively critical of the technical imperfections of the draft and the conceptions underlying it.

They helped us to find better drafting but all on the understanding that they reserved their attitude as a whole.

4. Our own position

At every stage here the problems of the transitional period seemed to be more difficult and their pattern less easy to see. This is becoming increasingly recognised, e.g. Board of Trade on Commercial Policy contemplate that Convention might be signed but put in cold storage for say three years with complete freedom to all signatories to be as discriminatory as they like, and then a penitential period of five years during which all countries would progressively go towards the full Convention.

I suppose we could adopt a similar technique with the Currency Scheme though it looks a little cock eye to fix very precise rules which are not to come into operation until the end of the period which may make the rules inappropriate. But I strongly dislike the idea of post-dated cheques in international conventions. The amount of wriggling to get out of the obligation would be terrible. If we signed the Currency Convention with the contracting out for the transitional period I think we would be morally on the defensive almost at every stage and if we shook ourselves free from such an inhibition and proceeded actively to work out the policy during that period which suited us we should probably be held to be very perfidious and cynical.

Currency Scheme is not a Statement of Principles despite its title. It is a fully detailed plan.

Chancellor's present and quite provincial view is that it may be necessary to see our way through transitional period with fairly free hands before we commit ourselves. I am coming more and more to that conclusion.

The questions raised by the discussions so affected the Treasury that when Mr Law's report on the Washington Discussions went to the War Cabinet, the part on monetary policy contained two sections. The first represented a statement in favour, in a form originally drafted by Keynes on 26 January and then shortened and re-ordered. The second began

This section of the note sets out the strong misgivings which are felt by some Treasury advisers about any decision at this stage to commend a scheme in its present form to the approval of the Dominions and Parliament.

Keynes's section ran as follows.

From The Proposal For an International Monetary Fund, Annex A of The Washington Conversations Article VII, Memorandum by the Minister of State, 7 February 1944

II. THE MAIN OBJECTS OF THE PLAN

6. The following is a statement of the main objects of the Plan and its attractions as seen more especially by our Washington representatives. Misgivings which are felt by some Treasury advisers are separately set out in the third section of this note.

7. (i) It is a characteristic of British foreign trade that it often suits us to sell predominantly in certain countries and to buy predominantly in others. Our best sources of supply are not always our best markets. It will, therefore, help the expansion of our trade if we can re-establish the conditions, generally prevailing before 1914, by which the proceeds of sales in one country can be freely applied to purchases in other countries. The Plan is calculated to secure this object after normal conditions have been reached, whilst requiring a full commitment to a multilateral clearing system in the transitional period, during which restrictions will be inevitable.

8. (ii) Nevertheless, this freedom from restrictions should apply only to current business and not to 'flights' or uncontrolled movements of capital funds. Experience between the wars clearly demonstrated the mischief of unregulated capital movements, which take no account of the balance of trade available for overseas investment. The Plan provides that members shall have full liberty of action to control such movements.

9. (iii) The ability of members to implement undertakings to secure the first objective above will be much increased if some attempt is made to redress the maldistribution of liquid reserves in the shape of gold and gold-convertible currencies. The provision now proposed is much smaller than in the Clearing Union Plan, but it enough to give the scheme a good

start and can be increased later on, if it proves necessary and if the scheme is working well in other respects. Under these proposals the quota of the United States would be £750 million, of Great Britain and her Colonies £325 million (with separate quotas for India and the Dominions), and of the world as a whole £2,500 million. The quota represents both the maximum liability on a country to support the Fund and also (in normal circumstances) the maximum assistance which a country can receive from the Fund. It also measures the member's voting power, except that no member is entitled to more than 20 per cent of the total votes. In our own case we shall be lucky if we end the transitional period with reserves so high as £325 million, so that the Plan is likely to double our resources to meet contingencies—a measure of assistance not to be rejected lightly. The amount of the gold subscription, where the United States representatives have gone a long way to meet our objections, is now put at 25 per cent of the quota or 10 per cent of a country's own reserves, whichever is least. In our own case this will probably work out at a little less than our Washington delegation was instructed to secure.

10. (iv) Some part of the responsibility for maintaining equilibrium should be placed on the creditor countries, instead of throwing the whole burden, as hitherto, on the debtor countries. The clause of the Plan dealing with this is of great importance, not least because it has been put forward on the initiative of the American representatives without amendment from our side, and concurred in by the State Department and the Federal Reserve Board, as well as by the United States Treasury. Under the Clearing Union Plan the liability on a creditor country to maintain equilibrium by supporting the Fund, if it had failed to do so in some other way, was more or less unlimited. The American representatives felt that Congress would never accept an unlimited liability in advance, and that some other means must, therefore, be

found for fixing responsibility on a chronic creditor country which was hoarding its earnings from the rest of the world and failed to return them to circulation either by consumption or by investment.

11. Put shortly in terms of the United States as an example, what the American representatives are offering the rest of the world is as follows. Up to an amount of £750 million they put at the disposal of the Fund the equivalent of any dollars which may accrue to them from a favourable balance of payments, as a result of their neither consuming nor investing what they earn from their imports. If it appears that the cumulative balance thus built up is in danger of exceeding this total, they have the option of getting rid of their surplus on imports or overseas investment, of increasing their contribution to the Fund which would have the effect of making more American currency available, or of accepting the conditions which become applicable when the Fund has declared dollars to be a 'scarce' currency. The conditions under this third alternative mean in effect that American exporters can no longer claim payment for their goods in excess of the amount which the United States is making available on the other side of the account by importing or by lending. All the other countries of the world become entitled forthwith to put any form of restrictions they choose in the way of accepting American goods and in the way of paying for any they do accept. To put this third alternative into effect would, it is true, cause great trouble and technical difficulty all round. It was, however, the view of the American representatives that from their point of view the third alternative would be so intolerable that it could never be allowed to come to this in practice and that their country would be forced to adopt one of the other alternatives. That, indeed, is what they wanted to see forced upon them. They also gave as an additional reason why this would be the outcome, that, if a heavy uncovered American surplus develops, this will most probably accompany slump

conditions in the United States. In such circumstances the American Administration could never afford to see the whole of its export industries thrown into confusion. The American representatives were fully aware of the implications of their own proposal. They were moved by their consciousness of how serious to the world any failure to solve the problem would be, and of the importance, therefore, of sufficient pressure to enforce a solution. Nevertheless, the offer is a signal mark of their courage, of their fair-mindedness and of their sense of responsibility to the other nations of the world.

12. This proposal represents, therefore, a revolutionary change for the better compared with the position in the inter-war period. The American representatives offer voluntarily on behalf of their country to abate its former stranglehold on the world's economy and to offer safeguards against its hoarding propensities forcing deflation on others. Moreover, this particular provision has been published and Congress is aware of it; yet, so far, it has not been the target of any particular criticism. It would seem rash on our part to reject so fair an offer and to risk a return to the chaos and irresponsibility of the former lack of system.

13. (v) Ministers will be particularly concerned with the adequacy of the provisions to secure elasticity of exchange rates. In this respect the American representatives have been persuaded to depart widely from their original proposals, which seemed to aim at extreme rigidity of exchange on the model of the former gold standard—or, at any rate, could be so represented. The Washington Delegation was authorised to state in plain terms that such arrangements could not be accepted by the British Cabinet and would be inevitably rejected by Parliament. As the result of prolonged discussions, the procedure set forth in Clause 5 of the Statement of Principles below emerged; it may be summarised as follows:–

(*a*) The principle of change both in the value of individual currencies and in the value of gold itself, to suit changing circumstances, is expressly recognised.

(*b*) A proposal for change by a member country has to be considered judicially by the Fund, from the point of view whether it is in fact required to remedy disequilibrium; and, if in the actual circumstances it is required, the Fund may not refuse it on the ground that the explanation of disequilibrium should be sought rather in the domestic, social or political policies of the applicant member, in which matters the Fund may not interfere.

(*c*) Changes not exceeding 10 per cent in the aggregate may be made by a member country acting, after consultation, but unilaterally.

(*d*) Changes of a further 10 per cent may be made unilaterally, unless the Fund has refused approval within two days of the application for a change having been made.

(*e*) If a member country is dissatisfied with the Fund's decision on this (or on any other) matter, it can terminate its membership of the Fund and resume its full freedom of action forthwith, without notice and without penalty.

(*f*) The Fund is particularly required to take into consideration the extreme uncertainties likely to prevail when the initial parities are fixed, and, during the transitional period, to allow a member asking for a change the benefit of any reasonable doubt.

14. These proposals seem to combine satisfactorily an orderly procedure for change with retaining a sufficient ultimate freedom of action to individual members. They certainly cannot be represented as being aimed at gold-standard rigidity. Their whole purpose is to provide a proper means to secure orderly changes in what is, of its nature, a two-sided transaction, and, therefore, a most proper subject for international consultation and adjustment.

15. Particular attention is invited to (*e*) above. The Ameri-

can representatives were at first most reluctant to accept this provision, but were in the end converted to the idea that an institution of this kind should be a free association of countries which believe membership to be to their mutual advantage, and that no attempt should be made to hold a dissatisfied country to a membership which had become irksome and undesired. In fact this freedom may help to hold the association together. The Fund is likely to be more reasonable if an aggrieved member is free to leave; and a member is more likely to acquiesce in a decision if he remains free at any time to change his mind.

16. (vi) If an international institution is to assume such wide responsibilities, it must be given some considerable measure of authority and of influence. At the same time it may seem alarming to entrust any wide measure of discretion to a new body which necessarily starts without traditions, under a management of whose wisdom and impartiality we have as yet no experience. Our object must be, therefore, to secure as much prior certainty as possible concerning the methods of those responsible for daily management, and to limit their initiative and discretion to cases where the rules and purposes of the institution are in risk of infringement, thus keeping them as an instrument, entirely passive in all normal circumstances, the right of initiative being reserved to the central banks of the member countries. The American representatives had set out in their Stabilisation Fund with quite a different conception of the functions of the new institution. In their eyes it should have wide discretionary and policing powers and should exercise something of the same measure of grandmotherly influence and control over the central banks of the member countries, that these central banks in turn are accustomed to exercise over the other banks within their own countries.

17. In the course of discussion, however, the American representatives were persuaded of the inacceptability of such

a scheme of things, of the undesirability of starting off by giving so much authority to an untried institution, and of the importance of giving the member countries as much certainty as possible about what they had to expect from the new institution and about the amount of facilities which would be at their full disposal. In the final draft, therefore, all the technical matters at issue, except one, have been in the end settled on the expert level.

18. The one matter outstanding which flows from an initial difference of approach by the Clearing Union and by the Stabilisation Fund respectively, is as follows. Under the Clearing Union proposals the member countries were to bank with the institution, where they would have accounts on which they were free to operate in terms of a new international unit of account, to be called bancor. Under the Stabilisation Fund proposals the institution was to bank with the member countries, holding accounts with their central banks on which it would be free to operate in terms of each member's currency, so that no new international unit would be necessary. An international money of account, unitas, was mentioned in the Stabilisation Fund proposals but was only mentioned to be forgotten and played no effective part. Now this difference, however important, is nevertheless only a matter of technical form. A given set of proposals can be drafted in terms of either set-up so as to be identical in substance and legal effect.

19. In the new draft Statement of Principles there is no new-fangled international unit of account. The United States Treasury and all the other American Departments, which have been parties to the discussion, are strongly of the opinion that this fact would help them greatly in their difficulties with Congress. In a recent message Dr White writes: 'While the emphasis on a new international currency would be attractive to some people it would rouse considerable opposition in this country among those who would feel that national currencies

are being replaced by a new and experimental currency. The task of gaining public support for international monetary co-operation would be increased by the high-lighting in the proposal of a new international currency.'

20. Moreover, if this set-up is adopted, it requires virtually no new legislation in the United States. No more is necessary than a motion of general approval in Congress followed by an appropriation of a part of the resources of the existing United States Stabilisation Fund. It is arguable that the other version would require special legislation which could be represented as tying up the dollar to a phoney international unit.

21. Whilst there are many advantages in the alternative involving a new international unit which the British technical experts would prefer, all the members of the British Delegation to Washington concerned in these discussions, who have had the opportunity of appreciating, face to face, the great efforts made on the other side to reach agreement, are of the opinion that on this remaining issue we should defer to the American view.

22. There remains the difficult matter of (vii) *the arrangements for the transitional period.* This was not discussed at Washington as thoroughly as it might have been. The clauses dealing with it, which the Delegation brought back, may have been adequate on a strict legal interpretation but were insufficiently explicit and, therefore, perhaps capable of leading to misunderstanding later on. A new draft of what is now clause 11 was, therefore, prepared and sent to Dr White together with a letter making clear the interpretation which we should want to put on it. Subject to drafting amendments, this clause has now been accepted by the United States Treasury. It preserves full freedom of action to us to enforce exchange control during the period before equilibrium has been restored sufficiently to enable us to remove restrictions. It also states clearly that it is not the purpose of the Fund to provide facilities for relief or reconstruction or to deal with

international indebtedness arising out of the war; and that members are entitled to be satisfied, before taking on the full commitments of the Plan, that they see their way to cover their balance of payments during the early post-war transitional period by means which will not unduly encumber their facilities with the Fund.

23. Nevertheless, Ministers will wish to assure themselves not only that we retain sufficient freedom of action during a period which is bound to be very difficult, but also that we do not prejudice our prospects of other outside aid during this period. It would be fatal if, in spite of the above assurance, we were to be pressed to use the resources of the Fund in the early years, with the result of depriving ourselves of reserves intended to support the commitments which we should be undertaking for the normal period. Although the probable position in the early post-war years is to a considerable extent conjectural and an estimate is still being worked at, it is only prudent to assume that our need for assistance in that period may be very large indeed. It may, therefore, be wise that we should take an early opportunity to express frankly to the United States Administration what is in our minds; namely that we cannot enter into this scheme unless there is an assurance of our not being expected to use its facilities prematurely, and that we cannot have any such assurance until they have given us some indication of the financial régime succeeding the lend lease phase which should, in their opinion, assist a steady progress by ourselves and others into the period when equilibrium can be secured without large-scale assistance from outside.

24. It might be argued that, in view of all this, we should postpone the whole scheme. If the scheme were of doubtful long-term advantage to us, this might be the prudent course. If, on the other hand, it is a good scheme from which we, not less than others, have much to gain, and without which we should risk a return to the inter-war chaos, we should be

unwise not to clinch the matter as soon as we have an opportunity to do so. Moreover, in certain respects the new institution may be of particular value during the early, difficult years. It is then that order and discipline in foreign exchange rates will be particularly important. And it is then that an authoritative organ of international discussion and consultation can play a specially significant part in finding the way out of the transition, where we should sit as equals, instead of waiting on the mat outside the United States Treasury. Those who have tasted the delights of the latter must be forgiven for showing some ardour in favour of the alternative. Further, it is very desirable that the new institution should have an opportunity to organise itself and find its feet before it has to undertake its full responsibilities. Above all a concrete example of international agreement for post-war economic policy will show that all the talk of such is not mere words. If the scheme is indefinitely postponed, it is exceedingly likely never to come into force.

When Mr Law's report was circulated to the War Cabinet with its appendices on 9 February, Lord Cherwell commented to the Prime Minister the same day,

The Chancellor, though, I believe, in favour of the proposals, is embarrassed by the existence of two rival factions in the Treasury. The one is headed by Lord Keynes, and supported by most of the Treasury, the Economic Section of the War Cabinet and officials of the Board of Trade. The other acts under the aegis of the Bank of England, and consists of Sir Hubert Henderson, an economist with Schachtian aspirations, and Sir Wilfrid Eady, who after a variegated Civil Service experience has only recently joined the Treasury.

When the War Cabinet met to discuss the Law Report on 11 February, largely as the result of a memorandum from Lord Beaverbrook, it agreed to set up a Committee on External Economic Policy consisting of Sir John Anderson, Mr Lyttleton, Lord Beaverbrook, Mr Dalton, Mr Law and Lord Cherwell to determine the instructions, on the assumption that Britain would proceed with the scheme, for the officials taking part in discussions with the Dominions on Article VII.

The Committee met six times between 14 and 18 February, with Keynes attending the second meeting on 15 February and discussing its progress with Lord Cherwell two days later. Keynes described the proceedings and surrounding atmosphere to S. D. Waley, who was away ill at the time.

From a letter to S. D. WALEY, *17 February 1944*

It is absolutely impossible to keep you up to date with the comings and goings here. It has been a complete bedlam, which only Hoppy's calm hand keeps in any sort of order. Ministers are in perpetual session, driving one another crazy with their mutual ravings, the Beaver being mainly responsible, his approach being nothing short of criminal. All the same, a certain amount of progress is being made, not all of it in the wrong direction. Instructions to the officials taking part in the Dominions talks will emerge, which will tell them to assume that something of the kind discussed at Washington is to proceed, but also instructing them not to take a definite line on any details. . . . . Ministers have now left Currency for Commercial Policy, and, as you may suppose, confusion is still worse confounded.

The Cabinet Committee reported on 18 February with Lord Beaverbrook dissenting. The majority recommended that discussions should proceed on the basis that Britain eventually would see its way clear to enter into the proposed post-war arrangements, with or without modifications, and that the discussions with the Dominions should be explanatory and exploratory. As regards the proposed monetary arrangements, the majority's misgivings concerned the passivity of the Fund in exchange markets, the position of the sterling area and the arrangements for the transitional period after the war, for which Britain would need assurances as to assistance before she could commit herself to the scheme. The majority also recommended that British negotiators should not open up any prospect of the end of Imperial Preference, but should look at the preference issue in the context of general tariff cuts and that in agricultural policy they should allow for state purchasing and subsidies.

Lord Beaverbrook's dissenting report recommended that Ministers should prepare an alternative scheme in consultation with certain of his supporters and the Bank of England. He, along with the Minister of Production on this issue alone, opposed a commodity scheme as likely to lead to either financial disaster or production restriction. He supported the Bank of England's criticisms of the monetary arrangements; that their gold basis would make sterling less acceptable than gold convertible currencies and thus make transitional arrangements based on the credit of sterling more difficult. He also regarded the monetary scheme as a gold standard and the commercial policy scheme as destroying Imperial Preference and re-ruining British agriculture.

When the War Cabinet met to discuss the reports of the Committee on External Economic Policy on 24 February, it also had before it a memorandum from Mr Amery entitled 'An Alternative Policy'. Before the meeting Keynes minuted the Chancellor.

To the CHANCELLOR OF THE EXCHEQUER, *23 February 1944*

The more I reflect on recent discussions, the more doubtful I feel whether the real issues are receiving sufficient emphasis or are clearly appreciated in all quarters. Many of the technical points, about which there has been so much disputation, are of no great importance one way or the other. Those who complain that the provisions for altering exchange rates in the Plan are too rigid, then proceed to support the definite linking of the pound to the dollar at 4. Most of these criticisms are not much more than stalking horses (this is not true of the question of suitable provisions for the transitional period, which is one of the real issues before us). What we are really discussing is something much more significant. I should like to try to indicate it briefly and, if you wish, at greater leisure, to set it all down more carefully as a memorandum to be circulated.

I. The Bank of England's alternative is essentially based on hoping to avoid any considerable financial dependence on U.S. The Bank make no bones about this. Their policy necessarily involves our not making our immediate plans on any confident expectation of a sizeable American loan. The attractions and advantages of this are obvious,—if it were possible. The Bank frankly face its full consequences,—

namely, extreme austerity in domestic consumption in the early post-war period, probably involving a level of consumption below what it is now, and the very opposite of an expansionist domestic policy, coupled with a high (though not perhaps a comparable) standard of discipline in the rest of the sterling area. But are Ministers facing these consequences? Do they appreciate that this alternative, whether it is right or whether it is wrong, would require them, as an act of ordinary prudence, to reverse, at any rate for the time being, a good many of the post-war decisions which they are now engaged in making. It is no good favouring currency arrangements seriously inconsistent with the other branches of their post-war policy.

This conclusion is admittedly essential to the Bank's alternative because no-one seriously supposes that we can form a currency bloc, which discriminates against American exports, and simultaneously ask America for large-scale financial assistance on easy terms for the purpose of providing this currency bloc with resources.

II. There are many attractions in an Empire bloc for trade and currency, but Canada is already out of it. The Bank admit that South Africa would almost certainly walk out. Those who know India say that India would certainly try to walk out, if she is allowed to,—and, sooner or later, we shall be letting her have her way. So, all in all, this seems a better way of breaking up the Empire than of retaining it.

III. On the currency side—and much the same thing applies *mutatis mutandis* to the other topics—there are three alternatives. (I am here thinking of the normal, rather than of the transitional, period):–

(1) A sterling currency bloc.

(2) An Anglo-American bloc offered as an international scheme.

(3) Dollar diplomacy.

We regard the choice as between (1) and (2). The Americans

regard it as between (2) and (3). They will not allow (1) (and it is only too easy for them to prevent it) except as a temporary expedient. We are not in fact strong enough to support (1) unaided. It follows that (2) is the only way of avoiding (3). The U.S. Treasury and State Department offer us (2) in a spirit of real disinterestedness; they do not like (3); but they will readily fall back on it—for, both politically and with the bankers, it is the line of least resistance—if they believe that we are throwing (2) over in favour of (1).

IV. We shall end the war owing to all our friends and close associates far more money than we can pay. We are in no position, therefore, to set up as international bankers, undertaking large and not closely defined liabilities, unless we can secure a general settlement on the basis of temporary American assistance followed by an international scheme.

(2) above is in fact the only basis which can leave us strong enough to continue our traditional banking business as heretofore with those who would vastly prefer to continue their traditional banking arrangements with us, if only they can.

V. The Bank is not facing any of the realities. They do not allow for the fact that our post-war domestic policies are impossible without further American assistance. They do not allow for the fact that the Americans are strong enough to offer inducements to many or most of our friends to walk out on us, if we ostentatiously set out to start up an independent shop. They do not allow for the fact that vast debts and exiguous reserves are not, by themselves, the best qualification for renewing old-time international banking.

Great misfortunes are not always avoided, even when there is no great difficulty in foreseeing them, as we have learnt through bitter experience. I feel great anxiety that, unless a decisive decision is taken to the contrary and we move with no uncertain steps along the other path, the Bank will contrive to lead us, in new disguises, along much the same path as that which ended in 1931. That is to say, reckless gambling in the shape of assuming banking undertakings beyond what we have any means to support as soon as anything goes wrong, coupled with a policy, conceived in the interests of the old financial traditions, which pays no regard to the inescapable requirements of domestic policies. Ministers should realise that these things, and not 'passivity' or the like, are what the trouble is all about.

The Cabinet meeting agreed to proceed with the discussions in the light of the majority report.

In the ensuing discussions with the Dominions, Keynes played an active role, making the introductory statement at the first meeting on currency policy on 24 February and entering into further discussions on the monetisation of unitas, scarce currencies, exchange rate policies, management and the transition period. During these discussions, after missing one meeting, he wrote to L. G. Melville.[38]

To L. G. MELVILLE, 14 March 1944

Dear Melville,

I have been reading the discussion of the fifth meeting on Monetary Policy on Wednesday, March 8th, at which I was very sorry not to be present.

There is one point in your remarks in paragraph 13 on which I should like to make a small comment. The 10 per cent *plus* 10 per cent depreciation measures, of course, only that amount of change which can be effected unilaterally. Further changes can be made with the approval of the Fund. I hope one can assume that, if there is a good and reasonable case, approval will be easily given. The discussion between ourselves and U.S. was not primarily on the question whether changes should be refused or allowed. They were from the

[38] Leslie Galfreid Melville (b. 1902); Professor of Economics, Adelaide University, 1929–31; Economic Adviser, Commonwealth Bank of Australia, 1931–49; Chairman, Australian delegation to Bretton Woods Conference, 1944; member, Advisory Council of Commonwealth Bank, 1945–51.

start entirely willing to accept our view that in the post-war world changes would often be required; but, on the question whether they should be made unilaterally or with the approval of the Fund. I think it is important not to confuse the amount of unilateral discretion with the question of changes generally. One wants to arrive at a state of affairs in which reasonable changes always take place with the Fund's approval.

I was much interested in the suggestion you made at the end of paragraph 14. Do you want to have a unilateral right to make changes for this reason or merely to have it stated as one of the considerations that the Fund should take into account?

My difficulty is that I find it extraordinarily difficult to see how an alteration in the exchanges could possibly be the right remedy for a catastrophic fall in some staple export commodity, such as wool. To maintain the incomes of the wool producers by greatly increasing the incomes of all other exporters and diminishing the purchasing power of the public generally, is something like burning down the house for roast pork. Also, if the cause of the collapse is excess supply, it cannot be wise, after all, to temper the wind to the shorn (and unshorn) lambs so easily. Moreover, in the contingency contemplated a quite enormous change might be necessary to do much good. I would suggest that, in so far as the remedy is to be found in the realm of external policy, it should take the form of great enthusiasm for buffer stocks. It is precisely to protect primary producers against such catastrophes that buffer stocks are proposed. I confess I have been rather disappointed by the lack of enthusiasm which the primary producers seem to feel for plans to keep their prices more stable. But is not this really the right line to press on?

I should also prefer to limit any change to listing the possibility in question as one of the considerations which the Fund should take into account, for the same reason as that given in an earlier paragraph. One does not want to act on the assumption that the Fund is an intrinsically unreasonable body, which always refuses everything. Much better that we should expect them too kind and complacent and reasonable when any respectable ground of change is produced.

Yours sincerely,
[copy initialled] K.

While the Dominions discussions continued, Keynes continued to advocate the monetary proposals in particular and the Article VII proposals in general in other places. After a discussion at the Other Club on 24 February, on 7 March Lord Beaverbrook sent Keynes a note on external monetary policy which he had circulated to the War Cabinet the previous day. On this Keynes replied.

To LORD BEAVERBROOK, *8 March 1944*

My dear Beaverbrook,

Thanks for letting me see the copy of your note on Monetary Policy. These are the notes I feel moved to make on it:–

(1) The Bank of England have never told me that they view the Monetary Plan as the gold standard, subject to the qualifications you mention.[39] It is, indeed, quite the opposite. Instead of setting out, as the gold standard, does, from the assumption of rigidity, it sets out from the assumption of appropriate changes to meet circumstances. Up to a point, members have a free discretion. Beyond that point, the Fund is to act in a judicial capacity. Surely it is not plausible to cast *me* for the role of a defender of the gold standard and the Bank for the role of pointing out what a shocking affair it is. You cannot have forgotten back history so much as to think that that makes sense!

(2) I agree with you that the Bank's suggestion of a pro-

[39] The qualifications were a 10 per cent spread for exchange rates and control over capital movements.

visional rate between sterling and the dollar is not a gold standard. That is to say, if it is interpreted, as I think it should be, as a rate which can be modified at any time without notice and without consultation.

(3) You speak of the Bank having a plan. I have never seen anything from them which deserves this name. They could be described as having a prejudice in favour of an atmosphere. But, as for a plan, it has never been produced.[40]

(4) I fear they have deceived you badly about the sterling area, as under their sterling area ideas there *is* an obligation of convertibility. That is the dilemma which makes the sterling area, unsupported by an international arrangement, indefensible. There is not the slightest chance of the countries of the sterling area agreeing to continue it unless we enter into an obligation of convertibility. There is no doubt that that is the Bank's intention. We are in no position to accept that obligation.

(5) Thus, in fact, it is only under the aegis of an international scheme that we can hope to preserve the sterling area. That is why I keep on repeating emphatically that the international plan is the essential conditions for the maintenance of the sterling area, to which I, like you, attach the greatest possible importance. With the international plan there is no reason in the world why any of the Dominions should want to disturb their existing arrangements with us. To ask them, on the other hand, to enter into a currency bloc with us on the basis of no obligation of convertibility with the outside world is to ask the impossible. Canada is already outside the sterling area. South Africa and India would walk out forthwith. So, I suppose, would Egypt, though I do not attach much importance to that.

(6) Twice in my life I have seen the Bank blindly advocating policies which I expected to lead to the greatest misfortunes and a frightful smash. Twice I have predicted it; twice I have

[40] The Bank of England's 'plan' involved no obligation of convertibility.

been disbelieved; twice it has happened. On both these occasions you and I were in agreement. My conviction is that here is a third occasion. The Bank is engaged in a desperate gamble in the interests of old arrangements and old-fashioned ideas, which there is no possibility of sustaining. Their plan, or rather their lack of plan, would, in my firm belief, lead us into yet another smash. Why, why, why should you be found, on this occasion, on their side? Simply, I believe, because you do not like the preference proposals in another part of these talks. But this is a totally separate matter, and should be kept totally separate in our minds.

(7) I wonder how far you appreciate that lying behind the Bank's approach to this question is the assumption that we should throw over practically all the ideas which Ministers now have for the post-war world, tighten our belts, reduce our rations below what they are now, and get through the post-war period with the least possible assistance from outside. Something, I agree, to be said for this austerity. But obviously it is not practical politics. We are not going to win the war and then put on a hair shirt. But the Bank's plan is even more impracticable than this, for their idea is that the rest of the sterling area, which will emerge from the war much richer in overseas resources than they entered it, would be prepared to imitate us in this austerity. The whole thing is sheer rubbish from beginning to end. For God's sake have nothing to do with it!

Yours ever,
[copy initialled] K.

Lord Beaverbrook responded.

From LORD BEAVERBROOK, *11 March 1944*

My dear Keynes,

You bring such charm to the discussion of economics that I am almost reconciled to disagreeing with you. For I can hardly suppose that you would trouble to preach with such eloquence to the converted.

417

I think it would be fair to say that the various aspects of the Plan that have emerged, partially at least, from the Washington discussions on Article VII must be regarded as portions of a single whole, with a coherent philosophy inspiring the structure.

The monetary plan leads us on to the commercial plan which, in turn, is linked to the commodity scheme. This is an expression of praise for the project as a logical, self-consistent entity. But it will explain to you why I find myself in disagreement with each portion of it. I am at variance with the underlying doctrine because it is essentially international and free-trade, and because my own beliefs are neither the one nor the other.

I put a value upon imperial preference and on the protection of domestic agriculture which is higher than anything assigned to them under the Plan. And I would not be prepared to support a proposition which destroyed the preference and sacrificed agriculture on account of compensations which appear to be both dubious and inadequate.

It is tacitly assumed in the Plan that a policy of expansion must necessarily proceed through a lowering of trade barriers. But I believe that it is possible to secure expansion within the Imperial ambit. Indeed, we shall build on a firmer foundation if we do so. This is a possibility that does not seem to have been properly explored so far, although I have no doubt that it will before we are finished with the subject.

Sir Stafford Cripps has been in here. He takes the view that we shall regulate the Americans. He appears to think that there will be a yoke but a yoke on the Americans' neck. And we shall be the controlling agency in the situation.

To me, this appears as a most perilous illusion. The days when we could control the Americans have passed away and there is no prospect of their return.

The situation in the United States does not in the least resemble the conditions that prevailed before the war. Congress has assumed an authority independent of the Executive and free from its control. For this reason, American leadership is not a development which we should welcome.

On the contrary, we are likely to have more than our fill of it before we are finished.

Yours ever,

B

In preparation for the Dominions discussions and later meetings with the Americans, Keynes prepared an analysis of the International Bank scheme formally passed to the British by Mr White the previous November.

His first draft, dated 21 February, was revised and circulated to the Dominions on 7 March. The March draft, printed below, differed from the first draft in that paragraphs 17–22 replaced a single, final paragraph that ran as follows:

> Can an organisation of such vast scale and importance hope to advance under so much camouflage? I should have thought not. Is any transmogrification of the Plan possible by which (a) all loans would be in terms of free exchange expendible in any market at the choice of the borrower arising, directly or indirectly, out of the main purpose of the loan, and (b) the responsibility for providing such free exchange arising out of old reserves or current trade? Professor Williams[41] of the New York Federal Reserve Bank wrote of the Plan recently—'I have the greatest difficulty in understanding how there can be an international bank, except in a formal or nominal sense, for very limited purposes, in a world which has only one large creditor country and many debtor countries.'

NOTES BY LORD KEYNES ON THE U.S. PROPOSALS FOR A BANK OF RECONSTRUCTION AND DEVELOPMENT
(circulated as A.S.D. (44) 8)

1. The Plan is based on making no distinction between countries, according as they have a surplus or a deficit in their balance of payments, in respect of their ability to provide overseas loans. It is understood that the reason for this is political, namely that the Plan should not appear to put any special responsibilities on U.S. This is, of course, out of relation to the facts; and no-one disputes that. Most of the other peculiar provisions of the Plan are, therefore, directed to bringing it back, by various obscure and devious devices and qualifications, towards commonsense.

2. In order that the above basic assumption should not cause a breakdown in the operation of the scheme from the start, it is further assumed that the Plan is primarily concerned with financing the export of capital goods *which*

---

[41] John Henry Williams (b. 1887); Professor of Political Economy, Harvard, 1933–57; Vice-President, Federal Reserve Bank of New York, 1936–47, Economic Adviser, 1933–56.

would not otherwise exist and is, therefore, a net addition to the overseas resources of the exporting country. This makes preliminary sense of the Plan because, on this assumption, a debtor country, which is called on to make a loan to finance additional exports, which are a net addition to what it would export otherwise, is no worse off than before. *Ergo* a country with an adverse balance of payments is in just as good a position to make overseas loans of this special character, as it would be if it had a favourable balance of payments.

3. There are two difficulties here. In the first place, it is most unlikely that none of the capital goods exports financed by the Plan would occur otherwise and that, in the absence of the Plan, there would be no alternative means whatever of financing any of them. Moreover, there is, perhaps, a let-out under IV (8) (*d*) by which subscriptions can be used to finance miscellaneous exports, which could be much less easily segregated as necessarily additional. (See also § 14 below; whether this is in fact the intention, I am far from sure.) In the second place, in so far as the assumption is fulfilled, the Plan can play no part in remedying or offsetting existing disequilibrium in the balances of payments between countries. It will leave these exactly as they were before. Dr White agreed emphatically that this was so. The Plan is intended to facilitate the capital improvement of undeveloped areas by financing works which otherwise could not exist. It is not intended to remedy disequilibria arising in the ordinary course of international trade, for which purpose (apart from the qualifications to be mentioned below) it is deliberately made quite useless. Indeed it is worse than this. For by insisting that international loans should always create *new* exports by the lending country, the Plan deprives us of what should be the normal instrument for preserving equilibrium in current trade.

4. The Plan provides that 'the Bank shall impose no condition upon a loan as to the particular member country in which the proceeds of the loan must be spent'. Some have

found this very comforting. But it is, unfortunately, deceptive. China, let us say, is given a loan of £20 million. China is, it is true, free to decide where she shall spend it. But if she decides to spend £5 million of it in U.K., then it is the U.K. which has to find the requisite £5 million finance. Thus the source of the exports and the source of the finance, so far from being left independent, are as closely tied up, one to the other, as is conceivable.

5. This provision leads inevitably to another. It is only possible to say definitely where the loan is spent, if the loan is tied to the purchase of capital goods directly imported for the purpose of the development which is being financed. The above technique cannot easily be applied to financing the import of, for example, consumption goods for the sustenance of the local labour employed on the capital works. If there is a loan for the drainage of the Yang-tse Valley, it can be used to pay for the bulldozers imported. But most of the expenditure incurred will be for the wages of coolie labour, the spending of which will indirectly cause increased imports of a variety of consumption goods. This expenditure is, in general, ineligible for the loan. Thus the loans under the Plan will only be attractive or practicable for the borrowing country if it is in a position to finance out of its own resources a large, and often a predominant, part of the capital works in view.

6. In general, the loans have to be serviced in gold or acceptable foreign currencies (subject to the qualification in IV (10c)). The service of the loans incurred in the earlier years cannot be met (as was so often the case with the British nineteenth-century loans) out of loans incurred in subsequent years, since loans under the Plan are not allowed to be used in this way. Before a loan is made 'a competent committee' has to certify 'that the prospects are favourable to the servicing of the loan'. An incompetent committee might, one feels, be more practically useful in this context.

7. The basic principles of the Plan, therefore, not only do

nothing to remedy existing disequilibria, but are also of only limited usefulness for promoting development. All this becomes so obvious when the nature of the Plan is understood that its authors, who are fully aware of these objections, have been at much pains to do something about it. Having offered this glowing tribute to the supposed preference of politicians and the public for what makes no sense, they then introduce a series of jokers and not too obvious qualifications which tend to bring the Plan back again to *terra firma*. It is these qualifications to which we must now turn, with a view to determining whether they are in fact sufficient to rescue the Plan.

8. There are two principal difficulties to overcome—

(i) the limitation on the usefulness of the loans to the borrowing country due to the condition that they can only be used to pay for capital goods directly required by the new investment;

(ii) the limitation on the usefulness of the Plan to remedy disequilibria due to the condition that the exporting country must always finance its own exports.

9. An attempt is made to deal with (i) in IV (8) (*d*). (IV (8) (*c*) merely means (e.g.) that China's own subscription to the Bank may, exceptionally, be released for expenditure in China). But the Bank's capacity to relax under this clause on any significant scale (unless the local currency subscriptions are intended to be available for this purpose, which is far from clear) is limited by the fact that the Bank has very little free foreign exchange with which to implement any relaxation. In order to provide at least some free exchange for this purpose, II (4) (*a*) requires some part of a member's initial subscription to be paid in gold, this proportion to be 20 per cent for a rich country and something less than this for a poor country. It seems doubtful whether, under this, much more than 10 per cent of the loans could be made available as free exchange. In addition to this a further 2 per cent per annum must be

put up in gold (II (7)) by those countries whose gold reserves are increasing. I believe that IV (5), under which the Bank may guarantee and sell a loan which it has made originally out of its subscribed funds, and also IV (15), are intended as means of furnishing the Bank with a supply of free exchange.

10. (ii) is dealt with to a very small extent by the provision just mentioned by which a creditor country pays a larger gold contribution than a debtor country. In the main, however, it is dealt with by a much more subtle and far-reaching provision.

11. This provision is as follows. The above limitations apply to loans which the Bank makes direct out of its own subscribed resources. But the Bank is also entitled to *guarantee* loans made through the usual investment channels out of new money raised currently in the market. I understand that the proceeds of such loans can be spent anywhere without restriction, and not merely in the country in which the loan has been subscribed. For example, if the Bank itself makes a loan of £20 million to China out of its subscribed funds, China's expenditure out of it has to be financed by the country where the expenditure is made. But if the Bank guarantees a loan of £20 million to China raised in the New York market, the spending of the proceeds of such a loan is in no way tied to the U.S.

12. In so far, therefore, as the Bank uses its power of guarantee, rather than that of direct lending, it is capable of remedying current disequilibria in the balance of payments of the lending country and of giving the borrowing country exchange which could be used to pay for any kind of imports, visible or invisible, and not restricted to specified capital goods. I pointed out to Dr White, when I was in Washington, that, if it were clear that this was the primary way in which the Bank would operate, the Plan would touch the spot more successfully than if it were to operate in the way in which it more obviously purports to operate. I suggested that, if the

subscribed capital of the Bank were to be wholly or mainly reserved as a guarantee fund, this would make better sense of the proposed participation of member countries having no available surplus on their balance of payments. To meet this Dr White introduced what is now II(5).

13. Nevertheless this procedure also is not free from difficulty. It is far from clear in what way the Bank is free to use its resources to implement any guarantee which falls due to be met. Presumably, however, it is intended that only the dollars originally subscribed by the U.S. Government would be available to compensate U.S. investors whose loans had been guaranteed. The sterling subscribed by the U.K. Government would only be available to compensate British investors. Thus each Government, so to speak, guarantees its own investors *via* the Fund. Nevertheless the clause, obviously required to deal with this, is at present missing.

14. It should be here interposed that §9 and §13 above are written on the assumption that clause II(8) of the Plan does not mean quite what it says. I believe that this clause means that the Bank's holdings of local currency 'shall be free from any special restrictions as to their use' *within the country*. For otherwise it would clearly be impossible for countries without a favourable balance of payments to subscribe to the Bank on the scale indicated. Even so interpreted, however, II(8) is dangerous. For it might mean that the part of the original subscription provided in local currency would be available to finance exports of consumption goods from the subscriber under the relaxation of the normal condition under IV(8)(d). In this case a member's subscription might be applied to finance its normal, and not merely its additional, exports, thus aggravating its balance of payments difficulties. If this is indeed the intention, it should be brought out more clearly.

15. Whilst the Plan is highly symmetrical as between countries having surpluses or deficits on their balance of payments respectively, it is highly unsymmetrical in its attitude

towards private enterprise in lending and in borrowing countries respectively. In the lending country there are elaborate provisions for allowing private enterprise a prior opportunity and for collaborating with it without the inter-position of the country's Government. But *every* loan in which the Bank participates, whether directly or by guarantee, must be fully guaranteed, by the Government of the borrowing country.

16. The subscription expected from U.K. would probably be about £250 million compared with £750 million from U.S. Obviously this does not correspond to the realities or the requirements of the actual conditions.

17. We do not want to express our criticisms to the United States Treasury in a way which is non-cooperative or obstruc-tive. We feel very strongly indeed that loans from creditor countries to debtor countries in the early post-war period are essential to avoid widespread economic chaos and much needless human suffering. Without them no International Monetary Plan can have a fair start and the reduction of barriers to trade will be frustrated by acute balance of pay-ment difficulties.

18. But it is essential that the loans made should be such as will achieve the purpose desired. Any loans, supported by an international institution, should satisfy the two conditions:–

(i) that the proceeds of the loan should be free exchange available to the borrower to expend in any market for re-quirements arising out of the project under finance whether the primary expenditure is inside or outside the borrowing country; and

(ii) that no country should be obligated to subscribe, directly or indirectly, to such loans, unless its monetary authority has approved such subscription as being within the capacity of the country's balance of payments at the time when it has to be made.

19. It follows that each individual loan, approved by such

an institution, must be actually subscribed by the government or in the market of the lending country after any necessary approval from the monetary authority. The part to be played by the international institution should be primarily concerned with the two functions following:–

(i) The expert examination of projects for international loans for which a guarantee by the United Nations Bank has been or might appropriately be sought, with regard to the degree of priority which should be accorded to each of such projects, to the reliability and technical capacity of those who would handle it, and to the prospects of servicing it in free exchange;

(ii) the guaranteeing of the service of the loan out of an internationally subscribed fund. If, even with the guarantee, a loan could not be raised at a low rate of interest on the market, it is important that the Government of the country by which the loan is to be made should itself make the loan (and obtain the benefit of the guarantee).

20. The facilitation of suitable loans from creditor countries to countries in need of reconstruction and development is so much in the general interests of the world economy and of equilibrium in the international balances of payment, that countries which fall into neither of these two categories can reasonably be asked to contribute to the guarantee fund within the limits of their reasonable capacity. It is, however, important to ensure, so far as possible, that any calls on the guarantees shall be kept within as narrow limits as possible and should be spread over as long a period as possible. For this reason it is suggested (i) that the service of the loans should take the form of terminable annuities covering both interest and repayment of principal, so that, in the event of default, no large capital sum falls due for repayment but only the continuance of the annuities; and (ii) that the institution should charge a substantial commission at a flat rate of (say) 1 per cent per annum on all loans

guaranteed by it, the accumulations of which would be drawn upon before calling on guarantees.

21. It should be made clear that the institution would be concerned with loans for post-war reconstruction as well as for new development.

22. Our first step must be to submit these essential principles to the United States Treasury. Until the principles are agreed, we feel that it would be a mistake to consider drafting amendments or detailed points, or to attempt to draw up the outlines of an alternative Plan. We feel that the best constructive contribution we can make to progress will be to set out the main principles which we regard as essential and to seek to obtain agreement on those principles.

K.

The discussions with the Dominions ended on 21 March. Before they ended, Keynes wrote to H. D. White.

To H. D. WHITE, *18 March 1944*

My dear White,

I have just received through Casaday[42] a message from you about the importance of arriving at an agreed, joint text with as little further delay as possible, and we have also had a report from Opie, who has very lately arrived. For reasons which will appear in this letter we are still, most unfortunately, not in a position to send you an official reply, and it has, therefore, seemed right that I should let you have this personal, unofficial letter to tell you how matters stand and what the explanation of the delay really is.

The experts on this side dealt with the outstanding questions as quickly as they could, and we were exceedingly appreciative of the way in which our suggestions were met at your end. The result of this was that you and Opie were able to arrive at a text, which was complete in respect of the

[42] L. W. Casaday was the American Treasury attaché in London, 1943–45.

427

discussions up to that point, except the question of the unitas version. Personally, I think it most unlikely that we shall make unitas a condition of acceptance, but we are not yet in a position to tell you so officially.

Meanwhile the representatives of the Dominions and India have arrived, and we have been discussing with them the draft reached by you and Opie. They have some interesting observations to make on these, which I hope we shall be transmitting to you shortly. Most of them are not much more than improvements in drafting, and, so far, no point of principle has been raised which is, in my opinion, likely to cause you difficulty. The most important proposal relates to the statement on quotas. Naturally the Dominions are not much inclined to leave this in a vague condition, and it has been widely felt—a view that we also have shared—that the smaller countries do not come off as well as one could wish.

As I say, I hope that we shall soon be telegraphing to you the suggestions of the Dominions. This will have the great advantage of having got over quite a considerable number of extra hurdles. We should, of course, like to have those suggestions, so far as you agree with them, embodied in the joint statement. In this case, there may not have been as serious a loss of time, in the final result, as appears on the surface. We should then be in a position to present Ministers with a final revised text, embodying, as I hope, the further suggestions emerging from these talks.

Assuming that all this goes according to programme—and you will appreciate that this is no more than a personal letter from me to put you wise as to what is going on behind the scenes—I do not anticipate that any objection will be felt to the course of procedure which you indicated to Opie some two or three weeks ago. If and when, that is to say, Ministers have agreed in principle to the early publication of the currency proposals, I should not expect that there would be any objection to the general line of procedure you indicate, namely, that you should be free to communicate the agreed draft forthwith to Brazil, Mexico and Cuba, and we to Holland, Belgium, Poland and Greece, and that, after about a fortnight, copies should go out to all the United Nations and be published on an agreed date, not much later. We may perhaps wish in our White Paper to precede the agreed text with some explanatory statement of our own.

No-one could agree more than I do with the point you make in the message you sent through Casaday that the inability to answer enquiries is an increasing handicap and that the effectiveness of a joint statement will be enhanced by prompt publication. On this side the Chancellor of the Exchequer is being constantly pestered by Members of Parliament with questions as to when they can hear more. There is obviously a good deal of restiveness, which can be largely explained, I think, by the lack of news. It is obvious that the proposals are most likely to be attacked on this side on the ground that, however we dress them up, they are no better than a revised gold standard, and they will be charged with submitting this country to the same yoke, from which it had escaped with so much difficulty but with so much ultimate relief in 1931. I hope that we have now got this part of the proposals in a form in which they can be adequately defended from this charge. But it is there, I am convinced, that the attack is likely to come.

Ever yours sincerely,
[copy initialled] K.

The conclusions of the Dominions discussions again saw a preference for a monetised unitas as the appropriate version of the Fund, but realised that such a proposal was not 'essential to the satisfactory working of the scheme' and that its acceptance by the United States could hardly be a condition for accepting the scheme as a whole. The discussions also saw requests for changes in the quotas of smaller countries and support for the British attitude towards the transitional period. The discussions on the Bank scheme resulted in the meetings seeing two functions for the Bank:

the examination of projects as to their priority, the capacity of those handling them and the prospects of servicing them in free exchange, and the guaranteeing of the servicing loans. The discussions also saw two principles as essential to the scheme: the proceeds of loans should be untied and cover primary expenditure both internally and externally and the subscriptions to loans should be dependent on balance of payments positions.

With the end of the Dominions talks, Keynes, before going off for a rest and only coming into the Treasury rarely, attempted to get permission for Mr Opie to tell the Americans the Dominions' views on the monetisation of unitas. He failed.

Attention now turned to another series of Cabinet discussions of an agreed Anglo-American draft. As Sir Wilfrid Eady turned to drafting a report on the outcome of the monetary discussions with the Dominions,[43] Keynes wrote from Gordon Square, providing drafting suggestions for Eady's factual record of the discussions, and continued

From a letter to SIR WILFRID EADY, *29 March 1944*

II. The question what to do next seems to me another matter. There is first of all the question of the relationship of the monetary scheme to the other schemes. The American Treasury's insistence, when we were in Washington, was that we should discuss it with them rather than with the State Department, though, in fact, they always invited the State Department as well as several other Departments to the party. It is also the case that, believing that the monetary proposals are practicable and the others less so, the American Treasury are inclined to press on with the one at a tempo obviously impossible for the others. But they did not expressly dissent from our frequent emphasis on the inter-connection between the schemes; though I should agree with them that, whilst the commercial scheme would find it difficult to function without the monetary scheme, the monetary scheme in no way needs the commercial proposals as an aid or support. I doubt,

[43] Eady's general position on the next stage of the talks had been one of delaying publication until further Anglo-American discussions had settled outstanding issues arising from the Dominions talks and on the transition.

therefore, whether the attitude of the American Treasury on this point can really be usefully separated from their general conception of the time-table, which you deal with in your paragraph 11. Thus, I think that the second half of your paragraph 10 would be better treated in conjunction with paragraph 11, and, as I have said, in a separate document from the report of the Discussions.

I come next to your section 11. I am quite sure that the second paragraph of this is not a sufficient statement of what White wants immediately, and I am certain it would not satisfy him. His idea is that, as soon as the document has been agreed at the technical level, it should be published. Moreover, that hitherto has been our idea too. Indeed the letter I exchanged with him commits us to that. It seems to me that it would be a grave reversal of every indication we have given him so far, if we were to attempt to postpone publication for more than a very short time further. The first stage of the procedure, to which, it seems to me, we are very nearly committed, is, as I see it, the following:

Opie will now do his best to persuade White to incorporate the Dominion amendments in the Statement of Principles. He will have to tell White whether or not we approve the unitas point. The sooner he does this, as I have already said, the better. The document will then be shown confidentially to each of us and to certain groups of countries. Shortly after that it will be published. It will then be before Congress. There will presumably be a debate in Parliament at some convenient time shortly after the Budget. That part of the programme we have put to White repeatedly, and I do not see any reason why we should go back on it.

What happens after that is an entirely different matter and must obviously depend on the reception the scheme receives in both our countries and also in other countries, and the nature of the criticisms that are made. Ministers, as I understand it, have a free hand as to whether or not they then remit

431

it to a drafting committee, ending in a conference. We have set that programme before White two or three times and have repeated it quite recently. It seems to me quite impossible to go back on it.

Though I much doubt if White has himself any very clear or cut-and-dried conception of what happens next, Grant's telegram Remac 233 of March 23rd is not perfectly clear; indeed, one would not expect a report of a general conversation of this kind to be cut-and-dried. The real point of difference which arises seems to me to be this. White would like us to pledge ourselves here and now to an international conference in the first week of June. Under the pledge Ministers have given to Parliament they clearly cannot commit themselves to this. But, nor, I should have thought, could the U.S. Treasury, if the proposed conference is to be on the lines hitherto envisaged, namely, to carry out principles which had been already agreed by both Governments after consultation with their legislatures. I should have thought that there was not any more chance of the U.S. Administration being in a position to enter into a conference on these lines in the first week in June than there is for ourselves. Accordingly, White was, if he really said this, talking, I should say, rather at random,—as he often does—and should not be taken too literally. Moreover, his electoral strategy does not seem to me to conform to that interpretation. What he wants is that the President should be able to make the monetary proposals part of his election platform. That implies that Congress have not yet swallowed it whole. For, if they had, it would be a *fait accompli*. Therefore, the conference he contemplates cannot be of the kind which he used to contemplate, namely, one which the delegates would enter with the full authority of their Governments and their legislatures to conclude. God knows what sort of international conference he has in mind. But all this seems to me just a frightful muddle, which we need not take seriously.

432

What we have to take seriously is early publication of the plan without full governmental commitment. If we agree to that, we are on absolutely firm ground in not, at this stage, making any further commitment. But to refuse early publication would, it seems to me, be quite fatal and lay us open to having seriously misled him about the time-table on more than one occasion. Indeed, I have very little doubt indeed that, as soon as a document has been agreed on the technical level, White will publish it whether we like it or not. That would make a very awkward situation with Parliament. So I do not see how the Chancellor can be advised otherwise than in favour of publication.

If the Cabinet were to decide that, in spite of the Dominion Report, they are sick of the whole thing and would like to drop it, that is a different matter. But, if they decide, as they are likely to, that we go on, then going on must include early publication. Indeed, I do not see what possible explanation the Chancellor could give to Parliament for not publishing.

If therefore, you still feel that you must put forward a recommendation on the lines of your clause 11, headed 'General Conclusions', I should feel that I had to put forward a counter-document on the above lines.

The upshot was that Eady's report became a flat, factual statement as to what had happened.

On 14 April, the War Cabinet, under considerable American pressure to get on with the scheme, agreed to publish the Joint Statement with a covering note that publication was to provide a basis for informed comment and discussion rather than to show any official commitment. The Cabinet also informed the Americans that the principles of the Fund would not apply to the transition, that it would begin operating in stages, that it would need supplementation for international reconstruction and development, and that Britain would not agree to the scheme until her transitional problems had found a solution. Before publication, Keynes, who was still away from the Treasury recovering from the heart trouble which had seriously troubled him in the early part of March, wrote to the Chancellor.

433

To SIR JOHN ANDERSON, *16 April 1944*

THE WHITE PAPER ON THE INTERNATIONAL MONETARY FUND

Mr Morgenthau and Dr White have only themselves to blame if the *Proposal for a Monetary Fund* reaches the British public prematurely and in an unsatisfactory way. Nevertheless, very serious dangers might ensue if, as a consequence of this unsatisfactory presentation, the character of the Proposal is misunderstood by the Press and by members of Parliament and an unfavourable public opinion is allowed to develop. I read in a recent report that some people in Washington are now saying that they feel an impulse to vote against President Roosevelt solely for the reason that his return means the return of Mr Morgenthau; and one can sympathise. It may be that, at the last lap, we shall not be dealing with Dr White. But I doubt if we shall find such a change as much a change for the better as some may expect, and, even if it happens, we should not have improved our position in the least by having appeared to reject his well-meant (and genuinely intended) efforts towards international cooperation.

These potential dangers, as I see them, are of several kinds. I would particularly emphasise the following aspects—

(1) If, on publication, the proposals enjoy a fair success with Congress and the American public, then a contrary development over here may lead to a position where Dr White, having secured widespread domestic and international support, adopts a take-it-or-leave-it attitude to us which will be extremely awkward and perhaps humiliating. If, on the other hand, which is at least as likely, he finds a somewhat doubtful reception in U.S., then undoubtedly he would attempt, and probably succeed, to put all the blame for a breakdown on us—with great prejudice to subsequent proposals. I have, all along, thought it vital that, if there is

434

a breakdown, there should be no excuse for saying that it came through us.

(2) If our attitude can be construed, not perhaps legitimately but plausibly, as a departure from, or repudiation of, our obligations under Article VII of the Mutual Aid Agreement, I have not a doubt that the Americans will retaliate by withdrawing from the rest of this Agreement. This could mean our losing the sheet-anchor of our post-war settlement of lend lease, namely the undertaking that the ultimate arrangements shall not be 'such as to burden commerce'. The President is already under criticism for having given us this.

(3) At a later stage we shall find ourselves in an excessively weak financial position vis-à-vis the U.S. Treasury. Dr White is a man with a memory. We may find ourselves in a position where we are forced to accept his general conditions without any of the admirable and far-reaching safeguards which we have worked, with such immense labour and forethoughtfulness, into the present document. In this event, he will, almost certainly, require as a condition of post-war aid a dollar-sterling exchange firmly fixed at 4 and the free use by the rest of the sterling area of the aid given to us, thus immediately introducing free convertibility of sterling at the cost of canalising as a dollar debt to U.S. what is now a sterling debt widely spread. Such conditions will appear entirely natural and proper to American opinion.

Therefore to allow a hostile public opinion to develop, not because the plan is bad but because it is inadequately explained and defended, would, surely, be playing with fire.

If the poor thing is brought into the world baldly and quite naked with no explanation of what it means and with no-one entitled to defend it, it will not have a fair chance.

I have two suggestions to make with a view to mitigating these dangers:–

(1) I have prepared below some introductory explanatory notes. I have endeavoured to use great discretion in the

preparation. They take the form of a comparison *seriatim* with the previously published White Paper on the Clearing Union. They are almost wholly explanatory. They would be put forward on the same technical level as the Proposal itself. The experts, who are publicly stated to have *agreed* this paper as being satisfactory, are surely entitled to offer some explanation why.

It is, in my opinion, *essential* that these notes should be printed as part of the White Paper itself, and not merely issued to the Press as an explanatory blurb. Otherwise they will never obtain the necessary textual circulation. Something of the kind which we prepared and circulated for the Clearing Union White Paper (which, indeed, stood in much less need of it) never saw the light of day at all.

A copy should be sent in advance to Dr White, but he should not be asked or expected to agree it. He has not earned such a privilege. And, in the circumstances, we should be acting as whipt curs to offer it. There is nothing in the Notes which goes beyond the terms of the agreed document or to which he is entitled to object.

(2) When the Clearing Union White Paper was issued which, like this, was without Cabinet commitment or authority beyond the agreement to allow publication, the late Chancellor agreed to allow me, and indeed strongly encouraged me, to see members of the Press beforehand and members of Parliament after publication with a view to answering questions and giving explanations,—quite privately, of course, and without any public reference to such conversations (a condition which was faithfully observed). I suggest that the same course might be followed on this occasion.

I hope that others also would help in the good work. But in certain respects the fact that I am not a Civil Servant and live in a limbo (though it be, in all respects, nearer hell than heaven) makes my interposition in such a way rather easier.

KEYNES

16 April 1944

On April Keynes received permission to brief the Prime Minister on the Joint Statement. The Joint Statement appeared as a White Paper on 22 April with the following explanatory preface by Keynes.[44]

From Cmd 6519, Joint Statement by Experts on the Establishment of an International Monetary Fund

I. EXPLANATORY NOTES BY UNITED KINGDOM EXPERTS ON THE PROPOSAL FOR AN INTERNATIONAL MONETARY FUND

Some of the more important respects in which the *Joint Statement by Experts on the Establishment of an International Monetary Fund*, set forth below as agreed between the British and American technical experts, differs from, or resembles, the *Proposals for an International Clearing Union* published as Cmd. 6437 are briefly explained below:–

(1) Under the *Clearing Union* the member countries might have been said to bank with the Union with which they were to keep balances or run overdrafts. Under the *International Monetary Fund*, on the other hand, the Fund may be said to bank with the member countries, which undertake to grant to the *Fund* facilities to hold and to draw on their local funds. Thus if under the *Clearing Union* a member country drew resources from the *Union* this meant that is own balance with the *Union* would be diminished and the balance of some other member would be increased; whereas, if a member country draws resources from the *Fund*, this means that the *Fund's* balances with that member are increased and its balances with some other member are decreased. These two arrangements represent alternative technical set-ups, capable of performing precisely the same functions. The same purposes and provisions in all other respects can be carried into effect under the one as under the other. It has, however, proved easier to obtain agreement on the mechanism of the proposed *Fund*,

[44] The Joint Statement itself appears as Appendix 4.

which has the appearance of being closer to what is already familiar.

(2) As a consequence of this, it is no longer necessary to introduce a new international unit, whether bancor or unitas, since it is only if the member countries bank with the Fund that the use of a new common unit becomes unavoidable.

(3) The provisions of the *Clearing Union*, by which only the central banks of member countries were in a position to engage in transactions with the *Union*, are replaced by the analogous provisions of III(1)(2) and (3) under which the *Fund* can only engage in transactions with the Monetary Authority of member countries and is not free to enter the market or deal with other banks or persons.

(4) The aggregate facilities, guaranteed by the initial subscriptions of the members under II(1), are smaller than were proposed for the *Clearing Union*. But they are substantial and, if necessary, can be increased later on by general agreement. It has been argued that the present proposals involve as large a commitment as it is prudent to ask in favour of an, as yet, untried institution. Moreover, in estimating the sufficiency of the facilities proposed, it is necessary to bear in mind x(1), where it is made clear that the facilities of the *Fund* are not intended to provide facilities for relief or reconstruction or to deal with international indebtedness arising out of the war.

(5) The *Clearing Union* proposals were criticised on the ground that they made insufficient provision for elasticity of exchange rates and for subsequent modification in the rates initially established. The new proposal explicitly provides for alteration of exchange rates, whilst maintaining the general principle that, exchange rates being two-ended so that a change in the parity of any currency affects the currencies of all countries, not only that of the country making the change, a proposed change is a proper subject for international consultation. The *Fund*, acting in a judicial capacity, is required under IV(3) to approve any change which is essential to the

correction of a fundamental disequilibrium, and shall, in determining the matter, accept the domestic, social or political policies of the country applying for a change as facts of the situation to be accepted and not criticised. Moreover, during the transitional period immediately after the war it shall under x(4) give the member country presenting a proposal the benefit of any reasonable doubt, and shall under IV(3) at all times take into consideration the extreme uncertainties prevailing at the time the parities of exchange were initially agreed upon. In addition member countries are allowed under IV(4) a certain margin for making unilateral changes. Finally, if a member feels unable to accept a decision of the Fund on this or on any other matter, it is entitled under VIII(1) to withdraw from membership without notice and without penalty, apart from an undertaking under VIII(2) to liquidate any outstanding obligations to the Fund within a reasonable time. Thus no member is under any obligation to continue its adherence to the conditions of membership if it comes to the conclusion that, taken as a whole, they are no longer to its advantage.

(6) The provisions for securing, apart from certain temporary relaxations, an eventual free inter-convertibility of all national currencies, on the basis of the parities of the exchange rates established for the time being, are the same in effect as those under the *Clearing Union*.

(7) Clauses III(5) and IX(3) provide that a member's obligation to maintain free convertibility of its currency applies only to transactions of a current account nature. It does not apply to capital transfers or to the removal of balances accumulated prior to the acceptance of the obligation of convertibility. Clause V(1) contemplates the control of the outflow of capital by members using the resources of the *Fund*, so as to ensure that the *Fund* shall not be drawn upon to finance a large or sustained outflow of a capital nature. Thus the proposal allows the maintenance of exchange control in

so far as it is required to carry out the above defined purposes, and may even require a member to exercise control of some kind.

(8) The proposals of the *Clearing Union*, to prevent a country from using up its quota too rapidly and from drawing on the *Fund* too freely in conditions in which its own resources are adequate without drawing on the *Fund*, are worked out more fully in clauses III (2) and (7) but without difference of intention. The provisions of II(3) and III(6) and (7) are new, under which the *Fund* has some gold resources which may be gradually increased with the intention that such gold in the hands of the *Fund* will be freely available in the interests of equilibrium.

(9) It was a feature of the *Clearing Union* proposals that they introduced certain provisions for placing on creditor countries, as well as on debtor countries, some pressure to share the responsibility in appropriate circumstances for maintaining a reasonable stability in the balances of international payments. These have been replaced in the new proposal by a different, but perhaps more far-reaching, provision with the same object in view. This is under VI, which provides that, if the requirements of the *Fund* for the currency of a country, in an unbalanced creditor position with the rest of the world, seem likely to exceed the supply of that currency which the *Fund* is in a position to acquire to meet the applications of the other members, the *Fund* shall issue a report covering the causes of the unbalanced position and containing recommendations designed to bring it to an end. Meanwhile the available supplies of the scarce currency will be apportioned, and the other members become entitled to resume complete freedom of action in relation to the affected currency. They are allowed to take any steps at their discretion to curtail imports from the country in question and to restrict and regulate exchange transactions, so as to keep their purchases in terms of the affected currency within the limits of their ability to pay. Rather than allow such a situation to develop,

it would be open to a creditor country to use any of various means to prevent the development of an unmanageable unbalanced situation with the rest of the world as a whole.

(10) The provisions for the management of the new Institution have not been worked out in detail in this Statement of Principles. This is an important matter left over for further discussion and development at a later date.

(11) The *Clearing Union* proposals, which were put forward at a relatively early stage of the war, did not attempt to deal adequately with the transitional arrangements in the period following the conclusion of hostilities. Whilst there are still too many uncertainties in other directions to allow of clear-cut conclusions, clause x of the Joint Statement carries matters somewhat further. It is there provided that a member need not assume the full obligations of membership until satisfactory arrangements are at its disposal to facilitate the settlement of its balance of payments difficulties arising out of the war. Furthermore x (2) contemplates a gradual evolution towards the attainment of the objects of the *Fund* by progressive stages and no country is committed to an immediate removal of war-time restrictions and regulations. Whilst the *Fund* may, within three years of the *Fund's* coming into force, make representations that the time has come for a further withdrawal of restrictions, no member is committed as to any fixed date for this final removal and is entitled to use its own judgment as to when it is strong enough to undertake the free convertibility of its currency which it has accepted as the desirable aim. The drafting of this clause, as the experts on both sides understand it, allows, during the transition period, the maintenance and adaptation by the members of the sterling area of the arrangements now in force between them. Nor is the scheme intended, when the obligation of free convertibility has been accepted, to interfere with the traditional ties and other arrangements between the members of the sterling area and London.

(12) In most other respects the general aims and purposes

of the new scheme are the same as those set forth in Cmd. 6437 in presenting the *Clearing Union Proposals*.

The day after publication, Keynes sent Redvers Opie his assessment of the situation.

To REDVERS OPIE, *23 April 1944*

My dear Redvers,

The utmost sympathy and at the same time the warmest congratulations on what you have been doing in the last week or two. We all think you performed miracles in carrying through to a successful conclusion. It must have been quite distracting, and I wonder how you survived. I hope that when the last lap came you collapsed and took a good rest.

It is not really possible to put you fully wise to all the comings and goings on this side by letter and at a distance. But I think I owe it to you to try to clear up a few matters.

Unfortunately, I was myself away from the Treasury, and until April 18th away from London. I saw the telegrams and tried to keep in as close touch as I could on the telephone and by notes, but, of course, one can scarcely ever in that way be either effective or in time. I did, in fact, get an agreement to tell White that we should no longer press the unitas version almost immediately after you left this country. Nevertheless, a long time elapsed before it was actually released to you, with the inevitable result that what might have been a most useful diplomatic weapon in your hands simply became the subject of our further humiliation apparently extracted from us by an ultimatum. When I got back to the Treasury on April 18th, I saw telegram Remac [ ], which seemed to me to put you in an impossible position, since you were not able either to assure White that these conditions added nothing new, nor, if they did add something new, to tell him what it was in any intelligible phrase. That telegram was really due to a confusion about certain provisos, which might have been going to be introduced at the ministerial level, if things had reached that point, but were not really, at this stage, appropriate to further conversations at the technical level. So I immediately drafted a telegram, Camer [ ], and got it agreed, which I hope helped you to clear matters up.

Personally, I really have no complaint about the line Harry took. Our delays have been so interminable, and the apparent confusion so great, that he naturally came to the conclusion that he would never get a move on unless he presented us with an ultimatum. It all meant a frightful hustle, but no real harm, in my opinion, was done.

The next thing was to get the document presented to public opinion in a way which would not lead to misunderstanding. I got the permission of the authorities to see all the more important press people so as to be quite sure that they really saw what it all amounted to. The result has been what I think you will agree is a very satisfactory press. I am sending the chief cuttings which have appeared in the first two days, April 22 and 23 (Saturday's and Sunday's papers) under separate cover. Next week I shall see groups of M.P.'s, with the same object in view. I suppose the matter will be discussed in Parliament sometime either in the week of May 1st or in the week of May 8th. But Parliamentary time is highly congested.

So far as the Investment Bank is concerned, you will have had a copy of the Chancellor's reply to Morgenthau. So far as I can judge from the newspaper reports, Morgenthau behaved quite well about that in Congress. What is the best means of making further quick progress along that line I am not yet quite sure. Perhaps the next stage of that can be tackled simultaneously with the proposed Conference, if, indeed, the Conference comes off on the due date, which personally I expect it will, although as the Chancellor pointed

443

out in his reply to Morgenthau, the latest security regulations make travelling extremely difficult, particularly for the Allies.

I have been reading in today's newspaper about how Hull has come out in enthusiastic support of the Monetary Fund. That makes it clear, I think, that the President and the whole Administration are behind this. That bit of news, in conjunction with the various indications you have been lately sending us, makes me see the situation along the following lines, and I am putting up a note today urging that it is greatly to our interest to facilitate rather than to obstruct progress along these lines.

In this note I point out that the President probably intends in his election platform to put emphasis on international collaboration over the economic field. Broadly speaking, he thinks this is a good issue on which to challenge the Isolationists and near-Isolationists, and that they will find it difficult and embarrassing to come out into open opposition. At the same time, in taking this stand, he must choose his wicket very carefully. On the one hand, the definite projects he fathers must seem fairly solid and to cover an adequate amount of ground. On the other hand, they must be as free as possible from political dynamite and of such a character that it is not too easy to raise political prejudice.

With this end in view the President is gradually building up an assemblage of projects which satisfy these conditions. First came POFA. Next UNRRA. Next the President's warm endorsement of the I.L.O. Now comes the Monetary Fund. I infer that they are very anxious to add the Reconstruction and Investment Bank to the list, and that is why there is urgency about that. It is very possible a declaratory statement about full employment on the lines that the Australians are pressing would also appeal to him in this context. (It is not clear how far this is before him. We have taken no steps, so far as I know, to communicate to the Americans the document drawn up at the Dominion Talks on the initiative of the

Australians.) All these projects taken together can be represented as a formidable first step towards international collaboration over the economic field. They are all of them politically innocent (or, at least, relatively so) and not very easy to attack. The Monetary Fund, in particular, has the great advantage that to the average Congressman it is extremely boring.

On the other hand, the President will go slow on the more dangerous issues, which undoubtedly include Commercial Policy, and very likely include Commodity Policy. Whatever goes on behind the scenes, I shall be surprised if anything clear-cut or in the nature of a draft agreement reaches the public on these matters before the election.

If the above is anything like a correct interpretation of what is in the mind of the Americans, I suggest that it also suits our book extremely well. It is vital that we should not fall out with the Americans on the issue of international collaboration in the economic field. There is no reason in the world (so far as I can see) why we need fall out with them on any of the matters listed above as being included, or perhaps included, in the President's immediate programme. I do not think he wants our ardent support along these lines. Indeed, it might embarrass him. All that he requires is that we should not obstruct this line of development or retard his time-table. It is important for him to be able to say that the various projects he is emphasising are all of them agreeable to the whole body of United and Associated Nations. He does not want to put too much of an Anglo-American complexion on it. On the other hand, politically it is much more difficult for the near-Isolationists to attack the programme, if he can represent it as being not merely a personal fad of his own but the first concrete constructive effort which the whole body of United and Associated Nations is concerned to forward.

Assuming any measure of correctness in this diagnosis, is there not much common-sense and political wisdom in it?

445

After the election, assuming that the President returns, very possibly with a Republican Congress, but nevertheless with a public endorsement of international collaboration which his return on this platform must be taken to confirm, then the more difficult subjects can be embarked upon.

I am also sending you under separate cover the Hansard report of the very important discussion in the House of Commons last Thursday and Friday on Empire unity in general and Preference in particular. It is important that you should read the actual text of this debate, not least of all the Prime Minister's statement of what he considers our commitments to be under Article VII.

You should read this debate in the light of the knowledge that there is at the moment in nearly all quarters a strong gust of sentiment in favour of closer relations with the Empire, coupled with more than a suspicion of anti-American prejudice. The chances of Parliament agreeing to give the Government a free hand about preferences in the near future are absolutely nil. This anti-American wave is essentially superficial and should not be taken too seriously, except as a momentary factor of the highest importance. I do not think that the Americans realise how the constant nagging that goes on gets on people's nerves over here. It would be much better if we reacted more violently on each particular occasion. But that, of course is not our nature. Our tendency is to say nothing at all on the particular occasion, play it down in public and then gradually under the surface get into a condition of extreme irritation. Take as a very small recent example, Colonel Knox's entirely mendacious testimony about alleged British action towards oil reserves in Saudi Arabia. This week's *Economist* comments on this—'This may be an effective way of gaining support for the pipe-line plan, but it can hardly foster good relations with America's Ally. It is, of course, the usual procedure in American politics, but the cumulative effect is to make the British resentful, distrustful and finally angry.' That is a very faithful description of the present mood. Or take another example, when Americans suggest that it is quite wrong of us to take the smallest interest in exports, although it is a matter of life and death to us. We may agree to all sorts of things, but the effect on mind and temper remains the same. Moreover, whilst we have to sit silent under the most malicious and ill-founded suspicions, it is considered as a great affront it we make any comment, however mild, on what goes on in America.

I mention all this because it is this background which is going to make necessary progress in ensuing weeks so frightfully difficult. On the Monetary Plan we have, as you will see, a very good press. But I shall have much more difficulty with the members of Parliament. They do not, of course, understand all the inwardnesses of the situation. But certain broad issues they do see and understand.

As I have said, I do not think all this should be taken too seriously. Anglo-American co-operation is absolutely certain to progress in the long run because, however much one may talk and rave, as soon as one seriously considers any alternative, one sees how hopeless and misguided it would be. The alternative simply is not thinkable; therefore, we must be of good courage.

The Americans are also, I suppose, both in their relations with us and with others, suffering from the usual prejudice against a benefactor. That does not alter the fact that, one way or another, the point is being reached when the average man finds it very difficult to keep his temper or conceal his feelings.

Yours ever,
[copy initialled] M. K.

P.S. Do read the Hansard Report right through. In my judgment, this was one of the rare occasions on which that mysterious, oracular force, British public opinion, often silent for years together, but which makes and unmakes Governments and ultimately settles all major matters of policy, declared itself. An ox has spoken in Apulia. The portent must be observed and the oracle accepted.

You may like to show Harry a selection of the press cuttings. Dacey in the *Observer* is one of the best. But the general impression created could not have been better.

The stage was set for the final Parliamentary discussions prior to the International Conference at Bretton Woods. The story continues in Volume XXV.

Appendix 1

CHANGES FROM DRAFT OF 4 AUGUST 1942 IN VERSION SENT TO H. D. WHITE ON 28 AUGUST 1942

page 168, title,	The previous title was 'The International Clearing Union (Not Utopia, but Eutopia)'.
page 168, lines 17–23,	The words 'that is to say...as heretofore' did not appear in the earlier draft.
page 169, line 6,	The word 'payments' replaced the word 'trade'.
page 169, line 8,	The words 'which must create' replaced the words 'from spreading and creating'.
page 169, line 33,	The word 'unavoidable' preceded the word 'measures' in the earlier draft.
page 170, line 25,	The word 'comprehensive' replaced the word 'comprehensible'.
page 171, line 19,	The words 'of assets and liabilities' followed the word 'debits' in the earlier draft.
page 171, lines 21–2,	The words 'can never be in any difficulty...drawn upon it' replaced the words '*itself* can never be in difficulties'.
page 171, line 22,	The words 'with safety' preceded the word 'make' in the earlier draft.
page 171, lines 30–1,	The words 'and perhaps one or more other members of the United Nations' did not appear in the earlier draft.
page 172, lines 1–2,	The words 'the charter...be drafted' replaced the words 'the United States and the United Kingdom (the former in consultation with the Pan-American countries and the latter with the other members of the British Commonwealth) could draft the charter and the main details of the new body'.
page 173, lines 2–3,	The words 'each country's' replaced the word 'its'.

449

page 173, line 10,	The word 'annual' followed the word 'average' in the earlier draft.
page 174, line 9,	The words 'to a figure' did not appear in the earlier draft.
page 174, lines 15–19,	The words 'Furthermore...its international balance' did not appear in the earliest draft.
page 175, line 13,	The word 'excessive' preceded the word 'tariffs' in the earlier draft.
page 175, line 19,	The word 'is' replaced the words 'would be'.
page 175, line 20,	The word 'a' replaced the word 'its'.
page 175, line 21,	The words 'since such balance is' replaced the words 'which would be'.
page 176, line 34 to page 177, line 13,	The words 'For the accumulation...or to consume' replaced the words 'For the accumulation of credit balances, just like the importation of actual gold represents those resources which a country voluntarily chooses to leave idle. They represent a potentiality of purchasing power, which it is entitled to use at any time. Meanwhile, the fact that the creditor country is not choosing to employ this purchasing power would not necessarily mean, as it does at present, that it is withdrawn from circulation and is exerting a deflationary and contractionist pressure on the whole world including the creditor country itself. No country need be in possession of a credit balance unless it deliberately prefers to sell more than it buys (or lends); no country loses its liquidity or is prevented from employing its credit balance whenever it chooses to do so; and no country suffers injury (but on the contrary) by the fact that the command over resources, which it does not itself choose to employ for the time being, is not withdrawn from use.'
page 177, line 24,	The sentences 'Now this can only be accomplished by the countries, whoever they may turn out to be, which are for the time being in the creditor position, showing themselves ready to remain so without exercising a pressure towards contraction, pending the establishment of a new equilibrium. This costs them nothing. The accumulation of bancor credit, as compared with an accumulation of gold, does not curtail in the least their capacity or their inducement either to produce

or to consume.' preceded the words 'The substitution of' in the earlier draft.

page 177, line 28,	The words 'the same objects' replaced the word 'this'.
page 178, line 3,	The words 'in addition to their greater complexity' did not appear in the earlier draft.
page 178, line 25,	A preliminary version of paragraph 16 below preceded paragraph 13 in the earlier draft.
page 179, line 29,	The words 'one of' did not appear in the earlier draft.
page 179, line 33,	The words 'and increased foreign lending' did not appear in the earlier draft.
page 179, line 35 to page 180, line 2,	The words 'as a result . . . frequent' replaced the words 'and gold movements lost their effect, the results of this change having been greatly aggravated by the breakdown of international borrowing credit and the'.
page 180, lines 9–13,	The words 'in terms of money . . . the world' replaced the words 'are hopelessly wrong, a change in the rate of exchange is inevitable. But if it possesses the productive capacity and the lack of markets as a result of restrictive policies throughout the world is its difficulty'.
page 180, lines 15–20,	The words 'We are . . . the contrary' did not appear in the earlier draft.
page 182, lines 30–1,	The words 'the states of a federal union' replaced the words 'the federated states of the American Union or of Australia'.
page 182, line 35,	The words 'except in the case of a specific loan from a member-state in credit with the Clearing Union to a member-state in debit' followed the word 'another' in the earlier draft.
page 183, line 24,	The words 'and the mainstay of its ability to act in the international field without anxiety for its own financial position' followed the word 'liquidity' in the earlier draft.
page 184, line 7,	The words 'against a clearance between them in the books of the Clearing Union' followed the word 'another' in the earlier draft.
page 184, line 29,	The words 'through the Clearing Union' followed the word 'dollars' in the earlier draft.
page 185, line 4,	The word 'Union' replaced the words 'bank'.
page 185, line 5,	The word 'excessive' replaced the words 'super-abundant for their legitimate purposes'.

451

page 185, lines 13-14	The words 'constitute an...fixed investment' replaced the words 'cannot safely be used for fixed investment and might turn it into a surplus country against its will and contrary to the real facts'.
page 185, line 9,	The words 'blocked or semi-blocked' preceded the word 'balances' in the earlier draft.
page 186, lines 11-19,	The words 'A country in...long-term expenditure' replaced the words 'In principle the use or removal of these must be regarded as an outward capital movement and therefore subject to the proposed control, since a country owing a large volume of such balances could not afford the risk of their being converted into bancor on a substantial scale, thus depleting at the outset the potential bancor resources of the country from which they are withdrawn. At the same time it is desirable that the countries holding these balances should be able to regard them as liquid,—at any rate, after having funded that part of them which they can afford to lock up in this way'.
page 186, lines 24-6,	The words 'there would...over a period' replaced the words 'the resulting strain on the bancor resources of the debtor country would be spread over a period'.
page 188, line 35,	The words 'Tariffs in excess of a moderate level' replaced the words 'excessive tariffs'.
page 189, line 6,	The words '(and the same applies to moderate tariffs)' replaced the words 'and tariffs'.
page 189, lines 28 and 32	The word 'bodies' is singular in the earlier draft.
page 189, lines 32-3,	The word 'rehabilitation' did not appear in the earlier draft.
page 190, line 9,	Before (2) there was the following additional item in the earlier draft with consequent renumbering: 'If the United States were to wish to effect a redistribution of gold reserves, the Clearing Union would provide a suitable channel for this purpose, the gold so redistributed being credited (e.g.) to the account of the Relief and Reconstruction Authority.'
page 190, line 25,	The words 'effectively attacked' replaced the words 'satisfactorily solved'.
page 191, line 5,	The word 'great' followed the word 'mutual' in the earlier draft.
page 192, line 9,	The words 'whenever he needs it' followed the word 'deposit' in the earlier draft.

Appendix 2

CHANGES FROM DRAFT SENT TO H. D. WHITE ON 28 AUGUST 1942 IN THE VERSION SENT AFTER THE DOMINIONS DISCUSSIONS, 9 NOVEMBER 1942

page 171, lines 29–32,
The words 'a draft plan of the Clearing Union shall be prepared by the United States and the United Kingdom, after such discussions with other parties as may be thought expedient and submitted for approval or amendment by the United Nations, who shall be invited to join them as founder states' replaced the words 'the Clearing Union...founder states'.

page 172, lines 5–9,
The sentence 'It would also mean...finally determined' disappeared.

page 172, line 12,
The words 'as are essential to the operation of this scheme' followed the word 'conduct'.

page 172, line 21,
The words 'or other appropriate authorities' followed the word 'banks'.

page 172, lines 24–5,
The words 'which will not be varied subsequently without their approval' disappeared.

page 173, lines 4–5,
The words 'and might be (say) 75 per cent of this amount' replaced the words 'being either...this amount'.

page 173, line 11,
The words 'rising to a five year average when figures for five post-war years are available' followed the word 'years'.

page 173, line 18,
A new clause (4), which runs as follows, preceded the previous clause (4) with consequent re-numbering:
'The Clearing Union, may at its discretion, charge a small commission or transfer fee in respect of transactions in its books for the purpose of meeting its

current expenses or any other outgoings approved by the Governing Board.'

page 173, line 32,   The additional words 'after consultation with the Governing Board' followed the word 'may'.

page 173, line 34,   The additional sentence 'The Governing Board may, at its discretion, remit the charges on credit balances, and increase correspondingly those on debit balances, if in its opinion unduly expansionist conditions are impending in the world economy' followed the word 'contributions'.

page 174, lines 3–4,   The words 'two years' replaced the words 'a year'.

page 174, line 6,   The words 'within a year' disappeared.

page 174, line 6,   The word 'consent' replaced the word 'permission'.

page 174, line 7,   The words 'but it shall not be entitled to repeat this procedure unless the Board is satisfied this procedure is appropriate' followed the word 'Board'.

page 174, line 8,   The sentences 'The Governing Board may require from a member State having a debit balance equal to *half* of its quota the deposit of suitable collateral against its debit balance. Such collateral shall, at the discretion of the Governing Board take the form of gold, foreign or domestic currency or Government bonds, within the capacity of the member state' preceded the word 'As'.

page 174, line 10,   The words 'all or any of the following measures' followed the word 'require'.

page 174, lines 22–3,   The words 'in the opinion of the Governing Board' replaced the words 'as measured by some formula laid down by the Governing Board'.

page 174, line 24,   The word 'or is increasing at an excessive rate' followed the word 'Union'.

page 174, line 27,   The word 'accordingly' replaced the words 'the figure in question'.

page 175, line 12,   The words 'money rates of earnings' replaced the words 'money wages'.

page 175, lines 15–16,   The words 'development loans' replaced the words 'loans for the development of backward countries'.

page 175, line 27,   A new clause (9), which runs as follows, preceded the previous clause (8) with further consequent renumbering: 'The monetary reserves of a member

State, viz. the central bank or other bank or Treasury deposits in excess of a working balance, shall not be held in another country except with the approval of the monetary authorities of that country'.

page 175, line 27, A new clause (10), which runs as follows, replaced the existing clause (8): 'The Governing Board shall be appointed by the Governments of the member states, those with the larger quotas being entitled to appoint a member individually, and those with smaller quotas appointing in convenient political or geographical groups, so that the members would not exceed (say) 12 or 15 in number. Each representative on the Governing Board shall have a vote in proportion to the quotas of the state (or states) appointing him, except that on a proposal to increase a particular quota, a representative's voting power shall be measured by the quotas of the States appointing him, increased by their credit balance or decreased by their debit balance, averaged in each case over the past two years'.

page 175, line 35, The following two new clauses (11) and (12), which run as follows, preceded the previous clause (9) with further consequent re-numbering:

(11) The Governing Board shall be entitled to reduce the quotas of members, all in the same specified proportion, if it seems necessary to correct in this manner an excess of world purchasing power. In that event, the provisions of paragraph 7(6) shall be held to apply to the quotas as so reduced, provided that no member shall be required to reduce his actual overdraft at the date of the change or be entitled by reason of this reduction to alter the value of his currency under 7(6) (9) [7(6)(a)],[1] except after the expiring of two years. If the Governing Board subsequently desires to correct a potential deficiency of world purchasing power, it shall be entitled to restore the general level of quotas towards the original level.

(12) The Governing Board shall be entitled to ask and receive from each member state any relevant statistical or other information, including a full dis-

---

[1] This error persisted into the next draft and was only removed in the 1943 White Paper.

closure of gold, external credit and debit balances and other assets and liabilities, both public and private. So far as circumstances permit, it will be desirable that the member states consult with the Governing Board on important matters policy likely to affect substantially their bancor balances or their financial relations with other members.'

page 176, line 11,   The words 'if the latter is in breach of agreements relating to the Clearing Union' followed the word 'notice'.

page 176, line 17,   The sentence 'The Governing Board shall make an annual Report and shall convene an annual Assembly at which every member State shall be entitled to be represented individually and to move proposals' preceded the words 'The principles'.

page 176, line 19,   The word 'Assembly' replaced the word 'Governing Board'.

page 176, line 20,   The following new Section III of three paragraphs followed paragraph 7 with consequent re-numbering.

III. WHAT LIABILITIES OUGHT THE PLAN TO PLACE ON CREDITOR COUNTRIES?

8. It is not contemplated that either the debit or the credit balance of an individual country ought to exceed a certain maximum—let us say, its *quota*. In the case of debit balances this maximum has been made a rigid one, and, indeed, counter-measures are called for long before the maximum is reached. In the case of credit balances no rigid maximum has been proposed. For the appropriate provision might be to require the eventual cancellation or compulsory investment of persistent bancor credit balances accumulating in excess of a member's quota; and, however desirable this may be in principle, it might be felt to impose on creditor countries a heavier burden than they can be asked to accept before having had experience of the benefit to them of the working of the plan as a whole. If, on the other hand, the limitation were to take the form of the creditor country not being required to accept bancor in excess of a prescribed

456

figure, this might impair the general acceptability of bancor, whilst at the same time conferring no real benefit on the creditor country itself. For, if it chose to avail itself of the limitation, it must either restrict its exports or be driven back on some form of bilateral payments agreements outside the Clearing Union, thus substituting a less acceptable asset for bancor balances which are based on the collective credit of all the member states and are available for payments to any of them, or attempt the probably temporary expedient of refusing to trade except on a gold basis.

9. The absence of a rigid maximum to credit balances does not impose on any member state, as might be supposed at first sight, an unlimited liability outside its own control. The liability of an individual member is determined, not by the quotas of the other members, but by its own policy in controlling its favourable balance of payments. The existence of the Clearing Union does not deprive a member state of any of the facilities which it now possesses for receiving payment for its exports. In the absence of the Clearing Union a creditor country can employ the proceeds of its exports to buy goods or to buy investments, or to make temporary advances and to hold temporary overseas balances, or to buy gold in the market. All these facilities will remain at its disposal. The difference is that in the absence of the Clearing Union, more or less automatic factors come into play to restrict the volume of its exports after the above means of receiving payment for them have been exhausted. Certain countries become unable to buy and, in addition to this, there is an automatic tendency towards a general slump in international trade and, as a result, a reduction in the exports of the creditor country. Thus, the effect of the Clearing Union is to give the creditor country a choice between voluntarily curtailing its exports to the same extent that they would have been involuntarily curtailed in the absence of the Clearing Union, or, alternatively, of allowing its exports to continue and accumulating the excess receipts in the form of bancor balances for the time being. Unless the removal of a

457

factor causing the involuntary reduction of exports is reckoned a disadvantage, a creditor country incurs no burden but is, on the contrary, relieved, by being offered the additional option of receiving payment for its exports through the accumulation of a bancor balance.

10. If, therefore, a member state asks what governs the maximum liability which it incurs by entering the system, the answer is that this lies entirely within its own control. No more is asked of it than that it should hold in bancor such surplus of its favourable balance of payments as it does not itself choose to employ in any other way, and only for so long as it does not so choose.

page 182, lines 7 and 15,	The word 'countries' replaced the words 'central banks'.
page 182, line 29,	The word 'country' replaced the words 'central bank'.
page 183, line 2,	The words 'monetary authorities', replaced the words 'central bank'.
page 185, lines 2–3,	The sentence 'It is proposed...change it' disappeared.
page 186, lines 3–4,	The words 'The power to vary its value might be excercised' replaced the words 'Clearly they might excercise this power'.
page 186, line 34 to page 187, line 4,	The words '(a) movement of funds from surplus countries to deficiency countries which will help to maintain equilibrium or develop the world's resources; and (b) speculative movements or flights out of deficiency countries or from one surplus country to another' replaced the words '(a) between movements...country to another'.
page 188, line 22,	The words 'The existence of the Clearing Union might make it easier' replaced the words 'It might also be possible'.
page 188, line 24,	The words 'between members of the Union' disappeared.
page 189, line 31,	The word 'preliminary' followed the word 'granting'.
page 190, line 1,	The words 'So far as this method is adopted it would be' replaced the words 'By this means it is'.

Appendix 3

CHANGES FROM THE DRAFT OF 9 NOVEMBER 1942 IN THE WHITE PAPER PUBLISHED ON 7 APRIL 1943 OTHER THAN THE PREFACE

(PRINTED ABOVE PP. 233–5)

paragraph 1(f)	disappeared, with consequent re-numbering.
paragraph 6	disappeared, with consequent re-numbering.
paragraph 7	As there were several alterations, the revised clause appears in full.

II. THE PROVISIONS OF THE PLAN

6. The provisions proposed (the particular proportions and other details suggested being tentative as a basis of discussion) are the following:–

(1) All the United Nations will be invited to become original members of the International Clearing Union. Other states may be invited to join subsequently. If ex-enemy states are invited to join, special conditions may be applied to them.

(2) The Governing Board of the Clearing Union shall be appointed by the Governments of the several member states (as provided in (12) below); the daily business with the Union and the technical arrangements being carried out through their central banks or other appropriate authorities.

(3) The member states will agree between themselves the initial values of their own currencies in terms of bancor. A member state may not subsequently alter the value of its currency in terms of bancor without

459

the permission of the Governing Board except under the conditions stated below; but during the first five years after the inception of the system the Governing Board shall give special consideration to appeals for an adjustment in the exchange value of a national currency unit on the ground of unforeseen circumstances.

(4) The value of bancor in terms of gold shall be fixed by the Governing Board. Member states shall not purchase or acquire gold, directly or indirectly, at a price in terms of their national currencies in excess of the parity which corresponds to the value of their currency in terms of bancor and to the value of bancor in terms of gold. Their sales and purchases of gold shall not be otherwise restricted.

(5) Each member state shall have assigned to it a *quota*, which shall determine the measure of its responsibility in the management of the Union and of its right to enjoy the credit facilities provided by the Union. The initial quotas might be fixed by reference to the sum of each country's exports and imports on the average of (say) the three pre-war years, and might be (say) 75 per cent of this amount, a special assessment being substituted in cases (of which there might be several) where this formula would be, for any reason, inappropriate. Subsequently, after the elapse of the transitional period, the quotas should be revised annually in accordance with the running average of each country's actual volume of trade in the three preceding years, rising to a five-year average when figures for five post-war years are available. The determination of a country's quota primarily by reference to the value of its foreign trade seems to offer the criterion most relevant to a plan which is chiefly concerned with the regulation of the foreign exchanges and of a country's international trade balance. It is, however, a matter for discussion whether the formula for fixing quotas should also take account of other factors.

(6) Member states shall agree to accept payment of currency balances, due to them from other members,

by a transfer of bancor to their credit in the books of
the Clearing Union. They shall be entitled, subject to
the conditions set forth below, to make transfers of
bancor to other members which have the effect of
overdrawing their own accounts with the Union, provided that the maximum debit balances thus created
do not exceed their quota. The Clearing Union may,
at its discretion, charge a small commission or transfer
fee in respect of transactions in its books for the
purpose of meeting its current expenses or any other
outgoings approved by the Governing Board.

(7) A member state shall pay to the Reserve Fund
of the Clearing Union a charge of 1 per cent per
annum on the amount of its average balance in bancor,
whether it is a credit or a debit balance, in excess of
a quarter of its quota; and a further charge of 1 per
cent on its average balance, whether credit or debit,
in excess of a half of its quota. Thus, only a country
which keeps as nearly as possible in a state of international balance on the average of the year will escape
this contribution. These charges are not absolutely
essential to the scheme. But if they are found acceptable, they would be valuable and important inducements towards keeping a level balance, and a significant indication that the system looks on excessive
credit balances with as critical an eye as on excessive
debit balances, each being, indeed, the inevitable
concomitant of the other. Any member state in debit
may, after consultation with the Governing Board,
borrow bancor from the balances of any member state
in credit on such terms as may be mutually agreed, by
which means each would avoid these contributions.
The Governing Board may, at its discretion, remit the
charges on credit balances, and increase correspondingly those on debit balances, if in its opinion unduly
expansionist conditions are impending in the world
economy.

(8)(a) A member state may not increase its debit
balance by more than a *quarter* of its quota within a year
without the permission of the Governing Board. If its
debit balance has exceeded a quarter of its quota on

the average of at least two years, it shall be entitled to reduce the value of its currency in terms of bancor provided that the reduction shall not exceed 5 per cent without the consent of the Governing Board; but it shall not be entitled to repeat this procedure unless the Board is satisfied that this procedure is appropriate.

(b) The Governing Board may require from a member state having a debit balance reaching a *half* of its quota the deposit of suitable collateral against its debit balance. Such collateral shall, at the discretion of the Governing Board, take the form of gold, foreign or domestic currency or Government bonds, within the capacity of the member state. As a condition of allowing a member State to increase its debit balance to a figure in excess of a half of its quota, the Governing Board may require all or any of the following measures:–

(i) a stated reduction in the value of the member's currency, if it deems that to be the suitable remedy;

(ii) the control of outward capital transactions if not already in force; and

(iii) the outright surrender of a suitable proportion of any separate gold or other liquid reserve in reduction of its debit balance.

Furthermore, the Governing Board may recommend to the Government of the member State any internal measures affecting its domestic economy which may appear to be appropriate to restore the equilibrium of its international balance.

(c) If a member state's debit balance has exceeded *three-quarters* of its quota on the average of at least a year and is excessive in the opinion of the Governing Board in relation to the total debit balances outstanding on the books of the Clearing Union, or is increasing at an excessive rate, it may, in addition, be asked by the Governing Board to take measures to improve its position, and, in the event of its failing to reduce its debit balance accordingly within two years, the Governing Board may declare that it is in default and no longer entitled to draw against its account except with the permission of the Governing Board.

(*d*) Each member state, on joining the system, shall agree to pay to the Clearing Union any payments due from it to a country in default towards the discharge of the latter's debit balance and to accept this arrangement in the event of falling into default itself. A member state which resigns from the Clearing Union without making approved arrangements for the discharge of any debit balance shall also be treated as in default.

(9) A member state whose credit balance has exceeded a *half* of its quota on the average of at least a year shall discuss with the Governing Board (but shall retain the ultimate decision in its own hands) what measures would be appropriate to restore the equilibrium of its international balances, including—

(*a*) Measures for the expansion of domestic credit and domestic demand;

(*b*) The appreciation of its local currency in terms of bancor, or, alternatively, the encouragement of an increase in money rates of earnings;

(*c*) The reduction of tariffs and other discouragements against imports;

(*d*) International development loans.

(10) A member state shall be entitled to obtain a credit balance in terms of bancor by paying in gold to the Clearing Union for the credit of its clearing account. But no one is entitled to demand gold from the Union against a balance of bancor, since such balance is available only for transfer to another clearing account. The Governing Board of the Union shall, however, have the discretion to distribute any gold in the possession of the Union between the members possessing credit balances in excess of a specified proportion of their quotas, proportionately to such balances, in reduction of their amount in excess of that proportion.

(11) The monetary reserves of a member state, viz., the Central Bank or other bank or Treasury deposits in excess of a working balance, shall not be held in another country except with the approval of the monetary authorities of that country.

(12) The Governing Board shall be appointed by

the Governments of the member states, those with the larger quotas being entitled to appoint a member individually, and those with smaller quotas appointing in convenient political or geographical groups, so that the members would not exceed (say) 12 or 15 in number. Each representative on the Governing Board shall have a vote in proportion to the quotas of the state (or states) appointing him, except that on a proposal to increase a particular quota, a representative's voting power shall be measured by the quotas of the member states appointing him, increased by their credit balance or decreased by their debit balance, averaged in each case over the past two years. Each member state, which is not individually represented on the Governing Board, shall be entitled to appoint a permanent delegate to the Union to maintain contact with the Board and to act as *liaison* for daily business and for the exchange of information with the Executive of the Union. Such delegate shall be entitled to be present at the Governing Board when any matter is under consideration which specially concerns the state he represents, and to take part in the discussion.

paragraph 23

As the new paragraph 22 varied considerably from the previous version, it appears below in full

22. Many Central Banks have found great advantage in centralising with themselves or with an Exchange Control the supply and demand of all foreign exchange, thus dispensing with an outside exchange market, though continuing to accommodate individuals through the existing banks and not directly. The further extension of such arrangements would be consonant with the general purposes of the Clearing Union, inasmuch as they would promote order and discipline in international exchange transactions in detail as well as in general. The same is true of the control of capital movements, further described below, which many states are likely to wish to impose on their own nationals. But the structure of the pro-

posed Clearing Union does not *require* such measures of centralisation or of control on the part of a member state. It is, for example, consistent alike with the type of Exchange Control now established in the United Kingdom or with the system now operating in the United States. The Union does not prevent private holdings of foreign currency or private dealings in exchange or international capital movements, if these have been approved or allowed by the member states concerned. Central Banks can deal direct with one another as heretofore. No transaction in bancor will take place except when a member state or its Central Bank is exercising the right to pay in it. In no case is there any direct control of capital movements by the Union, even in the case of 6(8)(*b*)(ii) above, but only by the member States themselves through their own institutions. Thus the fabric of international banking organisation, built up by long experience to satisfy practical needs, would be left as undisturbed as possible.

paragraph 25

The words 'United Kingdom and the United States' replaced the words 'Founder States' in the last sentence.

paragraph 36

As this paragraph was effectively replaced by two paragraphs they both appear below in full.

35. The advocacy of a control of capital movements must not be taken to mean that the era of international investment should be brought to an end. On the contrary, the system contemplated should greatly facilitate the restoration of international loans and credits for legitimate purposes. The object, and it is a vital object, is to have a means—

(*a*) of distinguishing long-term loans by creditor countries, which help to maintain equilibrium and develop the world's resources, from movements of funds out of debtor countries which lack the means to finance them; and

(*b*) of controlling short-term speculative movements or flights of currency whether out of debtor countries or from one creditor country to another.

36. It should be emphasised that the purpose of the overdrafts of bancor permitted by the Clearing Union is, not to facilitate long-term, or even medium-term, credits to be made by debtor countries which cannot afford them, but to allow time and a breathing space for adjustments and for averaging one period with another to all member states alike, whether in the long run they are well-placed to develop a forward international loan policy or whether their prospects of profitable new development in excess of their own resources justifies them in long-term borrowing. The machinery and organisation of international medium-term and long-term lending is another aspect of post-war economic policy, not less important than the purposes which the Clearing Union seeks to serve, but requiring another, complementary institution.

paragraphs
38–40

These were replaced by a single paragraph 38 with consequential re-numbering.

38. The existence of the Clearing Union would make it possible for member states contracting commercial agreements to use their respective debit and credit positions with the Clearing Union as a test, though this test by itself would not be complete. Thus, the contracting parties, whilst agreeing to clauses in a commercial agreement forbidding, in general, the use of certain measures or expedients in their mutual trade relations, might make this agreement subject to special relaxations if the state of their respective clearing accounts satisfied an agreed criterion. For example, an agreement might provide that, in the event of one of the contracting states having a debit balance with the Clearing Union exceeding a specified proportion of its quota on the average of a period it should be free to resort to import regulation or to barter trade agreements or to higher import duties of a type which was restricted under the agreement in normal circumstances. Protected by the possibility of

466

such temporary indulgences, the members of the Clearing Union should feel much more confidence in moving towards the withdrawal of other and more dislocating forms of protection and discrimination and in accepting the prohibition of the worst of them from the outset. In any case, it should be laid down that members of the Union would not allow or suffer among themselves any restrictions on the disposal of receipts arising out of current trade or 'invisible' income.

paragraph 43

This disappeared except for the last two sentences which were grafted on to paragraph 40 of the White Paper.

paragraphs 45, 46 and 47

These were drawn together in paragraph 42 of the White Paper as follows:

42. A reconciliation of these divergent purposes is not easily found until we know more than is known at present about the means to be adopted to finance post-war relief and reconstruction. If the intention is to provide resources on liberal and comprehensive lines outside the resources made available by the Clearing Union and additional to them, it might be better for such specific aid to take the place of the proposed overdrafts during the 'relief' period of (say) two years. In this case credit clearing balances would be limited to the amount of gold delivered to the Union, and the overdraft facilities created by the Union in favour of the Relief Council, the International Investment Board or the Commodity Controls. Nevertheless, the immediate establishment of the Clearing Union would not be incompatible with provisional arrangements, which could take alternative forms according to the character of the other 'relief' arrangements, qualifying and limiting the overdraft quotas. Overdraft quotas might be allowed on a reduced scale during the transitional period. Or it might be proper to provide that countries in receipt of relief or lend lease assistance should not have access at the same time to overdraft facilities, and that the latter

467

should only become available when the former had come to an end. If, on the other hand, relief from outside sources looks like being inadequate from the outset, the overdraft quotas may be even more necessary at the outset than later on.

Appendix 4

JOINT STATEMENT BY EXPERTS ON THE ESTABLISHMENT OF AN INTERNATIONAL MONETARY FUND

Sufficient discussion of the problems of international monetary co-operation has taken place at the technical level to justify a statement of principles. It is the consensus of opinion of the experts of the United and Associated Nations who have participated in these discussions that the most practical method of assuring international monetary co-operation is through the establishment of an International Monetary Fund. The principles set forth below are designed to constitute the basis of this Fund. Governments are not asked to give final approval to these principles until they have been embodied in the form of definite proposals by the delegates of the United and Associated Nations meeting in a formal conference.

I. *Purposes and policies of the International Monetary Fund*

The Fund will be guided in all its decisions by the purposes and policies set forth below:

1. To promote international monetary co-operation through a permanent institution which provides the machinery for consultation on international monetary problems.

2. To facilitate the expansion and balanced growth of international trade and to contribute in this way to the maintenance of a high level of employment and

469

real income, which must be a primary objective of economic policy.

3. To give confidence to member countries by making the Fund's resources available to them under adequate safeguards, thus giving members time to correct maladjustments in their balance of payments without resorting to measures destructive of national or international prosperity.

4. To promote exchange stability, to maintain orderly exchange arrangements among member countries, and to avoid competitive exchange depreciation.

5. To assist the establishment of multilateral payments facilities on current transactions among member countries and the elimination of foreign exchange restrictions which hamper the growth of world trade.

6. To shorten the periods and lessen the degree of disequilibrium in the international balance of payments of member countries.

II. *Subscription to the Fund*

1. Member countries shall subscribe in gold and in their local funds amounts (quotas) to be agreed, which will amount altogether to about $8 billion if all the United and Associated Nations subscribe to the Fund (corresponding to about $10 billion for the world as a whole).

2. The quotas may be revised from time to time, but changes shall require a four-fifths vote, and no member's quota shall be changed without its assent.

3. The obligatory gold subscription of a member country shall be fixed at 25 per cent of its subscription (quota) or 10 per cent of its holdings of gold and gold-convertible exchange, whichever is smaller.

III. *Transactions with the Fund*

1. Member countries shall deal with the Fund only through their Treasury, central bank, stabilization fund or other fiscal agencies. The Fund's account in

a member's currency shall be kept at the central bank of the member country.

2. A member shall be entitled to buy another member's currency from the Fund in exchange for its own currency on the following conditions:–

(a) The member represents that the currency demanded is presently needed for making payments in that currency which are consistent with the purposes of the Fund.

(b) The Fund has not given notice that its holdings of the currency demanded have become scarce in which case the provisions of VI, below, come into force.

(c) The Fund's total holdings of the currency offered (after having been restored, if below that figure, to 75 per cent of the member's quota) have not increased by more than 25 per cent of the member's quota during the previous twelve months, and do not exceed 200 per cent of the quota.

(d) The Fund has not previously given appropriate notice that the member is suspended from making further use of the Fund's resources on the ground that it is using them in a manner contrary to the purposes and policies of the Fund; but the Fund shall not give such notice until it has presented to the member concerned a report setting forth its views and has allowed a suitable time for reply.

The Fund may in its discretion and on terms which safeguard its interests, waive any of the conditions above.

3. The operations on the Fund's account will be limited to transactions for the purpose of supplying a member country on the member's initiative with another member's currency in exchange for its own currency or for gold. Transactions provided for under 4 and 7, below, are not subject to this limitation.

4. The Fund will be entitled at its option with a view to preventing a particular member's currency from becoming scarce: (a) to borrow its currency from a member country; (b) to offer gold to a member country in exchange for its currency.

5. So long as a member country is entitled to buy another member's currency from the Fund in exchange for its own currency, it shall be prepared to buy its own currency from that member with that member's currency or with gold. This requirement does not apply to currency subject to restrictions in conformity with IX (3) below or to holdings of currency which have accumulated as a result of transactions of a current account nature effected before the removal by the member country of restrictions on multilateral clearing maintained or imposed under X (2) below.

6. A member country desiring to obtain directly or indirectly the currency of another member country for gold is expected, provided that it can do so with equal advantage, to acquire the currency by the sale of gold to the Fund. This shall not preclude the sale of newly-mined gold by a gold-producing country on any market.

7. The Fund may also acquire gold from member countries in accordance with the following provisions:

(a) A member country may repurchase from the Fund for gold any part of the latter's holdings of its currency.

(b) So long as a member's holdings of gold and gold-convertible exchange exceed its quota, the Fund in selling foreign exchange to that country shall require that one-half of the net sales of such exchange during the Fund's financial year be paid for with gold.

(c) If at the end of the Fund's financial year a member's holdings of gold and gold-convertible exchange have increased, the Fund may require up to one-half of the increase to be used to repurchase part of the Fund's holdings of its currency so long as this does not reduce the Fund's holdings of a country's currency below 75 per cent of its quota or the member's holdings of gold and gold-convertible exchange below its quota.

IV. *Par values of member currencies*

1. The par value of a member's currency shall be agreed with the Fund when it is admitted to membership and shall be expressed in terms of gold. All transactions between the Fund and members shall be at par subject to a fixed charge payable by the member making application to the Fund; and all transactions in member currencies shall be at rates within an agreed percentage of parity.

2. Subject to 5, below, no change in the par value of a member's currency shall be made by the Fund without the country's approval. Member countries agree not to propose a change of parity of their currency unless they consider it appropriate to correct a fundamental disequilibrium. Changes shall be made only with the approval of the Fund subject to the provisions below.

3. The Fund shall approve a requested change in the par value of a member's currency if it is essential to correct a fundamental disequilibrium. In particular, the Fund shall not reject a requested change necessary to restore equilibrium because of domestic social or political policies of the country applying for a change. In considering a requested change, the Fund shall take into consideration the extreme uncertainties prevailing at the time the parities of currencies of member countries were initially agreed upon.

4. After consulting the Fund a member country may change the established parity of its currency provided the proposed change inclusive of any previous change since the establishment of the Fund does not exceed 10 per cent. In the case of application for a further change not covered by the above and not exceeding 10 per cent, the Fund shall give its decision within two days of receiving the application if the applicant so requests.

5. An agreed uniform change may be made in the gold value of member currencies, provided every member country having 10 per cent or more of the aggregate quotas approves.

473

V. *Capital transactions*

1. A member country may not use the Fund's resources to meet a large or sustained outflow of capital and the Fund may require a member country to exercise control to prevent such use of the resources of the Fund. This provision is not intended to prevent the use of the Fund's resources for capital transactions of reasonable amount required for the expansion of exports or in the ordinary course of trade, banking and other business. Nor is it intended to prevent capital movements which are met out of a member country's own resources of gold and foreign exchange, provided such capital movements are in accordance with the purposes of the Fund.

2. Subject to VI, below, a member country may not use its control of capital movements to restrict payments for current transactions or to delay unduly the transfer of funds in settlement of commitments.

VI. *Apportionment of scarce currencies*

1. When it becomes evident to the Fund that the demand for a member country's currency may soon exhaust the Fund's holdings of that currency, the Fund shall so inform member countries and propose an equitable method of apportioning the scarce currency. When a currency is thus declared scarce, the Fund shall issue a report embodying the causes of the scarcity and containing recommendations designed to bring it to an end.

2. A decision by the Fund to apportion a scarce currency shall operate as an authorization to a member country, after consultation with the Fund, temporarily to restrict the freedom of exchange operations in the affected currency and, in determining the manner of restricting the demand and rationing the limited supply amongst its nationals, the member country shall have complete jurisdiction.

VII. *Management*

1. The Fund shall be governed by a board on which each member will be represented, and by an executive committee. The executive committee shall consist of at least nine members including representatives of the five countries with the largest quotas.

2. The distribution of voting power on the board of directors and the executive committee shall be closely related to the quotas.

3. Subject to II(2) and IV(5), all matters shall be settled by a majority of votes.

4. The Fund shall publish at short intervals a statement of its position showing the extent of its holdings of member currencies and of gold and its transactions in gold.

VIII. *Withdrawal*

1. A member country may withdraw from the Fund by giving notice in writing.

2. The reciprocal obligations of the Fund and the country are to be liquidated within a reasonable time.

3. After a member country has given notice in writing of its withdrawal from the Fund, the Fund may not dispose of its holdings of the country's currency except in accordance with arrangements made under 2, above. After a country has given notice of withdrawal its use of the resources of the Fund is subject to the approval of the Fund.

IX. *The obligations of member countries*

1. Not to buy gold at a price which exceeds the agreed parity of its currency by more than a prescribed margin and not to sell gold at a price which falls below the agreed parity by more than a prescribed margin.

2. Not to allow exchange transactions in its market in currencies of other members at rates outside a prescribed range based on the agreed parities.

475

3. Not to impose restrictions on payments for current international transactions with other member countries (other than those involving capital transfers or in accordance with VI, above) or to engage in any discriminatory currency arrangements or multiple currency practices without the approval of the Fund.

X. *Transitional arrangements*

1. Since the Fund is not intended to provide facilities for relief or reconstruction or to deal with international indebtedness arising out of the war, the agreement of a member country to III(5) and IX(3), above, shall not become operative until it is satisfied as to the arrangements at its disposal to facilitate the settlement of the balance of payments differences during the early post-war transition period by means which will not unduly encumber its facilities with the Fund.

2. During this transition period member countries may maintain and adapt to changing circumstances exchange regulations of the character which have been in operation during the war, but they shall undertake to withdraw as soon as possible by progressive stages any restrictions which impede multilateral clearing on current account. In their exchange policy they shall pay continuous regard to the principles and objectives of the Fund; and they shall take all possible measures to develop commercial and financial relations with other member countries which will facilitate international payments and the maintenance of exchange stability.

3. The Fund may make representations to any member that conditions are favourable to the withdrawal of particular restrictions or for the general abandonment of restrictions inconsistent with IX(3), above. Not later than three years from the coming into force of the Fund any member still retaining any restrictions inconsistent with IX(3) shall consult the Fund as to their further retention.

476

4. In its relations with member countries the Fund shall recognize that the transition period is one of change and adjustment and in deciding on its attitude to proposals presented by members it shall give the member country the benefit of any reasonable doubt.

DOCUMENTS REPRODUCED
IN THIS VOLUME

Where Documents come from the Public Record Office, their call numbers appear before the date.

ACTIVITIES 1940–1944

MINUTES

To the Chancellor of the Exchequer (T247/47), 23 February 1944

To Hopkins, Sir Richard and H. Wilson-Smith (T247/115), 22 April 1942

UNPUBLISHED LETTERS

ACKNOWLEDGEMENTS

The Editors would like to thank the Controller of Her Majesty's Stationery Office for permission to reproduce Crown Copyright materials. They are also grateful to Mr J. K. Horsefield and Professor L. S. Pressnell for advice. They would also like to thank the Canada Council for financial assistance.

INDEX

486